1997

OCKHAM
ON THE
VIRTUES

**Purdue University Press Series
in the History of Philosophy**

General Editors
Arion Kelkel
Joseph J. Kockelmans
Adriaan Peperzak
Calvin O. Schrag
Thomas Seebohm

OCKHAM
ON THE
VIRTUES

Rega Wood

Purdue University Press
West Lafayette, Indiana

01   00   99   98   97   5   4   3   2   1

∞ The paper used in this book meets the minimum requirements of
American National Standard for Information Sciences—Permanence
of Paper Printed Library Materials, ANSI Z39.48-1992.

Printed in the United States of America

Interior design by Anita Noble

Library of Congress Cataloging-in-Publication Data
Wood, Rega.
    Ockham on the virtues / Rega Wood.
      p. cm. — (Purdue University Press series in the history of
philosophy)
    Includes Latin text of "De connexione virtutum" with Wood's
translation on facing pages.
    Includes bibliographical references and index.
    ISBN 1-55753-096-3 (alk. paper). — ISBN 1-55753-097-1
(pbk. : alk. paper)
    1. William, of Ockham, ca.1285–ca.1347. De connexione virtutum.
2. Virtues—History of doctrines—Middle Ages, 600–1500.
3. Virtues—Early works to 1800. I. William, of Ockham, ca. 1285–
ca.1347. De connexione virtutum. English & Latin. II. Title. III.
Series.
BV4630.W66 1997
179'.9'092—dc21   96-39436
                                         CIP

For the men in my life:
Stephen, Henry, and Allen

CONTENTS

PREFACE

Medieval philosophical ethics is undeservedly neglected today. It is written in reasonably simple and nontechnical language, and it provides insightful perspectives on ordinary issues of human conduct; it is no mere historical curiosity. Ockham's carefully considered and clearly written *De connexione virtutum* is particularly attractive in this regard. It is more polished than most of Ockham's works because it was prepared in fulfillment of a formal academic degree requirement. As I translated and commented on it, I was confident that intelligent readers would understand and care about the issues he raises. But I was also aware that Ockham's philosophy reflects a distant world, one that only medievalists are familiar with today. The relevance of Ockham's ethical thought to ordinary moral problems is more evident to medieval scholars than it will be to students, for a variety of reasons. Medievalists are familiar with the theological doctrines that Ockham accepted without question and with the examples he commonly used. They know what subjects he studied and what authors he respected, and usually they have a pretty good idea whose views he was out to refute. Trained to deal with informally reproduced works, never formally published by their authors, they also know when to consider variant readings. Some training of this sort is probably necessary to understand Ockham's writings today.

Ockham's views on many subjects have been misunderstood, even by medievalists—his views on ethics as much as any. This book was designed to avoid some pitfalls that arise in reading medieval philosophy generally, and Ockham in particular. Primarily intended for use by an intelligent undergraduate without much philosophical or historical training, I hope that *Ockham on the Virtues* will also be useful to more advanced scholars.

The introductory chapters provide first a summary account of Ockham's life and works. Next comes a discussion of his place in the history of philosophy and his influence, followed by a brief general guide to his views. Finally, there is a historical account of the medieval debate on the connection of the virtues, to which Ockham's treatise is an important contribution. Problems of interpretation are addressed in the commentary that follows the text and translation. I hope that the introduction, translation, and commentary will provide students of Ockham's treatise with the information they need to appreciate his approach to ethical issues and to challenge his arguments. If the gulf of time and culture can be bridged, I am confident that Ockham's *De connexione virtutum* can illuminate their thinking about moral problems.

This translation is intended to be as readable as possible. My hope was to present Ockham as he would wish to be presented in good modern English prose. Ockham's Latin is easy to follow. The translation cannot hope to be as spare and transparent as the original, but I have tried to keep some of the flavor; this has often meant shortening sentences. Where technical philosophical terms are concerned, however, I have sacrificed elegance to accuracy. The structure of the arguments and the terminology have been reproduced as faithfully and consistently as possible.

As mentioned above, Ockham's *De connexione virtutum* was his *Quaestio Biblica,* a formal academic exercise that met a degree requirement in theology for a public lecture or lectures on a biblical topic. In its written form, it is the work of a reporter, not its author, William of Ockham. Normally, the reporter records the author's words as he hears them, using the first person when the author does so. But when recording the author's references to his own works, the practice varies; in this case the reporter has used the third person on some occasions, referring not to "what I have said elsewhere" but to what "Ockham says elsewhere." Disconcerting as it is suddenly to realize that we are reading Ockham's spoken words as reported by someone else, rather than as he himself wrote them, it is a salutary reminder not to put too much weight on a single statement or one passage taken in isolation. On the whole, *reportationes* are reliable, though none can be treated like a modern book whose proofs have been corrected by the author. A *reportatio* is not simply a set of student's notes; it is a reasonably reliable, often an official, transcript. Some *reportationes* are more complete than others. But none is as untrustworthy as a modern student's notes, or as accurate and sure a guide to an author's views as an author's own revised version of the *reportatio,* an *ordinatio* or *scriptum.* Only the first part of Ockham's *Sentences* commentary was revised and approved for publication by Ockham. Like many other valuable and important works, the *De connexione virtutum* survives only as a *reportatio.*

The editor of the Latin text, Fr. Joseph Wey, CSB, has examined all the surviving manuscripts of the text. None of those manuscripts is perfect, or even nearly perfect. All are characterized by mistakes of omission, commission, and substitution. On the basis of the surviving manuscripts, Fr. Wey has attempted to reconstruct the original text; his critical edition not only provides the reader with an excellent approximation of the original, but also reports in the variant apparatus all the important rejected readings. It is a critical edition, because it is based on a critical reading of the surviving manuscripts and because it allows the reader to second-guess the editor. Looking at the variants, you can decide that manuscript T was correct to drop two paragraphs. You might come to believe that manuscripts BQ were right to substitute *illud* for *idem,* so that Ockham is saying that "no one can simultaneously know and be ignorant of that assumption" instead of "no one can simultaneously know and be ignorant of the same proposition." Or scholars might eventually conclude that Ockham really was talking about "depraved ignorance," as reported by FZ, instead of just "ignorance."

On the whole, however, since Fr. Wey is a very distinguished editor, the balance of scholarly opinion is likely to agree with his decisions. Consequently, readers of this book will not miss the variant apparatus too much. But where the reading is difficult, they should keep in mind that consultation of the Franciscan Institute's critical edition of Ockham's *Quaestiones variae* (St. Bonaventure, N.Y., 1984) may provide alternative readings that they would wish to consider. To facilitate reference to the critical edition, the text is reproduced with the line numbers that appear in Fr. Wey's edition, and the translation and commentary are numbered in accordance with those line numbers.

In addition to his painstaking and meticulous work with the manuscripts, Fr. Wey has also written Ockham's footnotes for him. The sort of footnotes to which we are accustomed were not provided in the Middle Ages. When Ockham refers to a passage in Aristotle or Scotus, Fr. Wey tells you just what page he has in mind. Similarly, Fr. Wey has verified Ockham's references to what he has already established or plans to treat later. Most importantly, when Ockham refers to a contemporary opinion without mentioning a name at all, Fr. Wey has usually been able to determine what author and what passage he has in mind. Fr. Wey's footnotes are reproduced at the bottom of the page with the Latin text. Their form and very occasionally their content have been revised on this occasion. In addition, a few short explanatory footnotes have been added.

Longer explanations and discussion are provided in the commentary, which indicates where there are relevant texts elsewhere in Ockham's works, provides specialized information, and contrasts his views with other important medieval thinkers. More generally, it raises problems of consistency, considers the structure of Ockham's arguments, and examines the implications of his views. Like the rest of the book, it is an attempt to make Ockham's reasoning accessible to the modern reader.

Not included in this book is a list of Ockham's works or a summary of current bibliography. For that information the reader is advised to consult J. Beckmann's *Ockham-Bibliographie 1900–1990* (Hamburg, 1992); Beckmann's presentation is brief, careful, complete, and well-organized.

In preparing the book, I have had a great deal of assistance. As always, my husband, Prof. Allen W. Wood, was the first to help. Last to help was Margaret Hunt, Purdue University Press's conscientious editor, whose pointed questions enabled me to catch many a mistake. An Alexander von Humboldt Stiftung fellowship allowed me to prepare a first draft of the translation. Fr. Wey, the distinguished editor of the *De connexione,* kindly checked the translation. Fr. Gedeon Gál, Ockham's general editor and biographer, read the introduction critically. The foremost Ockham scholar of our day, Prof. Marilyn McCord Adams, was generous enough to comment not only on the introduction but also on the commentary. Prof. Bonnie Kent, whose work on Ockham's *De connexione* is so important, also gave me the benefit of comments on parts of the book, as did my friend and fellow Scotus enthusiast Prof. Douglas Langston. Naturally, this distinguished group has saved me from many an error, and the book is much better because of their help, though not all of their recommendations have been accepted. As is to be expected in an exciting field where scholars are coming to terms with texts that have seldom been carefully studied for centuries, there are still substantial disagreements; the mistakes that remain are my own.

Reference from one article to another is by article and line number—e.g., a.1 41 refers to article 1, line 41.

Adams 1981 Marilyn McCord Adams and R. Wood, "Is to Will It as Bad as to Do It?" *Franciscan Studies* 41 (1981): 5–60. Cited by page number—e.g., Adams 1981, 16.

Adams 1987 M. McCord Adams, *William Ockham* (Notre Dame, Ind., 1987), 2 vols. Cited by volume and page—e.g., 1:114.

BFS Biblioteca Scholastica Franciscana Medii Aevi, Collegio S. Bonaventurae (Quaracchi, 1903–68; Grottaferrata, 1975–).

CCL Corpus Christianorum. Series Latina (Turnhout, 1953–).

Dial. Guillelmus de Ockham, *Dialogus de imperio et pontificia potestate,* Opera plurima 1 (Lyons, 1494); reproduced in facsimile by London's Gregg Press in 1962. Cited by part, book, chapter, and folio—e.g., 1.VI.77, fol. 90r–v.

Eth. Nic. Aristotle, *Nicomachean Ethics.* Cited by book and chapter and page, column (a or b), and line number in the I. Bekker edition (Berlin, 1831)—e.g., 6.2.1155b19.

Henr., *Quodl.* Henricus de Gandavo, *Quodlibet V* (Paris, 1518); *Quodlibet VI,* ed. G. Wilson (Leuven, 1987); *Quodlibet IX–X,* ed. R. Macken (Leuven, 1981, 1983). Cited by Quodlibet, question, and page or folio; whether it is the front (r: recto) or back (v: verso) of the folio is indicated—e.g., *Quodl. V* q.17, fol. 192r.

Kent 1984 Bonnie Kent, "Aristotle and the Franciscans: Gerald Odonis' Commentary on the *Nicomachean Ethics*" (Ph.D. diss., Columbia University, 1984). Cited by page number.

Lombard, *Sent.* Petrus Lombardus, *Sententiae in IV libris distinctae,* ed. I. Brady (Quaracchi, 1971 [books I–II], 1981 [III–IV]). 2 vols. Cited by book, distinction, and chapter and by volume and page number—e.g., III d.1 c.1, II: 202.

Lottin, *PM* Odon Lottin, *Psychologie et morale aux XIIe et XIIIe siècles,* vol. III (Louvain, 1949), 197–252; vol. IV (Louvain, 1954), 551–663. Cited by volume and page number, e.g., III: 197.

OP Guillelmus de Ockham, Opera Politica, 1940–63. Cited by volume number and page—e.g., OP I, 13.

Octo quaestiones de potestate papae, ed. J. Sikes: OP I, 13–221.

Opus nonaginta dierum c.1–6, ed. R. Bennett: OP I, 293–374.

Opus nonaginta dierum c. 7–124, ed. H. Offler: OP II.

Epistola ad Fratres Minores, ed. H. Offler: OP III, 6–17.

Tractatus contra Ioannem, ed. H. Offler: OP III, 29–156.

Tractatus contra Benedictum, ed. H. Offler: OP III, 165–322.

OPh Guillelmus de Ockham, Opera Philosophica, 1974–88. Page numbers in the introductions have asterisks. The works cited are:

Summa logicae, ed. G. Gál and S. Brown: OPh I.

Expositio in libros artis logicae, prooemium et expositio in librum Porphyrii de Praedicabilibus, ed. E. Moody: OPh II, 3–131.

Expositio in librum Praedicamentorum Arist., ed. G. Gál: OPh II, 135–339.

Tractatus de praedestinatione et de praescientia Dei respectu futurorum contingentium, ed. P. Boehner and S. Brown: OPh II, 507–39.

Expositio super libros Elenchorum Arist., ed. F. del Punta: OPh III.

Expositio in libros Physicorum, ed. V. Richter and G. Leibold; R. Wood, R. Green, G. Gál, J. Giermek, F. Kelley and G. Etzkorn: OPh IV, V.

OTh Guillelmus de Ockham, Opera Theologica, 1967–86. Cited by volume number and page— e.g., OTh I, 13. Page numbers in the introductions have asterisks. The works cited are:

Scriptum in I librum Sententiarum, ed. Gedeon Gál, S. Brown, G. Etzkorn, and F. Kelley: OTh I–IV.

Quaestiones in II Sententiarum, ed. G. Gál and R. Wood: OTh V.

Quaestiones in III Sententiarum, ed. F. Kelley and G. Etzkorn: OTh VI.

Quaestiones in II Sententiarum, ed. R. Wood and G. Gál: OTh VII.

De connexione virtutum, ed. J. Wey: OTh VIII, 323–407.

Quaestiones variae, ed. G. Etzkorn and F. Kelley: OTh VIII.

Q. disputatae: OTh VIII, 59–191.

Circa virtutes et vitiae: OTh VIII, 272–86.

Dubitationes addititiae: OTh VIII, 286–320.

Utrum voluntas possit habere actum virtuosum respectu alicuius obiecti respectu cuius est error in intellectu: OTh VIII, 409–50.

Quodlibeta Septem, ed. J. Wey: OTh IX.

Tractatus de Quantitate et Tractatus de Corpore Christi, ed. C. Grassi: OTh X.

PhB Les Philosophes Belges: Textes et études, L'Institut Supérieur de Philosophie (Louvain, 1901–41).

PL Patrologia Latina, ed. J. P. Migne (Paris, 1844–64).

Scotus, *Collatio* Ioannes Duns Scotus, *Collatio,* ed. L. Wadding, Opera omnia III (Paris, 1891).

Scotus, *Ord.* Ioannes Duns Scotus, *Ordinatio,* ed. C. Balic et al. (Vatican City, 1950–73). 7 vols. Cited by book, distinction, part, question, and paragraph numbers and by volume and page—e.g., I d.17 p.1 q.1–2 n.42, V: 155.

Scotus, *In Metaph.* Ioannes Duns Scotus, *Quaestiones in Metaph. Arist.,* Opera omnia VII (Paris, 1893); supplemented by reference to the new edition, ed. G. Etzkorn et al. (St. Bonaventure, N.Y., 1997). 2 vols. Cited by book, question, and paragraph numbers. Etzkorn page numbers are omitted because the work is at press.

Scotus, *Quodl.* Ioannes Duns Scotus, *Quodlibet,* Opera omnia XXV–XXVI (Paris, 1639); supplemented by reference to a slightly revised modern bilingual edition by F. Alluntis (Madrid, 1968), with articles. Reference is to question, number, paragraph number, and to page—e.g., *Quodl.* q.18 n. 6, XXVI: 236–37, Alluntis a.1 n.24, 637.

Scotus, *Rep.* Ioannes Duns Scotus, *Reportatio,* Opera omnia XXII–XXIV (Paris, 1894).

Scotus, *Sent.* Ioannes Duns Scotus, *Quaestiones in IV lib. Sententiarum,* Opera omnia VIII–XXI (Paris, 1893–94). Cited by distinction, question (except when there is only one), and paragraph numbers and by volume and page.

Thomas, *ST* Thomas Aquinatis, *Summa theologiae.* Cited by part, question, article, etc. I-II means the first part of the second part. Divisions of an article include resp.: reply; ad 3: reply to the third objection. When a part is not specified, reference is to the article as a whole—e.g., I-II q.56 a.3.

Wodeham, *L. sec.* Adam de Wodeham, *Lectura secunda in librum primum Sententiarum,* ed. R. Wood and G. Gál (St. Bonaventure, N.Y., 1990). Cited by distinction (or prologue) and question and by volume and page number—e.g., L. *sec.* prol. q.2, I: 50.

Wolter Allan B. Wolter, *Duns Scotus on the Will and Morality* (Washington, D.C., 1986). Revised text and modern translation. Most often used here to supplement references to Scotus's works, cited by page number where appropriate—e.g., Scotus, *Sent.* III d.36 n.12, XV: 630, Wolter 397.

P A R T
O N E

Introduction

CHAPTER
O N E | **Ockham's Life**

William of Ockham was born about 1287 near London in the village of Ockham, the county of Surrey, and the diocese of Winchester. His date of birth is calculated on the basis of information on his probable age when he was ordained a subdeacon and when he was licensed to hear confessions and first lectured on theology. In Ockham's day, subdeacons were ordained at eighteen; at thirty priests heard confessions for the first time and Franciscans lectured on theology. Ockham became a subdeacon in 1306 and heard confessions in 1318;[1] if he was eighteen in 1306 and thirty in 1318, he was born in late 1287 or early 1288. We date his birth in late 1287 because his first theology lectures appear to date from 1317 (OTh V, *14–18).

Ockham probably entered the Franciscan school at London at his parents' direction as a *puer oblatus* at the age of seven or eight,[2] like many of his confreres from families of modest means.[3] Tradition indicates that Ockham became a professed Franciscan as a youth (probably at the age of fourteen or fifteen).[4] He was ordained subdeacon, a step not taken before the age of eighteen, on 26 February 1306, the second Saturday in Lent, at Southwark Cathedral in the Diocese of Winchester.[5]

After receiving instruction in grammar and elementary logic, Ockham studied philosophy for eight years and theology for seven years; he probably began his Oxford theological studies when he was twenty-three, in 1310. His lectures on Peter Lombard's *Sentences* were delivered between 1317 and 1319 (OTh VII, *14–18); the earliest version of that commentary, called a *reportatio*,[6] need not have been given at Oxford.[7] The revised version of book 1, Ockham's *Scriptum* commentary on the *Sentences*, was certainly prepared at Oxford; on 18 June 1318, Ockham was an Oxford priest, as we know because he needed a license to hear confessions in the diocese of Lincoln.[8] Ockham's introductory lecture on the Bible, *On the Connection of the Virtues* (*De connexione virtutum*), was probably given in the summer or fall of 1319. *De compossibilitate actus virtuosi et intellectus erronei* probably followed soon thereafter (OTh VIII, *21–23). In all likelihood Ockham remained at Oxford for two years after his introductory lecture on the Bible, since the additional residence was required for anyone wishing to incept in theology at Oxford.[9]

It is unlikely that Ockham remained in Oxford after 1321. Instead he was at the Franciscan *Studium Generale* in London with Walter Chatton and Adam de Wodeham.[10] Most of Ockham's important philosophical works were produced in London, where he was a philosophy professor. In his London period, between 1321 and 1324, his output was prodigious: in addition to lectures on logic (OPh II, *13–22; OPh III, *13–14) and the *Physics* (OPh IV, *8–9), it includes his eucharistic treatises, *De quantitate* and *De corpore Christi* (OTh X, *23–27); and his most influential work (judging from the many manuscript copies that survive), the *Summa logicae*. His last theological work, the *Quodlibets*, was begun around 1322 in London and completed in Avignon around 1325; it includes a number of passages in which Ockham is replying to the papal commission at Avignon, which was investigating his works (OTh IX, *36–41).

Ockham was a very controversial philosophy professor. At Oxford, the Merton College master, Walter Burley, was an early and determined opponent. Ockham even encountered opposition among the Franciscans in London; Chatton attacked Ockham at every juncture. Wodeham tells us that Chatton's attacks were motivated by a contentious spirit, not by zeal for the truth. The atmosphere in this convent must have been poisonous: Ockham was not the only object of attack; Chatton's students accused him of heresy as well.[11] Very likely, intrigue at London led to Ockham's being called to justify his views at a provincial chapter meeting held in 1323.[12] But Ockham's troubles were not confined to England. In 1323,[13] John Lutterell, a former chancellor of Oxford University, received permission to travel to Avignon, where he brought complaints about Ockham's unorthodoxy to the attention of the papacy.

Ockham traveled to Avignon to defend his views not long afterward, arriving sometime between January and May 1324. His departure appears to have interrupted the completion of his *Physics* commentary. Numerous references indicate that he planned a full commentary on book 8 (OTh IV, 236, 353; OTh V,

138, 150, 159, 371, 396, 431); most of those references cannot be verified because the commentary breaks off after a few pages of book 8. He cannot have had much notice, since the references are still appearing early in book 7 (OTh V, 600, 608). Also left undone was a series of lectures on Aristotle's *Ethics* that Ockham intended (OTh II, 321; OPh I, 610, 615).

We date Ockham's arrival in Avignon from a statement made in his *Epistola ad Fratres Minores* (OP III, 6). In this letter, Ockham says that he had been in Avignon almost four years before becoming aware of Pope John XXII's heresy, and that he began studying the pope's views at the behest of the Franciscan minister general, Michael of Cesena. The minister general arrived at Avignon on 1 December 1327;[14] very likely he did not ask Ockham to study John's bulls immediately; from 1325 until his confrontation with the pope in April, Cesena had been urging discretion on his fellow friars, seeking to ensure that John encountered nothing but deference from Franciscans.[15] If we suppose that Cesena pursued this policy consistently, Ockham arrived in Avignon in early May 1324, almost four years before Cesena's confrontation with the pope in April 1328.

The examination of Ockham's works was a long and complicated process, and one in which the pope seems to have taken some interest. In 1325, John replied to a request from King Edward II that Lutterell return to England with the statement that he was needed for doctrinal investigations at Avignon.[16] The pope was actually present at a session where Ockham showed the commission his *Sentences* commentary. A report of that session indicates that Ockham's book showed additions and erasures; this probably indicates that it was a copy of the *Scriptum,* which underwent a number of revisions.[17] The members of the commission included a Dominican master, Durandus of St. Pourçain, who had espoused views on universals similar to those of Ockham. Joseph Koch has suggested that as the best-known theologian on the commission, Durandus was probably in charge and was responsible for the relative mildness of its initial pronouncements, which do not describe Ockham's views as heretical. Durandus withdrew before a sharper, second verdict was pronounced.[18] Yet no official papal condemnation of Ockham's theological or philosophical works was issued in the course of these proceedings.[19]

On May 26 1328,[20] Ockham left Avignon; he was at Pisa in June 1328, when Cesena drafted his famous appeal against Pope John XXII;[21] at Pisa the protesting Franciscans were joined by John's enemy, Emperor Louis of Bavaria. In 1330, Ockham traveled to the emperor's court in Munich. Most of the last twenty years of his life were occupied with treatises on ecclesiastical polity.[22] He dedicated himself to attacking John XXII and defending imperial rights on account of his allegiance to Franciscan poverty. In these endeavors, Ockham was a member of an interesting team of lawyers, theologians, and philosophers, including such important political theorists as Franciscus de Marchia and Marsilius of Padua, as well as the Franciscan Order's lawyer (*procurator generalis*), Bonagratia of Bergamo, who was a doctor of civil and canon law, and Louis's secretary, the Franciscan Henry of Thalheim. Together they produced an important body of ecclesiological theory that opposed ecclesiastical interference in the secular arena.[23] Effective as a polemical author, Ockham was excommunicated for his political views.[24] Notice of his excommunication is repeatedly reiterated in papal bulls, often accompanied by the demand that Ockham, as well as Cesena and Bonagratia, should be captured and imprisoned or transported; a letter to Tournay threatens that city with burning, should no action be taken.[25]

Throughout his life, Ockham's thought was marked by devotion to Franciscan theological precepts and logical rigor. At the end, he was very much alone. As early as 1336, Louis was willing to give up his Franciscan apologists for the sake of reconciliation with the papacy,[26] though he subsequently altered his policy. Bonagratia probably died in 1340.[27] Ockham inherited the seal of the order on 29 November 1342, when Cesena died. In 1344 Franciscus de Marchia, followed by Henry of Thalheim, was reconciled with the church.[28] Dying in April 1347,[29] at about the age of sixty, Ockham's allegiances never wavered despite the increasing hopelessness of his cause.

❙ NOTES

1. Ages for the offices of subdeacon and confessor are specified by the Clementine Constitutions (Clem. 1.6.3) adopted in 1311–12 and in the Franciscan Constitutions of 1316, respectively. True, Ockham became a subdeacon five years before the Clementines were promulgated, but this legislation only ratified the general ecclesiastical custom of ordaining earlier than ancient laws had permitted. The "Constitutiones Generales Ordinis Fratrum Minorum anno 1316 Assisi conditae" were edited by A. Carlini in *Archivum Franciscanum Historicum* 4 (1911): 517; the Clementines were edited by A. Friedberg in the *Corpus Iuris Canonici* (Graz, 1955), 2:1140.

On the dates in Ockham's life, see below. Regarding Ockham's place of birth, it is customary to note that he may have been born in another village called Ockham, but Ockham in Surrey is much the best-known medieval village in England of this name. What is more, when Pope John XXII was looking for Ockham, his June 1328 bull (*Analecta*

Franciscana 2 [1887]: 141–44) regarding Ockham is carefully registered on 1 December 1328 by the bishop of Salisbury (who had frequently dealings with clerics from the village of Ockham in Surrey). It was not registered by the bishop of York, so it seems unlikely that the philosopher Ockham came from the northern village. By contrast, the somewhat older secular cleric named William of Ockham is probably associated with Oakham in Rutland, since his clerical career is associated with the north and the Diocese of York. See *The Registers of Roger Martival, Bishop of Salisbury 1315–1330*, II.2, ed. C. Elrington, Canterbury and York Society 58 (Torquay, 1972), 593; *The Register of William Melton, Archbishop of York: 1317–1340*, ed. R. Hill and D. Robinson, Canterbury and York Society 70.71.96 (Torquay, 1977–78; York, 1988).

The basic biographical information about both Williams is found in A. Emden, *A Biographical Register of the University of Oxford to a.d. 1500* (Oxford, 1957), 2:1384–87. A good survey of Ockham's life and thought, similar to what is attempted here, was provided by William Courtenay, *Schools and Scholars in Fourteenth Century England* (Princeton, N.J., 1987), 193–218. Somewhat dated but still excellent are the classic accounts of Ockham's life by Leon Baudry, *Guillaume d'Occam* (Paris, 1949); and Philotheus Boehner, *The* Tractatus de Successivis *Attributed to William Ockham* (St. Bonaventure, N.Y., 1944).

The evidence for the lives of medieval thinkers permits little certainty. Strictly speaking, almost nothing we know about Ockham's life is indubitable; but a proliferation of 'possibly's' and 'probably's' would make an account of his life hard to read. Under the circumstances, it seems better simply to state the conclusions which are based on the best evidence we have. Expressions like 'probably' are reserved for likelihoods unsupported by early, specific evidence—such as the suggestion that Ockham was a *puer oblatus* at London.

2. The location is suggested by Ockham's ordination in Southwark. London Grey Friars was an important medieval school. In 1292, it was mentioned after Oxford and as on a par with Cambridge. Many well-known friars ended their lives and were buried in London, including Ockham's friend and disciple, Adam de Wodeham, who was born about five miles from Ockham. Its library included many works by Ockham: his commentaries on *Isagoge,* on the *Categories,* and on the *Sophistical Refutations,* as well other works (C. Kingsford, *Grey Friars of London* [Aberdeen, 1917], 21, 66, 234). The Franciscan custody of London included the diocese of Winchester (G. Weare, *The Friars Minors of Bristol,* British Society of Franciscan Studies, vol. 4 [Bristol, 1892], 20; G. Eubel, *Bullarium Franciscanum* 5 [1898]: 580). When Ockham was a boy, the bishop of Winchester pursued policies favorable to the Franciscans by arrangement with the Franciscan Warden in London (*Registrum Johannis de Pontissara . . . 1282–1304* [London, 1916–20], 254–57, 309).

Ockham's presence at a Franciscan school at an early age is a surmise based on a remark in Ockham's *Summa logicae* (OPh I, 67). Ockham indicates that he received instruction in supposition theory as a boy (*puerulus*), that is between the ages of seven and thirteen, before beginning his philosophical training (OPh I, 67). His earliest instruction in Latin probably was local, but the instruction Ockham received in the supposition of terms is more sophisticated than might have been expected in a village school.

On page 194 of his *Schools and Scholars in Fourteenth Century England,* Courtenay indicates that William Woodford notes that Ockham was a *puer oblatus* in his *Defensorium,* chapter 62. Reading through Oxford Magdalen 75 (178 folios), I was unable to verify this note. Woodford's *Defensorium* is a chapter-by-chapter refutation of Richard Fitzralph's *De pauperie Salvatoris* (or *De Christi pauperie*), which ends with a refutation of chapter 45. In part of that last chapter published by Eric Doyle, Ockham is mentioned as the first of a group of distinguished inceptors (cf. "A Bibliographical List by William Woodford OFM," *Franciscan Studies* 35 [1975]: 104). Earlier in the same chapter (fols. 174–75), Woodford replies to Fitzralph's charge that friars took young boys from their parents before the age of discretion. But he mentions no names. The two manuscripts of *Defensorium* are described in Doyle's "William Woodford's *Responsiones Contra Wiclevum et Lollardos,*" *Franciscan Studies* 43 (1983): 43–44.

   3. Regarding *pueri oblati,* see L. Oliger, "De pueris oblatis in ordine minorum," *Archivum Franciscanum Historicum* 8 (1915): 389–47; 10 (1917): 271–88; G. Mollat, "Les Ducs de Bourgogne," *Archivum Franciscanum Historicum* 30 (1937): 398. William Woodford contends that the practice was rare, saying in its defense that the *pueri oblati* were not allowed to profess before the age of fifteen (*Responsiones,* chapter 59, ed. Eric Doyle, "William Woodford's *Responsiones Contra Wiclevum et Lollardos,*" *Franciscan Studies* 43 (1983): 173. Cf. etiam Rogerus de Marston, *Quodlibeta quatuor II* q.28, ed. G. Etzkorn and I. Brady, BFS 26 (1968): 290–91.

   4. John Leland, who studied in the Franciscan archives for six years as Henry VIII's antiquarian, begins his entry for Ockham with the words: "Guilelmus Ochamus juvenis franciscanae religioni adjecit animae," quoted by L. Baudry, *Guillaume d'Occam* (Paris, 1949), 19.

   5. *Registrum Roberti Winchelsey, Cant.,* Canterbury and York Text Society 52 (Oxford, 1956), 981; A. Emden, *A Biographical Register . . . Oxford to 1500,* 3:1384.

   6. This work is called a *reportatio* because it was not written down by the author but by a reporter who attended the lectures. The earliest version of these lectures probably should be dated between 1317 and 1318 — after 1316 because of the citations of Peter Aureol (lect. circa 1316) and before 1319 because it antedates Ockham's revised lectures on the first book of the *Sentences,* the *Scriptum.* The *Scriptum* was completed not long after 14 July 1318, when Aureol became a doctor. There is a complete version and an incomplete version of the *Scriptum;* the complete version refers to Aureol as a doctor; the incomplete version does not. See Ockham, *Quaest. in IV Sent.,* ed. R. Wood & G. Gál (OTh VII, *14–18); *Chartularium Universitatis Parisiensis* II-I, n.772, ed. H. Denifle and A. Chatelain (Paris, 1891), 225; A. Emden, *A Biographical Register . . . Oxford to 1500,* 1:27.

   7. OTh VII, *15; W. Courtenay, "Ockham, Chatton and the London *Studium,*" *Die Gegenwart Ockhams,* ed. W. Vossenkuhl & R. Schönberger (Weinheim, 1990), 328–29.

   8. A. Emden, *A Biographical Register . . . Oxford to 1500,* 3:1384.

   9. *Statuta Universitatis Oxoniensis,* ed. S. Gibson (Oxford, 1931), 50. It is, however, possible that Ockham was hearing confessions at Reading as early as 1320, as Brampton argued ("Chronological Gleanings," *Archivum Franciscanum Historicum* 58 [1965]: 367–75). This seems somewhat unlikely, since the Franciscan William Ockham who was licensed to hear confessions in Reading was only replaced in 1328, while the Oxford philosopher left England in 1324 (*The Registers of Roger Martival, Bishop of Salisbury 1315–1330,* II.2: 504, 506). What seems more likely is that there was another Franciscan named William Ockham. The death of this second Franciscan in 1328 is listed in the records of the English Franciscan Province (A. G. Little, "Records of the Franciscan Province of England," *Collectanea Franciscana I,* ed. Little, James, and Bannister, British Society for Franciscan Studies, 5 [Aberdeen, 1941], 149).

The title by which Ockham is known, the Venerable Inceptor, suggests that he was successful in defending his views. Inception refers to a regent master's inaugural lecture. So if Ockham was prepared to incept at Oxford, he had received favorable depositions from the members of the theology faculty and a license from the chancellor of Oxford before his departure for Avignon in 1324. His name does not, however, appear in the list of Franciscan regent masters. Possibly, when Ockham was called to Avignon, Richard Drayton took his place as regent master (A. Emden, *A Biographical Register . . . Oxford to 1500,* 1:593; Eccleston, *De adventu Fratrum Minorum in Anglia,* ed. A. Little [Manchester, 1951]: 56). On the regulations governing Oxford inceptions, see A. G. Little and F. Pelster, "Oxford University Customs," *Oxford Theology and Theologian c. 1282–1302* (Oxford, 1934), 45–50. Other Oxford Franciscans known as inceptors include Roger Marston (A. Emden, *A Biographical Register . . . Oxford to 1500,* 2:1230–31) and Robert Cowton (Emden, 1:507).

10. References to London in Ockham's examples suggest this conclusion (OPh I, 743; OPh IV, 446), as does the company of Chatton and Wodeham. Chatton's first lectures on the *Sentences* were not given in Oxford (*in villa*). Like Ockham a member of the London Franciscan custody, Wodeham was the reporter for Chatton's theology lectures, which included attacks on Ockham, attacks that Wodeham showed to Ockham. Ockham, who was probably Wodeham's philosophy professor at the time, wrote replies to Chatton in the margin of that *Reportatio* (OPh I, *50). Courtenay, who has emphasized the hypothetical status of this conclusion, elsewhere relies on it without qualification; see "Ockham, Chatton and the London *Studium,*" 329–34; *Schools and Scholars,* 67.

11. Adam de Wodeham, *Lectura secunda,* ed. R. Wood and G. Gál (I, *12–16).

12. Vat. lat. 2148, fol. 146v; G. Etzkorn, "Ockham at a Provincial Chapter: 1323, a Prelude to Avignon," *Archivum Franciscanum Historicum* 83 (1990): 557–67; T. Stella, "Res generalis simplex est: Il Radicalismo Antilemorfico di Tommaso Barneby et di Giacomo di Carseto nella recensione di Pietro Tomás," *Salesianum* 38 (1976): 764. Here the problem is that the document refers to a provincial chapter meeting at Canterbury or Cambridge (Cantebr.), and as far as we know, the chapter meeting was held in Bristol that year (A. Little, "Records of the Franciscan Province of England," *Collectanea Franciscana* 1, British Society for Franciscan Studies 5 [Aberdeen, 1941]: 146). Possibly, what we have here is the place where Ockham heard the accusations. Normally only official delegates attended the provincial chapter; friars heard accusations directed against them at home; see M. Bihl, "Statuta provincialia Provinciarum Aquitaniae et Franciae: saec. XIII–XIV," Aquit. c.9 n.5; Franc. t.12 n.3, *Archivum Franciscanum Historicum* 7 (1914): 476, 500.

13. The royal permission is dated 20 August. Relevant information is summarized by Fritz Hoffmann (*Die Schriften des Oxforder Kanzlers Iohannes Lutterell*, Erfurter Theologische Studien 6 [Leipzig, 1959]). Hoffmann maintained that Lutterell's attack on Ockham was not self-serving (pp. 125–26). In a review of Hoffmann's book, Servus Gieben drew attention to a letter Lutterell received drawing his attention to the opportunities for advancement for theologians at the Curia (*Collectanea Franciscana* 30 [1960]: 343). For a further discussion of Lutterell's motives, see Frank Kelley, "Ockham: Avignon, Before and After," *From Ockham to Wyclif*, ed. A. Hudson and M. Wilks, Studies in Church History, Subsidia 5 (Oxford, 1987), 1–18.

14. Baluze, *Miscellanea*, ed. J. Mansi (Lucca, 1762), 3:237.

15. A. Carlini, "Constitutiones," *Archivum Franciscanum Historicum* 4 (1911): 533.

16. Calendar of the Close Rolls of Edward II (London, 1895), 3:373; A. Pelzer, "Les 51 articles de Guillaume Occam, censurés en Avignon, en 1326," *Revue d'histoire ecclésiastique* 18 (1922): 246–47.

17. J. Koch, "Neue Aktenstücke zu dem gegen Wilhelm Ockham in Avignon geführten Prozess," *Recherches de théologie ancienne et médiévale* 8 (1936): 195; G. Gál (OTh I, 30*).

18. Koch, "Neue Aktenstücke," 367–70; 8 (1936): 194.

19. Recently G. Knysh has made a number of suggestions for revising our view of Ockham's biography. Most useful is his suggestion that what happened to Ockham in Avignon was in two stages; the examination of Ockham's views by theologicians (masters of the sacred page) at Avignon that ended in 1326 was not an inquisition. An inquisition may have begun in 1327. See "Ockham's Avignon Period: Biographical Rectifications," *Franciscan Studies* 46 (1986): 64–65. Ockham's dissatisfaction with the procedure is reflected in his *Dialogus* 1.IV.17–20, fols. 27v–29r.

20. Baluze, *Miscellanea* 3:316; G. Eubel, *Bullarium Franciscanum* 5 (1898): 348.

21. It is not clear whether Ockham had been forbidden to leave Avignon. The pope asserted that he had, but Cesena called this a "false and malicious assertion" (*Appellatio in forma maiori*, Pisa, 18 Sept. 1328, cod. Paris. B. Nat. lat. 5154, fol. 119r): "Et praedictum fratrem Guillelmum de Ocham, cui falso et malitiose asserit se praecepisse ne de curia recederet, de facto excommunicavit, et alia gravamina michi et eis et dicto Ordini in nostrum et fidei catholicae praeiudicium fecit." Certainly, Ockham did not have permission to leave Avignon (Knysh, "Ockham's Avignon Period," 72–76; G. Eubel, *Bullarium Franciscanum* 5:346).

22. Ockham probably also returned to logic again at the end of his life and wrote the *Tractatus minor* and the *Elementarium logicae*. The authenticity of these works is suspect for a variety of reasons, most of which have to do with differences between them and the earlier works—there is, for example, almost no treatment of the topics that preoccupied

Ockham, such as quantity, relations, and universals. But as Ockham's editors noted when they questioned the attribution, as many or more arguments could be made for accepting their authenticity (OPh VII, *7–11). Those arguments have since been persuasively stated by Jürgen Miethke in "Der Abschluß der kritischen Ausgabe von Ockhams akademischen Schriften," *Deutsches Archiv für Erforschung des Mittelalters* 47 (1991): 180–84.

23. Cf. J. Miethke, *Ockhams Weg zur Sozialphilosophie* (Berlin, 1969); A. S. McGrade, *The Political Thought of William of Ockham* (Cambridge, 1974).

24. G. Gál, "Ockham Died Impenitent," *Franciscan Studies* 42 (1982): 90–91.

25. S. von Riezler, *Vatikanische Akten zur Deutschen Geschichte in der Zeit Kaiser Ludwigs des Bayern* (Innsbruck, 1891), 389, 404, 414, 421, 452.

26. Riezler, *Vatikanische Akten,* 639.

27. L. Oliger, "Fr. Bonagratia," *Archivum Franciscanum Historicum* 22 (1929): 302–3.

28. C. Schimitt, *Un pape réformateur et un défenseur de l'unité de l'église* (Quaracchi, 1959), 245.

29. G. Gál, "Ockham Died Impenitent," 90–95. Ockham's death in 1347 is also confirmed by the Chronica Anonyma (Argentinensi MS), edited by Lucas Carey (*Analecta Franciscana* 1 [1885]: 294). The entry for Munich includes the following sentence: "Item, frater Wilhelmus Ockham Anglicus et frater Bonagratia de Pergamo, doctor utriusque iuris, qui obierunt eodem anno, videlicet 1347; ille die Aprilis 10., hic vero III. calend. Iulii, in choro conventus sepulti." See also L. Oliger, "Fr. Bonagratia de Bergamo et eius Tractatus de Christi et Apostolorum paupertate," *Archivum Franciscanum Historicum* 22 (1929): 303, who quotes a fifteenth-century necrology that reads: "Anno D. MCCCXL obiit fr. Bonagracia de pergamo doctor utriusque iuris in die antonii, sepultus in choro ante altare cum magistro wilhelmo ockam, qui obiit quarto idus aprilis a.d. MCCCXLVII, et cum eis sepultus est fr. michahel generalis minister qui obiit in vigilia andreae apostoli a.d. MCCCXLII, qui omnes venerunt ad civitatem monacensem cum ludovico imperatore, qui proventus subitanea morte in venacione in nemoribus obiit in octa Francisci," transcribed by Wilhelm Preger, "Der kirchenpolitische Kampf unter Ludwig dem Baier," *Abhandlungen der Historischen Classe der Königlichen Bayerischen Akademie der Wissenschaften* 14 (1878): 34n.

| Ockham's Influence and
the Origins of His
Intellectual Isolation

The intellectual climate changed a great deal in Ockham's time. The English intellectual milieu between 1315 and 1325, when Ockham was most active as a philosopher-theologian, was much more hospitable to his views than it was a decade later. As William Courtenay has shown, Oxford in the early fourteenth century was less characterized by schools than was the later period. Views about what was and was not orthodox changed, as did attitudes toward Bl. John Duns Scotus and St. Thomas Aquinas.

Some of Ockham's most controversial views related to the Aristotelian categories—specifically, the categories of relation and quantity. Many of these views were anticipated in part by Peter John Olivi, an earlier Franciscan philosopher-theologian. Invited by Augustinus Triumphus to censure those views, the Council of Vienne, which censured some of Olivi's opinions, declined to condemn his views on the category of quantity (Clem. 1.1.1).[1] Olivi's views on quantity were attacked by Scotus,[2] who himself posited novel theses on the relations in the Godhead. Scotus's controversial discussion of nontemporal "instants" in the Godhead and relations between God and creatures is the probable object of a condemnation at Oxford in 1314.[3] Those views Ockham rejected as abusive or simply false (OTh III, 295). A staunch proponent of the condemnations of 1277, whose most controversial views had escaped censure in 1311–12 at the Council of Vienne, and an opponent of some of Scotus's more innovative views, Ockham must have thought himself reasonably secure in 1320. Yet he had to answer criticism of his own views on quantity and on relations as early as 1323.[4]

As an Oxford theologian, Ockham was preoccupied with the works of Scotus. Few of Ockham's important philosophical or theological doctrines can be fully understood without reference to Scotus's views. But Ockham's citation practice serves to conceal the extent of the influence. Ockham often borrows the basic elements of Scotus's view tacitly, naming Scotus only in connection with disagreements, even when the point in dispute is minor. Most notably, Ockham disagrees with Scotus on the problem of universals: Ockham denies the existence of common natures and attacks realism. But even when he disagrees with Scotus, his respect is evident; for example, when treating universals, he takes care to distinguish misinterpretations of Scotus from the views themselves, which he quotes extensively (OTh II, 100–173). Once, when criticizing Scotus, Ockham remarks that Scotus probably would not have disagreed, given his great knowledge of logic (OTh II, 344).

But respectful as he was, Ockham shows no special reverence in citing Scotus; he normally refers simply to John or Brother John, in *De connexione virtutum* (a.1 41) and in his early *Reportatio* commentary on the *Sentences* (OTh VII, 100, 348). Subsequently Ockham does refer to Scotus as the Subtle Doctor, adding that he is so called because he exceeds others in the subtlety of judgment (OTh II, 161), but noting that Scotus is not an authority for him in the same way as he is to his followers (OTh I, 44–47). Ockham does not mince words when he thinks Scotus is mistaken (OTh II, 321, 332).

Ockham's manner of reference contrasts with that of Adam Wodeham, his student, in about 1330, who refers to Scotus as "Our Doctor,"—that is, the Franciscan Order's doctor (*L. sec.* d.1 q.3 n.3, I: 230). Ockham did theology precisely in the period when Franciscans first began to venerate Scotus. Ockham's less deferential approach to Scotus may explain in part the hostility with which he was regarded by such fellow Franciscans as John Reading and Walter Chatton. The dispute between Ockham and Scotus's defenders was as much a matter of attitude as of doctrine, and it has served to obscure both the extent of Ockham's debt to Scotus and the degree to which Ockham influenced Scotists, such as Reading and Chatton.[5]

If Ockham's criticisms of Scotus were a product of intimate familiarity, his knowledge of Aquinas was much more limited.[6] Indeed, instead of discussing Aquinas, when contending against views associated today with Aquinas, he often has other medieval authors in mind. Not Aquinas but Giles of Rome is his probable opponent when discussing motion; when discussing quantity, the views under attack are those of Richardus Mediavilla, not Aquinas.[7] The ontological views he attacks resemble those stated in a standard logic text, the *Summulae logicales* of Peter of Spain (Adams 1987, 1:144).

At least at the beginning of his career, Ockham did not take Aquinas's views as seriously as he might have, because, as Courtenay says, if Scotism "was hardly dominant," . . . "Thomism was all but extinct at Oxford when Ockham was a student of theology."[8] Ockham's casual dismissal of Aquinas's views on some points as "fatuous" or "puerile" (OTh II, 495, 528) and even "rather pagan than Christian" (OTh V, 399) is less a reflection of animus than of disregard. This ill-advised disregard may have been based on the mistaken assumption that the condemnation of Aquinas, arranged by such champions of orthodoxy as Robert Kilwardby and Henry of Ghent in 1277 would remain permanently in force.

Where theological orthodoxy was concerned, for Ockham, as for his chief early Franciscan enemy, the touchstone was the Condemnations of 1277.[9] Apart from one article that he never tires of repeating,[10] Ockham cites the condemnations infrequently and does not distinguish carefully between the Oxford and the Paris condemnations, except in the *Quodlibets* (OTh IX, 24, 28, 160). But he, like his audience, was always aware of them, sometimes quoting from them without indicating his source (OPh I, 213; OTh X, 184). When he does indicate his source, he refers simply to an "article" (OTh III, 488; V, 324; VI, 22; VII, 142), knowing that no one would be in any doubt about what he has in mind. Among the rather strange assortment of views selected for condemnation in 1277, some are associated with Aquinas.[11] This is so much the case that in 1325, two years after Aquinas's canonization, the bishop of Paris felt it necessary to revoke the condemnations as far as they pertained to Aquinas.[12] Aquinas's rehabilitation was the result in part of his being championed by John XXII, whose interest in theology attracted to the papal court the man who became Ockham's most dangerous enemy, John Lutterell.[13]

Among the many philosophers who joined Ockham in rejecting realism and advocating terminist logic, only Wodeham seems to have championed Ockham personally. Wodeham wrote the introduction to Ockham's *Summa logicae,* commending Ockham not only for his genius but for the sublime truth of his teaching (OPh I, 5). Wodeham was probably both a student of philosophy under Ockham and the official reporter of Chatton's lectures on theology. As a young man, Wodeham defended Ockham in the classroom (OTh I, *29–30; OPh I, *53–55). Later on he was to devote substantial portions of his theological lectures to a defense of Ockham against Chatton (*L. sec.*, I: *12–18). Finally, shortly after his term as regent master at Oxford, Wodeham probably visited Ockham in Munich.[14]

Wodeham's boldness in arguing against Chatton in Chatton's own classroom in defense of Ockham's views did not protect Ockham from the rapid change in views about what theological orthodoxy required from theologians. Indeed Wodeham's own independence of mind has been made a ground for discounting Ockham's influence. Surely, that is the last thing that Wodeham, who was proud to have learned from Ockham, would have wished.

Aquinas's canonization by John XXII in July 1323, and the reversal of the condemnations of 1277 as they pertained to Aquinas, was part of a series of events that decisively shaped Ockham's life and future influence. In November 1323, John XXII asserted dogmatically that Christ and the apostles had had property and property rights. This meant that Franciscans could not view their renunciation of all property, both as individuals and as an order, as an imitation of Christ or call it evangelical poverty. These decrees constituted a radical change in policy on what Ockham probably regarded as settled questions. The Condemnations of 1277, like Nicholas III's papal bull officially sanctioning Bonaventure's teaching on Franciscan poverty in 1279, had been in effect for roughly a decade when Ockham was born.

Ordered by the Franciscan minister general to study the papal constitutions in 1328, Ockham concluded after a few weeks that the pope was a heretic. Ockham held that by contradicting his predecessor, Nicholas III, who defined Franciscan poverty as evangelical poverty, John XXII had advocated heresy openly. Based on his study of canon law, Ockham concluded further that this open heresy constituted a de facto renunciation of office by John XXII.

By maintaining this conclusion in defiance of John XXII publicly and effectively for many years, Ockham ensured that his subsequent philosophical reputation would be seriously compromised. No medieval Catholic wanted to cite a heretic as an authority in a philosophical, let alone a theological, controversy. That makes the business of determining influence, which is usually done by counting citations, more than usually problematic in Ockham's case.

From the point of view of the history of philosophy, the question debated today is whether Ockham should be regarded as the founder of an important school. Frederick Copleston says: "There is no adequate reason for challenging his reputation as the fountainhead of the terminist or nominalist movement."[15] By contrast,

Courtenay maintains that nominalism "included rather than stemmed from Ockham"; similarly, Katherine Tachau argues that it may be misleading to see Ockham's epistemology as central to the fourteenth century.[16] My own work has contributed to this trend emphasizing the continuity of Ockham's thought with that of Scotus. By contrast, Copleston claims that because Ockham "constantly attacked the system of Scotus, particularly his realism . . . Ockhamism was a strong reaction to, rather than a development of, Scotism."[17]

There is much to be said for Copleston's account. No one would dispute the correctness of his claim that Ockham "was an original thinker in the sense that he thought out his problems for himself and developed his solutions thoroughly and systematically,"[18] and the breadth of his philosophical project has been shown by Marilyn Adams.[19] Studies showing that a superficial reading of Ockham understates his debt to Scotus should not be taken as evidence of a lack of originality. They are a sign rather that we cannot understand Ockham without knowing Scotus. In the end, "a strong reaction" may be as important a manner of developing a philosophy as there is.

The serious study of more minor philosopher-theologians by Courtenay, Tachau, Hester Gelber, and others is altogether commendable. Perhaps inevitably as we learn more, our clear-cut notions of schools of thought—often the result of not reading the works in question—will be obscured by the tangled interactions characteristic of a reality populated by quite independent thinkers. Nonetheless, we should not confuse an absence of slavish followers or frequent citation by name with a lack of influence. As Philotheus Boehner wrote decades ago, there was no "Ockhamist school in the same sense as we encounter a Thomistic or a Scotist school,"[20] but that is because much of the influence exercised by Ockham was indirect, often mediated by thinkers powerful in their own right. Ultimately the test of influence is the ability to engage others in profound philosophical debate, not the number of times a name is cited. So it is likely that the traditional view is correct, and Ockham is a "primary source" of the revolutionary innovations in philosophical method characteristic of fourteenth-century England.[21] He was not alone. But the vigor, independence, and boldness of his thought was more marked than his contemporaries'; he was a great critic, and "he held certain clear convictions and principles which he was ready to apply courageously, systematically and logically."[22]

NOTES

1. *Corpus Iuris Canonici,* ed. A. Friedberg (Graz, 1955) 2:1133–34; Augustinus Triumphus, *Tractatus contra divinatores et sompniatores,* ed. R. Scholz, in *Unbekannte kirchenpolitische Streitschriften aus der Zeit Ludwigs des Bayern* (Rome, 1911), 2:485–90.

2. R. Wood, introduction to Adam de Wodeham, *Tractatus de indivisibilibus* (Dordrecht, 1988), 11–12, 25.

3. Frank Kelley, "Ockham: Avignon, Before and After"; and G. Etzkorn, "Codex Merton 284: Evidence of Ockham's Early Influence at Oxford," in *From Ockham to Wyclif,* ed. A. Hudson and M. Wilks, Studies in Church History, Subsidia 5 (Oxford, 1987), 7, 32–33.

4. G. Etzkorn, "Ockham at a Provincial Chapter: 1323, a Prelude to Avignon," *Archivum Franciscanum Historicum* 83 (1990): 557–67. Relation is the category chiefly discussed, but categories are discussed as well, as is the assertion that everything which exists is either a substance or a quality.

5. Wodeham notes the borrowing in *L. sec.* prol. q.6 n.12, I: 161. For Reading, see R. Wood, "Ockham on Essentially-Ordered Causes," *Die Gegenwart Ockhams* (Weinheim, 1990), 30–31. A systematic comparison of the views of Scotus and Ockham is provided in Marino Damiata, "Il contenzioso fra Duns Scoto e Ockham," *Studi francescani* 90 (1993): 233–354.

6. See Marino Damiata, "Ockham e San Tommaso d'Aquino," *Studi francescani* 91 (1994): 21–88, for a systematic comparison of the views of Aquinas and Ockham.

7. E. Moody, "Ockham and Aegidius of Rome," *Franciscan Studies* 9 (1949): 442; A. Maier, "Zu einigen Problemen der Ockhamforschung," *Archivum Franciscanum Historicum* 46 (1953): 178–80.

8. Courtenay, *Schools and Scholars,* 217.

9. Chatton's much more frequent citation is documented in Joseph Wey's edition, *Reportatio et Lectura super Sententias: Collatio ad Librum Primum et Prologus* (Toronto, 1989).

10. *Chartularium Universitatis Parisiensis* I, n.473 a.63, ed. H. Denifle and A. Chatelain (Paris, 1889), 1:547; R. Hissette, *Enquête sur les 219 articles condamnés à Paris le 7 mars 1277* (Louvain-Paris, 1977), 128. Ockham's use of this article, his principle of divine omnipotence is discussed below in chapter 4.

11. Hisette, *Enquête sur les 219 articles condamnés à Paris le 7 mars 1277,* 314–16.

12. *Chartularium Universitatis Parisiensis* II, n.838 (Paris, 1891), 280–81.

13. See note 6 above.

14. He traveled to the continent in the period when Edward III of England was allied with Louis of Bavaria. His presence is recorded in Basel, a little more than halfway to Bavaria on the main trade route between Paris and Munich, in 1339 (*Analecta Francescana* 2 [1887]: 177; 3 [1897]: 630–31, 637).

15. F. Copleston, *Ockham to Suarez.* Vol. 3 of *A History of Philosophy* (Westminster, 1953), 59.

16. Courtenay, *Schools and Scholars,* 218; K. Tachau, *Vision and Certitude in the Age of Ockham* (Leiden, 1988), xiv–xv.

17. Copleston, *Ockham to Suarez,* 59.

18. Ibid.

19. M. McCord Adams, *William Ockham* (Notre Dame, Ind., 1987).

20. P. Boehner, in Ockham, *Philosophical Writings* (Edinburgh-London, 1957), xi, li; the same point is made by Tachau, *Vision and Certitude,* xv.

21. Courtenay vigorously defends the other point of view. See *Schools and Scholars,* 218; "The Reception of Ockham's Thought in Fourteenth-Century England," in *From Ockham to Wyclif,* ed. A. Hudson and M. Wilks, Studies in Church History, Subsidia 5 (Oxford, 1987): 89–107. See also other studies by Courtenay listed in J. Beckmann's *Ockham-Bibliographie* (Hamburg, 1992).

22. Copleston, *Ockham to Suarez,* 59

CHAPTER
T H R E E | **Ockham's Thought**

Ockham has sometimes been hailed (or denounced) as the founder of modernity—emphasizing freedom, individuality, and economy of thought. He has been made responsible not only for modern progress in the sciences, but also for modern anxiety and uncertainty about the universe and the role of human reason.[1] Though he emphasized our complete dependence on God's will for salvation, he has been condemned not only as a Pelagian but also as a forerunner of the Protestant Reformation, whose leaders were extreme in their rejection of Pelagianism.

Most sweeping pronouncements on Ockham's philosophical radicalism and epoch-making historical significance are based on misunderstanding and on exaggerations of Ockham's originality. Responsible Ockham scholars today must repudiate many of the claims on which Ockham's philosophical reputation is based. Nonetheless, a reappraisal of Ockham must come to terms with the element of truth in the various extreme, and often contradictory, accounts of his doctrines and historical affinities.

The basis for such a reappraisal was laid by the pioneers of modern scholarly Ockham studies, Philotheus Boehner and Leon Baudry, beginning about 1926.[2] The completion of the Franciscan Institute's *Opera Philosophica et Theologica* in 1988 has made most of the material essential for such a reappraisal available.[3] Certainly, the reevaluation of Ockham's thought will continue for decades to come, but much has already been done.[4] A few elementary points about Ockham's epistemology, ontology, and theology and about the principles he most frequently evoked in argument will serve as an introduction to this commentary on Ockham's ethics.

I Principles of Argument

The compiler of the *De principiis theologiae,* working between 1328 and 1350, summarized all of Ockham's views under two principles: (1) God can do everything that does not include a contradiction and (2) the principle of economy (OTh VII, 507–639). Quite rightly he puts the 167 conclusions related to what I shall call the principle of abstract divine power first. But since Ockham's name has been associated with the principle of economy, which is often referred to as Ockham's (or Occam's) razor, we shall start with it.

I The Principle of Economy

As Ockham states the principle of economy, it reads "do not posit plurality unnecessarily" (pluralitas non est ponenda sine necessitate). Explanation frequently involves positing unobservable causes for observable effects. The principle of economy dictates that a minimum of such explanatory entities be posited.[5]

This principle is not original with Ockham, and despite the words of his compiler, Ockham seldom advanced it as a proof. As Boehner said, it is rather a methodological than an ontological principle for him.[6] So in regard to Ockham's razor, the question, Should we associate it with Ockham? has two parts: (1) Why not with others? and (2) Is it correctly associated with Ockham? As far as we know, Aristotle was the first to enunciate the principle of economy.[7] Moreover, Duns Scotus used the principle so often that John Reading called it "Scotus's rule."[8] In the seventeenth century, Sir Isaac Newton's first rule of reasoning in natural philosophy was based on a statement of the razor, which could have been quoted from Ockham (OPh I, 43): "it is vain to produce by many what can be produced by few [frustra fit per plura quod potest fieri per pauciora]."[9] But despite Newton's eminence and the popularity of the razor among scientists, we do not speak of Newton's razor or Scotus's rule. Probably that is because others followed the example of the compiler of *De principiis theologiae,* popularizing Ockham. They must have regarded the razor as an ontological principle, and since Ockham was famous for his sparse ontology, unlike Aristotle or Scotus, he was credited with the principle.

This brings us to our second question: Is it proper to associate the principle with Ockham? Adams, the foremost modern Ockham scholar, holds that it may mislead. Like Boehner, she points to theological difficulties with the principle: we cannot assume that God has acted economically; indeed we know that in the order of salvation God "does with more what he could do with fewer" (OTh III, 432; OTh IX, 450). Adams adds that for Ockham the principle of economy is "not his principal weapon in the fight against ontological proliferation; rather the Law of Noncontradiction is." Finally, she argues not only that this was not the weapon of choice, but that it would not have been effective if it had been, and that Ockham knew that. At best it can persuade opponents that they overestimate the "ontological commitments required by their basic tenets," or that hypostatization can be eliminated by revising their positions. Ordinarily, Ockham offers reasons independent of the principle of economy "for thinking his opponents' theses false or mutually incompatible" (Adams 1987, 1:156–61; 2:819–27).

Adams is correct to claim that Ockham offers logically more compelling arguments on most occasions. Nonetheless, even according to Adams, it is true that Ockham employed the principle of economy on a number of important occasions. He does this in connection with his arguments against positing relations of similarity distinct from the substances and accidents that ground them, in connection with his attack on quantity as something distinct from substance or quality, and in disputes about motion, quality, and temporal instants.

The case of motion is one in which Adams agrees that Ockham used the razor argument effectively. His opponents argue that we must postulate successives, such as time and motion, as well as permanent things—in this case, motion as well as movable objects and places. Arguing that it is unnecessary to postulate motion apart from movable objects in different places, Ockham begins by asking a question: "What is motion?" He replies that motion can be defined in terms of a movable object that is now where it previously was not. Motion is neither something absolute nor something relative. Not something relative, since everything relative can be reduced to something absolute. Not something absolute, since it is neither a substance nor an accident. There is no motion apart from a moving object, no additional entity inhering in a movable object that would explain the change of place we observe. All we need to posit is that movable objects are where they previously were not.

To this argument his opponents might reply that motion must be something apart from movable objects, since otherwise whenever there are bodies and places, there will be motion. Positing motion accounts for when there is and is not motion. No, Ockham might reply, I am not saying that the existence of a body and places implies motion. It is true that something does have to be added, but what is added need not be another thing. If we say that something is moving, we mean not only that there is a moving body and places, but in addition that that body is not simultaneously in both places, but rather in distinct places and nowhere at rest in a place (OPh IV, 431–36). And that is how the principle of economy normally functions for Ockham: an entity, such as motion, has been posited to explain appearances, and Ockham provides an equally satisfactory explanation that does not require us to posit such an entity.

Similarly, intelligible species are posited to explain intellection, and Ockham adduces the principle of economy in denying them. But whether his counterclaim stands or falls depends as much—or more—on the cogency of his arguments for direct realism as on his arguments that all of the phenomena that species explain have equally satisfactory alternate explanations. Thus Ockham's definition of intuitive cognition in terms of external objects (OTh V, 256–61) and his claim that it is problematic to suppose that intermediate beings rather than external objects terminate intellectual acts (OTh IV, 238–54) are more important than the argument that we do not need species to explain how external objects are represented to the mind (OTh V, 268, 272–76).[10]

The Principle of Abstract Divine Power

This brings us to the more important principle, the principle of abstract divine power: God can do everything that does not include a contradiction. While Ockham uses the principle of economy to justify his refusal to posit entities like motion and relations, he appeals to divine power, considered in abstraction from God's other attributes (de potentia Dei absoluta) to establish the possible independent existence of absolute entities.[11] De potentia Dei absoluta, accidents can exist without subjects (OPh I, 81–83, 599); quality can exist without quantity (OTh X, 58), and substance can exist without quantity (OTh X, 220). Ockham's views about logical impossibility are frequently stated in terms of what God cannot do de potentia absoluta. Thus de potentia Dei absoluta God cannot cause a proposition to be true and false simultaneously or undo the past (OPh II, 507–8; OTh VII, 132). But Ockham does not share all of our intuitions about what is or is not logically possible. Theological considerations dictate that the same thing can be in two places and that many bodies can be in the same place (OTh X, 101; OTh VII, 79, 97–101, 132). Many of the oddities of his views reflect the condemnations of 1277—for example, that God can cause more than three dimensions in the same place, or that God can cause accidents without a subject (OTh X, 183–84).[12]

The first consequence of the principle of abstract divine power drawn by the compiler of *De principiis theologiae* is the thesis that whatever God can do by means of secondary causes, he can do directly without intervening second causes. This thesis was established at Paris in 1277; its opposite was condemned in article 63: "Quod Deus non potest in effectum causae secundarie sine ipsa causa secundaria."[13] One application of this principle has to do with grace: *de potentia Dei absoluta* God could save people in the absence of the form of grace; this has been the basis of a charge of Pelagianism against Ockham.

More generally, Ockham's use of arguments based on what could be the case considering only God's power—absolute-power arguments—is responsible for his being blamed for the Reformation worldview and for modern uncertainty about the universe. Because he holds that God could have chosen to do everything differently, and still has the power to do so, it is suggested that Ockham's followers believe there is nothing dependable in the universe. We cannot believe what we see, since what appears to be the result of a secondary cause, God could be causing directly without any contribution from the secondary cause. Ockham describes a capricious God who might alter what he has ordained. Specifically, Ockham's detractors maintain that the order of salvation as understood by Ockham does not reflect justice and righteousness, because it is not necessary; *de potentia Dei absoluta* it could have been otherwise.[14]

This criticism of Ockham involves a mistaken interpretation of the distinction between God's power considered *de potentia absoluta* and *de potentia ordinata.* It is not as if God had the power to change his mind and could do one set of things *de potentia absoluta* and another *de potentia ordinata;* God is simple and his will is immutable. The distinction between absolute and ordained power does not refer to two separate powers in God. God never acts *de potentia absoluta,* according to Ockham. Properly understood, therefore, it is false to say that God can do absolutely what he cannot do ordinately (OPh I, 779–80). God's actual exercise of power is always ordinate, *de potentia ordinata.* The sentence "God can do x *de potentia absoluta,* but not *de potentia ordinata*" is true only if interpreted as follows: God can do x, though he has ordained that he will never do x; nevertheless, if God were to do x, it would be done *de potentia ordinata,* since if he were to do x, he would have ordained that he would do x (OP II, 726). Basically, absolute-power arguments refer to the scope of God's powers, to God's powers without considering whether he wills their exercise.

Ockham argues that God's power, considered simply as such, is unaffected by whether he chooses to exercise or not to exercise it. Theologians refer to God's undiminished capacity when they say that he could save without the habit of grace *de potentia absoluta* (OTh III, 452–53, 469; OTh VII, 58); and to the restriction implied by God's exercised or ordained power when they say that perhaps *de potentia ordinata* God could not fail to save once grace is posited (OTh VII, 233). God could have ordained otherwise (OTh VII, 206). But had he ordained the contrary, it would have been foreseen. Nothing actual has ever transpired or will ever transpire that is not preordained by God; everything actual is ordinate. The phrase *de potentia absoluta* always refers to what is possible, never to what is actual.

The suggestion that Ockham is a precursor of modern or Reformation theories of a capricious God is mistaken as far as human salvation is concerned. Ockham assumes without question that the order of salvation is preordained. What he seeks to avoid are presumptuous discussions about what it is fitting for God to will. That is the primary function of the absolute-power arguments; it explains Ockham's preference for considering God's power in the abstract, without discussing God's other attributes, such as his essence, wisdom, and justice.

Ockham does emphasize concepts of contingency in his picture of the natural world. So the charge that he is responsible for modern uncertainty about the universe can be justified to the extent that he emphasizes the total dependence of the world on God. In this respect, he is a faithful follower of the Franciscan tradition generally, and of Scotus in particular; and he does sharpen this emphasis on divine sovereignty over creation. Ockham, more than his predecessors, insists that without God no cause would have any effect; he claims that God could be the immediate, efficient cause of any and every effect (OTh V, 60–66; OTh X, 103, 115–18, 171). Thus if I see someone pushing a cart holding a plant down the street, it is true both that the plant will not move at all unless God cooperates with its movers and that it is possible that God is moving the plant by himself, and neither man nor cart has any effect. As Courtenay has pointed out, Ockham used the distinction between absolute and ordained power "to point up the contingent, non-necessary character of the world and its relationships."[15] Ockham's reflections on God's power, considered simply as such, were meant to point out the total dependence of creatures on God for their continued existence, their causal efficacy, and the completion of the ends for which they were created.

One could, therefore, view Ockham as a precursor of early-modern theocentric conceptions of causality, such as Nicolas de Malebranche's occasionalism, Gottfried von Leibniz's theory of preestablished harmony, or George Berkeley's repudiation of any but spiritual efficacy. But it would be important to add that in contrast to these views, Ockham holds only that God *could* substitute his own causal efficacy for that of creatures, not that God *actually* does so.

It is entirely mistaken to infer that Ockham argued that there was nothing certain in the universe or to hold him in any degree responsible for the skepticism that arose in the sixteenth and seventeenth centuries. For Ockham, there is absolute certainty; it derives from an immutable and all-powerful God. And though we may not be certain about the order of nature, we can be certain about the order of salvation. Unlike the order of nature, the order of salvation is not only preordained, but also proclaimed to the world in Scripture. It can be the basis for absolute security. Though we may be uncertain about the natural world, there is no reason for insecurity about our own final end. Ockham's focus on God's power in his discussion of the order of salvation was meant to evoke gratitude, not insecurity.

▮ Epistemology

Ockham's dubious standing as a forerunner of modern science rests in part on his claims for the evidence of experience. Ockham based all knowledge on reason, experience, and authority. His emphasis on experience was not particularly unusual in the Franciscan tradition, but his statements on the subject are clear. Moreover, if we are to understand Ockham, we must be clear about the philosophical functions of the triad of reason, experience, and authority. In addition to positing three sources of knowledge, Ockham endorses the five veridical habits postulated by Aristotle: art, prudence, intellect, science, and wisdom (*Eth. Nic.* 6.3.1139b15–17). Art is evident knowledge of things that can be made, prudence is evident knowledge about that we should do or not do (OTh I, 316), intellect is intellectual apprehension of such first principles as "the whole is greater than the parts," science is knowledge of the conclusions that can be based on such principles and other evident premises, and wisdom combines intellect and science (OTh I, 222). These five veridical habits are the province of reason and experience; they produce evident knowledge. In addition to the five veridical habits posited by Aristotle, Ockham posits a sixth one, faith, which results from authority and is a source of certain but not evident knowledge (OTh I, 200; OPh IV, 5).

Aristotelian science is restricted to knowledge of conclusions based on syllogistic reasoning from necessary first principles. By contrast, the modern concept of natural science emphasizes the experimental reliability of its evidence more than the logical coherence of its theories. From a terminological point of view, there is a considerable difference: when we speak of "knowing scientifically," we are referring to the results of a controlled experiment; Ockham is referring to knowledge of the conclusions of syllogistic reasoning. But this does not mean that there was no place for observation in Aristotelian science. Ockham affirms that necessary premises can be based on experience and observation (OTh VIII, 173). And like Aristotle, he holds that the process of knowing begins with the senses (OPh IV, 21).

Ockham argues that the number of theological truths that can be demonstrated conclusively is more restricted than his predecessors thought. He agrees with his predecessors that the existence of God can be demonstrated (OTh II, 395–96). Unlike his predecessors, however, he claims that there is no logically compelling argument for monotheism (OTh II, 337–57, 413). This does not mean for Ockham that there was a basis for justifiable doubt about God's unity, or that the possibility of certainty regarding theological propositions has been overestimated. The question is only which theological propositions can be demonstrated from evident premises and thus can claim the special status required for Aristotelian science.

Certainty for Ockham is not restricted to conclusions based on reason and experience. Certain knowledge is also based on authority (OTh IV, 290; OTh VIII, 288, 409–10). Speaking inexactly, Ockham sometimes even refers to theological conclusions known "scientifically" on the basis of authority (OTh IV, 290; OTh IX, 488). But elsewhere, recognizing that the principles of revealed theology are neither evident nor necessary (OPh IV, 5–6), Ockham explains that most theological propositions are not evident; our knowledge of them depends on faith (OTh I, 192, 197–99, 206).

What authority does Ockham recognize as certain? In the first place, ordinary, everyday teaching, which is necessary to know truths whose evidence is not otherwise accessible. When Ockham speaks of faith as *true* and *certain* but not *evident* belief, he is not referring exclusively to religious faith (OPh V, 5). His examples are such propositions as 'Rome is a large city' and 'this woman is my mother.' At least in his case, since he could not see Rome and was not present as a rational observer at his birth, neither of those propositions is or can be evident to him, but they are nonetheless true and certain or indubitable (OTh I, 200; OTh IV, 5). Unlike opinions, beliefs based on faith preclude error (OTh I, 341). Opinion is not a veridical habit, because we can equally opine true and false propositions (OTh I, 200, 206). Though he does not use the word 'justified,' it appears that for Ockham, faith is nonevident but justified true belief. Unlike evident knowledge and scientific knowledge, faith does not compel assent, but neither can it reasonably be doubted.

Ockham also often acknowledges the authority of the great philosophers of the past. When he disagrees with Aristotle and Averroes, however, Ockham does not scrupulously reproduce their views; instead he glosses them freely (OTh X, 35; OPh I, 479). Modern theologians, unapproved by the church, have even less weight with Ockham (OTh X, 70). The primary authority which provides knowledge that is in principle inaccessible to us is Scripture (OTh IV, 290; OTh VIII, 288).[16] Ockham is also prepared to prefer the conclusions of the saints and the church to other conclusions that might appear more probable if we had only reason and experience to guide us (OTh I, 17–18; OTh VI, 281; OTh VII, 138–40; OTh VIII, 191; OTh IX, 449–50; OTh X, 71, 213). Ockham holds that the universal church (though not any particular church office or group of ecclesiastical officials) is infallible; if one Christian weakens and abandons the faith, another will firmly maintain it.[17]

'Experience' refers to observation and a posteriori demonstration, as opposed to the science of a priori demonstrations. Ockham suggests that necessary propositions can be known a posteriori as well as a priori; 'heat can burn' is an example of a necessary proposition known only a posteriori (OTh VIII, 173). Our knowledge of the freedom of the human will is based on experience; its evidence cannot and does not depend on a priori demonstration. Similarly, we know evidently from experience that there are causes and effects. Known only by experience, the fact of causality is so certain that it can function as a premise in logical arguments (OTh IV, 665; OTh V, 62, 314). Finally, we know from experience that there is knowledge of our internal acts and the external world. By means of intuitive cognition we know evidently that we are thinking and whether external objects exist or not (OTh V, 256). Ockham affirms that knowledge can be and is based on experience. Of course not all experience leads to knowledge; we can be and sometimes are deceived. But Ockham quite rightly sees that the possibility of deceptive experience in no way implies that veridical experience does not exist. And as a matter of fact, he is not much interested in the question of how we distinguish veridical from deceptive experiences. He is neither skeptical about the evidential value of experience nor much interested in refuting skeptical arguments.

Nonetheless, Ockham has been accused of skepticism. This misapprehension is based on Ockham's definition of the two types of cognition involved in knowing by experience: abstract and intuitive. Intuitive cognition is immediate intellectual apprehension of existing things. As a result of intuitive cognition, we can know such propositions as 'Socrates is here' or 'Socrates is white.' It is knowledge of what is the case, here and now. By contrast, when such cognition supports no existential claim, but its evidentiary value is derived from intuitive cognition, it is called abstract cognition (OTh I, 30–33, 56, 64, 70; OTh V, 256–63). A prototypical example of something known by abstract cognition is the proposition 'heat burns.'

As stated thus far, Ockham shares these views with Scotus, from whom he took them. Attacks on Ockham are based on a controversial development of those views, Ockham's theory of intuitive cognition of nonexistents. This is an application of the principle of abstract divine power. Since God can take the place of a secondary cause as an external object of our faculties, he can cause intuitive cognition directly. God can cause intuitive cognition of a rose directly, in the absence of that rose. According to Ockham, intuitive cognition of a rose caused directly by God in the absence of the rose would result in the knowledge of the proposition 'this rose does not exist.' Even Ockham's champion, Adam de Wodeham challenged this claim. Holding that intuitive cognition of a rose always produces assent to the claim 'this rose exists,' Wodeham saw divinely caused intuitive cognition as a possible source of cognitive error and hence of uncertainty. Ockham, for whom cognition is always veridical, and for whom intuitive cognition is evident, would simply deny that the evidence provided by intuitive cognition of nonexistents could be the same as that provided by intuitive cognition of existing things. Thus Ockham saw no skeptical consequences in admitting the possibility of divine intervention in intuitive cognition.[18]

▌ Ontology

The most interesting and distinctive aspect of Ockham's ontology is his denial of common natures. If we ask what exists in the external world, he would reply "only individual substances and qualities" (OPh II, 240, 244, 257), making exceptions for some real relations posited for basically theological reasons. This view affects all other aspects of his thought. Thus he posits intuitive cognition only of primary substances and qualities. Since common natures do not exist, our concepts of universals—such as the concept 'animal'—do not correspond to any extramental reality. Universals themselves exist only as concepts in the soul. The evidential value of generalizations about universal concepts such as 'animal' or 'man,' called abstract cognitions, depends on intuitive cognition of individuals. A statement such as 'all men are animals' is true only if at least one man exists.

Theories of universals are usually described as *realist* or *nominalist.* Realists maintain that common natures really exist in the realm of ideas or in the external world, and that individuals are instantiations of those common natures. By contrast, nominalists maintain that common natures exist only as names describing groups of individuals. According to these definitions, however, Ockham was a neither a realist nor a nominalist, but rather a *conceptualist,* maintaining that common natures exist, but only in the form of acts of understanding or the products of those acts. Thus the common designation of Ockham as a nominalist is misleading. It correctly indicates his rejection of extramental common natures, but misrepresents his solution to the problem of universals in terms of mental concepts.

Ockham's denial of common natures affects his views on logic—most directly his theory of supposition. Medieval theories of supposition are theories about the way names can refer. Ockham distinguishes three important kinds of supposition (OTh V, 142, 227): personal, simple, and material. Taken in material supposition, reference is to the word itself, spoken or written; taken in simple supposition, reference is to the associated concept. Only in the case of personal supposition do terms refer to the real things they properly signify, singular individuals. The term 'man' is the usual example. In 'man is noun,' it has material supposition; in 'man is a species,' simple supposition; and in 'man is an animal,' personal supposition.

Composed of universal propositions, Aristotelian science does not deal with particular individuals. Realists would claim that it deals with common natures in the real world. Like some twentieth-century philosophers of science, Ockham denies that there are real common natures, but unlike Logical Positivists, he does not deny the existence of natural kinds. So when we say "man is an animal," we are not describing a shared characteristic of an arbitrarily selected group. And though 'humanity' has simple supposition, the term 'man' in 'man is an animal'—or rather 'every man is an animal'—has personal supposition; its subject term has personal supposition, it signifies real things (Adams 1987, 287–313). A real science, such as physics, is distinguished from logic because the concepts it includes signify external substances and qualities, while the concepts in logic signify thoughts in the mind, second intentions (OPh IV, 12).

Ockham reduces the number of categories with distinct extramental reference to three: substance, qualities (OTh IX, 416–24), and few real relations (OTh V, 15; OTh IV, 313, 369–74); quantity, place, time, position, action, and passion he views as logical functions of the other categories (OPh II, 205–24, 238–48, 298). He believes that categories other than substance and quality do not correspond to distinct individuals; rather they classify terms. Thus quantity and relation terms can signify the same things in different ways. For example, 'five feet tall' is a term that signifies Stephen as an extended substance, while 'son' indicates his relation to Allen. To account for the way things are, we do not have to postulate tallness or sonship.

Nonetheless, though Ockham believes he can explain motion without positing corresponding entities, he does not view acts or habits as functions of substance. Like all Scholastics, he regards them as species of quality. Acts and habits—and most importantly for us as we study Ockham's *De connexione virtutum,* human acts of intellect and will—belong to the category of quality and could exist independently outside the mind *de potentia Dei absoluta.*

I Theology and Ethics

Ockham follows Scotus in his description of God. God is a simply first, necessary, and infinite being (OTh II, 31–33, 424; OTh IX, 766, 774–75); by contrast creatures are contingent, finite, and dependent beings. Ockham agrees with Scotus that as an absolutely independent (*a se*), simply first being, God's existence can be demonstrated (OTh II, 335–37, 354–56). But unlike Scotus, Ockham thinks it impossible to demonstrate that there is only one God (OTh II, 340–57).

Ockham, like Scotus, holds that there is a concept of being which can be predicated of everything that exists—being can be predicated univocally of God, of substances, and of accidents (OTh II, 293–322, 333–34; OTh IX, 357–58). But he also holds that the concept of being does not correspond to any underlying similarity between beings. Thus although Ockham holds that the concept of being is predicated univocally of God and creatures (OTh II, 312), like Scotus he denies that that concept corresponds to anything that really exists and is common to God and creatures (OTh II, 300, 306–312). Our knowledge of God does not include any simple propositions that signify God in himself (OTh I, 203–5; OTh II, 404–5, 413). Noetically there is a distance between God and creatures, hence the importance of Scripture and ecclesiastical authority for knowledge of God. But though God is not knowable in himself in this life in a simple, proper concept, causally there is no distance between humankind and God. Without God's continual conservation, we would cease to exist at once; our dependence on God is constant and immediate.

Not only is Ockham more modest than his predecessors about what could be known scientifically about God, he is also more restrained about the claims of theologians. Theologians know more than the uneducated: they can expound Scripture and defend the faith. But they do not know more clearly. Since no one knows the truths of the faith evidently, an old woman may grasp a tenet of the faith as perfectly as a well-trained theologian (OTh I, 205). That theology is not a science is a basic tenet of Ockham's theology, maintained in self-conscious opposition to Aquinas; it is not a science because the principles on which it is based are not evident (OTh I, 184–90, 193, 199).

But though theology is a not a science based on self-evident principles, in one sense it is more certain than the sciences. We should adhere to its principles with greater firmness than to those of the sciences. Because it deals with greater truths and requires firmer adherence, theology judges the sciences, which serve it (OTh I, 200). The science of physics, for example, provides the theologian with a demonstration of God's existence.

Ockham's teaching on human salvation agrees in most respects with that of Scotus and differs sharply from that of Aquinas; it rejects accounts of the sacraments as instrumental, efficient causes (OTh VII, 12–14). Ockham distinguishes between grace understood as divine acceptance and grace understood as a habit informing the soul (OTh III, 471; OTh VII, 213–16). Like Scotus, Ockham holds that human salvation depends absolutely on divine acceptance. He minimizes the role of the kind of habit described by Aquinas and maximizes the direct role of divine acceptance. Salvation without divine acceptance would be logically impossible; hence it would not be possible even *de potentia Dei absoluta*. God has decreed that salvation requires the habit of grace, so no one will be saved without that habit (OTh IX, 241). But had God ordained otherwise, there would be nothing to prevent salvation without the habit of grace. *De potentia ordinata* the habit of grace is necessary; divine acceptance is necessary to salvation *de potentia absoluta,* regardless of what God ordains, because salvation without divine acceptance would be a contradiction in terms (OTh IX, 596–99).

Ockham's understanding of salvation in terms of acceptance is part of his emphasis on the role of God's will. What merits a divine reward can be nothing other than what God decides to accept. God is not obligated to allow people to achieve the end of their nature. Indeed, God cannot be obligated by anything external to his nature. There would be nothing unjust about God's willing our damnation; everything that God does he does justly (OTh VII, 55; OTh II, 48; OTh VI, 353).

Ockham's frequent reiteration of statements of this kind has mistakenly led many scholars to conclude that he is a divine-command theorist of morality, who defines goodness and moral virtue solely in terms of the dictates of God's arbitrary will.[19] This is not the case. Ockham maintains that acts of moral virtue must be elicited in conformity with right reason (OTh IX, 100, 260; OTh VIII, 362–63, 395). Basing himself on Aristotle's discussion of friendship or love *(philia) (Eth. Nic.* 8.2.1155b19), Ockham distinguishes three kinds of goods: the objects of love are either worthy (or virtuous), useful, or pleasant (OTh VIII, 442). As the supremely lovable object, in whom there is a plenitude of all goodness, God is the paradigm of goodness (OTh I, 447, 464; OTh IV, 683; OPh I, 28), but goodness is not defined in terms of God's dictates. Divine mercy and liberality are good because they are lovable. Statements like "God always acts for a good end" and "God cannot will evil" (OTh V, 342, 353) are not trivial analytical statements, but substantial claims.

As Adams has shown, Ockham distinguishes between positive and nonpositive morality;[20] he postulates two sets of norms: naturalistic (or nonpositive) dictates of right reason and voluntaristic (or positive) dictates. Dictates ascertainable from experience or moral science by human reason establish what is virtuous or vicious. Positive morality is the province of human or divine law; divine command establishes what is meritorious or sinful (OTh IX, 176–77).

In the area of ethics, Ockham's most radical departure from his predecessors is his insistence that we can will evil as evil. Here Ockham is at odds with Aristotle and with Scotus as well as with Aquinas. Scotus represents the common Scholastic doctrine when he maintains that we can will nothing except under the aspect of goodness; we cannot will unhappiness. Where the object is evil as evil, the only act of will we can elicit is rejection.[21] Of course, the Scholastics were aware that people do choose evils. Scholastics defended their position by arguing that people who make these choices misrepresent the evils as goods. Given his definition of goodness in terms of what is lovable, and his understanding of beatitude as the end proper to our nature, one might have expected Ockham to espouse a similar view, which he does. But he accepts the view only if taken in a trivial sense: if wickedness is defined as what we reject. Since we cannot choose what we reject, we cannot choose wickedness. Insofar as wickedness is defined apart from acts of will, however, we can choose wickedness as wickedness. On this subject, Ockham's most important claim is that we can choose against fruition—that is, against the enjoyment which is the appropriate end of our nature (OTh I, 504–7; OTh VII, 350; OTh VIII, 442–46).

More innovative than Scotus on the possible depravity of the human will, Ockham was more traditional than Scotus on the locus of moral responsibility. Scotus had maintained that moral goodness depended on external acts as well as on intentions (Adams 1981, 5–30).[22] Ockham rejects this view, claiming that only what we intend determines whether an act is good or evil. But though his moral theory focuses exclusively on acts of will, because they alone are within our control, he does not ignore the moral significance of the external circumstances of our actions in formulating and assessing acts of will; nor does he maintain that ignorance excuses. His *On the Connection of the Virtues* includes a detailed discussion of the impact of external circumstances on our moral assessment of human actions; his *On the Compatibility of Virtuous Acts and Errors of Intellect* presents his views on culpable ignorance. Like Aristotle, Aquinas, and many other authors, Ockham sharply limits the application of the dictum "ignorance excuses." Like Aquinas, Ockham distinguishes invincible ignorance, which excuses, from vincible ignorance, which does not.

Here an example may be helpful in describing Ockham's views. Being told that Ockham considers that only acts of will are culpable, Henry might conclude that he did nothing wrong when he sold beer late at night to a teenager who was subsequently killed in an automobile accident while intoxicated. If her parents sue the store, and Henry is fired, Henry might be outraged: "I didn't mean any harm, there's nothing wrong with selling beer, I didn't know she was only fifteen." Henry could easily be right about each of these claims and still have acted viciously, according to Ockham. He would argue that selling beer to a mature person at a reasonable time of day is an entirely different act from selling it to child at a dangerous time of night. Suppose Henry then repeats, "But I did not know she was only fifteen." An Ockhamist might reply: "It is wrong not to take steps to inform yourself about the age of people interested in buying alcohol." The store manager will remind Henry that he is supposed to ask for two forms of identification after 10:00 P.M. When something terrible happens as a consequence of his action, not intending harm excuses Henry only if he knows what he can be expected to know and has evaluated the circumstances intelligently.

Ockham differs from Aquinas on the question of the connection of the virtues; he opposes the Thomistic and Aristotelian view that virtues are necessarily connected, so that the virtues of honesty and generosity of spirit cannot fail to support and reinforce each other and have a common origin. By contrast Ockham holds that it is quite possible, for example, to find truthfulness in the absence of justice. His views on this subject were anticipated by Olivi and many other Franciscans, most remarkably by Scotus.[23]

As might be anticipated, Ockham does not entirely agree with Scotus, he allows some connection between the virtues. He argues that if the appropriate circumstances arise, higher degrees of virtue are incompatible with vice and do incline us to other virtues. This is because their purpose is obedience to right reason precisely for the sake of right reason, or obedience to God for the sake of love of God. Ockham's general discussion of virtue in this context is attractive and persuasive. Chapter 4 provides more information on the medieval controversy regarding the connection of the virtues and Ockham's place in that tradition.

I Conclusion

What is modern about Ockham? Chiefly four things: (1) his insistence that the external world consists primarily of individuals, not common natures, paired with (2) his emphasis on experience; (3) in theology, the modesty of his claim about demonstrative knowledge of the divine; and (4) in morals, his suggestion that human beings can knowingly choose evil. This assumes, of course, that the reader accepts certain generalizations about the modern as opposed to the medieval world: that modern thinkers have recognized the possibility of despairing, self-destructive human choices; that modern theologians emphasize the inadequacy of the human intellect to apprehend the divine; and that modern scientists have generally been empiricists, not realists. On such matters, our evaluation of medieval thinkers will change as our understanding of the modern world changes; a case in point is the philosophy of science, where some forms of realism have recently been persuasively advocated. Since anticipating modernity is an important part of Ockham's philosophical reputation, it is an issue that the reader needs to consider. For my purposes, however, when I say that Ockham's thought is modern, that means that Ockham shares assumptions common today; it does not mean that his views represent an advance on those of his predecessors.

Ockham's concern for freedom is modern in some respects but not in others. Modern is the insistence on evangelical liberty in the church found in his political works.[24] Of much greater significance for Ockham's theology are his views on divine freedom. His basic theological project is to describe God in the church and God in the universe in a manner compatible with divine freedom. In this context Ockham evaluates human liberty much more negatively than we would today. What we would call freedom Ockham describes as the liberty of mutability. It is no great advantage; it does not allow us to follow our inclinations or free us from coercion. Rather, it exposes us to sin and misery (OTh V, 354–56).

Since the view that human beings are free only to choose between slavery to sin and submission to the divine will is a commonplace of Christian theology, it is of little interest to the historian of ideas concerned with originality, and yet it was decisive for Ockham's evaluation of human freedom. Similarly, Ockham's affirmation that he wished his intellect to be captive to the authority of the church is totally unoriginal (OTh X, 71, 213). Indeed, it can be viewed as self-serving, since at the time Ockham made it, his works were being examined by a papal commission. And yet the sincerity of the statement is indubitable; it precisely reflects Ockham's own life choices. The foremost European logician for centuries and an original and immensely productive theologian, once he was recruited by Michael of Cesena for the defense of Franciscan poverty he wrote little other than political tracts. As far as we know, he seldom returned to rarefied theological questions or to abstract questions of ethics, epistemology, and ontology, though there is evidence that his interest in logic continued until near the close of his life.[25]

It may seem paradoxical to describe someone like Ockham, who so vehemently attacked the reigning pope and suffered excommunication as a result, as captive to the authority of the church. And yet in a sense it is accurate. It took only ten years for the theory of Franciscan poverty to go from being a doctrine defined by papal bull, a doctrine whose orthodoxy it was forbidden to dispute, to being regarded as a heterodox view. In the circumstances, it is not surprising to find people like Ockham, who in defending the theory considered themselves more orthodox, truer to the Christian faith, than the pope. Being true to the Christian faith was Ockham's highest ideal. In ecclesiology, his theory of the indefectibility and infallibility of the church admits the possibility that the true faith should be maintained only by a single, humble individual who holds no office in the church. On the one hand, this is an allusion to standard Christian doctrine, which maintains that only the Blessed Virgin maintained the faith in the time between Christ's crucifixion and resurrection.[26] On the other hand, Ockham surely also saw it as a vindication of his own defiant and increasingly lonely stance.

I NOTES

1. H. Blumenberg, *The Legitimacy of the Modern Age,* trans. R. Wallace (Cambridge, Mass., 1983).

2. L. Baudry, *Guillaume d'Occam* (Paris, 1949); *Lexique philosophique de Guillaume d'Ockham* (Paris, 1958). See also Philotheus Boehner, *Collected Articles on Ockham* (St. Bonaventure, N.Y., 1958). Other important pioneers include K. Michalski, E. Hochstetter, J. Koch, and E. Moody.

3. Also important are the works of Ockham's contemporaries: Peter Aureol, ed. E. Buytaert (St. Bonaventure, N.Y., 1952, 1956); John Lutterell, ed. F. Hoffmann, *Die Schriften* (Erfurt, 1959); Walter of Chatton, ed. J. Wey (Toronto, 1989); and Adam de Wodeham, ed. R. Wood and G. Gál, *Lectura secunda* (St. Bonaventure, N.Y., 1990).

4. Particularly important is Marilyn Adams's monumental study, *William Ockham* (Adams 1987). The many other important studies published between 1900 and 1990 are listed in Jan Beckmann's *Ockham-Bibliographie* (Hamburg, 1992).

5. The principle is usually stated in words not used by Ockham: "entities should not be unnecessarily multiplied" (entita non sunt multiplicanda sine necessitate). This wording is used by Ioannes Poncius (d. 1660), *Commentarii Theologici quibus Io. Duns Scoti Quaestiones in libros Sent.* III d. 34 q. unica (Paris, 1661), 4:387. He refers to the "common axiom . . . frequently used by Scholastics" (axioma vulgare . . . frequenter utuntur Scholastici: Non sunt multiplicanda entia sine necessitate).

6. William of Ockham, *Philosophical Writings: A Selection* (Edinburgh-London, 1957), xxi.

7. *Physica* 1.4.188a17–18; 6.189a14–15; 8.6.259a10–12; *Topica* 8.11.162a24–25. *Auctoritates Aristotelis* 2.26, ed. J. Hamesse (Louvain-Paris, 1974), 141: ". . . peccatum est fieri per plura quod potest fieri per pauciora."

8. G. Gal, "Quaestio Ioannis de Reading de necessitate specierum intelligibilium: Defensio doctrinae Scoti," n. 225–26, *Franciscan Studies* 29 (1969): 73, 133–134.

9. I. Newton, *Philosophiae naturalis principia Mathematica,* ed. A. Koyré and I. B. Cohen, assisted by A. Whitman (Cambridge, Mass., 1972), III:550 (a reprint of p. 387 in the 1726 edition).

10. See also below in the commentary, a.4 164.

11. A similar presentation of this distinction and its significance in Ockham's thought is found in J. Miethke's excellent article on Ockham in *Gestalten der Kirchengeschichte,* ed. M. Greschat (Stuttgart, 1983): 4:161–62.

12. *Chartularium Universitatis Parisiensis* I, n.473 a.138–41, ed. H. Denifle and A. Chatelain (Paris, 1889), 1:551; R. Hissette, *Enquête sur les 219 articles condamnés à Paris le 7 mars 1277* (Louvain-Paris, 1977), 287.

13. *Chartularium* I, n.473 a.63, 1:547; in Hissette, *Enquête,* 128.

14. R. Wood, "Göttliches Gebot und Gutheit Gottes nach Wilhelm von Ockham," *Philosophisches Jahrbuch* 101 (1993): 38.

15. Courtenay, "The Dialectic of Divine Omnipotence," *Covenant and Causality in Medieval Thought* (London, 1984), 14.

16. In his discussion of Ockham's views on the sources of Christian doctrine, Brian Tierney correctly observes that Ockham does not support the view that only Scripture can be a source of doctrine. In his generally excellent discussion, however, he also mistakenly suggests that Ockham did not give primacy to Scripture. Tierney points to a passage where Ockham is arguing against John XXII's eccentric views on beatific vision. Here Ockham says that if someone finds a passage in Scripture that appears to be contrary to what the universal church teaches, one should disregard it and either demand a truer codex, reject the translation, or doubt the interpretation (OP III, 73). Here the key word is 'appears'; Ockham would never agree that Scripture actually supported the pope's position on this matter. It was his view that Pope John, a canon lawyer who had been occupied in worldly litigation all his life, was unqualified to interpret Scripture. For Ockham, Scripture and reason are the chief sources of certainty, as can be seen in many of the passages that Tierney cites. Most of the passages in his theological works where Ockham defers to the authority of the church are instances where he reluctantly gives up a favored opinion consonant with Scripture and based on convincing argument in deference to the authority of the church; but he would not even have considered an opinion that was not consonant with Scripture. For a discussion of Ockham's efforts to define the extrabiblical sources of authority in his later political works, see Tierney, *Origins of Papal Infallibility: 1150–1350* (Leiden, 1972), 218–26.

17. *Dialogus* 1.V.5, fol. 36v: "communitas autem christianorum sic preservatur a Deo quod si unus a fide exorbitaverit, alius firmus in fide divino munere permanebit"; 1.V.8, fol. 38v: "illa autem ecclesia romana quae errare non potest est universalis ecclesia . . . nullum est collegium neque praelatorum neque religiosorum . . . [quod] non possit errare contra fidem; collegium tamen universaliter christianorum quod de facto comprendit viros et mulieres Deus nunquam permittet contra fidem errare"; 1.V.12, fol. 39v: "tota congregatio bonorum ubicumque sint potest ecclesia romana appelari." Tierney has traced the canonistic sources of Ockham's views in "Ockham, the Conciliar Theory, and the Canonists," *Journal of the History of Ideas* 15 (1954): 40–70; "Natural Law and Canon Law in Ockham's *Dialogus*," in *Aspects of Late Medieval Government and Society*, ed. J. Rowe (Toronto, 1986), 6–15. Tierney discusses Ockham's defense of the view that a pope can authentically define the faith immutably in his *Origins of Papal Infallibility*, 205–37. Here the key passage in Ockham comes from *Opus Nonaginta dierum* (OP II, 833). See also John Ryan, "Evasion and Ambiguity: Ockham and Tierney's Ockham"; and Tierney, "Ockham's Infallibility and Ryan's Infallibility," *Franciscan Studies* 46 (1986): 285–300.

18. For the fourteenth-century controversy on this subject, see R. Wood, "Intuitive Cognition and Divine Omnipotence: Ockham in Fourteenth-Century Perspective," in *From Ockham to Wyclif*, ed. A. Hudson and M. Wilks, Studies in Church History, Subsidia 5 (Oxford, 1987): 51–61; and Wood, "Adam Wodeham on Sensory Illusions," *Traditio* 38 (1982): 213–52. There is a vast literature on this, as on certain topics in Ockham's philosophy; see J. Beckmann, *Ockham-Bibliographie*, 143–44, 157. One good, brief article is M. Adams, "Intuitive Cognition, Certainty, and Scepticism in William Ockham," *Traditio* 26 (1970): 389–98.

19. This view has been generally accepted. Even the distinguished historian of philosophy Frederick Copleston maintained that for Ockham the act of loving God is good only *because* God commands it: "Authoritarianism has the last word" (*Ockham to Suarez*, 121). As recently as 1991, William Mann argued that for Ockham, "God's will determines what counts as created goodness" ("The Best of All Possible Worlds," in S. MacDonald, ed., *Being and Goodness* [Ithaca, N.Y., 1991]: 257). More moderate views are expressed by Ivan Boh, "An Examination of Ockham's Aretetic Logic," *Archiv für Geschichte der Philosophie* (1963): 253–68; and Kevin McDonnell, "William of Ockham and Situation Ethics," *American Journal of Jurisprudence* (1971): 25–35.

The best general discussion of Ockham's moral philosophy is found in Lucan Freppert, *The Basis of Morality According to William Ockham* (St. Bonaventure, N.Y., 1988). For a discussion of the different viewpoints expressed, see Adams 1981, 23n.

20. M. Adams, "William Ockham: Voluntarist or Naturalist," in *Studies in Medieval Philosophy*, Studies in Philosophy and the History of Philosophy 17, ed. J. Wippel (Washington, D.C., 1987), 234–39; Adams, "The Structure of Ockham's Moral Theory," *Franciscan Studies* 46 (1986): 1–35. Most other studies of Ockham's distinction between positive and nonpositive law focus on his political works. See Tierney, "Natural Law and Canon Law in Ockham's *Dialogus*," 15–20; A. S. McGrade, *The Political Thought of William of Ockham* (Cambridge, 1974), 136, 174–85. See also R. Wood, "Göttliches Gebot und Gutheit Gottes."

21. Scotus, *Collatio* 3 n.6, V: 153b; *Rep.* IV d.49 q.6 n.6–12, XXIV: 661–64; Thomas, *Summa Theol.* I-II q.10 a.2.

22. Note that Scotus, like Ockham, rejects the Thomistic view that moral acts are to be understood in terms of acts of understanding (*Sent.* IV d.49 q.6 n.5–9, XXI: 98–100).

23. B. Kent, "Aristotle and the Franciscans: Gerald Odonis' Commentary on the Nicomachean Ethics" (Ph.D. diss., Columbia University, 1984); J. Walsh, "Buridan on the Virtues," *Journal of the History of Philosophy* 24 (1986): 453–69; O. Suk, "The Connection of the Virtues According to Ockham," *Franciscan Studies* 10 (1950): 9–32, 91–113.

24. As John Morrall points out, "evangelical liberty," as Ockham understands it, is a restrictive and negative concept ("Some Notes on a Recent Interpretation of Ockham's Political Theory," *Franciscan Studies* 9 [1949]: 362–63). A. S. McGrade shows that Ockham extends to the political sphere the claim that government authorities should not encroach on natural and God-given freedoms (*The Political Thought of William of Ockham* [Cambridge, 1974], 64–71, 140–49, 180–82, 221). See also F. Kelley, "Ockham: Avignon, Before and After," 11–18; and Y. Congar, *L'Eglise de saint Augustin à l'époque moderne* (Paris, 1970), 294. It is a fact that Ockham condemned his ecclesiastical enemies harshly as heretics, but his views on dealing with heresy were not authoritarian. As McGrade has shown, he advocated the use of learning and argument in dealing with erring Christians.

25. The *Elementarium logicae* and *Tractatus minor,* which are plausibly attributed to Ockham, were composed between 1340 and 1347 (OPh VII, *11).

26. Bonaventura, *Sent.* III d.3 p.1 a.2 q.3 ad 2 (Quaracchi, 1887), III: 78; Thomas, *Sent.* III d.3 q.1 a.2 q.2 ad 1 (Parma, 1858), VII: 40.

| **The Medieval Debate on the
Connection of the Virtues**

Some people can be counted on to do the right thing. They enjoy
good food and take pleasure in their bodies, but they are not intemperate. They are not incontinent and at the mercy of their
emotions, but bravely face adversity. They are not greedy, but
treat other people fairly. Day in and day out, they know what
needs to be done to lead a worthy life. We describe people who
behave this way as morally virtuous—their actions are dictated
by the cardinal virtues of temperance, courage, justice, and prudence.

Are those virtues essentially connected? If someone is just,
will he or she also be courageous? Aristotle thinks so, and speaking for the Christian theological tradition, Jerome, Ambrose, and
Gregory agree that the virtues are connected.[1] Augustine writes:
"in like manner, although the virtues in the human soul each has
its own different meaning, yet they are in no way separated from
each other; so that whenever people are equal in courage, they
are also equal in prudence, temperance, and justice."[2]

For Aristotle, the connection is part of a harmonious picture
of the development of virtue. An excellent human being naturally
desires the good; practical wisdom is the intellectual virtue that
dictates acts by means of which goodness is achieved, and habitual virtues are the products of good training and the exercise
of repeated acts of practical wisdom. Thus in a well-functioning
human being, discerning practical wisdom—or prudence—will
naturally produce both justice and courage (*Eth. Nic.* 6.13.
1144b30–1145a6). For Christian theology, the unity of the virtues is viewed not as a consequence of the proper functioning of
human nature and human intellect, but as the result of the unity
of a single theological virtue, the virtue of love, or charity (*cari-*

tas), which is seen as a necessary and sufficient cause of every and all virtue. Without love there can be no virtue; if charity is once postulated, every other virtue follows.[3]

Since Aristotle and the Fathers of the Church agree on this central point, what issues can arise for Christian Aristotelianism? The answer is that medieval Scholastics disagreed as much about the proper interpretation of Aristotle and the Fathers as about the consequences of their views. As we shall see, they point, for example, to other texts from Augustine where he expresses reservations about the thesis that the virtues are connected.[4] Indeed, the question whether the virtues are connected was a standard and an unusually fruitful topic of controversy in the Middle Ages. Writing in the middle of the twelfth century, Peter Lombard, the author of the standard medieval textbook on theology, tells us that it was a customary topic for discussion (*Sent.* III d.1. c.1, II: 202), though he himself provides us only with citations from authorities in favor of the view that the virtues are connected. Jerome says that all virtues adhere together; if one virtue is lacking, all will be absent. Augustine says that charity is the mother of all virtues; if it is present, what can be lacking? To the degree that it is absent, there will be vice.[5]

Though Aristotle's conclusion agreed with those of the Fathers, when his ethical and metaphysical works became available, it was clear that his reasons for maintaining that conclusion were very different from those of Christian religious thinkers. For Aristotle, the unity of the virtues derives primarily from the unity of prudence, or right reason, directing us toward acts that lead to goodness (*Eth. Nic.* 6.13.1145a1). For the Fathers, the unity of the virtues derives from the unity of charity, or love of God. The Fathers emphasize love, or right willing; Aristotle, prudence (*phronesis*), which is the intellect deliberating about means to ends, a practical intelligence that grasps particulars. This difference in emphasis explains one focus of the debate on the connection of the virtues: an attempt to delineate the comparative roles of will and intellect in moral life.

Aristotle's example as well as his reasoning prompted debate. Neither he nor the other good pagans familiar to Christian scholars had been baptized. Since he did not have infused goodness, it would appear that he had no virtue, and yet his ethical wisdom was generally (though not universally) recognized. Moreover, Aristotle was primarily concerned with the virtues of the citizen and with intellectual virtues, not with such religious virtues as reverence, mercy, and humility. Accordingly, one topic for discussion was whether non-Christians were capable of virtue at all, while another concerned the question of the relation between the so-called political virtues and the theological virtues of faith, hope, and charity. Ockham uses the Aristotelian designation "moral virtues" rather than "political virtues" to refer to the group of virtues that includes the cardinal virtues of justice, courage, temperance, and prudence; those who prefer the phrase "political virtues" emphasize that these virtues fit us for life with our fellow human beings and contrast them with the theological virtues that orient us properly toward God.[6] Though some of his fellow Franciscans denied that pagans were capable of moral virtue,[7] Ockham held that true virtue was possible for non-Christians. But although he allowed even heroic virtue for pagans, he maintained that the highest degree, even of the moral virtues, was impossible without love of God.

The contrasts presented by Aristotelian and Christian ethics meant that discussion of the connection of the virtues developed in new ways when Aristotle's *Ethics, Politics,* and *Metaphysics* were read for the first time by Western medieval authors in the thirteenth century. But though there is considerable discussion of the connection of the virtues in commentaries on Aristotle's *Ethics,* most Scholastic discussion of the question was conducted by theologians, usually lecturing on Lombard's *Sentences.* And though Ockham's *De connexione virtutum* is his *Quaestio Biblica,* or *Principium Bibliae* (OTh IX, *20), his discussion is not a biblical commentary; nor is it based on patristic biblical exegesis. Rather it is an exercise in Scholastic theology, primarily based on the work of other medieval theologians who were seeking, like Ockham, to harmonize Aristotle with patristic theology. Its single most important source is John Duns Scotus's commentary on book 3 of Lombard's *Sentences.* Ockham's *Quaestio Biblica* is in effect an excerpt from a *Sentence* commentary, presented at a formal academic exercise that met the degree requirement for a public lecture on a biblical topic; it was written after his *Reportatio* (OTh V–VII) and before his *Summa logicae* (OPh I), his *Physics* lectures (OPh IV–V), and his *Quodlibets* (OTh IX).

In *De connexione virtutum,* Ockham concludes that the human commitment to right reason, or to God—essential to morality—is broad in scope. If people are brave primarily because they wish to bring their behavior into conformity with the dictates of right reason, they will not depart from the dictates of right reason when prompted by physical appetites. The determination to follow divine precept will produce not isolated virtues, but a uniform orientation toward worthy actions. Here Ockham is modifying a long tradition that found expression in the works of the first Franciscan theolo-

gian, Alexander of Hales. Alexander, and many Franciscans following him, saw such unity and stability only in theological virtues. As
a matter of fact, there are brave people who are greedy, and just
people who cannot control their appetites. Ockham does not disagree with this observation; in fact, he spends more time arguing
for the independence of the lesser virtues than for the connection
of the greater virtues. But his characteristically Franciscan emphasis on the preeminence of will in discussions of morality leads
him to see overarching significance and intrinsic value in willing
for the sake of God and right reason what God commands and
right reason dictates.[8]

┃ Alexander of Hales

If we are to understand Ockham's position as a whole, we need to
begin by looking at earlier developments in the theological tradition of which he was a part. First to adopt Lombard's *Sentences* as
a theology textbook, as well as the first Franciscan master of theology, Alexander believed that Aristotle opposed the view that the
virtues are necessarily connected. Alexander's interpretation of
Aristotle was influenced by the fact that he did not know the complete *Nicomachean Ethics* and had not seen book 6. Just as importantly, it is the result of an emphasis on the theory of virtues as
habits produced by acts, which can also be warranted from book 2
of the *Nicomachean Ethics* (1.1103b21–22; 6.1106a15–24). This
emphasis justifies medieval theories that deny the unity of the
virtues on the grounds that the virtues are as distinct as the acts
that produce them. Moreover, even after the *Nicomachean Ethics*
was known in its entirety, the theory that virtues are not connected was defended on this basis as an Aristotelian view. And
this is certainly true of Ockham, whose aim was to be not only as
theologically orthodox as possible, but also rigorous in applying
Aristotelian philosophical principles.

From Alexander's point of view, Aristotle and the Fathers
disagree. The Fathers hold that there is a connection among the
virtues conferred by grace; Aristotle holds that moral virtues are
not connected. Alexander reconciles the disagreement by allowing that the virtues conferred by divine grace, often called the
theological virtues—faith, hope, and charity—are connected,
while the virtues with which Aristotle had been concerned are
not. He contrasts Aristotle and the Peripatetics with the Stoics,
claiming that only the Stoics had advocated the connection of the
moral virtues.[9]

Moreover, unlike Lombard, Hales presents patristic authorities against the unity of the virtues. Confronted with the view that whoever has one virtue has them all, Augustine had replied that this view was the product of merely human ingenuity. The theological virtues are connected but not unified. They are connected because they are infused together, and charity is a universal virtue. But the theological virtues cannot be reduced to charity; they are distinct; each of the three is necessary, and there is a sense in which each can be independently intensified.[10]

Some theologians agree with Alexander on the independence of the moral virtues straightforwardly. William of Auxerre, for example, argues that the cardinal virtues—prudence, justice, temperance, and courage—differ as the acts associated with them differ.[11]

By contrast Alexander's contemporary Philip the Chancellor initially held that the moral virtues are connected because they are all products of well-ordered affection.[12] But Philip's final position is severely qualified; the virtues are independent to the degree that the faculties and the subjects to which they pertain are unrelated—a strawberry sundae, for example, can be the object of the virtue of temperance but not the virtue of courage. The virtues are related only by analogy, to the degree that their objects can be generalized. Moreover, though Philip holds that the theological virtues are clearly connected, unlike the moral virtues, he adds to the number of patristic and biblical authorities in favor of the view that even the theological virtues are independent.[13]

I Odo Rigaldus

Odo Rigaldus distinguishes between the cardinal virtues and the other political virtues.[14] He holds that noninfused moral virtues are independent, but treats the cardinal virtues as a special case. He argues that no individual moral virtues are necessarily connected, but holds that there is ambiguity concerning cardinal virtues. Cardinal virtues are so-called because not only can they be appropriated to designate single virtues, but they can also refer to general or common conditions requisite to virtue. Appropriated to designate a single or individual virtue, prudence is not necessarily connected with courage; but seen as a condition of virtue—namely, refraining from what is immoral—prudence is common to all completely virtuous people (Lottin, *PM*, III: 224–25).

In addition to distinguishing between singular and general virtues, Odo distinguishes degrees of virtue. He may have been the first thirteenth-century author to raise an important issue in the debate—the question of degrees of perfection (Lottin, *PM,* III: 223–25). Augustine had claimed, contrary to the Stoics, that there are degrees of virtue. It is not simply a question whether you are or are not virtuous. Christians are ordinarily practiced in virtue, but fall short of perfection. It is mistaken to restrict the term 'virtuous' only to the perfect. Following Augustine, medievals distinguish different degrees of virtue. Odo argues that only extraordinary perfect degrees of the cardinal virtue are connected, whereas proficiency in the singular virtue of temperance, for example—that is, refraining from excess in eating and drinking—is unrelated to proficiency in the individual virtue of courage.

An important source of ambiguity here are assumptions about what degree of virtue will be identified as virtue in the unqualified sense of the term.[15] Odo identifies even lesser degrees as virtues; he contrasts virtues understood without qualification with "perfect" virtues, by which he means the highest and most complete degree. Following common opinion, Odo holds that the theological virtues are connected, as are general cardinal virtues in their perfect degrees. Ordinary moral virtues, by contrast, are independent, as Alexander had held.

| Bonaventure

Bonaventure distinguishes more simply between cardinal virtues acquired by the process of habit formation described by Aristotle and cardinal virtues infused by grace.[16] Infused cardinal virtues are connected in a way that acquired cardinal virtues are not. Acquired cardinal virtues are political virtues, independent of one another. This is the same position taken by Alexander: virtues infused by grace are connected, and naturally acquired virtues are independent. Bonaventure also echoes Alexander's claim that only the Stoics held that the virtues were necessarily connected.[17]

Bonaventure follows Odo in distinguishing between the cardinal virtues as common and as singular virtues. Unlike Odo and many later authors, Bonaventure does not argue for the independence of moral virtues on the basis of the independence of intellectual virtues; he does not claim that examples of independent intellectual habits—such as the knowledge of arithmetic in those who know no geometry—suggests that we can be just without being temperate. Influential for the future was Bonaventure's agreement with Odo that extraordinary, perfect degrees of virtue are connected. Even in the case of the moral virtues, no one is perfectly virtuous unless he or she possesses all virtues, but the connection does not come from the essence of a virtue; rather a virtue is perfected when its association with the other virtues adds to its essence.[18]

Bonaventure is most concerned with the theological virtues, contrasting moral or political virtues with the virtues of grace. Bonaventure holds that distinct acts produce distinct virtues in the case of the political virtues. But in the case of the supernatural virtues, though the underlying habits differ formally, they are united in grace. To explain the connection of the theological virtues, Bonaventure considers a variety of theories. The most obvious connection is their common origin through divine infusion.[19] Then there is the connection provided by charity. But though Bonaventure holds that charity is sufficient by itself for merit and is necessarily connected with other perfect virtues, he denies that it is necessarily connected with hope and faith; this is probably because, as Scotus would point out later, neither faith nor hope characterizes the blessed.[20]

I Richard Rufus

The strongest advocate of the independence of the theological virtues among the early Franciscans is Richard Rufus, who sets out to counter the view that there is only one virtue, a view held by William of Auvergne.[21] Rufus argues that the virtues cannot be one, since the vices are not one. Since the virtues have different contraries—for example, not every fornicator is a murderer—there cannot be a single virtue. If the virtues are connected, it is because in their subject they constitute a single love, although the works of virtue are diverse.[22] Later Franciscans, including Ockham, argue that the habits are as distinct as the acts they incline us to. They adopt Rufus's practice of arguing for the independence of the virtues on the basis of the compatibility of the contrary vices.

I Albert the Great

Albert (Albertus Magnus) and Aquinas, by contrast with Alexander and Bonaventure, see Aristotle as an advocate of the connection of the virtues. A proponent of the connection of the virtues, Albert ascribes their unity to prudence. Following Aristotle, Albert assigns a broader function to prudence than did earlier authors. Prudence is right reason concerning acts (*Eth. Nic.* 6.5.1140b20–21); it directs us to act virtuously. It is true that some people are temperate without being courageous, but that can only be the result of their lacking prudence strictly speaking. Albert contrasts prudence as such (*simpliciter*) with the kind of imperfect prudence that could direct us to refrain from overindulgence, but might permit us to fail to act courageously in defense of a principle.[23] For Albert, prudence by itself performs the role ascribed to all four cardinal virtues seen as common conditions of virtue in Odo's theory. Not surprisingly, according to this view, the cardinal virtues themselves fade into obscurity—they are not so-called because they are more fundamental or have a greater degree of generality.[24]

Albert's distinction between perfect and imperfect prudence is reminiscent of the distinctions made by Franciscans. As Bonnie Kent has pointed out, superficially his position agrees with the Franciscans; imperfect virtues are independent, while perfect virtues are connected. But the Franciscans follow Augustine in regarding imperfect virtue as the normal Christian state, and when they speak of "virtue" without qualifying the term, they do not mean perfect virtue. By contrast, for Albert, virtue strictly speaking is perfect. People who are courageous in defense of a principle but incapable of avoiding drunkenness do not count as virtuous. Having discounted unconnected virtues, Albert has little regard for imperfect virtue. Not surprisingly, he provides a sympathetic interpretation of the Stoic view, which sees virtue not as characteristic of ordinary people, but as something rare and difficult, achieved only by the extraordinary. Albert dismisses the various Franciscan arguments for the independence of the virtues as valid only in the case of imperfect virtue, which is not virtue in an unqualified sense.[25]

Essential to Albert's theory is the view that there is no moral virtue without perfect prudence, and no perfect prudence without moral virtue.[26] Insofar as these theses characterize Albert's Aristotelianism, it was to remain controversial. The proper interpretation of the Aristotelian biconditional of *Ethics* 6 (*Eth. Nic.* 6.13.1144b30–32) is still controverted today.[27] Medievals like Aquinas, who accepted it, understood it to mean that the first principles of practical wisdom are determined by the virtues; prudence depends on the will to determine its ends (ST I-II q.56 a.3). Those like Scotus and Ockham, who rejected it, saw Aristotelian prudence as exclusively intellectual and claimed that practical moral knowledge unaccompanied by virtuous acts is possible. Albert's greater emphasis on prudence, like his more thoroughgoing Aristotelianism, was, however, generally accepted—by Ockham, among others (OTh VI, 422).

I Thomas Aquinas

Aquinas is the first author in the tradition we are discussing against whom Ockham explicitly contends in his *De connexione virtutum*. Like Albert, Thomas emphasizes the unifying role of prudence (ST I-II q.65 a.1);[28] indeed, his position resembles his teacher Albert's in many respects. This is scarcely surprising, given that Aquinas reported and revised Albert's *Ethics* commentary (Lottin, *PM*, III: 231).

Turning somewhat away from Albert in the direction of Bonaventure, Aquinas finds a role for cardinal virtues other than prudence. He adopts an argument for the connection of the virtues based on all four cardinal virtues. Like Albert, Thomas stresses prudence as a unique virtue rather than as one of the four cardinal virtues; it can be considered either as an intellectual or a moral virtue (ST I-II q.58 ad 1). But though prudence is the principal formal principle of virtue considered in itself, there are four cardinal virtues if we consider the subject matter of virtue. Prudence perfects the essentially rational, while the other three virtues perfect what participates in the rational, in that justice regulates the will; temperance, concupiscence; and courage, irascibility (ST I-II q.61 a.2). That this is an attempt at seeking consensus seems clear from Aquinas's claim that "almost everyone agrees" and his use of Bonaventure's description of the cardinal virtues as connective "common conditions." Cardinal virtues can be seen as describing what is necessary for virtue. Considered as conditions of virtue, prudence, justice, temperance, and courage become discretion, rectitude, moderation, and firmness (ST I-II q.65 a.1).

Another bow in Bonaventure's direction is Aquinas's discussion of degrees of virtue. Albert distinguishes between perfect and imperfect virtues simply in terms of virtues that are and are not connected with general prudence. By contrast, Thomas describes not imperfect virtues but inclinations prior to virtue, which either arise from human nature itself or result from training (*assuetudo;* ST I-II q.65 a.1). His account of perfect virtue ultimately requires a connection not just with general prudence but with infused virtues. Without the infused virtues, even the virtue that results from general prudence cannot be called virtue in the unqualified sense of the term (ST I-II q.65 a.2).

Two other areas in which Thomas further develops the views he shares with Albert can be seen as replies to objections. The first objection relates to virtues that cannot be exercised by everyone—such as liberality, which is appropriate only for the rich (*Eth. Nic.* 4.1.1120a9). The objection suggests that if virtues can and do occur without each other—for example, temperance without liberality—they cannot be necessarily connected. Here Aquinas's reply is based on the claim that occasions for the practice of most virtues are common to everyone. Only a few virtues are restricted to an elite few, whose wealth or power give them scope for certain special virtues. And though virtuous people who do not belong to the elite cannot actually have those virtues, they do have a proximate potential for them. Only the occasion is lacking; everything important is present (ST I-II q.65 a.1 ad 1). Hence the existence of virtues that can only be practiced by the few does not mean that the virtues are not connected.

Another objection, first raised by Odo and subsequently espoused by Ockham, is based on intellectual habits. Prudence is one of the five Aristotelian veridical habits, an intellectual disposition by means of which we apprehend truths (*Eth. Nic.* 6.3. 1139b15–17). The veridical habits also include wisdom, science, art, and the intuitive grasp of first principles. As a general rule, the products of veridical habits are not unified, even when they result from a single habit. Just as prudence is the means to virtue, scientific demonstration is the means to science. But the sciences of medicine and physics are not necessarily connected and do not form a unified whole. So why should the moral virtues that result from the exercise of prudence or practical wisdom be more unified than the sciences? Aquinas replies by claiming that the connection of the virtues is guaranteed not just by the unity of prudence, but also by the unity of prudence's subject matter; it concerns actions and passions determined by pleasures and pains (ST I-II q.65 a.1 c.). Just as Albert in his early writings maintained that the cardinal virtues all regard pleasure and pain,[29] Thomas holds that their unity is in part a result of the fact that passions and actions are disposed as an ordered set of related objects, not an unrelated aggregate. The claim that the objects of the virtues are connected (also made by Albert[30]) somewhat resembles Bonaventure's argument for the unity of the theological virtues.

Most original in Aquinas's reply to this objection is his claim that the veridical intellectual habits are not independent, as the objection maintains. Rather art, science, and wisdom are related to the veridical habit called *intellectio,* or the intuitive grasp of first principles, in the same way as prudence is related to moral virtue. Just as there can be no science that is not based on the grasp of first principles, there can be no prudence without the virtues that establish the ends in accordance with which prudence discerns the means. Here the term "virtue" is construed not as natural habit or excellence established by customary practice, but as the love of the good (ST I-II q.65 a.1 ad 3; a.2 c.).

I Henry of Ghent

This twofold understanding of moral virtues, considered either as the end toward which virtues are directed or as the acts they engender, was the object of attack by Henry of Ghent. By contrast with Thomas, Henry maintains that moral virtues are distinguished neither in terms of their end nor in terms of their acts, but solely in terms of their forms—that is, the forms of justice, courage, and so on; there are no different species of justice. Nor are justice and temperance distinguished in terms of their acts, since all virtuous acts are dictated by prudence. Moral virtues are not distinguished in terms of their ends, because avoiding drunkenness for the sake of good health and avoiding drunkenness for the love of God are specifically the same act. Christians with infused grace achieve higher grades of formally the same moral virtues practiced by the unbaptized. Moral virtues are, however, distinguished from theological virtues in terms of their end; infused theological, but not acquired moral virtues, aim at our final end, beatitude (*Quodl. VI* q.12, pp. 139–42).

Like Albert and Thomas, Henry distinguishes prudence from the other three cardinal virtues, speaking of three moral virtues (*Quodl. V* q.17, fols. 189v–191r). Here Henry is following Aristotle, who contrasts the intellectual virtue of prudence with the moral virtue of temperance (*Eth. Nic.* 1.13.1103a4–7). Henry also distinguishes general prudence and particular prudence (Lottin, *PM,* IV: 571). His claim that we must posit different kinds of particular prudence (*prudentiae*) corresponding to each moral virtue was very influential.

Like Thomas, Henry distinguishes inclinations prior to virtue and perfect virtues, distinguishing further two grades of the prior disposition and two grades of the perfect habit. The four grades of virtue are beginning and accomplished, perfect and superlative (*inchoatio, profectio, perfectio, excessio*) (*Quodl. V* q.17, fol. 190v)—in Aristotelian terminology, perseverance and continence, and temperance and heroic virtue (*Quodl. V* q.16, fol. 186v). As in other theories stressing the cardinal virtues, 'temperance,' 'continence,' and 'perseverance' are ambiguous terms referring to specific virtues, to general grades of virtue, and to common conditions of virtue. Considered as common conditions of virtue, Henry, like Thomas, calls the four cardinal virtues moderation, firmness, rectitude, and discretion (*Quodl. V* q.17, fol. 189r).

Henry scarcely needs an argument for the connection of the theological virtues—there is only one, charity, and a single prudence corresponds to it (*Quodl. VI* q.12, pp. 141–42). Of the various grades of moral virtue, the first are independent, and heroic virtue is necessarily connected; the situation regarding the intermediate case of perfect virtue, or temperance, is more complicated (*Quodl. V* q.17, fols. 189v–191v; Lottin, *PM, IV*: 572). Both Aquinas and Bonaventure had agreed that perfect virtues were connected, while imperfect virtues were unconnected. They disagreed in their understanding of "perfect virtues." Here Henry compromises. Unlike Bonaventure, the perfect virtues that he postulates as connected need not be extraordinary. In the degree of perfection characteristic of people who are not seriously tempted to such vices as adultery and drunkenness, the virtues are connected. But Henry emphasizes the supereminent and the superhuman when discussing the connection. For example, he glosses the Stoic claims for the connection of the virtues in terms of superhuman virtues, which stem from charity (*Quodl. VI* q.12, p. 142).

Henry's opinion is one of two that Ockham explicitly rejects in the *De connexione virtutum;* the other is Thomas's. The influence of Henry is greater than that of Thomas. Like Scotus, Ockham adopts Henry's theory of particular prudences and considers separately the connection of prudence with moral virtues. But unlike Henry (*Quodl. V* q.17, fol. 189v), both Scotus and Ockham reject the view that there can be no prudence without virtue. In some respects Ockham's views more closely resemble those of Henry than Scotus; like Henry, Ockham holds that the higher grades of each virtue cannot long survive without the other virtues (*Quodl. V* q.17, fol. 193r).

| Peter John Olivi

Olivi is much more an advocate of the independence of the virtues than Henry (Lottin, *PM, IV*: 629–31; Kent 1984, 548–52).[31] He classifies the arguments for the connection of the virtues, rejecting each in turn. He takes first the claims of prudence as a single virtue that directs all the moral virtues. In response to this argument, Olivi postulates a different particular prudence for each virtue, as did Henry.

The second argument Olivi rejects is the view first presented by Odo Rigaldus; it assigns a special place for the cardinal virtues. Olivi presents the version of Bonaventure and Aquinas, referring to general conditions for every virtue. Unless we act with rectitude, discretely, soberly, and firmly, we are not acting virtuously. Olivi replies that no individual virtue embodies these four qualities fully; remaining sober does not necessarily require rectitude, discretion, and courage. He argues by analogy. Just as humankind does not exemplify the entire genus animal, so the individual virtues need not exemplify the characteristics of virtue generally. Moreover, Olivi points out that some of the virtues that Henry considered to be specifically the same—the sexual abstinence of monks and marital chastity, for example—were not just unconnected but mutually incompatible.

Olivi finds most compelling the third argument for the connection of the virtues; indeed he identifies it as Augustine's considered position. The third argument—which is similar in some respects to the position that Ockham later espouses—claims that the virtues are connected because they have the same purpose. A person who loves goodness and worthiness generally will also esteem their particular manifestations. Contrary to this view, Olivi holds that general and specific volitions are different and not necessarily connected. He points to experience. A father can admire his son's intelligence and love his life, even be prepared to make sacrifices for him, without loving the lives of the rest of humanity or caring much for their intellectual contributions. Contrary to Henry, Olivi holds that virtues are distinguished in terms of their ends. Thus a father's courage is specifically distinct from a patriot's courage. Specifically different virtues result from acts with different ends; this thesis Ockham adopts.

Despite his objections, Olivi identifies himself as a proponent of the third argument. But in fact this is misleading. The three positions suggest that virtues are connected, because they (1) have a common source—prudence, (2) share common conditions—the cardinal virtues, or (3) share a common purpose—the pursuit of goodness. But Olivi argues for the connection of the virtues only in terms of a common subject—a justified person ordained for eternal life. One virtue is not essential to another; the virtues are independent. But all virtues taken together are essential to the total composite, which is rectitude in a virtuous person.

Aquinas's is the first position that Olivi sets out to refute. His main thesis is contrary to the type of Aristotelian connection that Aquinas held to be characteristic of the moral virtues. Olivi seeks to align himself with Bonaventure, suggesting that the virtues are more connected in their most perfect states. And he seems to make one major concession: the virtues, even the moral virtues, are connected, or at least exist concomitantly, in ordinary good Christians, since no one is fitted for eternal life without all the virtues. In fact, though he aims to reject Aristotle and the arguments of such Christian Aristotelians as Aquinas and Albert, in some ways Olivi's emphasis on the common human subject echoes Aristotle. He postulates a single habit, or virtuous complexion of rectitude and worthiness, the volitional counterpart of prudence as a single intellectual habit.

❚ John Duns Scotus

Scotus starts by sketching a hard-line position, employing against Henry the sorts of arguments provided by Olivi for the independence of the moral virtues (*Sent.* III d.36 n.7, XV: 606, Wolter 388). The virtues do not relate to a common subject matter (n.4, XV: 601, Wolter 382–84); they serve different purposes (n.9, XV: 622, Wolter 390; n.18, XV: 654, Wolter 408), and prudence does not connect them. Like Henry, Scotus postulates many different habits of prudence (n.11, XV: 627, Wolter 392; n.18, XV: 644, Wolter 408). But he rejects prudence as the connection between the virtues for radically different reasons, employing arguments that deeply influenced many future authors, including Ockham. Scotus maintains that the will can choose either not to act or to act contrary to the dictates of intellect (n.12–14, XV: 630–41, Wolter 398–402), so that prudence without virtue is possible. The will can err even in the presence of prudence or right reason.[32]

Like Aquinas and Albert, Scotus and Ockham hold that there can be no virtue at all without prudence. But Scotus and Ockham deny the other half of the Aristotelian biconditional, that the intellectual habit of prudence can exist without moral virtue (*Sent.* III d.36 n.12–14, XV: 630–41, Wolter 398–402; n.18, XV: 655, Wolter 408; n.20, XV: 654–55, Wolter 410). Following Henry, Scotus and Ockham distinguish prudence from the other cardinal virtues. Prudence is the intellectual habit of moral discernment; justice, temperance, and courage are moral virtues. Thus for Scotus, prudence is not a moral virtue but rather dictates the acts that effect moral virtue. When dealing in a less Aristotelian, more traditional context, Scotus associates prudence with modesty (*Sent.* III d.34 n.21, XV: 574, Wolter 374).[33]

Departing radically from early Franciscan authors, Scotus also holds that the theological virtues are independent. His proof is simple: charity can and does exist without faith and hope in the state of beatitude after death (*Sent.* III d.36 n.30, XV: 728, Wolter 416–18). Therefore it cannot necessarily be connected with the other theological virtues.

Also contrary to Bonaventure and earlier Franciscans, Scotus denies both that virtues in their perfect state are connected and that the cardinal virtues provide connection as common conditions of virtue. There can be perfect temperance without courage, just as there can be perfect sight without hearing (*Sent.* III d.36 n.8, XV: 617, Wolter 388). Similarly, perfect virtue, like imperfect virtue, can be lost (n.9, XV: 621, Wolter 388).

Fateful for its influence on Ockham is Scotus's reply to Henry's argument for the connection of perfect virtues. Henry claims that there are circumstances in which only a combination of virtues could safeguard any given virtue: unless there is courage as well as perfect continence, a chaste person can be induced to fornicate out of cowardice. Scotus distinguishes in reply between fornication that results from lust and fornication from cowardice: the one is incontinence *per se,* the other is incontinence *per accidens* (*Sent.* III d.36 n.9, XV: 621, Wolter 390). Connections between the virtues are accidental and contingent, not essential and necessary.

Taking the offensive, Scotus argues that if the possession of all the cardinal virtues were a condition of true virtue, then no virtue could be acquired. Courage and continence cannot be acquired together, since on the hypothesis each requires the other as a prior condition. Neither can one virtue be acquired first without the others (*Sent.* III d.36 n.6, XV: 605–6, Wolter 386). But moral virtues are absent at the outset and must be acquired. And since moral virtues are acquired and prior conditions cannot be mutual, the cardinal virtues cannot be connected as common conditions.

But despite these arguments, Scotus, like Olivi, postulates a connection between the virtues in a human being properly ordered toward the final end, and for the same theological reason: only divine charity destines us for beatitude. Because unconnected virtue is not meritorious and because the virtues are mutually reinforcing (*Sent.* III d.36 n.10, XV: 622, Wolter 390; n.25,

XV: 684, Wolter 412; n.30, XV: 728, Wolter 418), a moral Christian could be expected to develop the virtues concurrently and in association, not independently and disjointedly. Scotus's rigorous insistence on the independence of the virtues is a thesis about what is logically possible, not about what is ordinarily the case.[34]

Moreover, Scotus even adapts a form of Aquinas's argument for the connection of the virtues in terms of first principles. Olivi had argued that the paradigm provided by geometry showed that moral habits, like intellectual habits, were distinct and diverse (ed. Lottin, *PM*, IV: 630). On this subject, Scotus considers Aquinas's argument more cogent. Scotus holds that insofar as prudence is seen as the apprehension of first principles, from which dictates to perform particular acts of virtue can be deduced as practical conclusions, the virtues are virtually contained in prudence (*Sent.* III d.36 n.23, XV: 673, Wolter 412). The moral virtues can be seen as virtually contained in the apprehension of practical first principles, just as the conclusions of geometry are unified as conclusions following from Euclidean axioms.

I William of Ockham

Ockham follows Scotus in many respects. Like Scotus, he emphasizes will, not intellect. He holds that ordinary virtues are unconnected and that there can be theological virtue in the absence of moral virtue (Scotus, *Sent.* III d.36 n.27, XV: 684–85, Wolter 414; n.29, XV: 726, Wolter 416). He allows that there can be prudence without moral virtue, but not moral virtue without prudence. Moreover, he holds that true moral virtues can exist independently of theological virtue (Scotus, *Sent.* III d.36 n.29, XV: 726, Wolter 416).

Following Odo and Olivi, Ockham uses the analogy between moral and intellectual virtues as an argument for the independence of the virtues. He claims that if the sciences of physics and geometry are independent, it is equally likely that the virtues of justice and courage exist separately.

Most importantly, in contrast to Scotus and Henry, Ockham denies that there is only one virtue of justice or temperance. Ockham postulates five grades of each virtue. As the reader will see, Ockham's five grades form a rather awkward hierarchy that combines two kinds of ordering principles—intensity and purpose. Like most Franciscans, Ockham identifies the virtue of ordinary, imperfect people as virtue in the unqualified sense of the term. Successively higher degrees of virtue are characterized by greater willingness for sacrifice, by a more generalized commitment, and by a more elevated purpose. The intention to persist in virtue at all costs if needs be characterizes second-degree virtue; in fifth-degree, or heroic, virtue, the danger is actual. Acts virtuous in the third degree (true virtue) are performed chiefly for the sake of conformity with right reason; in the fourth degree (perfect virtue), for the love of God. One criticism of these degrees is the absence of the sort of neat mapping of the Aristotelian terms 'perseverance,' 'continence,' 'temperance' developed by Henry; only 'heroism' finds a place as fifth-degree virtue. One advantage of the grades postulated by Ockham is that they may be an attempt to reflect experience. Ockham's insistence that there are kinds of prudence that cannot be taught also suggests that his views are based in part on experience.

Unlike Scotus, Ockham returns to the common position, which affirms the connection of perfect (fourth-degree) individual virtues. This is because he defines virtue differently. Scotus had followed Henry in holding that virtues do not differ in terms of their ends. Distinguishing between intrinsically and extrinsically virtuous acts, Ockham argues that virtues with different ends differ specifically. For Scotus, the purpose of a virtuous act was a circumstance external to the act; for Ockham, it is the principal object of an intrinsically virtuous act. When an occasion requires the exercise both of a new virtue and an old virtue, Scotus did not see the old virtue producing the new virtue. For Ockham, such occasions give rise to the connection of the virtues—one virtue may be a partial cause of another. Third- and fourth-degree virtues, whose principal objects are respectively the determination to conform to right reason and to obey God, incline us to other virtues. Since Scotus described motivation as a circumstance, he understood this as an accidental connection; for Ockham, who sees the end or purpose of an act as the principal object of a virtue, the connection is nonaccidental.

Take the case of the chaste coward. For Scotus, she is essentially cowardly but only accidentally unchaste if she fornicates rather than face a beating. For Ockham, if she is truly chaste (third degree), she refrains from improper sexual connection for the sake of following right reason. As a result she will have to depart essentially from true chastity as well as courage if she abandons her commitment to right reason and chastity for fear of a beating. As Adams puts it, the connection that Ockham sees between the virtues is a consequence of how much he packs into the intensional objects of intrinsically virtuous acts.[35]

There are certain issues on which Ockham goes further than Scotus. He explicitly allows the compatibility of moral vice with moral virtue (Kent 1984, 565), which was implicit in cases considered by Scotus—for example, in accounting for the continent coward. Ockham also develops further the different ways of understanding prudence discussed by Scotus. Like Scotus, he distinguishes between prudence as the result of particular experience and prudence in discursive moral science, and he shows an awareness of the Aristotelian emphasis on practice and training. Because he allows essential connections between the higher degrees of the virtues in terms of their ultimate purpose, Ockham's is in some ways a more satisfactory account of natural moral development than Scotus's. Just as important is his uncompromising emphasis on will as the locus of imputability. For Ockham, not just will rather than intellect, but even intention rather than outcome, is the exclusive focus of moral life. This systematic and uncompromising commitment makes his *De connexione virtutum* a philosophically exciting and challenging work.

| NOTES

1. Ambrose, *De excessu fratri sui Satyri* I n. 57 (PL 16, 1366); *Exposito Evangelii sec. Lucam* V 49 (CCL 14, 152; PL 15, 1734); *De paradiso* c. 3 (PL 14, 297–99); Hieronymus, *Comment. in Esaiam* XV, lvi.1, ed. M. Adriaen (CCL 73, 629; PL 24, 558); Gregorius, *Homilia in Ezechielem* I h. 3 (PL 76, 808–9).

2. *De Trinitate* 6.4 (PL 42, 927; CCL 50, 233). A good translation is provided by W. Oates, *Basic Writings of Saint Augustine* (New York, 1948), 667–878, though the present translation is my own.

3. Lombard, *Sent.* III d.1 c.1: II: 202: "Cum caritas mater sit omnium virtutum . . . '[u]bi caritas est, quid est quod possit deesse? Ubi autem non est, quid est quod possit prodesse?' . . . quanto magis est [caritas] in homine, tanto magis est virtute praeditus; quanto vero minus, tanto minus inest virtus . . ."

4. For a modern account of Augustine's position, see John P. Langan, "Augustine on the Unity and Interconnection of the Virtues," *Harvard Theological Review* 72 (1979): 81–95.

5. This account of the medieval debate on the connection of the virtues has benefited much from the work of Bonnie Kent. An early version of her work is found in "Aristotle and the Franciscans: Gerald Odonis' Commentary on the 'Nicomachean Ethics,'" 512–608. Kent in turn found many important sources in the work of O. Lottin, "La connexion des vertus chez saint Thomas," *Psychologie et morale* (Louvain-Gembloux, 1949). For a fuller account than can be presented here, the reader should consult Kent's *Virtues of the Will* (Washington, D.C., 1995), her forthcoming publications, and Lottin as well as the primary sources mentioned here.

6. Bonaventura, *Sent.* III d.33 q.5 (Quaracchi, 1887), III: 723.

7. Matthaeus ab Aquasparta, *Quaestiones disputatae de fide,* BFS 1 (1957): 96.

8. Adams makes this point in "Scotus and Ockham on the Connection of the Virtues," in *John Duns Scotus: Metaphysics and Ethics,* ed. L. Honnefelder, R. Wood, and M. Dreyer, Studien und Texte zur Geistesgeschichte des Mittelalters (Leiden, 1996), 552.

9. Alexander de Hales, *Sent.* III d.36 n.21, BFS 14 (1954): 453.

10. Alexander de Hales, *Sent.* III d.34, BFS 14 (1954): 418; d.36 n.13–14, 28, BFS 14 (1954): 449–450, 455.

11. Guillemus Altissiodorensis, *Summa Aurea* III tr.19 c.1–2 (Paris, 1986), 386–87.

12. Philippus Cancellarius, *Summa de bono,* "De temperantia" q.5 (Bern, 1985), II: 877.

13. Philippus, *Summa de bono,* "De virtute in communi" q.1, II: 1071–79.

14. Kent (1984, 608) has rightly pointed out that Odo's contribution to the debate has been seriously underestimated.

15. I owe this point to Kent (1984, 529, 541).

16. Bonaventura, *Sent.* III d.33 q.5 (Quaracchi, 1887), III: 723.

17. Ibid., d.36 q.3, III: 797–99.

18. Ibid., q.1, III: 792; q.3, III: 798–99. The point about superadded perfections I owe to Bonnie Kent, letter of 16 March 1996.

19. Bonaventura, *Sent.* III d.36 q.1–2, III: 792–93, 795.

20. Ibid., d.27 a.1 q.1, III: 593; d.36 q.1, III: 792.

21. Guillelmus de Auvergne, *De virtutibus* c.11 (ed. Paris, apud Michaelem du-Neuf-Germain, 1674), I: 138a.

22. Richardus Rufus, *Sent. Oxon.,* III d.36, cod. Balliol 62, fol. 242ra–va.

23. Albertus Magnus, *Super Ethica* I l.8 n.43, ed. W. Kübel (Münster in Westf., 1968, 1987), I: 42–43.

24. Albertus, *Ethica* IV l.9 n.302, I: 259.

25. Albertus, *Ethica* VI l.18 n.593–95, II: 510–11.

26. Ibid., n.594, II: 511.

27. Cf. R. Sorabji, "Aristotle on the Role of the Intellect in Virtue"; A. Rorty, "The Place of Contemplation in Aristotle's NE," in *Essays on Aristotle's Ethics,* ed. A. Oksenberg Rorty (Berkeley-Los Angeles, 1980), 209–13, 384.

28. Like Ockham's account of Aquinas, this discussion is based on the *Summa theologica.* Another important discussion is found in Aquinas's *De virtutibus cardinalibus.*

29. Albertus, *De bono* tr.1 q.4 a.1, ed. H. Kühle, C. Feckes, B. Geyer, and W. Kübel (Münster in Westf., 1951), 45.

30. Albertus, *Ethica* I l.8 n.43, I: 43.

31. See also Olivi, *Quaestiones de virtutibus* q.6, ed. E. Stadter, BFS 24 (1981): 269–94; and J. Walsh, "Buridan on the Connection of the Virtues," *Journal of the History of Philosophy* 24 (1986): 456.

32. This account of Scotus is indebted to Adams, Stephen Dumont, and Allan B. Wolter, who has provided a revised edition of Scotus on the connection of the virtues, *Sent.* III d.36.

33. Scholarly opinion is divided on the question of whether we can speak of prudence when no acts are regulated. Cf. Scotus, *Sent.* III d.36 n.15–20, XV: 648–55, Wolter 404–10; Lottin, *PM,* IV: 652; Dumont, "The

Necessary Connection of Moral Virtue to Prudence According to John Duns Scotus," *Recherches de théologie ancienne et médiévale* 55 (1988): 193, 204; Adams, "Scotus and Ockham on the Connection of the Virtues," in *John Duns Scotus: Metaphysics and Ethics,* ed. L. Honnefelder, R. Wood, and M. Dreyer, Studien und Texte zur Geistesgeschichte des Mittelalters (Leiden, 1996), 507–8. It is my view that this dispute is merely terminological. Scotus considers two possibilities. If the definition of prudence includes the regulation of acts, then merely establishing what is the correct moral dictate without acting on that dictate does not count as prudence strictly speaking, but as potential prudence (a seed of prudence). But Scotus sees prudence primarily as the intellectual ability to determine what is the morally correct act, to provide proper dictates, whether or not those dictates are executed. Accordingly, he says that there can be prudence without moral virtues. He may in this case be speaking of prudence only in its strictest sense. But that hardly matters. The important point is that the intellectual ability—the disposition to correct judgment in matters of morals—can exist in the absence of virtuous acts or the will to conform to moral dictates.

34. Scotus admits an all-inclusive form of perfect virtue. Someone who as a result of divine liberality attains perfection as a whole, as opposed to the perfect form of an individual virtue, has all of the virtues (*Sent.* III d.36 n.9, XV: 617, Wolter 390). Here, Scotus is distinguishing between extensive and intensive perfection. What he seems to be saying is simply that if someone has all the virtues, his or her virtue is perfect extensively. This does not appear to be an important concession to the view that all perfect virtue is connected.

35. Adams, "Scotus and Ockham on the Connection of the Virtues," section 4.2, pp. 511–12.

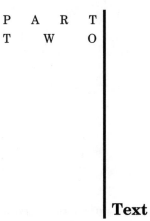

P A R T
T W O

Text

Utrum virtutes sint connexae

[Art. I: Conclusiones ad propositum necessariae]

Circa istam quaestionem[1] sunt quattuor facienda: p r i m o,
praemittendae sunt aliquae conclusiones necessariae ad propositum; s e c u n d o, aliquae distinctiones; t e r t i o, respon- 5
dendum est ad quaestionem; q u a r t o, movenda sunt aliqua
dubia, et solvenda.

[Conclusio prima]

Quantum ad primum est prima conclusio,[2] quod quanta est
distinctio habituum tanta est actuum, ita quod aequalis est. Hoc 10
probatur primo, quia omnia individua aeque perfecta inclinativa,
sive elicitiva sive receptiva, si sint eiusdem rationis, possunt in
effectus eiusdem rationis, et si non possunt in effectus eiusdem
rationis, illa principia non sunt eiusdem rationis; sed habitus generati ex actibus sunt effectus illorum, sicut alibi patet in tertio 15

---

    1. On the history of the question of whether the virtues are con-
nected, see chapter 4 above.

    a. In this translation, the paragraphs are numbered according to
the line numbers with which the paragraphs begin in the critical edition.
Apart from a few notes by the translator, most of the notes appear only
on the facing page with the Latin text. The Latin notes are taken for the
most part from the critical edition and have been slightly revised, chiefly
by changing their form not their content.

    2. Cf. OTh VI, 402–4; OTh I, 213–20.

I On the Connection of the Virtues

[Art. 1: Prefatory Conclusions]

3. Concerning this question,[1] there are four things we should do. First, we should preface the discussion with some conclusions necessary to the question being considered; second, we should make some distinctions. Third, we should reply to the question. Fourth, we should state and resolve some doubts.[a]

[First Conclusion]

9. As to the first article, the first conclusion[2] is that the distinction between habits is as great as the distinction between acts. That the distinction is equal is proved, first because all equally perfect individual things of the same kind—whether inclinative, elicitive, or receptive—are capable of producing effects of the same kind; if they are not capable of effects of the same kind, they are not principles of the same kind. But habits generated by acts are effects produced by those acts, as is evident elsewhere—in

O c k h a m,[3] et non semper sunt eiusdem speciei nec esse possunt, sicut patet de habitu respectu incomplexi et complexi, de
habitu respectu principii et conclusionis; igitur nec actus generativi
istorum.

    Praeterea si actus distinctorum obiectorum specie non distin-   20
guerentur specie, hoc non esset nisi q u i a causae[4] distinctae
specie possunt in eundem effectum specie, et ideo non obstante
quod habitus, qui sunt causa actuum, distinguuntur specie, tamen
ipsi actus possunt esse eiusdem speciei; v e l propter ordinem
obiectorum,[5] sicut est de principio et conclusione, respectu quorum   25
possunt esse actus eiusdem speciei propter ordinem eorum. Sed
primum[6] non impedit, quia si sic, cum actus sint causa habituum
sicut e converso, numquam erit via ad probandum distinctionem
specificam inter aliquos habitus, quia per te causae distinctae specie
etc.; igitur quantumcumque ponatur distinctio specifica in acti-   30
bus, numquam ponetur propter hoc quod erit in habitibus, quod falsum est. Nec secundum[7] impedit, quia habitus principiorum non
possunt generari ex actibus conclusionum nec ad tales actus inclinare; sed si actus principiorum et conclusionum essent eiusdem
speciei, possent habitus istorum ad tales actus inclinare; ergo ordo   35
obiectorum non impedit distinctionem specificam actuum.

    Praeterea, II *Ethicorum,*[8] habitus ex eisdem generantur et aug-
mentantur; sed actus, per quos habitus distinctarum specierum
augmentantur, sunt alterius speciei; igitur et actus ex quibus generantur.   40

    Praeterea [probatur] per idem argumentum per quod I o-
a n n e s probat in *Metaphysica*[9] distinctionem specificam inter
habitum principii et conclusionis: quia scilicet aliquis potest habitualiter scire principium et errare circa conclusionem, sed idem

---

    b. Here the reporter responsible for the written text has recorded
Ockham's reference to his own works in the third person. It is not a sign
that we should question the authenticity of *De connexione,* but that we
have a *reportatio,* not a written version approved by Ockham. See the
preface above.
    3. Cf. OTh VI, 397–98; OTh VI, 205.
    4. Cf. OTh I, 95.
    5. Cf. OTh V, 393.
    6. See lines 21–22.
    7. See lines 24–25.
    8. Cf. Aristotle, *Eth. Nic.* 2.2.1105a13–15; OTh VI, 392.
    9. Cf. Scotus, *In Metaph.* VI q.1 n.4, VII: 305; ed. St. Bonaventure
n.20–21.

Ockham's[b] commentary on the third book of the *Sentences*[3] — and habits do not always belong to the same species, nor could they belong to the same species, as is evident in the case of habits pertaining to complex and incomplex [objects], and habits pertaining to principles and conclusions. Therefore, neither do the acts that generate these habits belong to the same species.

20. Besides, if acts [terminating at] specifically distinct objects were not specifically distinct, this would only be because (1) specifically distinct causes[4] can [produce] specifically the same effect, and therefore, notwithstanding [the fact that] the habits that are the cause of the acts are specifically distinct, the acts themselves can be specifically the same; or (2) on account of the order of the objects,[5] such as principle and conclusion, in regard to which there can be acts of the same species because of their order. But the first [reason][6] does not stand in the way, since if it held, there would never be a way to prove a specific distinction between any habits. For acts are the cause of habits, just as conversely [habits cause acts], and according to you specifically distinct causes [produce distinct effects]. Therefore, however great the specific distinction of acts may be, there would never be [a distinction] among habits, which is false. Neither does the second [reason][7] stand in the way, since a habit concerning principles cannot be generated from acts in regard to conclusions or incline us to such acts; but if the acts [terminating at] principles and conclusions were specifically the same, habits could incline to such acts; therefore the order of objects does not stand in the way of [concluding that there is] a specific distinction between acts.

37. Besides, [according to] *Ethics,* book 2,[8] habits are generated and augmented by the same [acts]; but the acts by means of which specifically distinct habits are augmented are specifically distinct; therefore so, too, are the acts on the basis of which they are generated.

41. Besides, the same argument that John used in the *Metaphysics*[9] commentary to demonstrate a specific distinction between habits in regard to a principle and a conclusion proves this point. Namely, a person can habitually, scientifically know a

principium non potest simul habitualiter sciri et ignorari igno- 45
rantia dispositionis, igitur est distinctio specifica inter tales habitus. Idem argumentum concludit distinctionem specificam inter
actus cognoscendi principium et conclusionem. Quaere in Prologo
O c k h a m, de unitate theologiae.[10]

S i   q u a e r a s   utrum respectu omnium obiectorum distin- 50
guantur actus specie: r e s p o n d e o quod non, sed universaliter respectu illorum obiectorum, sive complexorum sive incom-
plexorum, respectu quorum sunt habitus distincti specie, respectu
illorum sunt actus distincti specie; et respectu quorum sunt habitus eiusdem speciei, sunt et actus eiusdem speciei. Et ideo respectu 55
eiusdem principii tam habitus quam actus generati in diversis in-
tellectibus sunt eiusdem speciei, et eodem modo est de obiecto
aliquo incomplexo.

[Conclusio secunda]

Secunda conclusio[11] est quod respectu obiectorum distincto- 60
rum specie sunt actus distincti specie. Hoc patet, quia aliter non
posset probari distinctio specifica actuum, quia si illi essent eiusdem speciei, multo magis actus respectu obiectorum eiusdem speciei essent eiusdem speciei, et sic omnes actus essent eiusdem speciei. 65

Praeterea habitus generatus praecise ex actibus respectu unius
obiecti numquam inclinat ad actum respectu alterius obiecti alterius speciei, quia aliter habens habitum respectu unius obiecti praecise, posset statim in actum respectu obiecti alterius speciei, quod
est manifeste falsum. Sed si actus [respectu] illorum obiectorum 70
essent eiusdem speciei, tunc habitus respectu unius posset inclinare
modo praedicto, quia si actus essent eiusdem speciei, et habitus,
ex prima conclusione;[12] et per consequens possent causare effectus
eiusdem rationis, ex eadem. Igitur etc.

Praeterea non est maior ratio quod aliqui actus habentes ob- 75
iecta distincta specie sint distincti specie quam alii, ut videtur; sed
aliqui distinguuntur specie, sicut patet de cognitione unius muscae
vel albedinis et Dei; igitur etc.

---

c. Know scientifically (*scire*) refers to the Aristotelian concept of
science in terms of logical demonstrations from first principles.
d. Dispositional ignorance is not knowing the truth because you believe something false—assent to the opposite of a true statement—not
simple ignorance.
10. Cf. OTh I, 213–20.
11. Cf. OTh I, 62–63.
12. See lines 9–11.

principle and be mistaken about a conclusion;[c] but a person cannot at the same time habitually know scientifically and be dispositionally ignorant of the same principle;[d] therefore there is a specific distinction between such habits. The same argument shows that there is a specific distinction between the acts of knowing a principle and a conclusion. See Ockham's prologue, his discussion of the unity of theology.[10]

50. If you ask whether the acts pertaining to all distinct objects are distinguished by species, my answer is no. Rather, it is universally true that when habits are specifically distinct (whether they pertain to complex or incomplex objects), the corresponding acts are specifically distinct; and when habits are specifically the same, acts are also specifically the same. And therefore, with respect to the same principle, both the habits and the acts generated in the intellects of different people are specifically the same; the same is true of any incomplex object.

[Second Conclusion]

60. The second conclusion[11] is that there are specifically distinct acts with respect to specifically distinct objects. This is evident; otherwise it would be impossible to prove that acts are specifically distinct. For if these acts belonged to the same species, then a fortiori acts with respect to objects of the same species would belong to the same species, and thus all acts would belong to the same species.

66. Besides, a habit generated precisely by acts with respect to one object never inclines us to an act with respect to another object of a different species. Otherwise someone with a habit with respect to precisely one object could immediately elicit an act with respect to an object of another species, which is manifestly false. But if an act with respect to those objects were specifically the same, then a habit with respect to one could incline in the aforesaid manner. For if the acts were specifically the same, so, too, the habits (from the first conclusion),[12] and consequently they could cause an effect of the same kind (from the same [conclusion]). Therefore, etc.

75. Besides, there is no more reason that some acts having specifically distinct objects should be specifically distinct than others, as it appears. But some [acts] are specifically distinguished, as is evident concerning cognition of one fly or [one] whiteness and cognition of God. Therefore, etc.

Praeterea respectu eiusdem obiecti numero possunt esse actus
distincti specie, sicut patet de cognitione intuitiva et abstractiva   80
respectu incomplexi, de actu sciendi et dubitandi respectu complexi; igitur multo magis respectu obiectorum distinctorum specie
sunt distincti actus specie.

Praeterea aliter posset, stante eodem actu in intellectu, aliquid
primo intelligi per illum actum et postea non intelligi, quod fal-   85
sum est. Assumptum patet, quia si per unum actum intelligam
obiectum aliquod praecise, et per alium actum intelligam illud
obiectum et aliud alterius speciei, cum secundum opinionem I o-
a n n i s[13] potest talis actus habens duo obiecta terminari ad
primum licet non ad secundum, igitur per secundum actum primo   90
intelligitur secundum obiectum et post non intelligitur, stante
secundo actu; igitur etc. Et tunc respectu illius primi obiecti erunt
simul duo actus eiusdem speciei, quod videtur inconveniens. Sed
quia istud argumentum fundatur super falsum, scilicet quod aliquid primo potest intelligi per aliquem actum, et postea, stante   95
eodem actu, non intelligitur, sicut patet in *Ordinatione* O c k-
h a m,[14] ideo huic non innitor.

[Conclusio tertia]

Tertia conclusio[15] est quod aliquis actus est necessario et intrinsece virtuosus. Hoc probatur, quia impossibile est quod aliquis   100
actus contingenter virtuosus, — sic scilicet quod potest indifferenter dici virtuosus vel vitiosus —, fiat determinate virtuosus propter
novitatem alicuius actus non necessario virtuosi, quia per nullum
actum contingenter virtuosum modo praedicto fit alius actus sive
denominatur determinate virtuosus. Quia si sic, aut ille secundus   105
actus, qui est contingenter virtuosus, erit determinate virtuosus
per aliquem alium actum qui est necessario virtuosus, aut per actum contingenter virtuosum. Si primo modo, tunc eadem ratione
esset standum in secundo, et similiter tunc habetur propositum,
quod est aliquis actus in homine necessario virtuosus. Si secundo   110
modo, erit processus in infinitum, vel stabitur ad aliquem actum
necessario virtuosum, et sic habetur propositum.

---

13. Cf. Scotus, *Ord.* I d.1 p.1 q.2 n.42–43, II: 26–30; Ockham, OTh I,
451–52.
14. Cf. OTh I, 453–55.
15. Cf. OTh VI, 359–62, 375, 385–87; OTh VIII, 263; OTh IX, 255;
Summa Halesiana, published as Alexander de Hales, *Summa theol.* II–II
n.388 (Quaracchi, 1930) III: 388b; Lottin, *PM* II: 421–23.

79. Besides, there can be acts that are specifically distinct with respect to numerically the same object, as is evident from intuitive and abstractive cognition regarding an incomplex object or from acts of knowing scientifically and doubting with respect to a complex object. Therefore, a fortiori there are specifically distinct acts regarding objects that are specifically distinct.

84. Besides, otherwise, with the same act remaining in the intellect, something could first be understood by means of that act and afterward not understood, which is false. The assumption is evident, since if we may understand some precise object by means of one act, and by means of another [second] act we understand that object and another, specifically different [object], then by means of that second act we can first understand the second object and afterward not understand it. This is because in John's opinion[13] such an act having two objects can be terminated at the first, and yet not at the second object. This could happen while the second act remains, therefore etc. And then with respect to that first object there will simultaneously be two specifically distinct acts, which is absurd. But I will not rely on this argument, because it is based on something false—namely, [the assumption] that something can first be understood by means of some act and afterward not understand while the same act remains, as is evident in Ockham's *Ordinatio*.[14]

[Third Conclusion]

99. The third conclusion[15] is that some act is necessarily and intrinsically virtuous. This is proved because it is impossible that some contingently virtuous act—namely, an act that can be called indifferently virtuous or vicious—be made determinately virtuous on account of some newly elicited act that is not necessarily virtuous; for no act that is contingently virtuous in the manner described makes another act determinately virtuous or causes it to be so denominated. For if this could happen, either the second act that is contingently virtuous will be determinately virtuous in virtue of some other act that is necessarily virtuous; or it will be determinately virtuous in virtue of a contingently virtuous act. If we choose the first alternative, then by the same reasoning the process will stop at the second act, and we have what we proposed to show—that there is some necessarily virtuous human act. If we choose the second alternative, there will be an infinite regress, or the process will stop at some necessarily virtuous act, so that we have what we proposed to show.

Sed actus hominis tam exteriores quam interiores, puta intelligere et velle, — secundum quod velle[16] est actus indifferens —,
sunt contingenter virtuosi. Exemplum: ire ad ecclesiam propter   115
finem debitum primo est actus virtuosus et, stante eodem ire ad
ecclesiam, propter malum finem est vitiosus, et per consequens
est contingenter virtuosus. Eodem modo est de intelligere et spe-
culari: primo propter debitum finem, erit istud intelligere virtuosum, et post, stante eodem actu in intellectu, mutata intentione,   120
scilicet quod talis actus continuetur propter indebitum finem, erit
illa speculatio vitiosa, et per consequens est contingenter virtuosa
illa speculatio.

Ideo dico quod est dare aliquem actum necessario primo virtuosum, qui est actus primo laudabilis et perfecte circumstantio-   125
natus, qui est ita virtuosus quod non potest fieri vitiosus, sicut
velle facere aliquid quia est praeceptum divinum, est ita virtuosus
quod non potest fieri vitiosus, stante praecepto divino. Et ex tali
actu generatur virtus, de qua dicunt S a n c t i[17] quod virtute
nemo potest male uti.   130

[Conclusio quarta]

Quarta conclusio[18] est quod actus primo et necessario virtuosus est actus voluntatis. Hoc patet primo, quia ille solus est primo
laudabilis vel vituperabilis, alii autem non nisi secundario et per
quandam denominationem extrinsecam, puta per hoc quod eli-   135
ciuntur conformiter actui voluntatis. Praeterea quilibet alius actus
ab actu voluntatis potest idem manens esse vitiosus vel virtuosus,
iste autem solus sic est virtuosus quod non potest fieri vitiosus, sicut patet supra in tertia conclusione. Praeterea secundum S a n c-
t o s[19] nullus actus est laudabilis vel vituperabilis nisi propter   140
intentionem bonam vel malam, intentio autem est actus voluntatis, igitur etc. Praeterea A n s e l m u s:[20] sola voluntas
punitur, sicut sola peccat, igitur etc.

[Conclusio quinta]

Quinta conclusio est quod nullus alius actus ab actu volun-   145
tatis est intrinsece virtuosus vel vitiosus, tum quia quilibet alius

---

16. Cf. OTh VI, 383–87.

17. Cf. Augustine, *De libero arbitrio* II c.19 n.50 (PL 32, 1268).

18. Cf. OTh VIII, 297; OTh VI, 359–62, 375; OTh VIII, 428.

19. Cf. Lombard, *Sent.* II d.40 n.2, I: 557; Aquinas, *ST* I–II q.19 a.7.

20. Cf. Anselm, *De conceptu virginali* c.4, ed. Schmitt (Rome, 1950)
II: 45.

113. But both the exterior and the interior acts of a man—
such as understanding and willing (insofar as the act of willing[16]
is a morally indifferent act)—are contingently virtuous. For example, going to church on account of the proper end is a virtuous
act at first, and yet the same act, continued on account of a wicked
end, is vicious; consequently the act is contingently virtuous. The
same thing can be said about understanding and speculating: the
act of understanding is first virtuous on account of a proper end,
and afterward, while the same act remains in the intellect, if our
intention changes—namely, so that the act is continued on account of an improper end—it will be vicious speculation; consequently that speculation is contingently virtuous.

124. Therefore I hold that some primary, necessarily virtuous act must be granted: a primary praiseworthy act in perfect
circumstances, an act so virtuous that it cannot be rendered vicious. Willing to do something because it is divinely commanded
is such an act; it is virtuous in such a way that it cannot be rendered vicious, given divine precept. The saints[17] are speaking of
the virtue generated by this kind of act when they speak of the
virtue that no one can abuse.

[Fourth Conclusion]

132. The fourth conclusion[18] is that a primary, necessarily virtuous act is an act of will. This is evident first because that act alone
is primarily praiseworthy or blameworthy, while other acts are
so only secondarily and in virtue of some extrinsic denomination—for example, in virtue of their being elicited in conformity
with an act of will. Besides, any act, other than an act of will, can
be either virtuous or vicious while remaining the same; but that
act of will alone is virtuous in such a way that it cannot be made
vicious, as it evident above in the third conclusion. Moreover, according to the saints[19] no act is praiseworthy or blameworthy unless on account of a good or a bad intention; but an intention is an
act of will; therefore etc. Besides, according to Anselm,[20] just as
only the will sins, only the will is punished, therefore etc.

[Fifth Conclusion]

145. The fifth conclusion is that no act other than an act of will is
intrinsically virtuous or vicious. For [1] any other act, while re-

idem manens potest indifferenter esse laudabilis et vituperabilis,
et primo laudabilis quando conformatur volitioni rectae, et post
vituperabilis quando conformatur volitioni vitiosae, sicut supra
patet in tertia conclusione; tum quia nullus actus est vitiosus nisi   150
sit voluntarius et in potestate voluntatis, quia peccatum adeo est
voluntarium[21] etc.; sed actus exterior potest primo esse in potestate voluntatis, puta quod aliquis dimittat se in praecipitium, et
post descendendo potest illum actum simpliciter meritorie nolle
propter Deum, sicut supra patet in dubitationibus istius quater-   155
ni;[22] igitur etc.

[Conclusio sexta]

Sexta conclusio[23] est quod nullus alius habitus ab habitu voluntatis est intrinsece et perfecte virtuosus, quia quilibet alius inclinat indifferenter ad actus laudabiles et vituperabiles.   160

---

21. Cf. Augustine, *De vera religione* 14 n.27 (PL 34, 133): "Nunc vero
usque adeo peccatum voluntarium est malum, ut nullo modo sit
peccatum, si non sit voluntarium" (Indeed, the wickedness of sin is voluntary to so great an extent that it is not sin at all if it is not voluntary).
   e. Here Ockham's truncated quotation has been completed.
22. Cf. OTh VIII, 263–64.
23. Cf. OTh VI, 366.

maining the same, can be praiseworthy or blameworthy indifferently; it can first be praiseworthy when it is in conformity with
right will, and afterward blameworthy when it is in conformity
with vicious will, as is evident above in the third conclusion. [2]
No act is vicious unless it is voluntary and in the power of the
will, because sin is such a voluntary[21] [evil that if it is not voluntary, it is not a sin at all];[e] but an exterior act can be first in the
power of the will [and afterward cease to be in the power of the
will]; therefore, etc. Suppose, for example, that someone throws
herself over a precipice: while falling she can simply and meritoriously reject this act for God's sake, as is evident in the case described above in the doubts found in this quire.[22]

[Sixth Conclusion]

158. The sixth conclusion[23] is that no habit other than a habit of the
will is intrinsically and perfectly virtuous, since any other habit inclines indifferently to praiseworthy and blameworthy acts.

❙ [Art. II: Distinctiones praeviae]

[Distinctio prima]

Circa secundum articulum est prima distinctio, quod prudentia accipitur quadrupliciter:[1] u n o m o d o, accipitur pro omni notitia directiva respectu cuiuscumque agibilis mediate vel imme-diate, sicut accipit A u g u s t i n u s prudentiam, I *De libero* 5
arbitrio.[2] Et isto modo tam notitia evidens alicuius universalis pro-positionis quae evidenter cognoscitur per doctrinam, quia procedit ex propositionibus per se notis, quae notitia scientifica proprie est scientia moralis, quam notitia evidens propositionis universalis quae solum evidenter cognoscitur per experientiam, quae notitia 10
etiam est scientia moralis, est prudentia. Exemplum primi: 'omni benefactori est benefaciendum'; exemplum secundi: 'quilibet ira-cundus per pulchra verba est leniendus'.

A l i o m o d o, accipitur pro notitia evidenti immediate directiva circa aliquod agibile particulare, et hoc pro notitia ali- 15
cuius propositionis particularis quae evidenter sequitur ex univer-sali propositione per se nota tamquam maiori et per doctrinam. Exemplum: 'isti est sic benefaciendum,' quae sequitur evidenter ex ista 'omni benefactori' etc.

---

1. Cf. Scotus, *In Metaph.* VI q.1 n.14, VII: 313–14; ed. St. Bonaventure n.68.
2. Cf. Augustine, *De libero arbitrio* I c.13 n.27 (PL 32, 1235).

| [Art. II]: Prefatory Distinctions]

[First Distinction]

2. The first distinction of the second article concerns prudence, which can be considered in four ways.[1] In one mode, it is taken as all knowledge directive with respect to any possible action whatever, whether mediately or immediately; this is the manner in which Augustine considered prudence in the first book of *On the Freedom of the Will*.[2] In this sense, prudence refers to two kinds of evident knowledge. It refers [1] to evident knowledge of some universal proposition that we evidently know from teaching, because it proceeds from self-evident propositions; this scientific knowledge is moral science properly speaking. Prudence also refers [2] to evident knowledge of a universal proposition that we can only know evidently in virtue of experience; this knowledge, too, is moral science. An example of the first kind of prudence is the proposition: "everyone who acts generously should be treated generously"; an example of the second, "any irascible person should be mollified with fine words."

14. In another mode, prudence is taken as evident knowledge that is immediately directive in regard to some particular possible action. In this sense it refers to knowledge of some particular proposition that evidently follows from teaching and from a self-evident universal proposition, as from a major proposition. For example: "this man should be treated generously," which follows evidently from the proposition "everyone who acts generously," etc.

T e r t i o m o d o, accipitur pro notitia immediate direc- 20
tiva accepta per experientiam solum respectu alicuius agibilis. Exemplum: 'iste iracundus est leniendus per pulchra verba'. Et haec
notitia est solum respectu alicuius propositionis particularis cogni-
tae per experientiam; et haec videtur esse prudentia proprie dicta
secundum intentionem P h i l o s o p h i,[3] prout distinguitur 25
a scientia morali.

Q u a r t o m o d o, accipitur[4] pro aliquo aggregato ex
omni notitia immediate directiva, sive habeatur per doctrinam
sive per experientiam, circa omnia opera humana requisita ad bene
vivere simpliciter. Et isto modo prudentia non est una notitia 30
tantum, sed includit tot notitias quot sunt virtutes morales requi-
sitae ad simpliciter bene vivere, quia quaelibet virtus moralis habet
propriam prudentiam et notitiam directivam.

Quod probatur, quia prudentia est notitia complexa; nunc autem ubi est aliud et aliud complexum, ibi est alia et alia notitia; 35
cum igitur aliud et aliud sit complexum, cuius notitia est immediate directiva respectu operationum unius virtutis et alterius, igitur
erit alia et alia prudentia.

Praeterea aliquis potest evidenter scire unam conclusionem
practicam cuius notitia immediate dirigit, circa materiam unius 40
virtutis, operationes, et ignorare ignorantia dispositionis per habitum erroris aliam conclusionem cuius notitia esset immediate
directiva operationum circa obiectum alterius virtutis. Sicut aliquis
potest scire evidenter istam conclusionem, quod homo debet velle
temperate vivere, et errare circa istam conclusionem, pro defen- 45
sione huius articuli 'Deus est trinus et unus' est moriendum vo-
luntarie, quia aliquis potest credere hunc articulum esse falsum.
Igitur notitia directiva respectu unius et alterius est alia et alia,
quia aliter impossibile esset scire evidenter unam conclusionem
practicam et ignorare aliam. 50

Et isto modo potest probari distinctio, non tantum numeralis
inter istas prudentias, sed etiam specifica, quia quandocumque
aliqua sunt eiusdem speciei, cum quocumque stat unum, et reliquum; et si cum aliquo alio stat unum cum quo non potest stare
reliquum, illa distinguuntur specie; exemplum de albedine et ni- 55

---

3. Cf. Aristotle, *Eth. Nic.* 6.5–9.1140a24–1142a16.
4. Cf. OTh VI, 419; Petrus I. Olivi, *Quaestio de connexione virtutum*
(Lottin, *PM* VI: 630); Scotus, *Collatio* I n.2–4, V: 132–34.
a. Dispositional ignorance is belief in the opposite of a truth. Cf.
the comment at a.1 41.

20. In a third mode, prudence is taken as knowledge, gained only in virtue of experience, immediately directive in regard to some possible action. An example is: "this irascible person should be mollified with fine words." This knowledge applies only to some particular proposition known by experience. It seems to be what the Philosopher[3] intends by prudence properly speaking, insofar as prudence is distinguished from moral science.

27. In a fourth mode, prudence is taken as an aggregate of all immediately directive knowledge,[4] whether gained from teaching or from experience, applied to all human works requisite for living well, considered absolutely or unconditionally. And in this mode prudence is not a single knowledge only, but it includes as many knowledges as there are moral virtues requisite to living well, considered absolutely. For any moral virtue has its own prudence and directive knowledge.

34. This can be proved because prudence is propositional knowledge. But where there are different propositional expressions, there are different knowledges. Therefore, since there are different propositional expressions whose knowledge is immediately directive in regard to the operations of different virtues, there are different prudences.

39. Besides, someone can evidently and scientifically know one practical conclusion, the knowledge of which immediately directs operations in regard to the subject matter of one virtue, and at the same time be ignorant of another conclusion (in virtue of a habitual error producing dispositional ignorance),[a] the knowledge of which would immediately direct operations in regard to the object of another virtue. For example, someone can evidently know scientifically this conclusion, "a man ought to wish to live temperately," and be mistaken about this conclusion, "one ought to be willing to die in defense of this article of faith 'God is three and one'"; for someone could believe that that article of faith was false. Therefore directive knowledge regarding one is different from directive knowledge of the other; otherwise it would be impossible evidently and scientifically to know one practical conclusion and be ignorant of another.

51. In this manner we can prove that there is not only a numerical distinction between these prudences, but also a specific distinction. For whenever two things belong to the same species, whatever is compatible with one is compatible with the other;

gredine et dulcedine in lacte. Sed scientia unius conclusionis stat
cum errore alterius conclusionis practicae, sicut patet prius, et
non stat cum errore eiusdem conclusionis simul propter repugnantiam formalem. Igitur scientia unius conclusionis et alterius
distinguuntur non tantum numero sed specie.   60

Si enim essent eiusdem speciei, sicut scientia stat cum errore
alterius conclusionis, sic staret cum errore istius conclusionis, quia
scientia alia alterius bene potest stare cum errore istius conclusionis. Sicut si albedo stat cum dulcedine in lacte et non stat cum
nigredine, ideo nigredo et dulcedo distinguuntur specie, quia si   65
non, sicut dulcedo stat cum albedine, sic nigredo staret cum dulcedine. De ista unitate quaere in I o a n n e et O c k h am,
de unitate scientiae et diversitate respectu diversorum principiorum et conclusionum speculabilium,⁵ et dicas uniformiter hic et
ibi, quia eadem est difficultas omnino et non maior neque minor.   70

Quomodo autem prudentia distinguitur a scientia morali et
quomodo non, et exempla de prudentia tribus primis modis accepta,⁶ quaere supra in isto quaterno, in dubitatione de virtutibus
moralibus.⁷

[Distinctio secunda]   75

Secunda distinctio est quod habituum moralium quidam sunt
geniti ex actibus imperativis exsecutionis formaliter, quidam sunt
geniti ex actibus respectu eorundem obiectorum, qui actus non
sunt formaliter imperativi exsecutionis sed tantum aequivalenter
imperativi, quia ad illos actus non inclinat habitus talis quando   80
est impedimentum exsecutionis, sed amoto omni impedimento,
tunc ad tales actus inclinat habitus de necessitate.

Exemplum p r i m i: aliquis vult patienter sustinere mortem
pro defensione fidei, et intentata sibi morte, imperat potentiis sustinere talem poenam sine rebellione. Istud imperium non est nisi   85
velle actualiter sine contradictione sustinere mortem quando mors

---

b. Milk is both white and sweet, but whiteness and sweetness are
distinct, since sweetness is compatible with blackness, but whiteness is
not. See line 65 below.

c. Here "whiteness" has been corrected from "sweetness," following
Augustinus de Ratisbona, since otherwise the example fails.

5. Cf. Scotus, *Quaest. in Metaph. Aristot.* VI q.1 n.4, VII: 305; ed.
St. Bonaventure n.20–21; Ockham, OTh I, 215–17; OTh VI, 287–89.

6. Lines 3–26.

7. Cf. OTh I, 317–21.

and if something is compatible with one and not compatible with the other, those things are specifically distinct; there is the example of whiteness, blackness, and sweetness in milk.[b] But scientific knowledge of one conclusion is compatible with error concerning another practical conclusion, as is evident from what was said above; and scientific knowledge is not consistent with error concerning the same conclusion at the same time, on account of formal incompatibility. Therefore scientific knowledge of one conclusion is not only numerically, but specifically distinct from scientific knowledge of another conclusion.

61. If they were of the same species, then, just as scientific knowledge is consistent with error concerning another conclusion, it would be consistent with error concerning this conclusion itself; for different scientific knowledge of another [conclusion] can well be compatible with error concerning this conclusion itself. Similarly, if whiteness is compatible with sweetness in milk and not with blackness, then blackness and sweetness are specifically distinct, since if they were not, then, just as sweetness is compatible with whiteness, so too blackness would be compatible with whiteness.[c] Concerning this unity, see John and Ockham on the unity of science and its diversity with respect to diverse speculative principles and conclusions.[5] And you should say the same thing here and there, since it is altogether the same difficulty, and neither greater nor lesser.

71. Now concerning how prudence is and is not distinct from moral science and the examples of prudence in the first three modes,[6] see above in this quire, in the doubt about the moral virtues.[7]

[Second Distinction]

76. The second distinction concerns moral habits. Some moral habits are engendered by acts that formally command execution. Others are engendered by acts with respect to the same objects but not by formally executive, imperative acts, only by equivalent imperative acts. For such a habit does not incline us to perform those acts when there is an impediment to their execution; although once every impediment is removed, that habit necessarily inclines us to such acts.

83. An example of the first kind of moral habit: someone wills patiently to sustain death for the sake of defending the faith; and intent on her death she commands her faculties to sustain this punishment without rebellion. This command is nothing other than willing without contradiction actually to sustain death

sibi offertur. Aliud exemplum est: aliquis habens multas divitias
vult actualiter illas dare pauperibus pro amore Dei, et imperat
actualiter, amoto impedimento, potentiis exsecutivis ut exsequan-
tur. Quod imperium non est aliud quam velle sic actualiter dare,   90
amoto omni impedimento; si enim esset impedimentum, tunc non
posset rationabiliter velle dare absolute sed tantum condicionaliter,
puta si tale impedimentum non esset.

Exemplum s e c u n d i: aliquis vellet sustinere mortem pro
defensione fidei, si mors immineret sibi, et non esset impedimen-   95
tum. Similiter, quantum ad aliud exemplum, aliquis vellet libenter
dare divitias pro amore Dei, si eas haberet, et non esset aliud impedimentum; sed quia non habet, ideo non potest rationabiliter
illas actualiter absolute dare propter impedimentum. Istud velle
est actus imperativus non formaliter sed tantum aequivalenter.   100

Ex istis actibus generantur distincti habitus specie, tum propter distinctionem obiectorum specificam, quia unus actus habet
impedimentum pro obiecto, alius, qui est formaliter imperativus,
non habet; tum quia quantumcumque habitus ille generatus ex
actibus imperativis aequivalenter augeretur in infinitum, num-   105
quam inclinaret ad actum imperativum formaliter. Distinctio istorum patet per separabilitatem actuum, quia aliquis potest habere
actum imperativum aequivalenter, etsi numquam habeat actum
imperativum formaliter.

[Distinctio tertia]   110

Tertia distinctio est quod iustitia et quaelibet una virtus moralis, secundum quod non est alia virtus nec formaliter nec aequivalenter, habet quinque gradus, non quidem eiusdem speciei, sed
distinctarum specierum.

[Quinque gradus virtutis]   115

P r i m u s g r a d u s est quando aliquis vult facere opera
iusta conformiter rationi rectae dictanti talia opera esse facienda
secundum debitas circumstantias respicientes praecise ipsum opus
propter honestatem ipsius operis sicut propter finem, puta intellectus dictat quod tale opus iustum est faciendum tali loco tali   120
tempore propter honestatem ipsius operis vel propter pacem vel
aliquid tale, et voluntas elicit actum volendi talia opera conformiter iuxta dictamen intellectus.

when death is at hand. Another example: someone possessing great riches wills actually to give them to the poor on account of love of God; and in the absence of an impediment, he actually commands his executive faculties to execute the act. That command is nothing other than willing actually to give in this manner, in the absence of an impediment; for if there were an impediment, then he could not rationally will to give absolutely, but only conditionally—that is, "if such an impediment did not exist."

94. An example of the second kind: someone might be willing to sustain death in defense of the faith if death were imminent and there were no impediment. Similarly, in the other example, someone would gladly will to give riches to the poor on account of love of God if he had them, and there were no other impediment; but since he does not have them, he cannot rationally, actually will to give riches unconditionally on account of the impediment. This act of will is not formally an imperative act, but only equivalently.

101. On the basis of these acts, specifically distinct habits are generated. They are distinct for two reasons: [1] because of the distinction in their specific objects, since one act has an impediment as an object and the other, which is formally imperative, does not; and [2] because, however infinitely much habits generated by equivalently imperative acts were augmented, they would never incline to a formally imperative act. The distinction between these acts is evident from the separability of the acts. For someone can have an equivalently imperative act, even if she never has a formally imperative act.

[Third Distinction]

111. The third distinction concerns justice and any other single moral virtue insofar as it is not another virtue, formally or equivalently. Such virtue has five degrees, which belong to distinct species, not to the same species.

[The Five Degrees of Virtue]

116. The first degree is when someone wills the performance of just works in conformity with right reason, as it dictates that such acts should be performed, according to the proper circumstances respecting precisely this work, on account of the worthiness of this work itself as an end. Suppose, for example, the intellect dictates that such a just work should be performed in such a place, at such a time, on account of the worthiness of the work itself or on account of peace or some such end, and the will elicits an act willing such work in conformity with the dictate of the intellect.

Secundus gradus est quando voluntas vult facere opera
iusta secundum rectum dictamen praedictum, et praeter hoc   125
cum intentione nullo modo dimittendi talia pro quocumque quod
est contra rectam rationem, etiam non pro morte, si recta ratio
dictaret tale opus non esse dimittendum pro morte; puta si homo
velit sic honorare patrem secundum rectum dictamen praedictum
loco et tempore etc., cum intentione et voluntate non dimittendi   130
illum honorem pro morte, si immineret.

Tertius gradus est quando aliquis vult tale opus
facere secundum rectam rationem praedictam cum intentione praedicta, et praeter hoc vult tale opus secundum circumstantias praedictas facere praecise et solum quia sic est dictatum a recta ratio-   135
ne.[8]

Quartus gradus est quando vult tale opus facere
secundum omnes condiciones et circumstantias praedictas, et praeter hoc propter amorem Dei praecise, puta quia sic dictatum est ab
intellectu, quod talia opera sunt facienda propter amorem Dei   140
praecise. Et iste gradus solum est perfecta et vera virtus moralis
de qua Sancti[9] loquuntur.

Quod autem sit proprie virtus moralis patet primo, quia generatur ex actibus moralibus et inclinat ad actus consimiles et dirigit in actibus respectu eorundem obiectorum, quod proprie per-   145
tinet ad virtutem moralem; secundo, quia variatio finis non variat
virtutem quantum ad moralitatem et non moralitatem, quia respectu diversorum finium possunt esse diversae virtutes morales,
hic autem solum variatur finis a praedictis gradibus; tertio, quia
vitium oppositum est proprie vitium morale, igitur istud est virtus   150
moralis.

Quintus gradus[10] est quando aliquis eligit tale
opus facere secundum praedictas condiciones excepto fine, quando[11] indifferenter potest fieri propter Deum tamquam propter
finem, et propter honestatem vel pacem vel aliquid tale, — quod   155
dico pro intentione philosophi[12] —, et praeter hoc eligit tale opus
facere actu imperativo formaliter, non tantum aequivalenter. Et
si tunc velit actu imperativo formaliter facere vel pati aliquid quod

---

8. Cf. a.4 451–67; Ockham, *Dial.* 1.VI.77, fol. 90r–v.
9. Cf. Augustine, *De civitate Dei* XIX c.25 (PL 41, 656); *De Trinitate*
XIII c.20 n.26 (PL 42, 1036); Ockham, ibid.
10. Cf. Ockham, OTh VIII, 275–78, 285–86.
11. Cf. a.3 322–29.
12. Cf. OTh VII, 58.

124. The second degree is when the will wills the performance of a just work in conformity with right reason as stated above, and beyond this has the intention never to give up such works for any reason whatever that is contrary to right reason, not even to avoid death, if right reason were to dictate that such a work should not be given up in order to avoid death. Suppose, for example, that a man wished to honor his father according to the aforesaid right dictate, at the proper time and place, etc., having the intention and the will not to give up honoring his father for the sake of avoiding an imminent death.

132. The third degree is when someone wills the performance of such a work in conformity with right reason as stated above, with the intention just discussed, and beyond this she wills the performance of such a work, in the aforesaid circumstances, precisely and solely because it is dictated by right reason.[8]

137. The fourth degree is when someone wills the performance of such a work according to all the conditions and circumstances discussed above, and beyond this wills that work precisely on account of love of God—because, for example, the intellect has dictated that such works should be performed precisely for the sake of love of God. Only this degree is the perfect and true moral virtue, about which the saints[9] speak.

143. That this is moral virtue properly speaking is evident, first, because this virtue is generated by moral acts, it inclines us to similar acts, and it directs us toward acts with respect to the same objects; and this properly pertains to moral virtue. It is evident, second, because varying the end does not result in a different virtue, as far as its being moral or immoral is concerned. For in regard to different ends there can be different moral virtues; but here only the end differs from the preceding degrees. Third argument: the opposite vice is moral vice, strictly speaking; therefore this is moral virtue.

152. The fifth degree[10] is when someone chooses to perform such a work according to the conditions described above, with the exception of the end, so that the end is indifferent,[11] and it can be for the sake of God as an end that the act is performed or for the sake of its worthiness or for peace or for some such end; I say this in order to take account of the intention of a philosopher.[12] Beyond this, in fifth-degree virtue someone chooses to perform such a work by a formally imperative act, not merely an equivalently imperative act. If that person then wills by a formally imperative

ex natura sua excedit communem statum hominum et est contra
inclinationem naturalem, vel si tale opus non excedit communem   160
statum hominum nec est contra inclinationem naturalem quantum
est ex natura actus, sed solum ex aliqua circumstantia est contra
inclinationem naturalem, talis inquam actus imperativus formaliter talis operis est generativus virtutis heroicae vel elicitus a virtute heroica secundum intentionem philosophi et secundum veri-   165
tatem, et nullus alius habitus generatus ex quibuscumque aliis
actibus est virtus heroica.

Exemplum p r i m i:[13] aliquis vult actualiter actu imperativo
formaliter, morte sibi imminente, pro defensione fidei, sive com-
bustione sibi imminente, sustinere mortem vel combustionem.   170
Exemplum s e c u n d i:[14] aliquis habens iustitiam, sic quod
pro nullo quod est contra rectam rationem vult deserere iustitiam
et facere iniustitiam, post exponitur igni vel carceri perpetuo nisi
faciat iniustitiam. Hoc nolle facere iniustitiam non excedit communem statum hominum, sed nolle sic, quantum ad illam circum-   175
stantiam quae est recta ratio universalis, excedit communem statum hominum. Si tunc ille citius vult actu imperativo formaliter
exsecutionis actus exterioris intrare ignem quam deserat iustitiam,
ille utique tam in primo casu quam in secundo est perfecte heroi-
cus, et non alius.   180

Distinctio numeralis istorum habituum et actuum[15] patet per
separabilitatem ipsorum. Distinctio specifica patet, p r i m o
per distinctionem specificam obiectorum partialium, quia pono[16]
quod illa quae ponuntur circumstantiae virtutum ab aliis, sunt
obiecta partialia et secundaria ipsius actus virtuosi, et ideo quando   185
talia obiecta variantur secundum speciem, actus et habitus istorum
variantur secundum speciem; sed actus cuiuslibet gradus ascen-
dendo habet aliquod obiectum et circumstantiam distinctam specie
quod non habet alius gradus inferior. S e c u n d o patet, quia
quantumcumque unus gradus augeretur in infinitum, numquam   190
inclinabit ad actum alterius gradus; sed illa quae sunt eiusdem
speciei, possunt habere effectum eiusdem speciei; igitur etc.

[Distinctio quarta]

Quarta distinctio[17] est quod virtus theologica accipitur dupli-
citer, large et stricte: l a r g e accipitur pro virtutibus adqui-   195

---

13. Lines 158–60.
14. Lines 160–63.
15. Namely, the fifth grade.
16. Cf. a.4 401–3.
17. Cf. OTh VI, 281–82.

act to do or undergo something [1] that naturally exceeds the common human state and that is contrary to his natural inclination; [2] or if, though the work does not exceed the common human state and is not contrary to his natural inclination as far as the nature of the act is concerned, it is contrary to his natural inclination on account of some circumstance; then I hold that such an act formally dictating such a work is generative of, or elicited by, heroic virtue according to a philosopher's intention and in truth; and no other habit generated by any other acts whatever is heroic virtue.

168. Example of the first:[13] someone actually wills in virtue of a formally imperative act, in the face of imminent death or burning, to sustain death or burning for the sake of defending the faith. Example of the second:[14] someone possesses the virtue of justice, so that he wills not to abandon justice and perform an injustice for any consideration that is contrary to right reason, and is afterward exposed to burning or perpetual incarceration unless he performs an injustice. This rejection of injustice does not exceed the common human state; but to reject injustice in this way, according to that circumstance which is universal right reason, does exceed the common human state. If such a person then wills to enter the fire, in virtue of an act dictating formally the execution of the exterior act, rather than abandon justice, then that act is certainly perfectly heroic, both in the first and in the second case, and the other act is not.

181. That there is a numerical distinction between these habits and acts[15] is evident from their separability. A specific distinction is evident first on account of a specific distinction among partial objects, because I maintain[16] that what others suppose are the circumstances of virtues are the partial and secondary objects of a virtuous act itself. And therefore when such objects vary by species, the acts and habits associated with these objects vary by species; but an act of any higher degree has some object and some specifically distinct circumstance that a lower degree does not have. A specific distinction is evident second because however much one degree is increased, even if it is increased infinitely, it will never incline us to an act of a different degree; but things that belong to the same species can have an effect of the same species; therefore, etc.

[Fourth Distinction]

194. The fourth distinction[17] concerns theological virtue, which is considered in two ways: loosely and strictly. Loosely speaking,

sitis, puta pro fide adquisita, spe adquisita, caritate adquisita, quia
isti habitus habent Deum pro obiecto; s t r i c t e accipitur
solum pro istis habitibus infusis.

[Distinctio quinta]

Quinta distinctio[18] est quod aliquis actus est intrinsece bonus   200
moraliter, aliquis intrinsece malus et vitiosus, aliquis neuter sive
indifferens. Exemplum primi: velle orare propter honorem Dei et
quia praeceptum est a Deo secundum rectam rationem etc. Exemplum secundi: velle orare propter vanam gloriam et quia contra
praeceptum Dei et contra rectam rationem. Exemplum tertii: velle   205
simpliciter orare sine aliqua circumstantia dictata a ratione, quia
nec propter bonum finem nec propter malum, quia propter nullum finem; et talis actus, sive interior sive exterior, solum dicitur
bonus denominatione extrinseca et nullo modo intrinsece, nec
vitiosus.   210

[Distinctio sexta]

Sexta distinctio[19] est quod aliquis actus est bonus ex genere
vel malus, aliquis ex circumstantia, aliquis ex principio meritorio.
Exemplum p r i m i quantum ad actum bonum ex genere: sicut
orare, dare eleemosynam, sive velle talia facere absolute sine aliqua   215
circumstantia bona vel mala. Exemplum quantum ad actum ma-
lum: velle furtum facere, velle fornicari, absolute sine aliqua circumstantia bona vel mala; de quibus dicit P h i l o s o p h u s
et S a n c t i dicunt,[20] quod statim nominata convoluta sunt
cum malitia.   220

Exemplum s e c u n d i: velle abstinere secundum circumstantias dictatas a recta ratione propter honestatem tamquam
propter finem vel propter conservationem naturae vel alium finem
quem intenderet philosophus paganus. Exemplum secundi quantum ad actum malum: velle fornicari contra rectam rationem, loco   225
indebito etc., et propter libidinem tamquam propter finem.

Exemplum t e r t i i: velle continere secundum rectam
rationem et alias circumstantias, et propter honorem divinum quia
talis actus est Deo acceptus.

---

18. Cf. a.1 99–130; OTh VI, 383–85; *Summa Halesiana,* published as
Alexander de Hales, *Summa theol.,* II–II n.388 (Quaracchi, 1930), III:
388b.

19. Cf. Scotus, *Sent.* II d.7 n.11–12, XII, 386–87; *Ord.* I d.17 p.1 q.1–
2 n.62, V: 163–64; *Rep.* II d.7 q.3 n.27, XXII: 636; d.40 n.2–3, XXIII: 209–
10.

20. Cf. Aristotle, *Eth. Nic.* 2.6.1107a8–12; Augustine, *Contra
mendacium* c.7 n.18 (PL 40, 528–29).

it is taken to refer to acquired virtues—as, for example, acquired faith, acquired hope, and acquired charity—since these habits have God as their object. Strictly speaking, 'theological virtue' refers to those habits only when they are infused.

[Fifth Distinction]

200. The fifth distinction[18] is that some acts are intrinsically good morally speaking, some acts are intrinsically wicked and vicious, and some acts are neutral or indifferent. An example of the first kind of act is willing to pray on account of God's honor and because it is commanded by God in accordance with right reason, etc. An example of the second kind of act is willing to pray on account of vainglory and because it contrary to God's command and contrary to right reason. An example of the third kind of act is simply willing to pray without some circumstance dictated by reason—that is, on account of no end, neither for a good end nor for a wicked end. Such an act, whether it is interior or exterior, is called good only by virtue of extrinsic denomination; in no sense is it intrinsically good or vicious.

[Sixth Distinction]

212. The sixth distinction[19] is that some acts are generically good or wicked; some acts, on the basis of a circumstance; and some acts, on the basis of a meritorious principle. An example of an act of the first kind, which is generically good, is to pray, to give alms, or to will to do such things unconditionally, in the absence of any good or wicked circumstance. An example of a wicked act is to will the performance of theft or adultery, absolutely, in the absence of any good or bad circumstance; concerning these last acts the Philosopher and the saints[20] say that the very names [of the acts] are immediately tied to wickedness.

221. An example of the second kind is to will abstinence in accordance with circumstances dictated by right reason on account of worthiness as an end, for the sake of conserving nature, or on account of another end, such as a pagan philosopher might intend. An example of a wicked act of the second kind is to will fornication contrary to right reason, in an inappropriate place, etc., on account of lust as an end.

227. An example of the third kind is to will continence in accordance with right reason and other circumstances, on account of divine honor, because such an act is acceptable to God.

[Distinctio septima]

230

Septima distinctio est quod habituum inclinantium ad actus quidam sunt subiective in parte sensitiva et quidam in voluntate. Primum membrum patet[21] per experientiam de brutis, furiosis et infatuatis, qui aliquos actus possunt elicere in absentia rerum sensibilium; non per intellectum et voluntatem, quia in eis non est usus rationis; igitur per phantasiam et alias virtutes sensitivas. Hoc non potest esse sine habitu genito ex actu qui habetur in praesentia illarum rerum, quia impossibile est quod aliquid transeat de contradictorio in contradictorium etc.; sed phantasia in talibus et appetitus sensitivus post primum actum possunt aliquem actum elicere quem non possunt ante primum actum; igitur ex illo actu aliquid generatur in tali potentia; non species,[22] quia illa non est ponenda, sicut alibi patet; si etiam ponatur, illa praecedit actum; et si illa sola ponatur, numquam potest in actum in absentia rerum si non habeatur actus in eadem potentia in praesentia obiecti; igitur ex illo actu causatur aliquis habitus in tali potentia; igitur etc.

235

240

245

Secundum membrum patet,[23] quia aliquis habitus est simpliciter virtus et primo, et non nisi voluntatis, quia nullus actus generativus habitus talis est primo virtuosus nisi actus voluntatis; igitur etc. Praeterea si non, hoc non esset nisi propter libertatem voluntatis, quae non potest determinate inclinari ad unam partem contradictionis; vel propter conformitatem eius ad rectam rationem, quia scilicet non potest discordare a recta ratione. Primum non impedit, quia secundum omnes caritas est ponenda in voluntate ad eliciendum actum meritorium, qui libere elicitur aliter non esset meritorius, et tamen inclinat voluntatem per modum naturae ad unum determinate. Nec secundum impedit, quia illud assumptum falsum est, sicut postea patebit.[24]

250

255

21. Cf. OTh VI, 356–57, 359.
22. Cf. OTh II, 314; OTh V, 253, 256, 269, 271–72, 302.
23. Cf. a.1 158–60; OTh VI, 357–58, 363, 365.
24. A.3 224–532, 690–95.

[Seventh Distinction]

231. The seventh distinction concerns habits that incline us to acts. Some are subjectively in the sensitive part of the soul, some in the will. The first member of the distinction is evident[21] from our experience with brutes, with madmen, and with the insane, who can elicit some acts in the absence of sensible things. They do not do this by virtue of the intellect or the will, since they do not have the use of reason. Therefore they do this by virtue of the imagination and other sensitive virtues. This cannot be without a habit generated by an act that occurs in the presence of those things, since it is impossible that something should make the transition from one contradictory to another, etc. (cf. a. 4, 129). But fantasy and the sensitive appetite can elicit some acts in such persons after the first act that it cannot elicit before the first act. Therefore something is generated from that act in such a faculty: not a species,[22] since that should not be posited, as is evident elsewhere; also [a species], if posited, precedes the act; and if only it is posited, [the faculty] can never be in act in the absence of things if an act would not occur in the same faculty in the presence of the object. Therefore, some habit is caused on the basis of that act in such a faculty, therefore, etc.

248. The second member of the distinction[23] is evident because some habit is simply and primarily a virtue; and this could only be a habit of the will because no act generative of such a habit is primarily virtuous except an act of will; therefore, etc. Moreover, if it were not an act of will, this would only be for one of two reasons: on account of the freedom of the will, which cannot be determinately inclined toward one part of a contradiction; or on account of the will's conformity with right reason—namely, because it cannot diverge from right reason. The first consideration is no obstacle to the conclusion, since everyone agrees that charity must be posited in the will to elicit a meritorious act; a meritorious act is freely elicited, otherwise it would not be meritorious, and yet charity inclines the will toward a single act in the manner of a natural cause. Nor does the second consideration stand in the way of the conclusion, since that assumption is false, as will be evident later.[24]

▎[Art. III: responsio ad quaestionem]

Circa tertium articulum principalem sunt quattuor articuli:
p r i m u s est de connexione virtutum moralium inter se; s e-
c u n d u s est de connexione earum cum virtutibus theologicis;
t e r t i u s est de connexione earum cum habitibus partis sen-   5
sitivae; q u a r t u s est de connexione earum cum prudentia.

[Opiniones de connexione virtutum moralium inter se]

[Opinio Thomae Aquinatis]

Quantum ad primum articulum est una opinio T h o m a e,
prima secundae, q.65,[1] quod aliquae sunt virtutes quae perfici-   10
unt hominem secundum communem statum, quantum ad ea quae
communiter omni homini occurrunt, cuiusmodi sunt virtutes
cardinales; quaedam sunt quae perficiunt hominem quantum ad
statum specialem et quantum ad illa quae conveniunt homini secundum illum statum, sicut magnificentia, magnanimitas, quae   15
conveniunt homini exsistenti in dignitate, potestate et honore,
et aliis virtutibus. Loquendo de primis, dicitur quod illae sunt
connexae; loquendo de secundis, illae non sunt connexae.

Quantum autem ad connexionem virtutum cum prudentia,
dicit[2] quod prudentia non potest esse sine virtutibus moralibus,   20
quia prudentia est recta ratio agibilium, quae procedit ex finibus
virtutum. Quaere in T h o m a.

---

1. Cf. Aquinas, *ST* I-II q.65 a.1 ad 1.
2. Cf. Aquinas, *ST* I-II q.58 a.5 resp.

| [Art. III: Reply to the Question]

2. The third principle article itself has four articles: the first concerns the connection of the moral virtues among themselves; the second concerns their connection with the theological virtues; the third, their connection with the habits of the sensitive part of the soul; the fourth, their connection with prudence.

[Opinions Concerning the Connection of the Moral Virtues]

[Thomas Aquinas's Opinion]

9. Concerning the first article there is Thomas's opinion in the *Summa theologicae,* first part of the second part, q.65.[1] According to Thomas there are some virtues that perfect a person according to the common state, having to do with things every person encounters; the cardinal virtues are of this kind. Other virtues perfect a person according to a special state and have to do with matters appropriate to a person in that state—such as magnificence, magnanimity—which are appropriate to a person who holds a position of dignity, power, and honor, and other virtues. Speaking of the first virtues, it is said that those virtues are connected; speaking of the second, that those virtues are not connected.

    19. As to the connection of the virtues with prudence, Thomas[2] says that prudence cannot exist without the moral virtues because "prudence is right reason regarding possible actions," which is derived from the ends of the virtues. See Thomas.

Item P h i l o s o p h u s, VI *Ethicorum:*[3] "Malitia est cor-
ruptiva principii", principium autem est prudentia, igitur non stat
cum vitio. Item, III *Ethicorum:*[4] "Omnis malus est ignorans . . . ," 25
igitur scientia sive prudentia non stat cum malitia.

[Contra opinionem Thomae Aquinatis]

Contra istam opinionem: p r i m o, quia concedit propositum, scilicet quod non omnes virtutes necessario sunt connexae,
quia illae quae perficiunt hominem in determinato statu, non sunt 30
connexae cum aliis quae perficiunt hominem secundum communem statum. S e c u n d o, quia possibile est quod alicui occurrat materia unius virtutis, quae perficit hominem secundum
communem statum, et non alterius, sicut possibile est quod alicui
occurrat materia temperantiae et non fortitudinis, et per conse- 35
quens potest se exercere circa materiam illius virtutis, adquirendo
temperantiam et non fortitudinem, per rationem suam. T e r-
t i o, quia videtur contradicere sibi ipsi, quia dicit quod prudentia
non potest esse sine virtutibus moralibus, quia qua ratione prudentia separatur ab una virtute morali, et ab alia; et per conse- 40
quens qua ratione non potest esse sine virtutibus de primo genere,
nec potest esse sine virtutibus de secundo genere. Confirmatur,
quia non omnis prudens[5] est perfecte virtuosus.

[Opinio Henrici Gandavensis]

Ideo est alia opinio G a n d a v e n s i s, *Quodlibet V,* q.17,[6] 45
quod in adquisitione virtutis sunt quattuor gradus, scilicet perseverantia, continentia, temperantia, virtus heroica; et in adquisitione habitus vitiosi sunt alii quattuor gradus, scilicet incontinentia, imperseverantia, intemperantia, bestialitas, secundum
P h i l o s o p h u m, VII *Ethicorum,* in principio.[7] Dicit enim 50
ibi in responsione ad argumentum,[8] quod aliquis potest exerceri
circa materiam unius virtutis et non alterius, ut adquirat perseve-

---

3. Cf. Aristotle, *Eth. Nic.* 6.5.1140b19–20; Henry, *Quodlibet* V q.17,
fol. 190r.
4. Cf. Aristotle, *Eth. Nic.* 3.2.1110b28–29; Scotus, *Sent.* III d.36
n.11, XV: 627–28; Henry, *Quodl.* X q.10, pp. 268–71.
5. Note that the words 'omnis prudens,' translated "every prudent
person," were not found in any manuscript, only in the printed edition of
1495 (=Z).
6. Cf. Henry, *Quodl.* V q.16, fol. 186v.
7. Cf. Aristotle, *Eth. Nic.* 7.1.1145a15–1145b7.
8. Cf. Henry, *Quodl.* V q.17, fols. 192v–193r; fols. 190v–191r);
Scotus, *Sent.* III d.36 n.2, XV: 599–600.

23. The next argument is from the Philosopher, *Ethics* 6:[3] "Wickedness is destructive of the principle," but the principle is prudence, therefore prudence is not compatible with wickedness. The next argument is from *Ethics* 3:[4] "Every wicked person is ignorant . . . ," therefore scientific knowledge or prudence is not compatible with wickedness.

[Against Thomas Aquinas's Opinion]

28. Against this opinion there are three arguments. First, Aquinas concedes what we set out to prove—namely, that not all virtues are necessarily connected, because those that perfect a man in a determinate state are not connected with other virtues that perfect a person according to the common human state. Second: it is possible that someone should encounter subject matter for one virtue that perfects a person according to the common human state, and not the subject matter of another. For example, it is possible that someone should encounter the subject matter for temperance in the absence of the subject matter for courage; consequently such a person can practice temperance but not courage, according to Thomas's argument. Third: Aquinas seems to contradict himself, because he says that prudence cannot exist without the moral virtues. For if prudence can be separated from one moral virtue, it can be separated from another for the same reason. Consequently if prudence cannot exist without virtues in the first genus, it cannot exist without virtue in the second genus for the same reason. This is confirmed, since not every prudent person[5] is perfectly virtuous.

[Henry of Ghent's Opinion]

45. For these reasons, Ghent defends another opinion, in *Quodlibet* V, question 17,[6] according to which there are four degrees in the acquisition of virtue—namely, perseverance, continence, temperance, and heroic virtue; in the acquisition of a vicious habit another four degrees are found—namely, incontinence, lack of perseverance, intemperance, and brutishness, as the Philosopher indicates at the beginning of the seventh book of the *Ethics*.[7] In reply to an objection, Ghent[8] says that someone could be practiced in the subject matter of one virtue and not another, so that he would acquire perseverance [and] continence; he

rantiam et continentiam et temperantiam in duobus gradibus,
scilicet quantum ad inchoationem et augmentationem, sed non
quantum ad complementum et perfectionem naturae, in quo gradu 55
simpliciter meretur dici virtus absolute, nec quantum ad virtutem heroicam; ita quod in eodem habitu numero ponit praedictos
quattuor gradus, et in duobus primis possunt esse non connexae,
et aliquo modo in tertio gradu; sed in tertio gradu perfecto et
quarto necessario sunt connexae, quia sic requiritur connexio alia- 60
rum sicut fulcimentum, quia non posset diu conservari nisi fulci-
retur, nec diu persistere absque aliis eam fulcientibus.

Pro ista opinione arguitur multipliciter. Tangam rationes ali-
quas: primo sic: non est vera virtus quae in contrarium fini suo
obliquari potest; secundo, quia una sine alia non potest delectabi- 65
liter operari; tertio, quia una non perfecte perducit ad finem virtutis sine alia. Confirmatur, quia virtus[9] est quae habentem perficit
et opus eius bonum reddit. Praeterea, VI *Ethicorum,* virtutes sunt
sorores.[10] Item A u g u s t i n u s, VI *De Trinitate.*[11] Item
G r e g o r i u s, X *Moralium.*[12] Quaere haec et alia in G a n- 70
d a v e n s i et I o a n n e.[13]

[Contra opinionem Henrici Gandavensis]

Contra istam opinionem, quia multipliciter peccat: p r i m o,
quia male allegat P h i l o s o p h u m, quia non ponit nisi
tria membra, sicut patet in principio septimi,[14] ubi ponit conti- 75
nentiam, temperantiam et virtutem heroicam ex una parte, et ex
alia parte ponit incontinentiam, malitiam et bestialitatem. Sed
capitulo 9 et 10,[15] ponit quattuor, scilicet perseverantiam, continentiam ex una parte, et ex alia parte ponit mollitiem et incontinentiam. Et distinguit inter ista, quia continentia et incontinentia 80
sunt circa delectationes, perseverantia et mollities circa tristitias.
Unde dicit sic, 9 capitulo:[16] "hic autem circa delectationes incontinens, hic autem continens; hic autem circa tristitias mollis, hic
autem perseverans."

---

9. Cf. Aristotle, *Eth. Nic.* 2.5.1106a 15–17.
10. Cf. Eustratius, *In Eth. Nic. Commentaria,* ed. G. Heylbut,
Comm. in Aristot. Graeca (Berlin, 1892), XX: 309.
11. Cf. Augustine, *De Trinitate* VI c.4 n.6 (PL 42, 927).
12. Cf. Gregorius, *Moralium Libri* XXII c.1 n.2 (PL 76, 211–12).
13. Cf. Henry, *Quodl.* V q.17, fols. 188v–189v; fols. 191v–192v;
Scotus, *Sent.* III d.36 n.3, XV: 600.
14. Cf. note 7 above.
15. Cf. Aristotle, *Eth. Nic.* 7.1.1145a35–36, 2.1145b8–10.
16. Cf. Aristotle, *Eth. Nic.* 7.8.1150a13–15.

could even acquire two degrees of temperance (namely, beginning and increasing virtue), but not its natural completion and perfection, which is the degree that is worthy of being called virtue, simply and absolutely; nor could he acquire heroic virtue. Thus Ghent posits these four degrees in numerically the same habit. In the first two degrees, the virtues need not be connected, and this is also the case in some sense in the third degree. But in the perfect third degree and in the fourth degree, the virtues are necessarily connected. This is so because in these last two degrees, a connection with other virtues is needed as a support, since such virtue could not be preserved for long unless it were supported, nor could it persist for long without the support of other virtues.

63. Many arguments support this opinion; I should mention some of them. First, what can be bent into the contrary of its end is not true virtue. Second, there is no pleasure in the practice of one virtue without another. Third, no one virtue without another leads perfectly to the end of virtue.[9] This is confirmed because virtue perfects those who possess it and renders their work good. Besides, according to book 6 of the *Ethics,* the virtues are sisters.[10] Then there is a citation from Augustine, in book 6 of *De Trinitate.*[11] Next there is a quotation from Gregory, book 10 of the *Moralia.*[12] These and other references may be found in Ghent's work and in that of Scotus.[13]

[Against Henry of Ghent's Opinion]

73. Since this opinion is mistaken in many ways, I will argue against it. First, the reference to the Philosopher is bad; the Philosopher posits only a three-part distinction, as is evident at the beginning of book 7,[14] where he posits continence, temperance, and heroic virtue on the one hand, and incontinence, malice, and brutishness on the other hand. In chapters 9 and 10,[15] he posits a four-part distinction—namely, perseverance and continence on the one hand, and softness and incontinence on the other hand. He distinguishes between them as follows: continence and incontinence pertain to pleasures; perseverance and softness, to pains. That is why he says in the ninth chapter:[16] "those regarding pleasures are continence and incontinence; those regarding pains are softness and perseverance."

Quod sic intelligo,[17] quod continens est ille qui habet pravas   85
concupiscentias et delectationes in appetitu sensitivo, et non sequitur eas sed sequitur rectam rationem; incontinens, qui dimittit
rectam rationem et sequitur illas delectationes. Ideo continentia et
incontinentia habent proprie fieri circa delectabiles concupiscentias. Perseverans est ille qui habet virtutem, sed in illa aliquando   90
perseverat cum tristitia propter aliquid extrinsecum annexum ma-
teriae illius virtutis. Mollis est, qui propter illud extrinsecum, ex
quo sequitur tristitia, dimittit actum virtutis, quia non vult illum
actum exercere cum tristitia.

Exemplum: si aliquis esset virtuosus in surgendo ad matuti-   95
num ad laudandum Deum, si esset frigidus vel piger vel aliquid
tale sibi accideret, et exerceret tunc actum illius virtutis, hoc esset
cum quadam tristitia, et diceretur talis perseverans, continuando
actum virtutis. Si autem dimitteret actum virtutis et non exerceret
illum quia non vult talem actum exercere cum tristitia, tunc dice-   100
retur mollis.

Quod autem bestialitas distinguatur per obiecta a virtute, patet
per eum, capitulo 7:[18] "Dico autem bestiales...". Quomodo autem
isti gradus quos ponit P h i l o s o p h u s distinguuntur,
patebit postea.[19]   105

S e c u n d o, ponendo quod essent gradus tales in virtute
sicut non sunt, adhuc non valet quod dicit de connexione.[20] Primo,
quia possibile est materiam unius virtutis occurrere et numquam
alterius, et per consequens circa materiam illius virtutis potest
generari virtus in gradu heroico sine aliqua alia virtute, maxime   110
cum secundum eum[21] isti sint gradus unius quantitatis, et una
potest augmentari usque ad gradum supremum possibilem sibi
sine alia, quando non occurrit materia alterius.

Praeterea virtus sufficit ad fulciendum seipsam sine quacumque alia; igitur etc. Antecedens patet, quia stante vitio opposito   115
alteri virtuti, quamvis non in complemento, sufficit; igitur sine illa
virtute sufficit. Patet enim per experientiam quod aliquis intempe-
ratus citra complementum intemperantiae potest velle exercere
opera iustitiae et facere, igitur multo magis potest talia opera
exercere sine temperantia. Ideo dixi 'in complemento,' quia tunc   120
aliquis est in complemento vitii quando propter actum vitiosum
vult omnino deserere actum virtuosum, et ideo intemperantia in
tali gradu non stat cum iustitia.

---

17. Cf. OTh VIII, 272–73, 275, 281.
18. Cf. Aristotle, *Eth. Nic.* 7.6.1148b 19–21.
19. Cf. OTh VIII, 272–86.
20. Lines 57–62; cf. OTh VIII, 284–85.
21. Cf. Henry, *Quodl.* V q.17, fol. 192r; q.16, fol. 187r; q.17, fol. 191v.

85. I understand[17] this to mean that a continent person is someone who experiences depraved desires and pleasures in the sensitive appetite and does not follow them, but follows right reason instead; an incontinent person follows those pleasures and abandons right reason. Therefore, the proper operation of continence and incontinence pertains to pleasurable desires. A persevering person is someone who possesses a virtue, but because of something extrinsically connected with the subject matter of that virtue, sometimes experiences pain and perseveres. A soft person abandons a virtuous act on account of something extrinsic that has pain as a sequel, because he does not will the practice of the act when associated with pain.

95. Consider an example. Suppose someone virtuously got up at matins to praise God. If that person felt cold or sluggish (or something similar occurred) and still performed that virtuous act, it would be with some pain; and a person continuing that virtuous act would be said to persevere. However, if a person abandoned that virtuous act and did not practice it because she did not will its practice with pain, she would be called soft.

102. Brutishness is distinguished from virtue by its objects, according to the Philosopher, as is evident from chapter 7:[18] "I mean the brutish states . . ." But how the degrees posited by the Philosopher are distinguished will be evident later.[19]

106. Second, this opinion errs, because, even positing nonexistent degrees of virtue, what he says about their connection is not valid.[20] This is clear, first, because the subject matter of one virtue can occur where that of another never does. Consequently, regarding the subject matter of that virtue, a heroic degree of that virtue can be generated without any other virtue. This is particularly so, since according to Ghent,[21] these are degrees of a single quantity, and one virtue can be augmented without another, attaining the supreme degree of which it is capable in the absence of the subject matter for another virtue.

114. Besides, one virtue suffices to support itself without any other virtue. The antecedent is evident, for one of two virtues suffices in the presence of a vice opposed to the second virtue, as long as that vice is not complete; therefore it suffices in the absence of that virtue. For it is evident from experience that an intemperate person can will the practice of works of justice and can perform them, provided her intemperance is not complete; so much the more, therefore, in the absence of temperance. I have spoken of "complete" vices because someone is in a state of complete vice when she wills to desert virtuous action entirely on account of a vicious act; consequently intemperance in such a degree is not compatible with justice.

Praeterea quando[22] aliqua causa nata est generare aliquem effectum augmentabilem, illa approximata generabit et perducet ad   125
perfectionem tantam quantam potest; sed sic est de causis genera-
tivis unius virtutis sine alia.

Praeterea secundum[23] istam viam multi Sancti et Confessores
non habuissent aliquam virtutem moralem perfecte, quia multi
fuerunt quibus numquam materia fortitudinis occurrit nec materia   130
regiminis.

S i d i c a s quod occurrebat eis in cognitione et fuerunt
parati mortem sustinere, si materia eis occurrisset, et eodem modo
ad bene regendum: c o n t r a, forte numquam cogitabant de
materia fortitudinis nec de regimine, nisi tantum forte in generali,   135
saltem hoc est possibile. Sed sic cogitare non sufficit ad virtutem
moralem in speciali, quia ad illam requiritur prudentia in speciali, sicut
prius dictum est.[24]

[Conclusiones auctoris de connexione virtutum inter se]

[Conclusio prima]   140

Ideo respondeo ad istum articulum, et sit haec prima conclusio, quod virtutes morales omnes connectuntur in quibusdam
principiis universalibus, puta 'omne honestum est faciendum,'
'omne bonum est diligendum,' 'omne dictatum a recta ratione est
faciendum,' quae possunt esse maiores et minores in syllogismo   145
practico concludente conclusionem particularem, cuius notitia est
prudentia immediate directiva in actu virtuoso. Et potest idem
principium numero esse maior cum diversis minoribus acceptis
sub, ad concludendum diversas conclusiones particulares, quarum
notitiae sunt prudentiae directivae in diversis actibus virtuosis,   150
sicut de ista conclusione dictum est diffuse in *Reportatione* O c k-
h a m in materia morali.[25] Quaere ibi.

---

22. Lines 66–67 above; cf. OTh VI, 420–21, 424; Scotus, *Sent.*III d.36
n.9, XV: 617.

23. Cf. Scotus, *Sent.* III d.36 n.4, XV: 600–601.

24. See a.2 30–50.

a. Here the reporter responsible for the written text has recorded
Ockham's reference to his own works in the third person. It is not a sign
that we should question the authenticity of *De connexione* but that we
have a *reportatio,* not a written version approved by Ockham. See the
preface.

25. Cf. OTh VI, 425–26.

124. Besides, when[22] some cause is designed to generate an augmentable effect, and that [cause] is proximate, it will generate and attain such perfection as it can. But this is the case for causes that generate one virtue without another.

128. Furthermore, according to this opinion,[23] many saints and confessors would not have possessed any moral virtue perfectly, since there were many who encountered neither the subject matter for courage nor the subject matter for [virtuous] governance.

132. Someone might object that courage occurred to them in thought, and they were prepared to sustain death if the subject matter had occurred; and similarly they were prepared to govern well. On the contrary, I reply: perhaps they never thought about the subject of courage or government, except perhaps merely in general; at least this is possible. But such [general] thinking does not suffice for a particular moral virtue, since particular moral virtue requires particular prudence, as was indicated above.[24]

[Author's Conclusions about the Connection of the Virtues]

[First Conclusion]

141. Therefore in reply to the first article of the third principle article, let this be the first conclusion: All moral virtues are connected in certain universal principles, which can serve as major premises and as minor premises in a practical syllogism proving a particular conclusion; the knowledge of these conclusions is the prudence that is immediately directive of a virtuous act. I have in mind such principles as, 'everything worthy should be done,' 'everything good should be loved,' 'everything dictated by right reason should be performed.' Numerically the same principle as the major premise, together with different subordinate minor premises, can serve to prove different particular conclusions; the knowledges of these conclusions are the prudences that are directive of different virtuous acts, as was discussed at length in Ockham's *Reportatio*[a] in the section on morals.[25] See that passage.

[Conclusio secunda]

Secunda conclusio[26] est ista, quod una virtus perfecta sufficienter cum voluntate et recta ratione sive prudentia inclinat ad pri-   155
mum actum alterius virtutis qui est generativus illius virtutis;
et intelligo per virtutem perfectam virtutem in tertio et quarto
gradu, de quibus supra dictum est.[27] Quia si aliquis vult aliquid
solum quia dictatum est a recta ratione quantum ad tertium gradum, vel quia solum dictatum est a recta ratione et propter hono-   160
rem divinum, tunc vult omne dictatum a recta ratione; et ita dictante recta ratione quod actus virtuosus sit eliciendus circa materiam alterius virtutis, statim ista virtus, licet sit alterius speciei
in uno gradu vel in alio, inclinat voluntatem sufficienter ad eliciendum actum primum alterius virtutis. Patet exemplum de iustitia   165
et temperantia.

Et si quaeras utrum virtus in secundo gradu[28]
inclinet sufficienter modo praedicto ad primum actum alterius
virtutis: respondeo quod aliquando inclinat, aliquando
non. Universaliter enim, quando occurrit materia alterius virtutis   170
cum aliqua circumstantia repugnante conservationi istius virtutis
in secundo gradu, tunc inclinat ad primum actum alterius virtutis,
in secundo gradu sicut in tertio vel quarto. Quando autem occurrit cum circumstantiis impertinentibus, tunc non inclinat.

Exemplum: si enim aliquis sit iustus et immineat sibi mors   175
nisi faciat actum iniustitiae, talis iustitia in secundo gradu inclinat
statim modo praedicto ad actum primum fortitudinis, quia actus
illius virtutis est nolle deserere iustitiam pro aliquo quod est contra
rectam rationem; et ideo si recta ratio dictet quod citius sustinenda
est mors quam fiat actus iniustitiae, statim illa iustitia in tali gradu   180
inclinat ad actum primum fortitudinis. Sed si aliquis habeat iustitiam in praedicto gradu et immineat sibi mors nisi faciat actum
intemperantiae, puta nisi fornicetur, ibi non inclinat iustitia in
gradu praedicto ad primum actum temperantiae, quia potest istam
iustitiam conservare secundum rectam rationem et tamen facere   185
actum intemperantiae, quia hic nulla est repugnantia inter actus
nec inter circumstantias actuum.

Sed utrum iustitia in primo gradu[29] inclinat ad primum
actum alterius virtutis? Respondeo quod non, quia potest

---

26. Cf. OTh VI, 426; *Dial.* 1.VI.77, fol. 90r–v.
27. See a.2 132–42.
28. See a.2 124–31.
29. See a.2 116–23.

[Second Conclusion]

154. This is the second conclusion:[26] One of two perfect virtues, together with the will and right reason or prudence, sufficiently inclines to the first act of another virtue, an act capable of generating that other virtue. Here I understand by "perfect virtue" third- or fourth-degree virtue, as was indicated above.[27] For if someone wishes something precisely because it is dictated by right reason in the third degree, or precisely because it is dictated by right reason and for the sake of divine honor, then he wishes everything dictated by right reason. Hence, one of two virtues sufficiently inclines the will to elicit a first act of another virtue, as soon as right reason dictates that an act of virtue should be elicited concerning the subject of the second virtue. This is evident in the example of justice and temperance.

167. Someone might ask whether second-degree[28] virtue would sufficiently incline us to the first act of another virtue in the manner described. My answer is that a second-degree virtue sometimes does and sometimes does not function in this manner. For it is universally the case that when the subject matter for one virtue occurs, together with some circumstance that is incompatible with the preservation of that second-degree virtue, second-degree virtue inclines us to elicit the first act of another virtue, and it would do so whether it is in the second degree or the third or the fourth degree. However, when it occurs with circumstances that are not pertinent, then it does not so incline us.

175. For example, suppose death is imminent for someone just unless she performs an unjust act. Such second-degree justice immediately inclines her to the first act of courage in the manner described, because to reject the abandonment of justice for the sake of something that is contrary to right reason is an act of that virtue. Therefore if right reason were to dictate that she should sustain death rather than perform an act of injustice, that degree of justice inclines her to the first act of courage at once. But if death is imminent for someone who is just in the aforesaid degree unless he performs an act of intemperance—unless he fornicates, for example—justice in the aforesaid degree does not incline him to the first act of temperance because he can preserve this justice according to right reason and yet perform the intemperate act, since neither the acts nor the circumstances are incompatible here.

188. But does first-degree[29] justice incline us to perform the first act of another virtue? My answer is that it does not. For

aliquis velle facere opera iusta conformiter rectae rationi absque 190
hoc quod plus inclinetur ad volendum actum temperantiae conformiter rectae rationi, quia tam isti actus quam circumstantiae
actuum sunt impertinentes ad invicem; et ideo habitus a quo elicitur unus actus, non inclinat ad alium actum impertinentem.

De hac conclusione, quomodo scilicet una virtus inclinat ad 195
actum primum alterius, quaere in O c k h a m ubi prius.[30]

S i q u a e r a s utrum iustitia, secundum quod est virtus
heroica,[31] inclinet sufficienter ad actum alterius virtutis: r e s-
p o n d e o quod aliquando inclinat, aliquando non. Nam occurrente materia alterius virtutis cum aliqua circumstantia necessario 200
sequente iustitiam vel repugnante, puta si oporteret aliquem deserere actum iustitiae vel facere inhonestum, vel sustinere carcerem,
ibi inclinaret sufficienter ad actum fortitudinis. Si autem occurrat
materia alterius virtutis cum circumstantiis omnino impertinentibus, puta si oporteret aliquem bona sua perdere nisi faceret actum 205
intemperantiae, in tali casu non inclinat sufficienter.

S i q u a e r a s utrum iustitia in uno gradu inclinet ad
actum iustitiae in alio gradu: r e s p o n d e o, primus gradus
non videtur inclinare ad secundum, quia secundus habet circumstantiam omnino impertinentem ad primum, nec sequentem nec 210
repugnantem sibi; nec eadem ratione secundus inclinat ad tertium
nec ad quartum. Sed tam secundus quam tertius quam quartus
inclinant ad quintum, puta ad heroicam.

[Conclusio tertia]

Tertia conclusio[32] est quod nulla virtus moralis in quocumque 215
gradu necessario coexigit aliam virtutem in quocumque gradu.
Hoc probatur, quia aliquis potest se exercere circa materiam unius
virtutis in quocumque gradu supradicto absque hoc quod exerceat
se circa materiam alterius virtutis, quia possibile est quod non
occurrat materia cuiuscumque alterius virtutis, et non videtur 220
maior ratio quare potest se exercere magis in uno gradu quam in

---

30. Cf. OTh VI, 426.
31. See a.2 152–67.
32. Cf. OTh VI, 420–21, 424.

someone can will the performance of just works, in conformity with right reason, without being more inclined to will an act of temperance in conformity with right reason, since neither the acts nor the circumstances of the acts are pertinent to each other. Therefore a habit from which one act is elicited does not incline us to perform another, impertinent act.

195. Concerning this conclusion—namely, the discussion of how one virtue inclines us to perform the first act of another virtue—see Ockham, in the passage just cited.[30]

197. Someone might ask whether justice as a heroic virtue[31] sufficiently inclines us to an act of another virtue. My answer is that sometimes it does, and sometimes it does not. When the subject matter of the second virtue occurs together with some circumstance necessarily consequent on justice or necessarily incompatible with justice, it would sufficiently incline someone to an act of courage. Suppose, for example, a just person would have had to sustain imprisonment if he had not abandoned an act of justice or performed an unworthy act. If, however, the subject matter of the other virtue occurred together with entirely impertinent circumstances, heroic justice would not sufficiently incline a person to an act of another virtue. If, for example, a just person would have to act unjustly or lose his possessions unless he performed an intemperate act, that would be a case of an impertinent circumstance.

207. Someone might ask whether justice in one degree inclines to an act of justice in another degree. I would say in reply that the first degree does not appear to incline to the second because second-degree justice includes a circumstance that is entirely impertinent to first-degree justice, a circumstance that neither follows from, nor is incompatible with, first-degree justice. For the same reason second-degree justice does not incline to third- or fourth-degree justice. But second-, third-, and fourth-degree justice do incline us to heroic, or fifth-degree, justice.

[Third Conclusion]

215. The third conclusion[32] is that no moral virtue in any degree whatever necessarily requires another virtue in any degree whatever. A proof of this is that someone can practice the subject of one of two virtues in any of the aforesaid degrees whatever, without practicing the subject of the second virtue, since the subject matter of the second virtue need not occur. There seems to be no more reason why a person should be more capable of the practice of a virtue in one degree than another; consequently a person should

alio, et ita in quolibet vel in nullo; et si quandoque occurrat materia alterius virtutis, hoc accidit.

[Conclusio quarta]

Quarta conclusio[33] est quod duo primi gradus virtutis stant   225
cum vitio contrario alteri virtuti et[34] recto iudicio rationis, non
tantum respectu istius virtutis quae stat cum vitio, sed respectu
alterius virtutis cum cuius opposito stat ista virtus; et similiter
stat cum vitio opposito et errore respectu alterius virtutis, et hoc
quantumcumque virtus in illis gradibus intendatur.   230

Prima pars probatur per experientiam, quia aliquis potest temperate agere secundum duos primos gradus temperantiae et tamen
velle iniuste agere, etiam dictante ratione recta quod talia opera
iniusta non sunt facienda sed opposita sunt facienda. Etiam stante
ratione recta tam respectu temperantiae quam respectu iustitiae,   235
potest aliquis propter libertatem voluntatis velle oppositum unius,
sicut post patebit,[35] et ita potest velle facere opera iniusta et post
esse iniustus.

Praeterea quando[36] aliquis actus sine circumstantiis stat cum
alio actu, idem actus saltem genere, — non dico numero, quia   240
non potest esse idem actus numero primo sine circumstantiis et
postea cum circumstantiis —, stat cum eodem actu cum circumstantiis impertinentibus. Hoc patet, quia si stat cum eo sine circumstantiis, non posset sibi repugnare nisi propter aliquam circumstantiam repugnantem alicui circumstantiae illius virtutis.   245
Puta, si aliquis vellet facere opera iniusta quia inhonesta vel quia
contra rectam rationem, hic videtur repugnantia inter actum temperantiae in primo gradu et secundo, et inter actum iniustitiae,
quia actus temperantiae tam in primo quam in secundo elicitur
propter honestatem et quia conformis rectae rationi; et ideo ille   250
qui elicitur quia inhonestus vel quia contra rectam rationem, videtur repugnare actui temperantiae propter istas duas circumstantias;

---

33. Cf. Ockham, OTh VIII, 284–85, 421.
34. Namely, et cum recto iudicio rationis.
35. Lines 521–22, 691–93 below.
36. Cf. lines 170–74 above.

be capable either of any degree or of none. Moreover, if at one time or another the subject matter of another virtue occurs, that is coincidental.

[Fourth Conclusion]

225. The fourth conclusion[33] is that the first two degrees of one virtue are compatible with reason judging correctly and[34] with a vice contrary to some other virtue—that is, these degrees of virtue are compatible with vice even when right reason judges correctly not only with respect to original virtue, but also with respect to the other virtue, whose opposite is compatible with the original virtue. Similarly, the first two degrees of one virtue are compatible with error in respect to the other virtue and with a vice opposite to the other virtue. This is the case, however much the [original] virtue is intensified in those degrees.

231. The first part of the fourth conclusion is proved on the basis of experience, since in the first two degrees of temperance someone can act temperately and yet will injustice, even when right reason dictates that such unjust works should not be performed but rather the opposite works. Even when reason dictates correctly, both in respect to temperance and in respect to justice, someone can will the opposite of temperance or justice because the will is free, as will be evident later;[35] thus a person can will the performance of unjust works and thereafter be unjust.

239. Besides, when[36] one act without circumstances is compatible with a second act, generically the same act is compatible with the same second act in the presence of impertinent circumstances. (I say generically the same act, since it is not numerically the same act if it occurs first without circumstances and afterward with circumstances.) This is evident because if it is compatible with the second act in the absence of circumstances, it could not be incompatible unless on account of some circumstance that is not compatible with some circumstance of the second virtue. Suppose, for example, someone were to will the performance of unjust works because they were unworthy or because they were contrary to right reason. In this case, there appears to be incompatibility between an act of temperance, both in the first and the second degree, and an act of injustice. For both in the first and in the second degree, an act of temperance is elicited because of its worthiness and because it conforms to right reason; consequently that act elicited because it is unworthy or because it is contrary to right reason appears to be incompatible with an act of temperance on account of these two circumstances.

igitur sublata omni repugnantia inter circumstantias et stante im-
pertinentia inter eas, videtur quod isti actus possunt aequaliter
simul stare sicut quando unus fuit sine circumstantiis. Patet igitur   255
maior.[37]

Sed pro minori, patet quod velle facere actum temperantiae,
prout est actus indifferens et sine circumstantiis, stat cum actu
vitioso volendi facere opera iniusta, sicut patet per experientiam.
Et potest primo elici actus in primo gradu et secundo cum cir-   260
cumstantiis omnino impertinentibus, ut si aliquis vellet facere
opera iniusta quia nociva proximo vel destructiva vel huiusmodi,
ubi ponuntur circumstantiae omnino impertinentes circumstantiis
temperantiae in praedictis gradibus. Igitur virtus temperantiae in
praedictis gradibus potest stare cum iniustitia.   265

Secunda pars[38] patet, quia si iniustitia potest stare cum temperantia et recta ratione respectu iustitiae, multo magis potest
stare cum errore in ratione respectu iustitiae, puta si ratio erronea dictaret quod talia opera iniusta non sunt mala sed bona vel
honesta.   270

[Conclusio quinta]

Quinta conclusio est quod tertius gradus virtutis[39] non stat
cum vitio opposito alteri virtuti et recto dictamine respectu illius
virtutis; sed si sit ignorantia in ratione vel error respectu alterius
virtutis, tunc potest stare cum vitio opposito.   275

Prima pars probatur, quia quando aliquid est volitum quia
aliquale praecise, nihil scitum esse tale potest esse nolitum. Exemplum: si diligo Sortem quia est homo, impossibile est, stante
prima dilectione, quod ego odiam aliquem quem scio esse hominem, et per consequens diligo omnem quem scio esse hominem,   280
quia aliter sequeretur quod diligam omnem quem scio esse hominem per primam propositionem, et tamen odirem aliquem quem

---

37. Lines 225–28.
38. Lines 228–30.
39. A.2 132–36; cf. OTh VIII, 285–86; *Dial.* 1.VI.77, fol. 90r–v.

Therefore, leaving aside any incompatibility between the circumstances, as long as the circumstances are impertinent, it appears that these acts can be just as compatible as they were when one of them was without circumstances. Consequently the major premise[37] is evident.

257. But as for the minor, it is evident that willing the performance of an act of temperance, insofar as it is an indifferent act without circumstances, is compatible with a vicious act of willing to perform unjust works, as is evident on the basis of experience. The act can also be first elicited in the first and second degree, together with circumstances that are entirely impertinent, as when someone wills the performance of unjust works because they are harmful to his neighbor or destructive or something similar, where the circumstances posited are entirely impertinent to the circumstances of temperance in the degree we have discussed. Therefore the virtue of temperance is compatible with injustice in the aforesaid degrees.

266. The second part[38] of the fourth conclusion is evident. For if injustice is compatible with temperance and right reason in respect to justice, it is much more compatible with error in human reason regarding justice. Consider the case where an erring reason dictates that such unjust works are not wicked, but good or worthy.

[Fifth Conclusion]

272. The fifth conclusion is that third-degree virtue[39] is not compatible with a vice that is opposed to another virtue when reason dictates correctly in respect to the second virtue. But if there is ignorance in reason or error in respect to the second virtue, then third-degree virtue is compatible with a vice opposed to the second virtue.

276. The first part of this fifth conclusion can be proven as follows. When something is willed because it is something of a certain kind, nothing scientifically known to be of this kind can be rejected. For example, if I love Socrates because he is a man, it is impossible that I should hate someone whom I know to be a man, as long as my first love remains. Consequently, I love everyone whom I know scientifically to be a man. Otherwise it would follow that I love everyone whom I know to be a man in virtue of the first proposition, and yet I would hate someone whom I know

scio esse hominem, quod includit contradictionem. Sed in tertio
gradu diligo vel volo facere opera iusta praecise quia conformia
rectae rationi. Igitur impossibile est quod sciam aliquid esse con-   285
forme rectae rationi, et tamen quod nolim illud.

S i d i c a s quod licet non possim nolle illud dictatum a
recta ratione, tamen possum velle oppositum illius dictati; puta,
possum velle actum incontinentiae quantumcumque ratio dictet
continentiam esse volendam. Nunc autem vitium non tantum   290
generatur ex actu nolendi continentiam, sed ex actu volendi incontinentiam. Igitur etc.

R e s p o n d e o quod stante prima volitione et recta ratione
praedicta, impossibile est aliquem velle actum incontinentiae propter repugnantiam formalem, quia si vult facere actum iustitiae   295
propter honestatem et praecise quia est sic dictatus a recta ratione,
tunc consequenter vult necessario omne dictatum a ratione recta,
stante prima volitione. Et per consequens si dictatur a ratione
quod sit continendum propter honestatem, necessario vult illum
actum. Igitur non potest simul velle oppositum, quia volitiones   300
talium oppositorum sunt oppositae.

S i d i c a s quod tunc ista secunda volitio respectu continentiae non est actus virtuosus, quia non est in potestate voluntatis: r e s p o n d e o quod sic, quatenus potest suspendere
primum actum.[40]   305

Secunda pars[41] conclusionis patet, quia si aliquis ignoret actum
incontinentiae esse malum vel erret credendo illum actum esse
bonum, tunc cum primo actu voluntatis et tali errore potest stare
vitium oppositum alteri virtuti, quia hic non videtur aliqua repugnantia.   310

[Conclusio sexta]

Sexta conclusio est quod iustitia in quarto gradu[42] cum nullo
vitio stat nec errore culpabili. Hoc probatur, quia si aliquod vitium
staret, aut illud esset peccatum ex ignorantia, vel ex malitia, vel
ex passione. Non primum, quia illa ignorantia aut esset vincibilis   315
aut invincibilis; si secundo modo, non est tunc ignorantia culpabilis; si vincibilis, tunc necessario vincit et amovet impedimentum,

---

40. Lines 295–96.
41. Lines 274–75.
42. A.2 137–42; cf. *Dial.* 1.VI.77, fol. 90r–v.

scientifically to be a man, which is a contradiction. But in third-degree justice, I love—or will the performance of—just works precisely because they conform to right reason. Therefore it is impossible that I should scientifically know that something conforms with right reason and yet reject it.

287. Someone might object that although I could not reject what is dictated by right reason, yet I can still will the opposite of that dictate. For example, I can will an incontinent act, however much reason dictates that continence should be willed. But vice is generated not only when continence is rejected, but also when incontinence is willed. Therefore, etc.

293. My response is that as long as right reason remains, together with the first act of will mentioned above, it is impossible for someone to will any incontinent act on account of formal incompatibility. For if she wills an act of justice in order to be worthy precisely because it is so dictated by right reason, and if the first act of will remains, she necessarily wills everything dictated by right reason. Consequently, if reason dictates that she should be continent in order to be worthy, she necessarily wills that act. Therefore, she cannot will the opposite act at the same time, since acts in which opposites are willed are themselves opposite.

302. Someone might say that then this second volition in respect to continence is not a virtuous act, since it is not in the power of the will. I reply that it is virtuous to the extent that she can suspend the first act.[40]

306. The second part[41] of the fifth conclusion is evident, since if someone does not know that an act of incontinence is wicked, or if he mistakenly believes that that act was good, then a vice opposite to another virtue can be compatible with the first act of will and with such an error; there does not appear to be any incompatibility here.

[Sixth Conclusion]

312. The sixth conclusion is that justice in the fourth degree[42] is compatible neither with any vice nor with culpable error. This is proven because if some vice were compatible with fourth-degree justice, it would be a sin committed either from ignorance, malice, or passion. Ignorance is not a possibility, since the ignorance would be either vincible or invincible. If it is invincible, then it is not culpable; if it can be overcome, then, if a person loves God or

si diligat Deum vel honorem Dei ordinate. Non secundo modo
nec tertio, quia si sic, sequitur quod aliquid plus diligeretur quam
Deus, et ita corrumperetur illa virtus qua diligo aliquid propter   320
amorem Dei ordinate.

[Conclusio septima]

Septima conclusio est quod iustitia in quinto gradu,[43] prout est
virtus heroica perfecta in uno christiano, qui talem actum impe-
raret propter honorem Dei, non compatitur secum aliquod vitium   325
nec defectum culpabilem propter eandem causam. Tamen virtus
heroica alicuius philosophi bene compatitur aliquod vitium, quia
illae sunt alterius speciei, quia una habet Deum pro obiecto, alia
non.

[Conclusiones de connexione virtutum moralium   330
cum virtutibus theologicis: Conclusio prima]

Quantum ad secundum articulum istius tertii articuli sit ista
prima conclusio, quod virtutes morales in tribus primis gradibus
non necessario coexigunt virtutes theologicas stricte vel large ac-
ceptas.[44] Hoc patet, quia theologicae virtutes non possunt haberi   335
sine cognitione finis in particulari, eo modo quo cognoscitur pro
statu isto, in conceptu sibi proprio.[45] Sed virtutes morales in praedictis gradibus possunt adquiri sine tali cognitione finis,[46] sicut
patet in simplici pagano, qui posset talia facere secundum rectam
rationem sine investigatione ad habendum conceptum proprium   340
de illo fine. Igitur etc.

[Conclusio secunda]

Secunda conclusio: quod duo primi gradus stant cum contrariis
virtutum theologicarum. Hoc patet, quia stant cum dubitatione

---

43. A.2 152–67. The text of the first part of this conclusion is uncertain. As can be seen in the apparatus of variants, most of it is found only
in the printed edition, Z, and in codices E and L, which are not credible
witnesses. Wey has followed E and L, but notes that the authenticity of
Z's text seems to be confirmed from what Ockham says elsewhere. See
OTh VI, 427–28, and a.4 353–66.

b. The three theological virtues are faith, hope, and charity. On the
origins of the phrase 'theological virtues,' see O. Lottin, *PM* III: 100–102,
citing Peter of Poitiers, *Sent.* III c.20 (PL 211, 1087).

44. A.2 194–98.
45. Cf. OTh II, 402–3.
46. Cf. OTh VII, 58.

God's honor ordinately, he necessarily overcomes his ignorance and removes the impediment. Neither malice nor passion need be considered, since these would imply that a person loved something more than God, consequently the virtue of loving something ordinately for the sake of love of God would be destroyed.

[Seventh Conclusion]

323. The seventh conclusion is that for the same reason, fifth-degree[43] justice, insofar as it is a perfect, heroic virtue in a Christian who would command such an act for God's honor, is not compatible with any vice or culpable defect. Nonetheless, heroic virtue in a philosopher is indeed compatible with some vice. This is so because those virtues belong to different species, since one has God as its object, and the other does not.

[Conclusions Regarding the Connection of Moral and Theological Virtues]

[First Conclusion]

332. This brings us to the second article of the third [principal] article. Here the first conclusion is that the first three degrees of moral virtues do not necessarily require the theological virtues,[b] considered either strictly or loosely.[44] This is evident because we cannot have theological virtues without particular knowledge and a proper concept[45] of the end, in the manner in which it is known in this state. But moral virtues in the aforesaid degrees can be acquired without such knowledge of the end.[46] This is evident in the case of a simple pagan, who does these things according to right reason, without seeking to acquire the concept proper to that end. Therefore, etc.

[Second Conclusion]

343. Second conclusion: the first two degrees of moral virtue are compatible with the [vices] contrary to theological virtues. This is evident because they are compatible with doubt and dissent in

et dissensu respectu credendorum, patet in philosopho;[47]   345
et cum desperatione, quia nullus sperat quod non credit;
et cum odio Dei, quia potest virtuosus in praedictis gradibus odire
sectam christianorum.

Praeterea non est maior connexio virtutum moralium et theologicarum quam unius virtutis ad aliam, nec maior repugnantia   350
inter virtutes morales in praedictis gradibus et opposita theologicarum quam inter unam virtutem moralem et vitium oppositum
alteri virtuti. Sed una virtus moralis in praedictis gradibus stat
cum vitio opposito alteri virtuti.[48] Igitur eodem modo in proposito.   355

[Conclusio tertia]

Tertia conclusio est quod virtus moralis in tertio gradu non
compatitur secum contrarium virtutis theologicae nisi propter
defectum rationis. Probatur per omnia sicut quinta conclusio alterius articuli,[49] ideo nunc transeo.   360

[Conclusio quarta]

Quarta conclusio est quod virtus moralis in quarto gradu necessario coexigit virtutes theologicas, et hoc de potentia Dei ordinata. Hoc patet, quia non potest esse amor creaturae vel alicuius
creati propter Deum nisi talis amet Deum super omnia, quia prop-   365
ter[50] quod unumquodque etc.; talis[51] autem amor de potentia Dei
ordinata non potest esse sine fide, spe et caritate infusis, nec sine
eis aliquo modo adquisitis.

[Conclusio quinta]

Quinta conclusio est quod virtus in quinto gradu, quae est   370
heroica perfecti christiani, coexigit necessario de potentia Dei
ordinata virtutes theologicas, non autem virtus heroica philosophi.
Probatur quantum ad primam partem sicut praecedens conclusio.
Probatur etiam quantum ad secundam partem, quia ipse non im-

---

47. Cf. OTh VI, 280; OTh V, 291. Or see perhaps Vincentius
Bellovacensis, Speculum Hist. (ed. Douai, 1624), cc. 70–71.

Here the text of the critical edition has been changed, the word "second" found in three of the fifteen manuscripts has been omitted, and the
note has been changed accordingly.

c. The Latin word "secta" refers to schools of thinking; unlike the
modern English 'sect,' it does not connote error.

48. Lines 225–26 above.

49. Lines 271–305 above.

50. Cf. Aristotle, *Anal. Poster.* 1.2.72a 29–30.

51. Cf. OTh VI, 281–82, 312.

regard to what we ought to believe, as is evident in the case of the Philosopher[47] in the second book. They are also compatible with despair (since no one hopes for what he does not believe) and with hatred of God (since a person virtuous in the aforesaid degrees can hate the Christian school).[c]

349. Besides, there is no greater connection between the moral virtues and the theological virtues than between one virtue and another. Nor is there greater repugnance between moral virtues in the aforesaid degrees and the vices opposite to theological virtues than between one moral virtue and a vice opposed to another moral virtue. But in the aforesaid degrees, one moral virtue is compatible with the vice opposed to another moral virtue.[48] Therefore, similarly in the case under consideration [the first two degrees of moral virtue and theological virtues are not connected].

[Third Conclusion]

357. The third conclusion is that third-degree moral virtue is not compatible with the contrary of theological virtue, except on account of defective reason. This is proved in entirely the same way as the fifth conclusion of the other article,[49] therefore I will pass over it now.

[Fourth Conclusion]

362. The fourth conclusion is that fourth-degree moral virtue necessarily requires the theological virtues; this is true according to God's ordained power. It is evident because no one can love a creature or anything created for the sake of God unless she loves God above all, since "that on account of which we love is better loved."[50] But by God's ordained power, such love[51] cannot exist without infused faith, hope, and charity, or without faith, hope, and charity acquired in some manner.

[Fifth Conclusion]

370. The fifth conclusion is that fifth-degree virtue, which is perfect, heroic Christian virtue, necessarily requires the theological virtues by God's ordained power; while heroic philosophical virtue does not. The first part is proved in the same manner as the preceding conclusion. The proof of the second part is that a

peraret talem actum propter honorem Dei nec diligeret Deum   375
super omnia, igitur etc.

[Conclusio sexta]

Sexta conclusio est quod virtutes theologicae non necessario
coexigunt omnes alias virtutes morales; sunt tamen causae suffi-
cientes mediantibus actibus suis, — ubi concurrunt tam virtutes   380
theologicae adquisitae quam infusae, quia infusae[52] sine adquisitis
non inclinant ad aliquem actum —, cum recta ratione, si occurrat
materia virtutis moralis, ad causandum actum virtuosum.

Haec conclusio probatur quantum ad primam partem, quia
rectitudo circa finem potest esse sine rectitudine circa ea quae sunt   385
ad finem; potest enim aliquis credere articulos fidei, sperare spe-
randa et ordinate diligere Deum, etsi nullam creaturam velit vel
diligat. Sed virtutes morales in tribus gradibus maxime inclinant
ad actus rectos circa creaturam praecise. Igitur etc. Sed virtutes[53]
theologicae stricte sumptae non infunduntur de potentia Dei ordi-   390
nata alicui adulto habenti usum rationis sine virtute morali in
quarto gradu, quia in eo requiritur bonus motus praecedens.

Secunda pars[54] patet, quia qui habet virtutes theologicas infu-
sas et adquisitas, occurrente materia virtutis et dictante ratione quod
actus virtuosus sit eliciendus, statim illae virtutes cum recta   395
ratione inclinant sufficienter ad talem actum virtuosum. Et hoc
est quod dicit G r e g o r i u s,[55] quod "probatio dilectionis
exhibitio est operis".

Et ex hoc sequitur quod virtutes theologicae maxime infusae
non possunt diu conservari sine illis virtutibus, quia ratione dic-   400
tante quod actus virtuosus sit eliciendus, occurrente materia et
aliis inclinantibus modo praedicto et ipso non eliciente, statim[56]
demeretur conservationem virtutum theologicarum.

[Conclusio septima]

Septima conclusio est quod virtutes theologicae nullum vitium   405
morale compatiuntur. Hoc patet, quia rectitudo circa finem ulti-

---

52. Cf. OTh VI, 281–82, 291–92; OTh VII, 57.
53. Cf. OTh VII, 218–21.
54. Lines 379–83; cf. OTh VII, 51, 57–58; Scotus, *Sent.* III d.36 n.29,
XV: 726.
55. Cf. Gregorius, *XL Homiliarum in Evang.* II h.30 (PL 76, 1220 C).
56. Cf. Scotus, *Sent.* II d.37 q.1 n.10, XIII: 359–60.

philosopher's [will] would not dictate such an act for the sake of God's honor; nor would he love God above all; therefore, etc.

[Sixth Conclusion]

378. The sixth conclusion is that theological virtues do not necessarily require all other moral virtues. Nonetheless, it is by means of moral acts that theological virtues sufficiently cause a morally virtuous act, when accompanied by right reason, if the subject matter of moral virtue occurs. Here, both acquired and infused theological virtues concur because in the absence of acquired virtues,[52] infused virtues do not incline us to perform any act.

384. The first part of the conclusion is proved as follows. Rectitude concerning the end can exist without rectitude concerning those things that pertain to the end. For someone can believe the articles of the faith, hope for what we should hope for, and love God ordinately, even if he neither loves nor wills any creature. But the [first] three degrees of moral virtue maximally incline us to correct acts regarding creatures precisely. Therefore, etc. But the theological virtues,[53] taken strictly, are not infused in any adult having the use of reason without moral virtue in the fourth degree. This is by God's ordained power, because baptism requires a preceding good motion in adults.

393. The second part[54] is evident because in a person who has the infused and acquired theological virtues, when the subject matter of virtue occurs and right reason dictates that a virtuous act should be elicited, those virtues together with right reason immediately and sufficiently incline that person to perform such a virtuous act. This is what Gregory[55] means when he says that "the proof of love is a display of work."

399. From this it follows that the theological virtues—most of all, the infused theological virtues—cannot long be preserved without those [moral] virtues. For when reason dictates that a virtuous act should be elicited, and the subject matter of virtue is present together with other factors inclining us to virtue in the aforesaid manner, and a person does not elicit a virtuous act, he immediately[56] ceases to merit the preservation of the theological virtues.

[Seventh Conclusion]

405. The seventh conclusion is that the theological virtues are not compatible with any moral vices. This is evident because rec-

mum repugnat omni deformitati circa ea quae sunt ad finem; quia
si non, aut[57] illa deformitas procedit ex ignorantia vincibili, et
tunc vincit si potest, aliter non est rectitudo circa finem; aut
invincibili, et tunc non est culpabilis; aut procedit ex malitia aut   410
ex passione, et sive sic sive sic, destruitur rectitudo circa finem
ultimum.

Patet etiam, quia qui recte diligit Deum, diligit Deum super
omnia; qui autem habet aliquod vitium, diligit obiectum illius
plus quam Deum; ista non stant simul.   415

Patet tertio, quia qui recte diligit Deum, diligit[58] omne quod
Deus vult diligi, et odit omne quod Deus vult odiri; sed si sit
vitiosus, tunc non diligit omne quod Deus vult diligi, quia non
virtutem, quam Deus vult diligi; similiter diligit aliquid quod
Deus non vult diligi, quia vitium; haec repugnant. Patet igitur   420
maior.[59]

Sed si sit deformitas circa ea quae sunt ad finem, illa procederet
ex ignorantia vel malitia etc. Igitur non stant simul.

[Conclusio octava]

Octava conclusio[60] est quod virtutes theologicae stricte sump-   425
tae compatiuntur secum vitia moralia habitualia, sed non actualia;
sed theologicae adquisitae non compatiuntur habitualia nec actualia.

Prima pars probatur[61] de adulto vitioso nunc baptizato, cui
infunduntur virtutes theologicae, et tamen vitia habitualia non   430
corrumpuntur, quia ita pronum sentit se adhuc post baptismum ad
actus vitiosos sicut ante; igitur remanet habitus aequaliter nunc
inclinans sicut prius.

Secunda pars patet, quia quilibet actus vitiosus moraliter cor-
rumpit illas virtutes demeritorie, quia non stant simul rectitudo   435
circa finem et deformitas circa ea quae sunt ad finem, patet ex
conclusione praecedenti.[62]

---

57. Lines 314–21 above.
58. Cf. OTh VI, 284, 298; Anselm, *De libero arbitrio* c.8, ed. F.
Schmitt (Edinburgh, 1946), I: 220.
59. Lines 406–7.
60. Cf. a.4 344–99.
61. Cf. OTh VII, 52, 59–60; Scotus, *Sent.* III d.36 n.27, XV: 684–85.
62. Lines 405–23; cf. OTh VII, 60.

titude concerning the final end is not compatible with any deformity of character concerning those things that pertain to the end. For otherwise, either that deformity of character proceeds from vincible ignorance,[57] and it will be overcome if it can, otherwise there is no rectitude concerning the end; or it proceeds from invincible ignorance, and then it is not culpable; or it proceeds from malice or passion, either of which destroys rectitude concerning the final end.

413. This conclusion is also evident because a person who loves God correctly loves God above all; but a person who has some vice loves the object of that vice more than God; these [loves] are not compatible.

417. A third argument for the conclusion is that a person who loves God rightly loves everything that God wills us to love,[58] and hates everything that God wills us to hate. But if that person were vicious, he would not love everything that God wills us to love, since he would not love a virtue that God wills us to love; similarly he would love something that God does not will him to love, since he would love a vice; the two are not compatible. Therefore the major premise is evident.[59]

422. But if there were deformity of character concerning those things that pertain to the end, that would proceed from ignorance or malice, etc. Therefore, [theological virtue] is not compatible [with moral vice].

[Eighth Conclusion]

425. The eighth conclusion[60] is that, taken strictly, the theological virtues are compatible with habitual moral vices, but not with actual vices. On the other hand, acquired theological virtue is compatible with neither habitual nor actual [moral vice].

429. The first part of this conclusion is proved[61] in the case of a [formerly] vicious and now baptized adult in whom the theological virtues are infused, and yet habitual vices are not destroyed. For such a person feels himself as much prone to vicious acts after baptism as before; therefore the habit, which equally inclines him before and after, remains.

434. A proof of the second part of this conclusion follows: Any morally vicious act corrupts those virtues demeritoriously. For rectitude concerning the end is not compatible with deformity of character concerning those things that pertain to the end, as is evident from the preceding conclusion.[62]

Tertia pars patet, quia⁶³ universaliter ubi actus aliquorum habituum repugnant, illi habitus repugnant; sed actus vitiorum moralium et virtutum theologicarum adquisitarum repugnant, quia   440
actus caritatis adquisitae est diligere Deum super omnia, actus
autem vitiosus est plus diligere aliud quam Deum, vel diligere
aliquid quod Deus non vult diligi, vel odire aliquid quod Deus
vult diligi; igitur etc.

[Conclusiones de connexione virtutum moralium cum habitibus]   445

[Conclusio prima]

Circa tertium articulum huius tertii articuli principalis sit haec
prima conclusio,⁶⁴ quod nulla virtus moralis necessario exigit habitum consimilem in parte sensitiva. Hoc patet, quia⁶⁵ quantumcumque actus eliciantur in appetitu sensitivo generativi habituum,   450
tamen potest esse tanta rebellio carnis ad spiritum quod causatio
talis habitus potest omnino impediri. Exemplum de Paulo,⁶⁶ qui
habuit stimulum carnis qui non potuit ab eo naturaliter per actus
naturales auferri, sicut satis patet, et tamen ipse fuit castus et
temperatus.   455

Praeterea quando duo contraria generantur, augmentantur vel
conservantur ex distinctis causis, quantumcumque una causa sit
approximata, fortior poterit impedire eam. Igitur quantumcumque causa generativa habitus virtuosi denominative approxime-
tur in appetitu sensitivo, — quae aliquando potest esse voluntas   460
et volitio, quia non est mihi inconveniens quod voluntas causet
et conservet aliquem habitum in parte sensitiva, sicut in quarto
O c k h a m dictum est,⁶⁷ aliquando actus imperati a voluntate
generant talem habitum, sicut patet de actibus temperantiae et
aliis virtutibus quae requirunt actus in parte sensitiva —, tamen   465
causa contraria impediens potest esse ita fortis, quod totam illam
activitatem destruet et generationem habituum impediet. Et hoc⁶⁸
aliquando potest esse cibus bonus, aliquando bona complexio naturalis vel calor vel sanitas vel aliquid tale.

63. Cf. OTh VII, 60; OTh VIII, 317–18.
64. Cf. OTh VI, 373–74; OTh VIII, 279–80.
65. Cf. OTh VI, 368, 417–19.
66. Cf. 2 Cor. 12:7.
67. Cf. OTh VII, 282–83; OTh VI, 411–12; OTh VIII, 279–80. Perhaps, however, the reference is to article four of this question. See a.4
410–26.
68. Cf. OTh VI, 395–97, 399; OTh VI, 204.

438. The third part of the conclusion is evident because it is universally true that when the acts proceeding from certain habits are irreconcilable,[63] those habits are irreconcilable. But the acts proceeding from moral vices and from acquired theological virtues are irreconcilable, since the act proceeding from acquired charity is to love God above all; but the vicious act [proceeding from habitual moral vice] is to love something other than God, or to love something that God does not will us to love, or to hate something that God wills us to love. Therefore, etc.

[Conclusions Concerning the Connection of Moral Virtues with Habits of the Sensitive Soul]

[First Conclusion]

447. Concerning the third article of this third principal article, let this be the first conclusion:[64] No moral virtue necessarily requires a similar habit in the sensitive faculty. This is evident because,[65] however much acts generative of habits are elicited in the sensitive appetite, the flesh can still rebel against the spirit, so much so as entirely to impede the generation of such a habit. Consider the example of Paul,[66] who was possessed of a fleshly urge, which he could not naturally remove by means of natural acts, as is sufficiently evident, and yet he was chaste and temperate.

456. Moreover, when two contraries are generated, augmented, or preserved on the basis of different causes, however near one cause draws, a stronger cause will be able to impede it. Therefore, however near a cause generative of a habit draws in the sensitive appetite, a contrary impeding cause could be so strong as to destroy the whole of that activity and prevent the generation of habits denominated vicious; here I have in mind [causes like] good food, a good natural constitution, heat, health, or something similar. And sometimes the [faculty of] will and an act of will can be such a cause, for I see no objection to holding that the will might cause and preserve some habit in the sensitive faculty, as was mentioned in Ockham's commentary on the fourth book of the *Sentences*.[67] As is evident in the case of acts of temperance and other virtues that require an act in the sensitive faculty,[68] sometimes imperative acts of will generate such a habit.

[Conclusio secunda]   470

Secunda conclusio est quod quicumque habitus partis sensitivae inclinans ad opera bona ex genere, sicut habitus partis sensitivae inclinans ad temperate comedendum, compatitur secum quodcumque vitium in voluntate, etiam contrarium virtuti voluntatis respectu illius obiecti. Quod autem compatiatur vitium disparatum   475 quod respicit aliud obiectum omnino, patet, quia nulla est repugnantia.

Quod autem compatitur vitium oppositum virtutis quod respicit obiectum istius habitus, probatur, quia[69] talis actus in parte sensitiva potest indifferenter fieri bona intentione et mala: propter   480 bonum finem conformiter rectae rationi, vel deformiter. Et si primo fiat bona intentione, tunc stat cum virtute in voluntate inclinante ad illum actum; si post fiat mala intentione, tunc corrumpitur virtus et generatur vitium, et semper stat idem habitus in parte sensitiva. Et ideo ille habitus et actus in appetitu sensi-   485 tivo, qui est virtuosus et vitiosus denominatione extrinseca et non intrinsece, potest primo denominari virtuosus et post vitiosus, stante semper eodem actu uniformiter non variato in appetitu sensitivo, propter solam variationem actus voluntatis.

[Conclusiones de connexione virtutum moralium cum prudentia]   490

[Conclusio prima]

Quantum ad quartum articulum huius tertii articuli sit haec prima conclusio,[70] quod nulla virtus moralis nec actus virtuosus potest esse sine omni prudentia, quia nullus actus est virtuosus nisi sit conformis rectae rationi, quia recta ratio ponitur in defini-   495 tione virtutis, II *Ethicorum*;[71] igitur quilibet actus et habitus virtuosus necessario requirit aliquam prudentiam.

E t s i q u a e r a s utrum post generationem virtutis possit elici actus virtuosus sine actu prudentiae: r e s p o n d e o quod non, quia nullus virtuose agit nisi scienter agat et ex liber-   500 tate. Et ideo si aliquando talis actus voluntatis elicitur a tali habitu sine actu prudentiae, non dicetur virtuosus nec est, sed[72] magis elicitur sicut actus appetitus sensitivi habituati, sicut in fatuis patet

---

69. Cf. OTh VI, 359–62.

70. Cf. OTh VI, 421–22; OTh VIII, 409–10, 412–13, 414; Scotus, *Sent.* III d.36 n.20, XV: 654–55.

71. Cf. Aristotle, *Eth. Nic.* 2.6.1106b36–1107a2. **72.**   Cf. OTh VI, 356–57, 360–62.

72. Cf. OTh VI, 356–57, 360–62.

[Second Conclusion]

471. The second conclusion is that any habit of the sensitive faculty whatever that inclines us to generically good works—such as a habit in the sensitive faculty inclining toward temperate eating—is compatible with any vice in the will whatever; it is even compatible with the [vice] contrary to that virtue in the will with respect to that [same] object. That it is compatible with a disparate vice in respect to an entirely different object is evident because there is no repugnance.

478. That it is compatible with the vice contrary to that virtue in respect to the object of that habit is proved as follows:[69] Such an act in the sensitive faculty can equally be produced by a good and by a wicked intention, on account of a good end and in conformity with right reason or contrary to right reason. If it is first produced by a good intention, then it is compatible with the virtue in the will inclining us to that act; if it is afterward produced by a wicked intention, then it corrupts the virtue and generates vice; the habit in the sensitive faculty always remains the same. Therefore that habit and the act in the sensitive appetite that is virtuous and vicious by extrinsic, not intrinsic, denomination can be first virtuous and afterwards vicious on account of a variation only in the act of will, while the sensitive act always remains uniformly the same, with no variation in the sensitive appetite.

[Conclusions Concerning the Connection of Moral Virtues with Prudence]

[First Conclusion]

492. Let this be the first conclusion[70] of the fourth article of the third [principal] article: There can be no moral virtue and no virtuous act without any prudence. For no act is virtuous unless it is in conformity with right reason, since right reason is posited in the definition of virtue (see the *Ethics*, book 2).[71] Therefore any virtuous act or habit necessarily requires some prudence.

498. Someone might ask whether after the generation of virtue, a virtuous act could be elicited without an act of prudence. My answer is no, since no one acts virtuously unless he acts knowingly and freely. And therefore, if on some occasion such an act of will is elicited on the basis of such a habit without an act of prudence, it will neither be, nor be called, virtuous. Rather it is elicited in the manner of an act of habituated, sensitive appetite.[72] This is evident in the case of the insane, who will some-

quod aliquid volunt, quod prius virtuose voluerunt, propter habitum derelictum in voluntate, qui inclinabat ad actus virtuosos   505
quando fuit in bono statu, sed nunc non est actus virtuosus, quia
nec est laudabilis nec vituperabilis propter actus suos. Et tota ratio
est, quia nescit quid facit, eo quod non habet prudentiam sive
rectam rationem.

S i q u a e r a s de actu prudentiae, in quo genere causae   510
se habet ad actum virtuosum, ex quo necessario requiritur per te,
et effectus sufficienter dependet ex causis suis essentialibus etc.:[73]
r e s p o n d e o quod est causa efficiens necessario requisita
ad actum virtuosum, sine qua impossibile est actum esse virtuosum, stante ordinatione divina quae nunc est, quia ad actum vir-   515
tuosum necessario requiritur activitas actus prudentiae et activitas
voluntatis, ita quod illae duae causae sunt causae partiales cum
Deo respectu actus virtuosi.

[Conclusio secunda]

[Probatio prima]   520
Secunda conclusio est quod prudentia primo modo[74] potest
esse sine omni actu virtuoso et habitu. Hoc probatur primo sic:
ille[75] actus qui necessario conformatur alteri et qui de necessitate
ponitur altero posito, non est primo virtuosus formaliter. Hoc
patet, quia ille actus qui necessario conformatur alteri, non est   525
primo laudabilis, nec propter illum laudamur nec vituperamur.
Patet etiam per exemplum de actu appetitus sensitivi, qui necessario ponitur posita apprehensione sensitiva; ideo non est primo
laudabilis. Sed si actus virtuosus necessario poneretur posita recta
ratione, necessario conformaretur sibi, et sic ille actus non esset   530

---

73. Cf. Scotus, *Ord.* I d.3 p.3 q.2 n.414, III: 251; Ockham, OTh V,
269; OTh VIII, 417–18.
74. See a.2 3–13. Concerning this conclusion, cf. lines 224–70; OTh
VI, 421; Scotus, *Sent.* III d.36 n.14, 20, XV: 640–41, 654–55; II d.43 q.2
n.2, XIII: 493–94; Ioannes de Bassolis, *Sent.* II d.25 q.2 (Paris, 1517), fols.
133–35. On the controversy concerning the freedom of the will in respect
to a dictate of the intellect, see A. San Cristobal-Sebastian, *Controversias
acerca de la voluntad desde 1270 a 1300* (Madrid, 1958); Lottin, *PM* I:
225–89, especially pp. 382–89; III: 621–50; R. Hissette, *Enquête sur les
219 articles condamnés à Paris le 7 mars 1277* (Louvain, 1977), 230–63.
75. Cf. Scotus, *Sent.* II d.25 n.2, XIII: 197–98; III d.36 n.12, XV: 630–
31; *Collatio* III n.1, V: 149–50; Richardus de Mediavilla, *Sent.* II d.38 a.2
q.2, 4 (Brescia, 1591), 467–68, 471; Godefridus de Fontibus, *Quodlibet* XV
q.4, ed. J. Hoffmans & A. Pelzer, PhB XIV: 20–21.

thing that they previously willed virtuously on account of a residual habit in the will that inclined them to virtuous acts when their condition was good. In their present state, however, this is not a virtuous act because they are neither praiseworthy nor blameworthy on account of their acts. The entire reason for this is that they do not know what they are doing, since they do not have prudence or right reason.

510. Someone might ask about an act of prudence: How is it related to a virtuous act? What genus of cause does it belong to? Since in your view prudence is necessarily required, and it is also true that an effect sufficiently depends on its essential causes, etc.,[73] my answer is that it is an efficient cause, necessarily requisite to an act of virtue, without which it is impossible that an act should be virtuous, according to the present divine ordination. For a virtuous act necessarily requires the activity of an act of prudence and an act of will, so that these two causes are partial causes, together with God, with respect to a virtuous act.

[Second Conclusion]

[First Proof]
521. The second conclusion is that the first mode[74] of prudence can exist without any virtuous act and without any virtuous habit. The first proof of this is as follows: When the second of two acts[75] necessarily conforms to the first act, and the second act is necessarily posited when the first is posited, the second act is not primarily, formally virtuous. This is evident because the second act, which necessarily conforms to the first, is not primarily praiseworthy, nor are we praised or blamed on account of such an act. It is also evident from the example of an act of the sensitive appetite, which is necessarily posited when sensitive apprehension is posited and therefore is not primarily praiseworthy. But if a virtuous act were necessarily posited when right reason had been posited, it would necessarily conform to right reason, and thus that act would not be primarily virtuous; rather an intellec-

primo virtuosus sed actus intellectus, cuius oppositum est prius
probatum.[76]

[Probatio secunda]
Secundo sic: actus qui de necessitate elicitur altero elicito, non
est primo in potestate voluntatis, quia quando ad primum necessa-   535
rio sequitur secundum, tunc secundum non est in potestate voluntatis nisi quia primum est in potestate voluntatis. Sed si volitio
necessario conformatur rationi, posita ratione necessario poneretur
volitio. Igitur actus voluntatis non est in potestate voluntatis nisi
quia actus intellectus est in potestate voluntatis. Consequens est   540
falsum, quia[77] actus intellectus non est primo virtuosus nec est in
potestate voluntatis, quia actus primo et essentialiter et intrinsece
virtuosus non potest idem manens esse vitiosus; sed actus intellectus idem manens potest; igitur etc. Assumptum patet, quia
aliquis primo intelligens aliquid cum bona intentione, potest eun-   545
dem actum continuare cum mala intentione; iste actus intelligendi
idem numero manens est primo virtuosus et post vitiosus; igitur
non est primo virtuosus nec primo in potestate voluntatis.

S i   d i c a t u r   quod propositio particularis non potest
sciri cum mala intentione propter certitudinem et rectitudinem: 550
c o n t r a, tanta est rectitudo in propositione universali sicut in
particulari, et certitudo; igitur si una potest sciri mala intentione,
et alia.

[Probatio tertia]
Tertio sic: secundum omnes theologos aliquod est peccatum   555
ex malitia, aliquod ex ignorantia. Tunc quaero, aut[78] peccans ex
malitia habet notitiam tam universalem quam particularem, aut
tantum universalem. Si primo modo, habetur propositum, quod
habens tam universalem quam particularem notitiam potest ex
malitia facere contra utramque. Si secundo modo, ita peccans ex   560
ignorantia habet notitiam universalem sicut[79] peccans ex malitia,
quia peccans ex ignorantia scit tales maiores: omne iustum est

---

76. See a.1 132–56.

77. See a.1 99–130.

78. Cf. Aegidius Romanus, *Quodlibet* I q.19 (Louvain, 1646), 39b.

79. As the variant apparatus indicates the end of this sentence
(from "as much . . .") is found only in the printed edition. At this point,
the elliptic Latin text should be expanded.

tual act would be primarily virtuous. The opposite conclusion has already been proved [a.1 132].[76]

[Second Proof]

534. The second proof is as follows: When one of two acts necessarily follows from another, it is not primarily in the power of the will. For when a second act necessarily follows the first, the second is in the power of the will only because the first act is in the power of the will. But if an act of will necessarily conforms to reason, then if reason were posited, an act of will would necessarily be posited. Therefore an act of will would be in the power of the will only because an intellectual act is in the power of the will. The conclusion is false. For an intellectual act is not primarily virtuous,[77] nor is it in the power of the will, because no act primarily, essentially, and intrinsically virtuous can be made vicious while remaining unchanged; but an intellectual act can, while remaining the same, be made vicious; therefore, etc. The assumption is evident, since someone who first understands something when his intention is good can continue the same act of understanding when his intention is wicked; that act of understanding can be first virtuous and afterward vicious while remaining numerically the same; therefore it is not primarily virtuous, nor is it primarily in the power of the will.

549. Someone might say that a particular proposition cannot be scientifically known by someone whose intention is wicked, on account of the rectitude and certitude of scientific knowledge. My answer is that there is as much rectitude in a universal proposition as in a particular proposition—and as much certitude. Therefore, if one can be scientifically known with a wicked intention, so can the other.

[Third Proof]

555. The third proof is as follows: All theologians agree that some sin is based on malice; other sin, on ignorance. I ask, then, is a malicious sinner in possession of both universal and particular knowledge or only universal knowledge?[78] If both, I have what I set out to prove—namely, that someone in possession of both universal and particular knowledge can act maliciously contrary to both universal and particular knowledge. If a malicious sinner has only universal knowledge, then an ignorant sinner has as much[79] universal knowledge as a malicious sinner. For an ignorant sinner scientifically knows major premises—such as 'every-

faciendum, omne honestum, omne quod placet Deo etc.; sed ig-
norat minores, puta quod hoc est iustum, hoc est honestum, hoc
est placitum Deo. Si igitur peccans ex malitia non plus sciret,   565
tunc aequalem scientiam haberet peccans ex malitia et ex ignoran-
tia, et ita aequaliter dicetur unus peccans ex malitia sicut alius,
et[80] eodem modo ex ignorantia.

S i   d i c a s: in[81] scientia universalium sunt gradus: c o n-
t r a, aut intelligis quod sunt gradus respectu eiusdem proposi-   570
tionis, quia scientia in peccante ex malitia est intensior quam in
peccante ex ignorantia, et hoc nihil ad propositum, quia sive intensior sive non, semper ignorans potest habere notitiam universalem; aut respectu diversarum propositionum universalium, et
tunc adhuc stat argumentum praedictum, quia omnem notitiam   575
quarumcumque propositionum universalium quam habet peccans
ex malitia, potest habere peccans ex ignorantia; igitur solum differunt penes cognitionem particularium.

[Probatio quarta]
Quarto sic: secundum communiter opinantes contrarium,[82]   580
natura angelica non potest transmutari. Tunc sic: angelus malus
inducit homines ad peccatum et vult efficaciter eos peccare. Et
tamen ipse habet notitiam universalem istius 'nullus est inducen-
dus ad faciendum contra praeceptum Dei sui,' quia haec videtur
per se nota; et habet notitiam particularem istius, quod istud pec-   585
catum ad quod homo inducitur per angelum malum est contra
praeceptum Dei sui, quia non videtur rationabile negare ab eo notitiam propositionum quarum notitiam communiter habent homines. Et tamen facit contrarium. Igitur etc.

S i   d i c a s quod habet bene notitiam speculativam proposi-   590
tionum, sed non practicam: c o n t r a, illam aliquando habuit,
et non potest transmutari per te, igitur etc. Praeterea si corrumpitur, quaero a quo. Non a passione, quia talis non est in ange-
lo, igitur a malitia. Sed illa praesupponit notitiam practicam tam
maioris quam minoris, sicut prius patet.[83] Igitur etc.   595

---

80. Namely, "et eodem modo dicetur unus peccans ex ignorantia
sicut alius."

81. Cf. Scotus, *In Metaph.* VI q.1 n.3, VII: 304; ed. St. Bonaventure
n.18–19).

82. For example, Aegidius Romanus, *Quodlibet* I q.19 (Louvain,
1646), 39–41; Godefridus de Fontibus, *Quodlibet* VIII q.16, ed. J. Hoffmans, PhB IV: 165–66; Durandus a S. Porciano, *In Sent. Commenta-
riorum* III d.36 q.2 (Venice, 1571; reprint, Ridgewood, N.J.: Gregg Press,
1964), fol. 279ra, n.10.

83. See lines 555–78.

thing just should be done,' 'everything worthy should be done,' 'everything that pleases God should be done'—but he is ignorant of minor premises—such as 'this is just,' 'this is worthy,' and 'this is pleasing to God.' If, therefore, a malicious sinner knew no more, then the scientific knowledge of someone sinning from malice would be equal to that of someone sinning from ignorance, and thus both people will equally be said to sin from malice; and[80] the same could be said of ignorance.

569. Someone[81] might say that there are degrees of universal scientific knowledge. In reply I would ask: Do you mean that there can be such degrees in regard to the same proposition, so that the scientific knowledge of the malicious sinner is more intense than that of the ignorant sinner? If so, that is irrelevant, since whether it is more intense or not, the ignorant sinner can always have universal knowledge. If, on the other hand, you mean degrees in regard to different universal propositions, then the same argument holds. For the ignorant sinner can have all the knowledge of any universal propositions whatever possessed by the malicious sinner; therefore they differ only in respect to particular cognition.

[Fourth Proof]

580. The fourth proof is as follows: According to the common opinion of those who hold the contrary opinion,[82] angelic nature cannot be changed. If that is the case, then a wicked angel induces men to sin and efficaciously wills them to sin. Nonetheless, the angel himself possesses the universal knowledge of the proposition, 'no one should be induced to do anything contrary to the precept of his God'; this appears to be a self-evident proposition. He also knows the particular proposition, 'the sin that a wicked angel induces a man to commit is contrary to the precept of his God,' since it does not appear rational to deny the wicked angel the knowledge of propositions that are commonly known by men. Yet he does the contrary. Therefore, etc.

590. Someone might say that the wicked angel does indeed possess speculative knowledge of the propositions, but not practical knowledge. My answer is that at some time he did have practical knowledge, and in your view he cannot change, therefore, etc. Moreover, if the practical knowledge is destroyed, what destroys it? Not passion—there is no such thing in an angel. So it must be malice. But malice presupposes practical knowledge of both the major and the minor premises, as was evident before.[83] Therefore, etc.

[Probatio quinta]

Quinto, secundum P h i l o s o p h u m, I *Posteriorum,*[84]
impossibile est simul scire maiorem et minorem et tamen ignorare
conclusionem, quia secundum eum necessario simul inducens cognovit. Sed aliquis incontinens scit quod nullum inhonestum est   600
faciendum, et scit evidenter per experientiam quod hoc est inhonestum; igitur scit quod hoc non est faciendum, quia scit principia
istius conclusionis; et tamen facit contrarium. Igitur etc.

S i d i c a s quod[85] incontinens habet duas maiores, scilicet
quod nullum inhonestum est faciendum, et omne delectabile est   605
faciendum; et sub secunda maiori solum accipit minorem, puta
quod hoc est delectabile; et ideo ex istis tantum concludit quod
hoc est faciendum: c o n t r a, impossibile est quod simul
assentiat illis maioribus, quia isti assensus opponuntur. Similiter,
dato quod sic, adhuc potest evidenter scire primam maiorem, mi-   610
norem et conclusionem, et tamen potest facere oppositum; igitur
potest facere oppositum illius quod est dictatum a recta ratione.

[Probatio sexta]

Sexto, ostendo[86] quod posito quod voluntas necessario conformetur rationi in eliciendo actum, quod voluntas non erit liberior   615
appetitu sensitivo, quia quando sunt aliqua duo indifferentia ad
contraria quae possunt causari a diversis, si utrumque illorum
aequaliter et aeque necessario respicit ad causalitatem illorum, utrumque illorum est aeque liberum. Sed posita hypothesi, voluntas
aeque indifferenter se habet ad velle et nolle et aeque necessario   620
respicit [ad] causalitatem illorum sicut appetitus sensitivus ad ap-
petere et fugere, quia iudicante sensu et apprehendente quod hoc
est nocivum vel delectabile, appetitus sensitivus statim fugit vel
appetit nec potest resistere; ita iudicante intellectu quod hoc est
volendum vel nolendum, voluntas statim necessario vult vel non   625
vult. Igitur est aequalis libertas utrobique.

84. Cf. Aristotle, *Anal. Poster.* 1.1.71a 19–21; Aegidius Romanus,
Quodlibet I, q.19 (Louvain, 1646), 39b.

85. Cf. Aquinas, *ST* I-II q.77 a.2 ad 4; *Quaest. disp. De malo* q.3 a.9
ad 7.

86. Cf. Henry, *Quodl.* IX q.5, pp. 127–28.

[Fifth Proof]

596. The fifth proof is taken from the Philosopher, book 1 of the *Posterior Analytics*.[84] It is impossible at one and the same time to know the major and the minor premises and yet be ignorant of the conclusion. According to the Philosopher, [someone who knows these premises] taken together necessarily [already] has known [virtually]. But an incontinent person knows that nothing unworthy should be done, and she knows evidently on the basis of experience that this [particular thing] is unworthy; therefore she knows that this thing should not be done, because she knows the principles that lead to this conclusion; and yet she does the contrary. Therefore, etc.

604. Someone[85] might object that an incontinent person has knowledge of two major premises—namely, 'nothing unworthy should be done' and 'everything enjoyable should be done'—but accepts only the minor premise subordinate to the second major—for example, 'this is enjoyable.' On the basis of these premises, he therefore concludes only that 'this should be done.' I answer that it is impossible to assent simultaneously to these two major premises because two such assents militate against each other. Similarly, granted that such simultaneous assent is possible, the incontinent person posited can still evidently and scientifically know the first major premise, the minor, and the conclusion and yet do the opposite; therefore he can do the opposite of what is dictated by right reason.

[Sixth Proof]

614. In the sixth proof,[86] I show that if we posit that the will necessarily conforms to reason in eliciting an act, the will will not be any more free than the sensitive appetite. For when two things are indifferent to contraries that can be produced by different causes, if each of them relates equally and equally necessarily to their causality, each of them is equally free. But on the hypothesis, the will is equally indifferent to acts of willing and to acts of rejection, and it is as necessarily related to their causality as the sensitive appetite is related to acts of grasping and acts of avoidance. For once the sense apprehends that something is enjoyable or judges something noxious, the sensitive appetite immediately acts to attain or avoid it, and the sensitive appetite cannot resist. Thus if the intellect judged that something should be willed or rejected, the will would will or not will necessarily. Therefore, there is equal liberty [in the will and in the sensitive appetite on the hypothesis].

S i   d i c a s[87] quod voluntas potest impedire iudicium rationis per imperium, quia potest imperare intellectui quod consideret
illud obiectum vel aliud, et ita est libera respectu illius imperii,
quia in potestate sua: 630

C o n t r a, aut intellectus dictat illud imperium esse eliciendum, aut non. Si sic, igitur voluntas necessario conformatur illi
iudicio imperando, igitur hoc non est in potestate sua. Si non,
igitur voluntas potest aliquid velle quod non est dictatum a ratione, cuius contrarium dicunt.[88]   635

Praeterea non plus dependet voluntas in volendo ab intellectu
quam appetitus sensitivus a sua cognitiva; sed appetitus sensitivus
potest in actum suum facta sola ostensione obiecti sine omni iudicio vel dictamine; igitur multo magis voluntas.

Praeterea aut actus intellectus necessario elicitur, aut non. Si   640
sic, tunc sic: in essentialiter ordinatis quae sic se habent quod
posito primo, necessario ponitur secundum, secundum non est in
potestate voluntatis nisi primum sit in potestate voluntatis; sed
dictante intellectu quod tale imperium sit eliciendum, necessario
elicitur per te; igitur istud imperium non est in potestate volun-   645
tatis primo. Si non necessario elicitur actus intellectus sed libere,
sequitur idem, quod[89] ille actus intellectus sit primo in potestate
voluntatis.

Praeterea[90] illud imperium, per quod voluntas potest impedire
iudicium rationis, est actus voluntatis elicitus, igitur est conformis   650
rectae rationi; et non isti iudicio rationis cuius imperium est destructivum, certum est, quia si sic, non esset eius destructivum;
igitur est conformis alteri iudicio rationis. Et de illo iudicio quaero
sicut de primo: ex quo potest impediri per imperium, hoc non
erit per imperium conforme sibi, quia illud conformiter elicitur   655
rectae rationi, igitur per aliquod aliud imperium. Et illud est actus
voluntatis et per consequens necessario conformatur alicui iudicio
rationis; non autem illi cuius est destructivum, sicut patet; igitur

---

87. Cf. Scotus, *Sent.* II d.25 n.7, XIII: 201; III d.36 n.12 ad finem,
XV: 631; Richardus de Mediavilla, *Sent.* II d.38 a.2 q.4 (Brescia, 1591),
471–72.
88. Cf. note 82.
89. Cf. lines 539–42 above.
90. Cf. Scotus, *Sent.* III d.36 n.13 ratio 3&4, XV: 631.

627. Someone[87] might hold that the will can impede the judgment of reason by means of an imperative act of will, because it can direct the intellect to consider this or that object, and thus the will is free in respect to that directive, because this is within its power.

631. I ask in reply: Does the intellect dictate that that directive should be elicited, or not? If it does, then the will necessarily conforms to that judgment by issuing that directive; therefore that is not within its power. If it does not, then the will can will something that is not dictated by reason, contrary to the proponents of this view.[88]

636. Moreover, there is another reply: In producing an act of will, the will no more depends on the intellect than the sensitive appetite depends on the cognitive faculty; but the sensitive appetite need only be shown an object in order to produce an act; it can act without any judgment or dictate [of reason]; therefore, so much more the will.

640. A further reply: Either the act of intellect is necessarily elicited, or it is not. If it is, then we argue as follows: When [causes] are essentially ordered—so that if a first object is posited, the second is [also] necessarily posited—the second is not in the power of the will unless the first is in the power of the will; but when the intellect dictates that such a directive should be elicited, it is necessarily elicited according to the objection; therefore that directive is not primarily in the power of the will. If the act of intellect is not elicited necessarily but freely, the same thing follows: That act of intellect would be primarily in the power of the will.[89]

649. A further reply:[90] The directive by means of which the will can impede the judgment of reason is an elicited act of will, therefore it conforms to right reason; and it is certain that it does not conform to that judgment of reason that the directive destroys, since otherwise the directive would not destroy it; therefore it conforms to another judgment of reason. Concerning that second judgment, I object as [I objected against] the first, since you hold that that act can be impeded by a directive: It will not be impeded by a directive in conformity with that act itself, since that act is elicited in conformity with right reason, therefore [if it can be impeded, it will be] by some other directive. That other directive will be an act of will, and consequently it will necessarily conform to some judgment of reason, but not in conformity to that judgment that it destroys, as is evident; therefore it will be

alteri priori. Et de illo tertio, ex quo potest impediri, potest quaeri
sicut de primo et secundo; et sic erit processus in infinitum in 660
iudiciis et imperiis, vel stabitur ad aliquod imperium quod non
elicitur conformiter rectae rationi, sed solum libere ex nuda ostensione. Et qua ratione statur in secundo vel in tertio imperio, eadem
ratione in primo. Igitur etc.

Praeterea appetitus sensitivus potest impedire iudicium, sicut 665
aliquae passiones possunt esse ita vehementes in appetitu sensitivo
quod totaliter impedient iudicium rationis; et tamen propter hoc
non est liber; igitur nec eodem modo in proposito.

Confirmatur, quia[91] ratio aliquando errat. Tunc quaero, aut
hoc est in potestate voluntatis, aut non; si non, non peccat ex 670
ignorantia, quia nullus obligatur ad impossibile; si sit in potestate
voluntatis, aut immediate aut mediante actu voluntatis.

S i d i c a s[92] quod ipsa intentio est primo in potestate
intellectus: c o n t r a, intellectus[93] nulli adhaeret nisi propter evidentiam rei vel propter auctoritatem vel propter imperium 675
voluntatis; sed sive sic sive sic adhaereat, semper necessario adhaeret posito alio, puta evidentia rei vel imperio voluntatis, nec potest
istis stantibus non adhaerere; igitur non est in potestate intellectus.

Praeterea, tunc primum peccatum esset in intellectu, non in 680
voluntate, quia consistit in illo actu qui primo est in potestate
nostra; et per consequens tunc posset peccatum non esse voluntarium, quod est contra A u g u s t i n u m et alios S a n c-
t o s.[94]

Confirmatur: non videtur impossibile Deum posse suspendere 685
actionem causae secundae et facere actum priorem sine actu posteriori; igitur posset facere illum actum intellectus esse sine actu
voluntatis, et sic peccatum esset in intellectu, nullo exsistente in
voluntate.

---

91. Cf. Godefridus de Fontibus, *Quodlibet* V q.12, ed. M. de Wulf &
J. Hoffmans, PhB III: 51.

92. Cf. Godefridus de Fontibus, *Quodlibet* VIII q.16, ed. J. Hoffmans,
PhB IV: 160–61; *Quodlibet* VI q.10, ed. M. de Wulf & J. Hoffmans, PhB
III: 207.

93. Cf. Scotus, *Collatio III* n.1, V: 149–50.

94. Cf. Augustine, *De vera religione* c.14 n.27 (PL 34, 133); Aquinas,
ST I-II q.74 a.1 Resp.

in conformity with a third judgment. Concerning that third judgment, since it can be impeded, we can make the same objection as was made in the case of the first and second judgments. So there will either be an infinite regress of judgments and directives, or there will be a halt at some directive that is not elicited in conformity with right reason, but freely, presupposing only the bare manifestation [of an object]. Moreover, there is the same reason to make a halt at the first act, as at the second or third. Therefore, etc.

665. A further reply: The sensitive appetite can impede judgment, as is the case with some passions in the sensitive appetite that can be so vehement that they totally impede the judgment of reason; and yet the sensitive appetite is not for that reason free; therefore similarly neither in the case under consideration.

669. A confirmation:[91] Reason sometimes errs. Then I ask, Is this error in the power of the will, or not? If not, then we do not sin from ignorance, since no one is obligated to the impossible. If such error is in the power of the will, then this is either immediately or mediately by an act of will.

673. Someone[92] might object that the [erring] intention itself is primarily in the power of the intellect. My answer is that the intellect does not adhere to a view except for one of three reasons:[93] either on account of authority, or because of the evidence a thing presents, or on account of an imperative act of will. But for whatever reason the intellect adheres to a view, it always adheres necessarily, once one of these grounds for adherence is posited—as, for example, the evidence a thing presents or an imperative act of will; and the intellect cannot fail to adhere when such grounds are present. Therefore, the [erring intention] is not in the power of the intellect.

680. A further reply to this objection: It would follow from the objection that the first sin was in the intellect, not in the will, since sin consists in an act that is primarily in our power; and consequently sin could be involuntary, contrary to Augustine and other saints.[94]

685. A confirmation follows: It does not appear impossible that God could suspend the action of a second cause and produce a prior act without a posterior act. Therefore he could produce that act of intellect without an act of will, and thus there would be sin in the intellect without sin in the will.

[Conclusio tertia]   690

Tertia conclusio est quod prudentia secundo modo dicta,[95] pro
notitia immediate directiva alicuius particularis evidenter illatae ex
universali, potest esse sine virtute morali. Haec probatur per eas-
dem rationes per quas prior[96] probatur, quia dictante intellectu
de aliquo in particulari, potest voluntas in contrarium etc.   695

S i   d i c a t u r[97] quantum ad priorem conclusionem et
istam similiter, quod voluntas non est libera quia potest facere
contra iudicium rationis, sed quia potest libere imperare exsecutionem operationum exteriorum; et respectu illius imperii dicitur
libera, non autem respectu alicuius actus eliciti conformiter vel   700
deformiter cum ratione:

C o n t r a, quando aliqua sic se habent quod posito primo,
necessario ponitur secundum, impossibile est primum poni nisi
ponatur secundum, et per consequens secundum non est in potestate voluntatis nisi quia primum est. Sed recta ratione dictante   705
quod aliquid sit omnino operandum, et voluntate volente efficaciter illud operari, necessario operatur et exsequitur secundum
potentias exteriores, si non impediatur; igitur necessario sequitur
imperium exsecutionis.

Maior patet ex praedictis.[98] Minor probatur per G r e g o-   710
r i u m:[99] "probatio dilectionis exhibitio est operis." Similiter,
P h i l o s o p h u s, IX *Metaphysicae,*[100] potentia rationalis
valet ad opposita, et dicit ibi quod cum sit oppositorum, oportet
aliquid esse determinativum, scilicet appetitum et prohaeresim.
Unde dicit sic: "Quod[101] enim desiderabit principaliter, hoc faciet,   715
quando ut possit exstiterit et appropinquaverit passivo. Quare
potens secundum rationem necesse, quando desiderat cuius habet
potentiam, et ut habet, hoc facere; habet autem praesente passivo...". Sequitur igitur conclusio.

S i   q u a e r a s utrum imperare exsecutionem actus exte-   720
rioris sit alius actus ab illo quo vult efficaciter dictatum a recta

---

95. A.2 14–19.
96. Namely, conclusion 2, lines 522–24.
97. Cf. Godefridus de Fontibus, *Quodlibet* XV q.4, ed. J. Hoffmans &
A. Pelzer, PhB XIV: 30.
98. Lines 534–37, 641–43 above.
99. Cf. Gregorius, XL *Homiliarum in Evang.* II h.30 (PL 76, 1220 C).
100. Cf. Aristotle, *Metaph.* 9.5.1048a 8–15 t.c. 10; Scotus, *Sent.*II
d.25 n.2, VI: 874; Ockham, OTh VII, 358–59.
101. Ockham here uses the same version that is found, for example,
printed with Aquinas's works. See *In lib. Metaphysicorum Aristot.
expositio* IX lect. 4, c.5 n.765 (ed. Marietti, 1950), 434.

[Third Conclusion]

691. The third conclusion is that prudence in the second mode[95] can exist without moral virtue—that is, prudence as knowledge that is immediately directive of some particular act evidently inferred from a universal proposition. This is proved with the same arguments that proved the prior conclusion,[96] since the will can elicit a contrary act when the intellect dictates something particular.

696. As far as this conclusion and the prior conclusion are concerned, someone[97] might similarly object that the will is free not because it can act contrary to the judgment of reason, but because it can freely direct the execution of exterior operations. It is called free in respect to that directive, not in respect to some act elicited in conformity with or contrary to reason.

702. On the contrary, when things are so related that when the first is posited, the second is necessarily posited, it is impossible to posit the first without positing the second, and consequently the second is only in the power of the will because the first is. But when right reason dictates that some operation should be done without fail, and the will efficaciously wills that operation, the operation is necessary, and so is its execution in the exterior faculties, if there is no impediment. Therefore the direction to execute [the exterior operation] follows necessarily.

710. The major premise is evident from what has been said above.[98] The proof of the minor premise comes from Gregory:[99] "The proof of love is a display of work." Similarly, according to the Philosopher, in book 9 of the *Metaphysics*,[100] "the rational faculty is capable of contrary effects." As the Philosopher says there, since the rational faculty is capable of opposite operations, something must make the determination—namely, desire or choice. Consequently, the Philosopher[101] says: "What [an animal] principally desires, it will do, when the possibility is present and the passive object is within range. Hence when the possessor of a rational faculty desires something for which he has the potential and in circumstances in keeping with the potential, he does that thing necessarily; but he has the potential when the passive object is present . . ." The conclusion follows.

720. Someone might ask whether the act directing the execution of an exterior act is different from the act by which some-

ratione: r e s p o n d e o, si actus ille quo vult dictatum a
ratione sit actus imperativus formaliter, qualis est actus virtutis
heroicae,[102] tunc est idem actus omnino quo vult dictatum et
quo imperat exsecutionem, quia ipso posito, statim exsequitur   725
amoto impedimento, sicut prius patet,[103] et hoc sine omni alio
actu voluntatis. Si autem sit imperativus aequivalenter,[104] puta aliquis vult dictatum a ratione si esset opportunitas et nisi esset impedimentum, si post imperet exsecutionem actus exterioris habita
opportunitate, ibi imperare est alius actus a primo, quia primus   730
est imperativus solum aequivalenter, secundus formaliter; primus
habet impedimentum pro obiecto, secundus non; secundus habet
tempus praesens pro obiecto, primus non; et per consequens sunt
diversi actus.

[Conclusio quarta]   735

Quarta conclusio est quod aliqua prudentia tertio modo dicta[105] potest esse sine virtute morali, et aliqua non. Hoc patet,
quia aliqua talis propositio potest cognosci per experientiam acceptam respectu actus alterius hominis, aliqua non potest evidenter
cognosci nisi per experientiam acceptam respectu proprii actus.   740

Exemplum primi: 'iste iracundus est mitigandus per pulchra
verba, quia aliquando vidi eum sic mitigatum per alium vel per
me.' Notitia evidens istius potest esse sine omni virtute morali,
quia aliquis potest evidenter illam propositionem cognoscere, et
tamen nolle eum simpliciter mitigare, sicut patet per experien-   745
tiam. Et probatur haec pars per rationes prius factas pro secunda
conclusione.[106]

Exemplum secundi: 'aliquis enim eliciendo frequenter actum
continentiae et temperantiae magis disponitur ad Dei cognitionem
et dilectionem et ad studendum'; similiter hic: 'aliquis diligendo   750
Deum maiorem habet delectationem quam in aliqua re temporali';
et similiter: 'diligens perfecte Deum et actum temperantiae propter Deum, facile contemnit actus intemperantiae,' et huiusmodi,
sunt propositiones quae non possunt evidenter esse verae nec evidenter ab aliquo sciri sine actu proprio elicito generativo virtutis. 755
Nullus enim potest evidenter scire istas, quod actus temperantiae
est frequenter eliciendus quia disponit hominem ad Dei dilectionem,

---

102. A.2 76–109, 152–57.
103. Lines 705–8.
104. A.2 76–109.
105. A.2 20–26.
106. Lines 522–24.

one effectively wills a dictate of right reason. My answer is that if the act by means of which we will a dictate of reason is a formally imperative act—as in the case of an act of heroic virtue[102]—then the act by means of which we will the dictate is entirely the same as the act by means of which we direct its execution, since once the will is posited, it is immediately executed, in the absence of an impediment, as was evident above;[103] no other act of will would be required. But if the act is equivalently imperative[104]— as in the case where someone wills a dictate of reason if it is opportune and there is no impediment—then, if the execution of the exterior act is subsequently directed when it is opportune, that directive is a different act from the first. The first act is only equivalently imperative; the second, formally. The first act has the impediment as its object; the second does not. The second act has the present time as an object, the first does not. Consequently, these are different acts.

[Fourth Conclusion]

736. The fourth conclusion is that prudence in the third mode[105] can sometimes be without moral virtue, and sometimes not. This is evident because some such propositions can be known by means of experience acquired in reference to the acts of another person, other propositions can be known evidently only by means of experience acquired in reference to one's own acts.

741. An example of the first kind of proposition is: 'This irascible person should be mollified with fine words,' because I have seen him mollified in this way at some time either by myself or by someone else. Evident knowledge of this proposition can exist without any moral virtue, because someone can evidently know that proposition and yet not will to mollify him at all, as is evident from experience. This part of the conclusion is proved by the arguments advanced above for the second conclusion.[106]

748. An example of the second kind of proposition is: 'By frequently eliciting acts of continence and temperance, one is more disposed to know, to love, and to study God.' Similarly: 'Someone who loves God finds more enjoyment than in temporal things,' 'Someone who perfectly loves God and an act of temperance for the sake of God finds it easy to condemn acts of intemperance.' Such propositions cannot be evidently true, nor can they be evidently known scientifically by anyone without eliciting an act generative of virtue on his own. That 'an act of temperance should be elicited frequently because it disposes men for the love

vel quod Deus sit diligendus propter delectationem quae habetur in
eo plus quam in aliqua alia re, nisi quia per experientiam in seipso
aliquando cognovit quod ipsemet eliciendo frequenter actum tem-　760
perantiae magis sic disponitur; similiter in diligendo Deum habuit
ipsemet maiorem delectationem quam in aliqua alia re temporali,
quia istae propositiones et similes non possunt evidenter sciri per
propositiones per se notas, nec possunt evidenter sciri per experientiam acceptam respectu actus alterius hominis, quia de actibus　765
talibus alterius hominis non possum habere experientiam pro statu
isto.

　　Ad hoc igitur quod habeam notitiam evidentem talium naturaliter, necesse est quod virtus moralis insit habenti talem prudentiam, virtus inquam generata ex illis actibus de quibus accipitur　770
notitia evidens et certa, vel saltem quod prius infuit virtus aliquo
tempore, licet forte modo non inest. Quod dico, quia possibile
est quod maneat habitus in intellectu inclinans evidenter ad assen-
tiendum illis propositionibus prius acceptis per experientiam, et
quod omnis habitus voluntatis corrumpitur; et tunc talis actus　775
prudentiae non requirit necessario actum virtuosum.

　　Ideo intelligendum est illud dictum[107] quantum ad generationem primam actus virtuosi et prudentiae, quia primus actus talis
prudentiae non potest causari sine actu virtuoso, quia respectu
illius actus prudentiae actus virtuosus est causa partialis, et post　780
generationem habituum hinc inde, potest unum esse sine alio.

　　S i   q u a e r a s utrum actus prudentiae qui necessario
requirit vel praesupponit actum virtuosum, sit directivus respectu
illius actus quem praesupponit: r e s p o n d e o quod non,
quia dirigere[108] non est nisi causare actum; sed actus virtuosus　785
causat illum actum prudentiae; igitur non causatur ab eo, aliter
idem esset antequam esset.

[Conclusio quinta]

Quinta conclusio est quod prudentia quarto modo dicta,[109]
qua aliquis dicitur prudens quantum ad totum vivere, secundum　790

---

107. Lines 753–55; cf. OTh I, 320.
108. Cf. Ockham, OTh VIII, 418.
109. A.2 27–33.

of God' or that 'God should be loved on account of our enjoyment of God, which is greater that the enjoyment we find in other things' are conclusions that no one can know evidently and scientifically, unless by means of his own experience at some time. A person would have to experience himself that by frequently eliciting an act of temperance, he is more inclined to love God, or that he personally has found greater enjoyment in loving God than in some other, temporal thing. For these, and [other] similar propositions, cannot be evidently and scientifically known by means of self-evident propositions, nor can they be evidently and scientifically known by virtue of the experience accepted on the basis of other men's acts, since in this life we cannot experience such acts as other people experience them.

768. Therefore moral virtue must inhere in a person who has such prudence if she is to have evident knowledge of such propositions naturally. Here I mean the virtue generated by those acts from which we receive evident and certain knowledge—or at least virtue must have inhered at some previous time, although perhaps it does not now. I say this because it is possible that every habit of will be corrupted while a habit remains in the intellect, inclining someone to assent evidently to those propositions previously accepted on the basis of experience. In that case, such an act of prudence would not necessarily require a virtuous act.

777. What was said above[107] should be understood as having to do with the first generation of a virtuous and a prudent act. The first such act of prudence cannot be caused without a virtuous act, since a virtuous act is a partial cause in respect to that act of prudence. But after the generation of habits in both areas, one can exist without the other.

782. Someone might ask whether an act of prudence that necessarily requires or presupposes a virtuous act is directive in respect to the act that it presupposes. I would reply that it is not directive,[108] because to direct only means to cause an act; but a virtuous act causes that act of prudence; therefore it is not caused by the act of prudence. Otherwise, one and the same thing would be before it existed.

[Fifth Conclusion]

789. The fifth conclusion is that prudence in the fourth mode[109] can exist without some virtues, but not without others. When

quod includit notitias directivas omnium virtutum quae requiruntur ad perfecte vivere hominis, potest esse sine aliquibus virtutibus, et sine aliquibus non potest esse. Hoc patet, quia prudentia sic accepta includit prudentiam tribus primis modis acceptam, et aliqua istarum prudentiarum potest esse sine virtute morali,   795
sicut patet de duobus primis modis, et de tertio modo quantum ad aliquam prudentiam; et alia non, sicut patet de tertio modo quantum ad aliquam prudentiam.[110]

[Conclusio sexta]

Sexta conclusio est quod quaelibet virtus moralis potest esse   800
sine prudentia primo modo et secundo modo dicta, quia ad hoc quod actus virtuosus eliciatur, non requiritur quod notitia immediate directiva causetur per propositiones per se notas, quo modo causatur prudentia secundo modo dicta, quia illa eadem notitia potest causari per propositiones per se notas vel per experientiam,   805
et sufficit quod altero illorum modorum causetur. Exemplum: ad hoc quod virtuose benefaciam isti, non requiritur quod haec propositio 'isti est benefaciendum' sequatur ex ista 'omni amico est benefaciendum' etc., sed sufficit quod huic evidenter assentiam quia vidi vel aliter expertus sum quod ipse mihi benefecit. Sed   810
ad hoc quod actus virtuosus eliciatur, necessario requiritur prudentia secundo modo vel tertio modo dicta.

Et eodem modo, ad virtutem moralem non requiritur prudentia primo modo dicta, quia ut patet, notitia particularis cuiuscumque immediate directiva potest haberi per experientiam, ad quam   815
non requiritur notitia alicuius universalis. Si tamen notitia evidens alicuius particularis non posset haberi per experientiam, tunc virtus illa, cuius notitia particularis esset directiva, requireret necessario prudentiam primo modo et secundo, sed non tertio.

---

110. Conclusions 2–4, lines 521–23.

someone is called prudent in the fourth mode, that refers to every aspect of life, in that prudence in this mode includes directive knowledge of all the virtues requisite to the perfect life of a human being. The fifth conclusion is evident because prudence in this mode includes prudence in the three previous modes, and some of these forms of prudence can exist without moral virtue, as is evident for the two first modes. This is also evident for the third mode of prudence as regards some prudence; but another form of prudence in the third mode cannot exist without moral virtue, as it evident for the third mode of prudence.[110]

[Sixth Conclusion]

800. The sixth conclusion is that any moral virtue can exist without prudence in the first and second mode. For eliciting a virtuous act does not require that the immediately directive knowledge be caused by self-evident propositions, in the manner in which prudence in the second mode is produced. The same knowledge can be caused either by self-evident propositions or by experience, and one of the two means suffices to cause that knowledge. For example, that I should virtuously help or do something good for someone does not require that the proposition "this person should be helped" follow from this proposition "every friend should be helped," etc. Instead it suffices that I evidently assent to this because I saw (or in some other way experienced) that that person helped me. But eliciting a virtuous act necessarily requires prudence in the second or third mode indicated above.

813. In the same manner, moral virtue does not require prudence in the first mode indicated because, as is evident, experience can provide knowledge of any particular, immediately directive proposition whatever; knowledge of a universal proposition is not required. But if experience does not provide evident knowledge of some particular proposition, then the virtue directed by that particular knowledge would necessarily require prudence in the first and second modes, but not the third.

[Art. IV: Dubia circa quaestionem]

[Dubium primum]

Circa quartum articulum sunt aliqua dubia movenda. Primum est utrum[1] aliquis actus voluntatis sit indifferens, sic quod primo sit indifferens ad bonum et malum, et post idem numero fiat bonus vel malus. Videtur quod sic, quia omnis actus elicitus conformiter rectae rationi est simpliciter virtuosus; sed potest aliquis primo elicere actum indifferentem sine ratione recta, et post continuare eundem cum ratione recta; igitur etc.

Et[2] eodem modo potest probari quod actus primo et intrinsece bonus potest fieri intrinsece malus, quia si primo elicitur conformiter rectae rationi, et post continuetur contra rectam rationem, erit primo intrinsece bonus et postea erit intrinsece malus, igitur etc. Eodem modo, si eliciatur primo contra rectam rationem, et post continuetur secundum rectam rationem, erit primo intrinsece malus, et post intrinsece bonus, igitur etc.

[Dubium secundum]

Secundum dubium est, quia non videtur quod[3] recta ratio, finis, locus et tempus etc. sint obiecta secundaria et partialia actus virtuosi; p r i m o, quia istae sunt circumstantiae talis actus,

1. Cf. a.1 99–143; a.2 200–210; OTh VI, 423, 383, 385.
2. Cf. OTh VI, 371–72.
3. Cf. a.2 183–85; OTh IX, 265–66.

I [Art. IV: Uncertainties Concerning the Question]

[First Doubt]

3. The fourth article raises some doubts. The first doubt is whether there is any indifferent act of will[1]—such that that act would at first be indifferent as to goodness or wickedness, and afterward numerically the same act would be rendered good or wicked. It appears that this could happen, since every act elicited in conformity with right reason is simply virtuous; but someone could first elicit an indifferent act without right reason and afterward continue the same act with right reason; therefore, etc.

10. In the same way,[2] it can be proven that a primarily and intrinsically good act can be rendered intrinsically wicked. For if it is elicited first in conformity with right reason and afterward continues contrary to right reason, then it will first be intrinsically good and thereafter intrinsically wicked; therefore, etc. Similarly, if it were elicited first contrary to right reason and afterward continued in conformity with right reason, then it will first be intrinsically wicked and thereafter intrinsically good; therefore, etc.

[Second Doubt]

18. The second doubt arises because it does not appear that right reason, end, place, time, etc.[3] are secondary and partial objects of a virtuous act for the following reasons: [1] these are the circum-

igitur non sunt obiecta illius actus, quia idem non potest esse
obiectum et circumstantia; s e c u n d o, quia tunc idem actus
esset actus volendi et nolendi, quia aliquis potest nolle peccatum,
odire et detestari propter Deum tamquam propter finem; sed iste
actus, ut terminatur ad Deum, non potest esse actus nolendi et   25
odiendi, quia est actus virtuosus et nullus virtuose odit Deum,
igitur est actus volendi ut sic terminatur; sed ut terminatur ad
peccatum, est actus nolendi, igitur etc.

[Dubium tertium]

Tertium est, quia videtur quod[4] actus exterior habeat propriam   30
bonitatem et malitiam; p r i m o, quia aliter non magis quis
vituperaretur propter malum actum exteriorem quam propter interiorem tantum; s e c u n d o, quia distincta praecepta cadunt
super exteriorem et interiorem, igitur sunt distincta peccata.

[Dubium quartum]   35

Quartum dubium est, quia P h i l o s o p h u s[5] ponit
virtutes in parte sensitiva, scilicet in irrationali, igitur videtur
quod[6] non solum sunt in voluntate.

[Dubium quintum]

Quintum dubium est de distinctione de virtute morali, quia   40
non videtur quod[7] virtus moralis sic potest esse circa obiectum
supernaturale, cum, — quia distincti habitus inclinant ad distincta
obiecta —, cum igitur obiectum naturale et supernaturale sint
distincta, erunt distincti habitus sic inclinantes; igitur si unus erit
moralis, puta ille qui inclinat ad actus circa obiectum naturale,   45
alius erit supernaturalis.

[Dubium sextum]

Sextum dubium est, quia videtur quod illa probatio[8] sit insufficiens qua probatur distinctio specifica inter habitus: quia error
circa conclusionem potest stare cum notitia principii et non cum   50
scientia conclusionis, igitur istae notitiae distinguuntur specie.
Similiter: una[9] virtus potest stare cum vitio respectu alterius vir-

---

4. Cf. a.1 132–56; OTh VI, 370.
5. Cf. Aristotle, *Eth. Nic.* 3.13.1117b23–24; OTh VI, 353, 369.
6. Cf. a.1 158–60; a.2 231–59.
7. Cf. a.2 137–51.
8. A.1 41–47; a.2 56–60.
9. A.3 225–29; a.2 181–89.

stances of such an act, therefore they are not the objects of that act, since the same thing cannot be both object and circumstance; [2] the same act would then be an act of willing and rejecting, since someone can reject, hate, and detest sin for the sake of God as an end. But insofar as this act terminates at God, it cannot be an act of hatred and rejection, since it is a virtuous act, and no one virtuously hates God; therefore it is an act of willing insofar as it terminates at God. But insofar as it terminates at sin, it is an act of rejection. Therefore, etc.

[Third Doubt]

30. The third doubt: It appears that an exterior act[4] would have its own goodness and wickedness. First, this is because otherwise a person would not be blamed more on account of a wicked exterior act than on account of an interior act alone. Second, exterior and interior acts are covered by distinct precepts, therefore the sins are distinct.

[Fourth Doubt]

36. The fourth doubt: The Philosopher[5] posits virtues in the sensitive faculty—namely, in the nonrational faculty. Therefore it appears that virtues are not found only in the will.[6]

[Fifth Doubt]

40. The fifth doubt concerns the distinction regarding moral virtue. For it does not appear that moral virtue can pertain to a supernatural object in this way[7]—since distinct habits incline to distinct objects. Since therefore natural and supernatural objects are distinct, distinct habits incline us to will these objects. Therefore, if one moral habit inclines us to acts regarding a natural object, the other habit will be a supernatural one.

[Sixth Doubt]

48. The sixth doubt: It appears that the proof[8] that demonstrated a specific distinction between habits was insufficient. This was the proof: Error concerning a conclusion is compatible with knowledge of the principle and not with scientific knowledge of the conclusion; therefore these types of knowledge are specifically distinct. Similarly: One of two virtues is not compatible with its own opposite vice,[9] but is compatible with vice in respect

tutis et non cum vitio sibi opposito, igitur distinguuntur specie.
Quia instantia est: potest[10] enim dilectio unius hominis stare cum
odio alterius et non cum odio respectu eiusdem; et tamen nullus   55
dicit quod istae dilectiones distinguuntur specie.

[Dubium septimum]

Septimum dubium est, quia videtur quod illa distinctio[11] de
virtute morali sit insufficiens, quia P h i l o s o p h u s, VII
Ethicorum,[12] distinguit in virtute: continentiam, perseverantiam   60
et temperantiam, quae sub nullo istorum membrorum continen-
tur, igitur etc.

[Dubium octavum]

Octavum dubium est, quia videtur quod virtus heroica[13] non
distinguitur a fortitudine, nec sit ponere virtutem heroicam in   65
aliquo genere virtutis nisi tantum in fortitudine, quia talis habitus
generatur ex actibus imperativis exsecutionum quae sunt contra
communem cursum naturae, puta sustinere mortem, vulnera, carcerem etc.; sed circa tales actus generatur fortitudo solum; igitur
etc.   70

[Solutio dubii primi: Opinio Scoti]

Ad primum istorum respondet I o a n n e s in primo, in
materia de caritate, et in secundo, ubi quaerit utrum aliquis actus
voluntatis sit indifferens, et in *Quolibet,* ubi quaerit utrum actus
dilectionis naturalis et meritoriae sint eiusdem speciei, quod[14] tam   75
habitus quam actus voluntatis potest esse indifferens, sic quod
idem habitus abstinentiae generatus solum in esse naturae, cuius
actus solum est actus naturalis, potest postea per coexsistentiam
actus prudentiae esse intrinsece bonus.

S e c u n d o, dicit in *Quolibet,*[15] quod idem actus non solum   80
specie sed numero potest primo esse indifferens, sic quod erit solum naturalis actus nec laudabilis nec vituperabilis, et postea idem

---

10. Cf. OTh I, 216; note the addition in codex D at line 8.
11. A.2 111–13.
12. Cf. Aristotle, *Eth. Nic.* 7.1.1145a 16–20, 35–36; and Averroes, ad
loc. (ed. Iuntina, 1574, III, fol. 94C).
13. A.2 152–67; a.3 197–206.
14. Cf. Scotus, *Ord.* I d.17 p.1 q.1–2 n.62–65.92–97, V: 163–68, 184–
88; *Sent.* II d.41 n.4, XIII: 435–36; *Quodl.* q.18 n.16, XXVI: 249.
15. Cf. Scotus, *Quodl.* q.17 n.6–7.13, XXVI: 211–12, 224–25; q.18
n.8.6, XXVI: 238, 236–37.

to the second virtue, therefore virtues are specifically distinct. For there is the following objection: Love of the first of two men is compatible with hatred of the second,[10] but not with hatred of the first; and yet no one says that these loves are specifically distinct.

[Seventh Doubt]

58. The seventh doubt arises because it appears that the distinction drawn in regard to moral virtue[11] is insufficient. For in the *Ethics,* book 7,[12] the Philosopher distinguishes within virtue continence, perseverance, and temperance; and these [degrees] are not included in any division listed; therefore, etc.

[Eighth Doubt]

64. The eighth doubt arises because it appears that heroic[13] virtue is not distinct from courage. Nor should we posit heroic virtue in any other genus of virtue, except courage, since such a habit is generated by imperative acts of execution, contrary to the common course of nature—as, for example, when one is willing to sustain death, injury, incarceration, etc. But only courage is generated by such acts. Therefore, etc.

[Reply to the First Doubt: John Duns Scotus's Opinion]

72. John[14] replies to the first doubt in the first book [of his *Sentences* commentary] when discussing the subject of charity; in the second book, where he asks whether any act of will is indifferent; and in the *Quodlibet,* where he asks whether the acts of natural and meritorious love are specifically the same. He says that both a habit and an act of will can be indifferent, so that the same habit of abstinence that is generated solely by nature and whose act is merely natural can afterward be intrinsically good by virtue of the coexistence of an act of prudence.

80. Second, in the *Quodlibet,*[15] he says that not only specifically the same, but numerically the same, act can be first indifferent, so that it would be a merely natural act, neither praiseworthy nor blameworthy; and subsequently, without changing at all, that

manens omnino potest esse virtuosus et moraliter bonus, et tertio
idem manens potest esse actus meritorius; quia secundum eum
bonitas moralis vel meritoria non addit super substantiam actus   85
nisi quosdam respectus ad circumstantias actus, vel tantum unum
respectum ad rationem rectam plene dictantem de circumstantiis;
et ille respectus secundum eum oritur ex natura rei.

T e r t i o, dicit in secundo, ubi tractat de peccato originali,[16]
quod peccatum sive deformitas in actu peccati non est nisi carentia   90
rectitudinis, non quidem quae inest actui nec quae aliquando infuit, quia actus idem est et per consequens non alteratur ab opposito
in oppositum, sed solum est carentia rectitudinis quae debuit inesse actui tali, quam rectitudinem tenebatur voluntas sibi dare.

[Contra opinionem Scoti]   95

Contra p r i m u m,[17] impossibile est quod de actu non
virtuoso fiat virtuosus per aliquem actum pure naturalem qui nullo
modo est in potestate voluntatis, quia[18] propter talem nullus lau-
datur nec vituperatur, ex quo solum est actus naturalis; sed actus
prudentiae secundum eum[19] et secundum veritatem est solum   100
actus naturalis et nullo modo in potestate nostra plus quam actus
videndi; igitur impossibile est quod actus voluntatis indifferens
et non virtuosus fiat virtuosus per solam coexsistentiam prudentiae.

Praeterea numquam de actu non virtuoso intrinsece potest fieri   105
virtuosus nisi per actum intrinsece virtuosum, et non solum extrinsece et contingenter, quia aliter esset processus in infinitum,
sicut patet supra;[20] sed sicut supra dictum est,[21] solus actus voluntatis est intrinsece virtuosus vel vitiosus, et nullus alius nisi extrinseca denominatione, quia quilibet alius, — tam actus intel-   110
lectus quam exterior —, potest idem manens fieri successive bona
intentione et mala, et per consequens est contingenter bonus vel
malus, et non necessario et intrinsece; igitur impossibile est quod
aliquis actus voluntatis non bonus fiat bonus per solum actum
prudentiae.   115

Praeterea secundum istam viam videtur quod actus virtuosus
non est unus et simplex actus, sed quod includit formaliter duos

---

16. Cf. Scotus, *Sent.* II d.37 q.1 n.6, XIII: 356–57; *Quodl.* q.18 n.16,
XXVI: 249.
17. Lines 75–79 above.
18. Cf. Aristotle, *Eth. Nic.* 2.4.1105b28–1106a4; OTh IX, 182.
19. Cf. Scotus, *Sent.* II d.40 n.4 ad 2, XIII: 427.
20. A.1 100–112.
21. A.1 145–56.

act can be virtuous and morally good; and finally, the same act can be meritorious. For according to John, moral goodness or meritorious goodness adds nothing to the substance of an act except certain relations to the circumstances of the act, or a single relation to right reason, when it fully dictates circumstances. This relation arises from the nature of things according to him.

89. Third, in the second book, where he deals with original sin,[16] John says that sin—or the deformity found in an act of sin—is nothing but a lack of rectitude. It cannot be rectitude that inheres in the act, or has at some time inhered in an act, since it is the same act and consequently does not change to something contradictory. Rather it is a lack of the rectitude that ought to inhere in such an act, a rectitude that the will was obligated to supply.

[Against Scotus's Opinion]

96. Contrary to the first part[17] of John's reply we argue as follows: It is impossible that an act which is not virtuous should be rendered virtuous by any purely natural act, which is in no sense in the power of the will. For no one is praised or blamed for such an act,[18] since it is a merely natural act. But according to John,[19] and in truth, an act of prudence is a merely natural act; it is no more in our power than an act of seeing. Therefore it is impossible that an indifferent act of will, which is not virtuous, should be rendered virtuous solely by the coexistence of an act of prudence.

105. Moreover, an act that is not intrinsically virtuous cannot be rendered virtuous except by an intrinsically virtuous act; it cannot be rendered virtuous by extrinsically and contingently virtuous acts, since otherwise there would be an infinite regress, as was evident above.[20] But as was also mentioned above,[21] only an act of will is intrinsically virtuous or vicious; no other act is virtuous except by extrinsic denomination, since any other act— whether intellectual or exterior—can, while remaining unchanged, be produced successively with good and wicked intentions; consequently any act other than an act of will is contingently good or wicked, not necessarily and intrinsically. Therefore it is impossible that any act of will that is not good should be rendered good by an act of prudence alone.

116. Besides, on this view, it appears that a virtuous act would not be a single, simple act. Instead it would formally include two acts—the indifferent act and an act of prudence; for an

actus, puta actum illum indifferentem et actum prudentiae, quia
numquam de actu non bono intrinsece nec formaliter potest fieri
bonum formaliter et intrinsece nisi per aliquid formaliter et intrin-   120
sece bonum; et sic actus virtuosus includit formaliter duos actus,
quod videtur absurdum.

Si dicis quod solum includit respectum conformitatis ad
prudentiam ultra substantiam actus: hoc videtur magis
absurdum, quod aliquis actus fiat formaliter virtuosus per unum   125
respectum qui naturaliter oritur posito extremo, quod etiam naturaliter ponitur secundum eum,[22] quia prudentia naturaliter causatur, et ipsa posita naturaliter oritur ille respectus, igitur etc.

Contra secundum,[23] quia impossibile est fieri transitum
de contradictorio in contradictorium ceteris paribus sine omni   130
adquisitione et destructione positivi;[24] sed quando de actu non
bono moraliter vel meritorie fit actus bonus moraliter vel meritorius, est talis transitus; igitur etc. Sed nihil destruitur per te et
secundum veritatem, igitur aliquid de novo adquiritur, aut absolutum aut respectivum. Si primum, aut habitus aut species aut ac-   135
tus. Non primum et secundum, quia illa possunt aequaliter mane-
re cum actu non virtuoso et vitioso sicut cum virtuoso, sicut
patet consideranti. Igitur producitur novus actus; non solum in
intellectu, quia sicut prius patet,[25] per solum actum intellectus
non potest de actu non bono intrinsece fieri bonus intrinsece;   140
igitur necessario erit alius actus voluntatis, — qui nunc est intrinsece bonus moraliter vel meritorie —, ab actu non bono sive in-
differenti.

Si producatur novus respectus,[26] contra, secundum eum in
primo in materia de caritate, ille respectus est intrinsecus adve-   145
niens, sed secundum eum in prima quaestione tertii,[27] numquam
causatur talis respectus sine productione alicuius absoluti de novo;
igitur necesse est ponere quod hic producatur aliquid de novo
absolutum quod est formaliter et intrinsece bonum. Tale nihil
potest esse ex natura sua nisi solus actus voluntatis, licet alius   150
actus posset dici intrinsece bonus ex causa extrinseca acceptante,

---

22. Cf. Scotus, *Ord.* I d.17 p.1 q.1–2 n.63–64, V: 164–66; *Sent.* II d.40
n.4 ad 2, XIII: 427.
23. Lines 80–88 above.
24. Cf. OTh III, 506; OTh V, 14–15; OTh VII, 323.
25. Lines 105–15 above; a.1 100–115.
26. Line 135 above.
27. Cf. Scotus, *Sent.* III d.1 q.1 n.14–15, XIV: 40–41; *Ord.* I d.17 p.1
q.1–2 n.63–64, V: 164–66.

act that is not intrinsically and formally good cannot be rendered formally and intrinsically good except by something formally and intrinsically good. Thus a virtuous act would formally include two acts, which appears absurd.

123. Someone might say that apart from its substance, the virtuous act includes only a relation of conformity to prudence. This appears more absurd. It is absurd to suggest that some act should be rendered formally virtuous by a relation that arises naturally once the extremes are posited. The relation even arises naturally, according to John,[22] since prudence is caused naturally, and once it is posited, the relation arises naturally. Therefore, etc.

129. Contrary to the second part[23] of John's reply, we argue as follows: All things being equal, a transition from one contradictory to another without adding or destroying something positive is impossible;[24] but there is such a transition when an act that was not morally good or meritorious is rendered morally good or meritorious; therefore, etc. But, in your view and in truth, nothing is destroyed, therefore something new is acquired, either absolute or relative. If it is absolute, then what is new is either a habit, a species, or an act. The first two can be excluded because they can remain just as much when an act is not virtuous (or vicious) as when an act is virtuous, as is clear to anyone who considers the case. Therefore, a new act is produced, and this cannot be in the intellect alone because, as was evident above,[25] an act that is not intrinsically good cannot be rendered intrinsically good by an intellectual act alone. Therefore, the new act will necessarily be another act of will, an act that now is intrinsically morally good or meritorious and is distinct from the act that was [morally] indifferent or not good.

144. If [someone suggests that] a new relation[26] might be produced, this should be denied on the basis of John's own views, as expressed in the first book, on the subject of charity, where he says the relation is something intrinsic that occurs. In the first question of the third book,[27] however, he says that such a relation is never caused without the production anew of something absolute. Therefore, it is necessary to posit something newly produced here, something absolute that is formally and intrinsically good. Nothing, on the basis of its own nature, can be of this kind except only an act of will. Some other act could, however, be called in-

quo modo Deus nunc solum acceptat actum voluntatis, quia si
acceptaret actum intellectus sicut voluntatis, tunc ita posset actus
intellectus dici bonus intrinsece sicut voluntatis.

Contra t e r t i u m,[28] quaero quid intelligit per rectitu-   155
dinem debitam inesse. Aut intelligit quod peccatum et deformitas
in actu est carentia rectitudinis debitae inesse voluntati peccanti,
et tunc verum dicit, quia voluntas elicit actum quem non debuit
elicere quia contra voluntatem et praeceptum divinum, et similiter
non elicit actum rectum quem debuit elicere secundum praecep-   160
tum divinum, et ita peccat peccato commissionis et omissionis;
sed isti actus sunt distincti non solum numero sed specie propter
distinctionem obiectorum.

Aut intelligit quod deformitas in actu peccati est carentia rectitudinis debitae inesse actui illius peccati vel quae potest sibi inesse   165
in posterum. Sed[29] hoc est impossibile, quia quaero quid est illa
rectitudo sic nata inesse actui: aut aliquid absolutum, aut respectivum. Si primum, aut habitus aut species aut actus. Non species
nec habitus, quia illi possunt stare cum actu peccati, igitur non
sunt rectitudo illius actus. Si actus, non potest esse actus intellec-   170
tus, patet, tum quia talis actus non est natus inesse actui voluntatis, tum quia actus voluntatis non est natus esse rectus per actum
intellectus, igitur erit actus rectus voluntatis. Sed ille non est natus
inesse actui vitioso, quia illi actus sunt contrarii respectu eiusdem
obiecti, et per consequens non compatiuntur se, sed potius unus   175
est destructivus alterius et non natus sibi inesse sicut eius perfectio.
Si autem illa rectitudo sit respectus, erit respectus intrinsecus ad-
veniens ex natura extremorum, et per consequens non est natus
inesse alicui cui non inest nisi propter novum fundamentum absolutum. Hoc autem non potest esse nisi actus voluntatis rectus,   180
sicut patet supra,[30] qui non est natus inesse actui peccati. Igitur
etc.

---

28. Lines 89–94 above.
29. Cf. OTh VII, 195–97.
30. Lines 144–50 above.

trinsically good because an extrinsic cause accepts it, as God accepts an act of will now, because if he were to accept an act of intellect as he does an act of will, then an act of intellect could be called intrinsically good, just as an act of will is called intrinsically good.

155. Contrary to the third part[28] of John's reply, we argue as follows: What does he understand by "rectitude that ought to inhere"? Does he means that sin (and the deformity of an act) is the lack of a rectitude that ought to inhere in the will of the sinner? If so, he speaks the truth, since the will elicits an act that it ought not to elicit, because it is contrary to divine precept and to the divine will; similarly the will does not elicit a correct act that it ought to elicit according to divine precept; and thus the will sins by commission and omission. But these act are specifically, not merely numerically distinct, because the objects of these acts are distinct.

164. Or does he mean that the deformity of an act of sin is the lack of the rectitude that ought to inhere (or can inhere subsequently) in that sinful act? This is impossible,[29] since I can ask what is that rectitude that is designed to inhere in the act; it must either be something absolute or relative. If rectitude is an absolute, it must be either a habit or a species or an act. It cannot be a species or a habit, since species and habits are compatible with an act of sin, therefore the rectitude of that act is not a species or a habit. If rectitude is an act, it evidently cannot be an act of intellect, both because such an act is not designed to inhere in an act of will, and because an act of will is not designed to be rectified by an act of intellect. Therefore, if rectitude is an act, it must be an act of right willing. But that act is not designed to inhere in a vicious act, since right willing and acting viciously are contraries in respect to the same object, and consequently they are not compatible. Rather, one is destructive of the other; neither is designed to inhere in the other as its perfection. If rectitude is a relation, it will be a relation based on things intrinsic to the nature of the terms and consequently not a thing designed to inhere in something in which it only inheres because of a new absolute foundation. But this new absolute foundation can only be an act of right willing, as was evident above,[30] and right willing is not designed to inhere in an act of sin. Therefore, etc.

[Solutio propria auctoris]

Ideo dico quantum ad istud dubium, quod actus potest dici
virtuosus vel intrinsece vel extrinsece. Primo modo, impossibile   185
est quod actus indifferens fiat bonus moraliter per coexsistentiam
actus prudentiae, quia impossibile est quod aliquis actus non virtuosus, per mere naturale fiat virtuosus. Secundo modo, bene
potest, sed hoc non erit solum per coexsistentiam prudentiae, sed
cum hoc per novam volitionem.   190

Exemplum: aliquis vult studere circumscribendo omnem circumstantiam. Iste actus est bonus ex genere. Et post intellectus
dictat quod iste actus volendi sit continuandus secundum omnes
circumstantias requisitas, et voluntas vult primum actum continuare secundum dictamen rectae rationis. Iste secundus est per-   195
fecte virtuosus, quia conformis rectae rationi complete dictanti,
et est intrinsece virtuosus; et primus est solum virtuosus denominatione extrinseca, quia scilicet conformatur secundo actui. Et
est secundus actus distinctus a primo; patet per separabilitatem
eorum et per distinctionem obiectorum, quia secundus habet rec-   200
tam rationem pro obiecto, primus non. Unde si solum esset primus actus, — et ideo iste primus actus non est aliter bonus quam
actus exterior potentiae apprehensivae vel exsecutivae, sicut patet
in *Reportatione* O c k h a m[31] —, cum actu prudentiae, non
diceretur virtuosus intrinsece nec extrinsece. Quod non intrinsece, 205
patet ex praedictis;[32] quod non extrinsece, patet, quia numquam
actus est extrinsece bonus nisi quia conformatur alicui actui intrinsece bono, cuiusmodi non est actus prudentiae sed solum actus
voluntatis, ut patet ex praedictis.[33]

Et quando arguitur[34] de actu primo intrinsece bono et post   210
malo, dico quod casus iste impossibilis est, quia istae rationes sunt
contrariae, quia prima dictat quod talis actus sit eliciendus et continuandus, secunda dictat quod ille actus non est continuandus, et
impossibile est quod istae rationes stent simul in intellectu propter
formalem repugnantiam. Et sicut istae rationes repugnant, ita   215
volitiones conformiter elicitae istis rationibus: velle enim studere
secundum rectam rationem et velle studere circa idem obiectum
contra rationem sunt volitiones oppositae propter rationes opposi-

---

31. Cf. OTh VI, 375, 389.
32. Lines 96–115 above; a.1 99–130.
33. Lines 96–115 above; a.1 132–36.
34. Lines 10–14 above.

[The Author's Own Solution]

184. Therefore, in reply to this doubt, I say that an act can be called virtuous, either intrinsically or extrinsically. In the first sense, it is impossible that an indifferent act should be rendered morally good by the coexistence of an act of prudence, since it is impossible that any act that is not virtuous should be rendered virtuous by something merely natural. In the second sense, it can indeed occur, but this will not be solely on account of the coexistence of prudence, but rather on account of a new act of will together with prudence.

191. Here is an example: In abstraction from any [particular] circumstance someone wills study. That act is generically good. Subsequently the intellect dictates that this act of will should be continued according to all requisite circumstances, and the will wills to continue the first act according to the dictate of right reason. That second act is perfectly virtuous, since it conforms to a complete dictate of right reason, and it is intrinsically virtuous. The first act is virtuous only by extrinsic denomination—namely, because it conforms to the second act. The second act is distinct from the first act, as is evident from their separability and the distinction in their objects, since the second act has right reason as an object, and the first does not. The goodness of the first act is no different from the goodness of an exterior act of the apprehensive or executive faculty, as is evident from Ockham's *Reportatio*.[31] Hence, if only the first act existed, together with an act of prudence, it would not be called virtuous, either intrinsically or extrinsically. That it would not be intrinsically virtuous is evident from what was said above.[32] That it is not extrinsically virtuous is evident because an act is never extrinsically good unless because it conforms to some intrinsically good act; prudence is not this sort of act; only an act of will is, as is evident from what was said above.[33]

210. When someone argues [against this view][34] on the basis of an act that is first intrinsically good and afterward wicked, I reply that the hypothesis is impossible. For these acts of reason are contraries: the first dictates that such an act should be elicited and continued, the second dictates that that act should not be continued, and it is impossible that these acts of reason should coexist in the intellect, on account of their formal incompatibility. Moreover, just as these acts of reason are incompatible, so also are the acts of will elicited in conformity with them. For to will study according to right reason and to will study of the same object contrary to [right] reason are opposite acts of will, on account

tas, quae sunt obiecta istarum volitionum. Et similiter primus actus
volendi virtuosus non posset naturaliter elici nec continuari   220
sine recta ratione, quae est causa partialis eius tam in eliciendo
quam in conservando, et ideo destructa illa recta ratione, destruitur ille actus volendi; destruitur autem illa ratio quando actus
oppositus elicitur; igitur etc. Et ideo actus primo intrinsece bonus
non potest fieri post intrinsece malus nec indifferens nec extrinsece   225
malus nec e contra.

Quantum ad secundum[35] quod dicit I o a n n e s, dico
quod impossibile est quod actus quicumque sit primo indifferens
et naturalis solum, et postea intrinsece bonus moraliter vel meritorie, et hoc propter transitum de contradictorio in contradictorium,   230
qui non potest salvari sine novo actu voluntatis, sicut prius patu-
it.[36]

Quantum ad tertium[37] quod dicit, dico quod deformitas in
actu vel peccatum in actu non est carentia rectitudinis debitae
inesse actui qui dicitur peccatum, propter rationem prius dictam,[38]   235
sed est carentia rectitudinis debitae inesse voluntati; quod nihil
aliud est dicere nisi quod voluntas tenetur et obligatur aliquem
alium actum elicere secundum praeceptum divinum quem non
elicit, et sic peccat peccato omissionis;[39] et ita rectitudo nihil absolutum vel respectivum est aliud quam ipse actus qui debuit elici   240
secundum rectam rationem et voluntatem Dei.

Et ex hoc patet quod imaginatio I o a n n i s et aliorum est
falsa, — quod rectitudo sit respectus conformitatis ad circumstantias sive ad rectam rationem —, propter rationes prius dictas.[40]
Et hoc videtur sequi ex dictis suis, nam dicit[41] quod deformitas   245
non est carentia rectitudinis quae aliquando infuit actui et modo
non inest, quia actus ille, cum sit idem simpliciter, non potest
alterari ab opposito in oppositum. Tunc arguo sic: si deformitas
non potest esse carentia rectitudinis quae infuit et modo non inest,
propter illum transitum de contradictorio in contradictorium, igi-   250
tur eodem modo non potest esse carentia rectitudinis quae modo
inest et prius non infuit, propter eandem causam; et per consequens impossibile est etiam secundum eum quod actus voluntatis
sit primo indifferens sive virtuosus moraliter vel meritorie, et post
idem actus fiat intrinsece virtuosus.   255

---

35. Lines 80–88 above.
36. Lines 129–50 above.
37. Lines 89–94 above.
38. Lines 164–82 above.
39. Cf. lines 156–61 above.
40. Lines 177–82 above.
41. Lines 90–93 above.

of the opposite acts of reason that are the objects of these acts of will. Similarly, the first virtuous act of will could not naturally be elicited or continued without right reason, which is a partial cause, both in eliciting and in preserving the act; and therefore, when that right reason is destroyed, so is that act of will; but that act of reason is destroyed when the opposite act is elicited; therefore, etc. And therefore an act that is at first intrinsically good cannot subsequently be rendered indifferent or intrinsically or extrinsically wicked; nor is the converse possible.

227. As to John's second point,[35] I hold that it is impossible that any act whatever should be first [morally] indifferent and strictly natural, and subsequently morally intrinsically good or meritorious. This is because there is a transition from one contradictory to another, no account of which can be preserved without [positing] a new act of will, as was evident above.[36]

233. In regard to John's third point[37] I maintain that the deformity in an act—or the sin in an act that is called a sin—is not a lack of rectitude that ought to inhere in the act, on account of the argument advanced above.[38] Instead, it is the lack of rectitude that ought to inhere in the will. This is no different from saying that the will sins by omission[39] when it is bound and obligated by divine precept to elicit some other act that it does not elicit. Hence rectitude is nothing, either absolute or relative, other than the act itself that ought to be elicited according to right reason and God's will.

242. From this it is evident that John and others are mistaken when they imagine that rectitude is a relation of conformity with circumstances or with right reason, for the reasons previously stated.[40] That they are mistaken seems to follow from John's own words,[41] for he says that deformity is not a lack of rectitude that at some time inhered in, and does not now inhere in, an act. For that act cannot change from one opposite to another, since the act is simply identical. Accordingly, I would argue as follows: If deformity cannot be a lack of rectitude that inhered and does not now inhere, on account of the transition from one contradictory to another, then in the same manner it cannot be a lack of rectitude that now inheres and previously did not inhere, for the same reason. Consequently, even in John's view, it is impossible that the act of will should first be indifferently virtuous in regard to morals or merit and subsequently be rendered intrinsically virtuous.

Unde[42] omnes istae imaginationes, quae dicunt quod rectitudo
in actu addit aliquid super actum absolutum vel respectivum, fal-
sae sunt, quia nihil aliud est quam ipsemet actus. Et ideo carere
rectitudine in actu est carere tali actu. Et similiter voluntas elicit
aliquem actum quem tenetur non elicere quia elicit contra rectam   260
rationem et praeceptum Dei, et sic peccat peccato commissionis;
et si voluntas teneatur ad actum oppositum, tunc deformitas in
isto actu est carentia rectitudinis debitae inesse voluntati, quia
est carentia alterius actus oppositi quem voluntas tenetur elicere;
et si voluntas non teneatur ad oppositum actum, — si[43] hoc esset   265
possibile alicubi invenire —, tunc deformitas non esset carentia
alicuius rectitudinis debitae inesse nec illi actui nec voluntati per
positum, sed esset ipsemet actus elicitus contra Dei praeceptum
et nullius esset carentia.

[Corollaria: Materiale et formale in peccato]   270

Ex hoc etiam patet quod non bene dicitur[44] quod actus positivus est materiale in peccato, et carentia iustitiae debitae inesse
est formale; quia aut est peccatum commissionis, aut omissionis in
voluntate, aut utrumque simul. Si primum solum, puta si voluntas
eliciat aliquem actum contra rectam rationem et praeceptum divi-   275
num, et non teneatur elicere oppositum actum, tunc solum est
ibi in voluntate actus peccati sine omni carentia rectitudinis vel
iustitiae debitae inesse, et per consequens carentia non est ibi formale. Si secundum solum sit in voluntate, puta quia voluntas
tenetur aliquem actum elicere quem non elicit, tunc solum est   280
ibi carentia rectitudinis sine omni materiali, quia sine omni actu
elicito. Si tertium detur, puta quando voluntas elicit aliquem actum contra praeceptum Dei, et ad oppositum tenetur, tunc est
ibi duplex peccatum: commissionis et omissionis. Peccatum commissionis est actus ille positivus solum, peccatum omissionis est   285
carentia alterius actus debiti inesse.

Et per consequens nihil aliud erit dicere quod in peccato sunt
talia duo, materiale et formale, quam quod peccatum commissum
est materiale et omissum est formale; et per consequens ubi[45] so-

---

42. Cf. OTh VI, 387–89.
43. Cf. Ockham, OTh VIII, 432–33, 437–42.
44. Cf. Scotus, *Sent.* II d.37 q.1 n.7, XIII: 357; q.2 n.9, XIII: 374–75.
45. Concerning this text (ubi . . . commissionis, or where . . . commission), see the variant apparatus. Wey has followed codex L. But if that
codex appears untrustworthy to the reader, s/he should adopt the reading
in codices BHPQS—that is, "ubi solum est peccatum commissionis."

256. Hence all those who imagine that the rectitude of an act adds something to the act, whether absolute or relative, are mistaken;[42] for rectitude is nothing other than the act itself. Therefore, to lack rectitude in an act is to lack this sort of act. Similarly, the will elicits some act that it is obligated not to elicit, because it elicits contrary to right reason and God's precept, and thus the will sins by commission. If the will is obligated to elicit the opposite act, then the deformity in this act is a lack of the rectitude that ought to inhere in the will; it is the lack of another act—the opposite act—which the will is obligated to elicit. And if the will is not obligated to elicit the opposite act—if such a case could be found anywhere[43]—then, on the hypothesis, the deformity would not be the lack of some rectitude that ought to inhere either in that act or in the will; instead, it would be the act itself, elicited contrary to God's precept, and it would not be a lack of any thing.

[Corollaries: On What Is Formal and Material in Sin]

271. From what has been said, it is also evident that it is not good to say that what is material in sin is the positive act,[44] and what is formal is the lack of justice that ought to inhere. For sin in the will involves either commission or omission, or both at once. Take the case of commission alone: if the will elicits some act contrary to right reason and divine precept, and if it is not obligated to elicit the opposite act, then there is only an act of sin in the will and no lack of rectitude or justice that ought to inhere; consequently what is formal in that case is not a lack of anything. If there is only omission in the will—because, for example, the will is obligated to elicit some act that it does not elicit—then there is only a lack of rectitude there without anything material, since no act is elicited. If there is both commission and omission, as when the will elicits some act contrary to God's precept, and it is obligated to elicit the opposite act, then the sin is twofold: commission and omission. The sin of commission is solely that positive act, the sin of omission is the lack of another act that ought to inhere.

287. Consequently, to say that there are two things in sin—something material and something formal—is no different from saying that a sin of commission is material and a sin of omission is formal. And thus where[45] there is only a sin of omission or only

lum est peccatum omissionis vel solum peccatum commissionis,   290
non erit assignare talia duo secundum imaginationem eorum; quia
si imaginentur quod carentia iustitiae vel rectitudinis sit sic formale in peccato, quod rectitudo illa sit aliquid positivum absolutum vel respectivum natum vel possibile inesse actui, per quod
ille actus peccati fieret virtuosus, et hoc praeter actum rectum   295
quem voluntas tenetur elicere, imaginatio est impossibilis, sicut
prius probatum est.[46]

[Quomodo peccatum est privatio]

Ex hoc etiam patet quomodo[47] peccatum dicitur privatio, quia
peccatum omissionis formaliter est privatio, et aliud peccatum,   300
commissionis, non est privatio, sed est actus positivus quem voluntas tenetur non elicere, et ideo est peccatum. Si[48] tamen cum
isto peccato sit semper peccatum omissionis, tunc cum omni peccato erit privatio quae est peccatum. Non tamen omne peccatum
est privatio, quia solum peccatum omissionis est privatio.   305

[Causa peccati]

Et ex hoc patet quid est causa efficiens peccati, quia peccati
omissionis nulla est causa positiva, quia ipsum nihil est positivum,
sed tantum habet causam defectivam; et illa est voluntas quae
tenetur actum oppositum illi carentiae elicere, et non elicit. Si   310
autem loquamur de peccato commissionis, sic[49] non tantum voluntas creata est causa efficiens illius actus, sed ipse Deus, qui omnem actum immediate causat, sicut quaecumque causa secunda; et
ita est causa positiva deformitatis in tali actu sicut ipsius substan-
tiae actus, quia sicut dictum est,[50] deformitas in actu commissionis   315
non est nisi ipsemet actus elicitus contra praeceptum divinum,
ita[51] quod iste conceptus vel vox 'deformitas' significat ipsum actum et connotat sive dat intelligere ipsum esse causatum contra
praeceptum divinum, et nihil penitus aliud dicit.

    E t s i d i c i s quod tunc Deus peccaret causando talem   320
actum deformem, sicut voluntas creata peccat quia causat talem
actum: r e s p o n d e o: Deus[52] nullius est debitor, et ideo nec

---

46. Lines 233–41 above.
47. Cf. OTh VII, 223–25.
48. Cf. note 43.
49. Cf. Scotus, *Sent.* II d.37 q.2 n.14, XIII: 378; Ockham, OTh IV, 681–83.
50. Lines 259–61, 265–68 above.
51. Cf. OTh VII, 225; OTh IV, 622.
52. Cf. OTh V, 343; OTh VII, 198, 225–26.

a sin of commission, those who hold this view should not assign two such things. For if they imagine that a lack of justice or rectitude is something formal in sin, so that that rectitude is something positive, either absolute or relative, that can inhere in, or is designed to inhere in, an act that renders that act of sin virtuous apart from the right act that the will is obligated to elicit, the view is impossible [to defend], as was proven earlier.[46]

[Sin as a Privation]

299. From what has been said, it is also evident in what sense sin is called a privation;[47] for a sin of omission is formally a privation, and a sin of commission is not a privation but a positive act that the will is obligated not to elicit, and therefore it is a sin. If, however, a sin of commission[48] always involves a sin of omission, then every sin will include a privation that is a sin. But not every sin is a privation, since only a sin of omission is a privation.

[The Cause of Sin]

307. It evident on this basis what the efficient cause of sin is. For a sin of omission has no positive cause, since it is nothing positive itself; instead, it has only a defective cause; and that cause is the will, which is obligated to, and does not, elicit an act opposite to that privation. However, if we speak of a sin of commission,[49] in this case the efficient cause of that act is not solely the created will, but God himself, who is as much the immediate cause of every act as any second cause. God is as much the positive cause of the deformity found in such an act as he is a cause of the substance of the act itself, since, as has been said,[50] the deformity in an act of commission is nothing but the act itself, elicited contrary to divine precept. Thus the word or concept 'deformity'[51] signifies the act itself and connotes or allows us to understand that the act caused is contrary to divine precept; it indicates absolutely nothing else.

320. Someone might say that then God would sin by causing such a deformed act, just as a created will sins by causing such an act. My reply is that God is a debtor to no one,[52] and therefore he

tenetur illum actum causare nec oppositum actum, nec illum actum non causare, et ideo non peccat quantumcumque illum actum causet. Voluntas autem creata tenetur per praeceptum divinum　325
illum actum non causare, et per consequens in causando illum actum peccat, quia facit quod non debet facere. Unde si voluntas creata non obligaretur ad non causandum illum actum vel oppositum, quantumcumque causaret illum, numquam peccaret sicut nec Deus.　330

[Aversio a Deo, conversio ad Deum]

Ex isto etiam patet quomodo aliquis per peccatum avertitur a Deo,[53] quia non omne peccatum etiam commissum est actus odiendi Deum. Potest enim aliquis velle facere opera iniusta contra rectam rationem, et nec diligere Deum nec odire. Sed ideo dicitur　335
omne peccatum avertere a Deo, quia omnis peccans mortaliter vel facit aliquid quod Deus non vult eum facere quia praecipit illud non fieri, vel non facit quod Deus vult fieri quia Deus praecipit illud fieri; et sic talis videtur diligere aliud a Deo plus quam Deum, et sic avertitur a Deo quia non diligit Deum super omnia, quod　340
tamen tenetur facere. Et similiter per actum gratiae et caritatis aliquis convertitur ad Deum, quia tali actu diligit Deum super omnia.

Et si quaeras[54] utrum conversio ad Deum per caritatem et aversio a Deo per actum peccati formaliter repugnant:　345
respondeo, aut quaeris de caritate habituali aut actuali; et similiter aut quaeris de actu peccati quo aliquis odit Deum, aut de actu quo diligit aliquam creaturam quam Deus non vult diligi.

Si quaeras utrum conversio ad Deum actu caritativo et aversio ab eo actu odiendi Deum opponuntur formaliter, dico quod sic,　350
quia diligere Deum super omnia et odire Deum sunt actus contrarii.

Si quaeras de conversione ad Deum actu caritativo et aversione actu quo diligitur creatura quam Deus non vult diligi, puta actum fornicandi, sic non repugnant illi formaliter et naturaliter inter　355
se, sed compatiuntur se in eodem quantum est ex natura actuum; sed solum repugnant per causam extrinsecam, puta per Deum

---

53. Cf. Ockham, OTh VIII, 313–18; Scotus, *Sent.* II d.37 q.1 n.8, XIII: 358.
54. Concerning this objection and the following replies, cf. a.3 425–44.

is not obligated to cause either that act or the opposite act; nor is he obligated not to cause that act. Therefore, however much he might cause that act, God does not sin. But the created will is obligated by divine precept not to cause that act, and consequently it sins by causing that act because it does what it ought not to do. Hence, if the created will were not obligated not to cause that act or its opposite, however much it caused that act, it would not sin, just as God does not sin.

[Aversion from God and Conversion to God]

332. On this basis it is also evident how someone is averted or turned away from God by sin,[53] since not every sin, not even every sin of commission, is an act of hating God. For someone can intend to perform unjust works contrary to right reason and neither love nor hate God. But all sin is said to avert one from God, because everyone sinning mortally either does something that God does not intend her to do because he commands her not to do it, or she does not do what God intends her to do because he commands her to do it. Thus such a person seems to love something other than God more than God; thus she turns away from God because she does not love God above all, which, however, she is obligated to do. Similarly, someone is converted to God by an act of grace or charity, because in such an act she loves God above all.

344. You might ask whether conversion to God by virtue of charity and aversion from God by virtue of an act of sin are formally incompatible.[54] I would ask in reply whether you are asking about habitual or actual charity; and similarly whether you ask about an act of sin by virtue of which someone hates God, or about an act by which someone loves a creature whom God does not intend us to love.

349. If you ask whether conversion to God in an act of love and aversion from God in an act of hating God are formally opposed, I reply that they are, since to love God above all and to hate God are contrary acts.

353. Someone might ask about conversion to God by an act of charity and aversion from God in an act by virtue of which we love a creature whom God does not intend us to love, as in the case of an act of fornication. These acts are not formally and naturally irreconcilable; rather, they are compatible in the same subject as far as the nature of the acts is concerned. They are incompatible only by virtue of an extrinsic cause—namely, God,

ordinantem talem creaturam nullo modo a voluntate creata diligi;
et ita voluntas diligens talem creaturam non diligit Deum super
omnia, quia si sic, non diligeret aliquam creaturam quam Deus   360
odit vel vult non diligi; et ideo propter ordinationem talis causae
extrinsecae videtur solum repugnantia. Quod patet, quia si lex
statuta revocaretur, iam isti actus diligendi compaterentur se in
eodem; et si lex illa praeciperet illam creaturam diligi, tunc posset
non tantum simul stare cum alio actu, sed tunc meritorie diligeret   365
illam creaturam.

Si autem quaeras de conversione ad Deum per caritatem habi-
tualem et aversione ab eo per actum peccati actualis, sic dico quod
caritas habitualis infusa et peccatum actuale sive primo modo sive
secundo modo acceptum[55] non repugnant formaliter, quia nulla   370
forma naturalis repugnat formae supernaturali, — licet aliquando
differat ab ea specie —, sed solum repugnant per causam extrinsecam statuentem numquam dare caritatem exsistenti in tali actu.

Et similiter posset aliquis habere habitum odiendi Deum, et
tamen caritatem infusam, quia inter illos habitus non est repug-   375
nantia. Quod patet, quia aliquis sic odiens Deum habitualiter,
post paenitens iustificatur, et per consequens gratia sibi infunditur;
et per unum actum poenitentiae non corrumpitur totus habitus
ille odiendi Deum; igitur manet ille habitus cum caritate secundum multos gradus. Quod credo esse verum, quia post primum   380
actum paenitentiae experitur talis se plus inclinatum ad odiendum
Deum quam ad diligendum, et ad odiendum plus quam si nullum
actum odii prius habuisset; et ista inclinatio non potest esse nisi
per habitum odiendi; igitur etc.

Si quaeras utrum caritas adquisita habitualis et peccatum actu-   385
ale primo modo vel secundo[56] opponantur formaliter et intrinsece,
dico quod non, quia aliquis habens caritatem adquisitam potest
Deum odire vel creaturam aliquam diligere quam Deus non vult
diligi, quia aliter numquam posset peccare peccato commissionis;
et per illum actum odiendi Deum non corrumpitur tota caritas   390
adquisita, probatur sicut praecedens conclusio de odio;[57] igitur
manet iste actus odiendi cum caritate adquisita in eodem, et per
consequens non repugnant formaliter et intrinsece. Sed caritas adquisita habitualis et odium habituale respectu Dei repugnant formaliter.   395

---

55. Lines 347–48 above.
56. See note 55.
57. Lines 374–80 above.

who ordains that the created will should in no way love a certain creature, so that by loving such a creature the will does not love God above all. For if the will did love God above all, it would not love another creature whom God hates or intends it not to love. Hence the incompatibility appears to be solely on account of the ordination of such an extrinsic cause. This is evident, since if the statutory law were revoked, these acts of love would thenceforth be compatible in the same subject. Moreover, if the law were to command that that creature be loved, then not only could the acts coexist, but the will would then love that creature meritoriously.

367. On the other hand, someone might ask about conversion to God by means of habitual charity and aversion from God by means of an act of actual sin. I reply that infused, habitual charity and actual sin (whether taken in the first or second sense)[55] are not formally incompatible. For although sometimes a natural form differs specifically from a supernatural form, no natural form is incompatible with a supernatural form; instead, they are only incompatible by virtue of an extrinsic cause that establishes that charity is never granted to someone who exists in such an act.

374. Similarly, someone could have a habit of hating God and still have infused charity, since there is no incompatibility between those habits. This is evident in the case of someone who, after hating God habitually in this way, repents and is justified, and consequently grace is infused in him. One act of penitence does not destroy that entire habit of hating God, therefore many degrees of that habit remain together with charity. This is true, I believe, since after the first act of penance, such a person finds from experience that he is more inclined to hate than to love God; he is more inclined to hatred than if he had never had an act of hatred; and this inclination cannot exist unless on account of a habit of hatred. Therefore, etc.

385. Someone might ask whether acquired, habitual charity and actual sin—in the first or the second sense[56]—are formally and intrinsically opposed. I say that they are not, since someone with acquired charity can hate God or love some creature that God does not intend us to love (otherwise there would never be a sin of commission); and that act of hating God does not destroy all acquired charity, as was proved in the preceding conclusion regarding hatred.[57] Therefore this act of hatred remains together with acquired charity in the same subject, and consequently they are not formally and intrinsically incompatible.

E t s i q u a e r a s quomodo per illum actum odiendi
Deum frequenter elicitum corrumpitur caritas adquisita, si nulla
sit repugnantia formalis inter caritatem adquisitam et actum odiendi: r e s p o n d e o[58] . . .

[Solutio dubii secundi]   400

Ad secundum dubium[59] dico quod tam finis quam recta ratio
et omnes aliae circumstantiae sunt obiecta partialia secundaria actus virtuosi. Cuius ratio est, quia aliquis est actus voluntatis qui
est intrinsece et necessario virtuosus, stante ordinatione divina
quae nunc est, et nullo modo contingenter virtuosus. Nunc au-   405
tem, si illa quae dicuntur circumstantiae non essent obiecta actus
virtuosi, nullus actus voluntatis esset necessario et intrinsece virtuosus sed solum contingenter et extrinsece, cuius oppositum est
prius probatum.[60]

Assumptum patet, quia omnis actus voluntatis idem omnino   410
manens potest continuari et conservari, facta sola apprehensione
et ostensione obiecti illius actus, quia ad causandum actum voluntatis non videntur plura requiri quam Deus et ipsa voluntas et
apprehensio obiecti; et ista sufficiunt ad causandum, sicut causae
partiales, omnem actum volendi, qui non requirit aliquid aliud   415
tamquam obiectum in esse reali; igitur ista sufficiunt ad conser-
vandum talem actum sine omni alio posito in esse reali.

[Recta ratio]

Si igitur recta ratio, sive actus assentiendi qui vocatur recta
ratio,[61] non sit obiectum actus virtuosi, puta temperantiae, sed   420
solum circumstantia, et cibaria sunt obiecta talis actus, sequitur
quod apprehenso cibo, sine omni recta ratione, immo forte cum
ratione erronea, posset voluntas elicere actum virtuosum perfecte.
Et sicut potest causare actum virtuosum, posita hypothesi, sine
omni ratione recta, ita potest conservare actum elicitum cum recta   425
ratione, postea sine recta ratione; et sic ille actus erit primo virtuosus et post non virtuosus vel vitiosus, et ita contingenter, non
necessario.

S i d i c i s quod actus prudentiae requiritur sicut causa
essentialis et partialis ad actum virtuosum, — secundum I o a n-   430

---

58. The reply is lacking, but cf. OTh VII, 224.
59. Lines 18–28 above; cf. OTh VI, 380–83, 423; OTh VIII, 414–15,
418–19, 425, 413–14; OTh VIII, 292–93.
60. A.1 99–156.
61. Cf. OTh VI, 422–23.

393. Nonetheless, acquired, habitual charity and habitual hatred in regard to God are formally incompatible. And if you ask how acquired charity is corrupted by means of that act of hating God, frequently elicited, if there is no formal incompatibility between acquired charity and the act of hating, I reply[58] . . .

[Reply to the Second Doubt]

401. In reply to the second doubt,[59] I maintain that both the end and right reason, and all other circumstances, are partial, secondary objects of a virtuous act. The reason for this is that there is an act of will that is intrinsically and necessarily virtuous and in no sense contingently virtuous, given the present divine ordination. Moreover, in the present state of affairs, if what are called circumstances were not the objects of a virtuous act, no act of will would be necessarily and intrinsically virtuous but only contingently and extrinsically virtuous; the opposite conclusion was proven above.[60]

410. The assumption is evident, since every act of will, while remaining entirely the same, can be continued and preserved, given only the apprehension and manifestation of the object of that act. For causing an act of will appears to require nothing more than God, the will itself, and the apprehension of an object. Acting as partial causes, these three suffice to cause every act of will, which does not require the real existence of anything else as an object. Therefore they suffice to preserve such an act without positing the real existence of anything else.

[Right Reason]

419. Suppose, therefore, that right reason,[61] or the act of assent that is called right reason, is not the object of an act of virtue—for example, temperance. But if only a circumstance and nourishment are the objects of such an act, then it follows that once the food is apprehended, the will could elicit a perfectly virtuous act without right reason, even perhaps when reason errs. On this hypothesis, just as the will can cause a virtuous act in the absence of all right reason, so it can subsequently preserve an act elicited with right reason in the absence of right reason. Consequently, that act will first be virtuous and afterward vicious or not virtuous, and be so contingently, not necessarily.

429. Someone might say that according to the opinion advanced here and according to John,[62] an act of prudence is re-

n e m et istam opinionem[62] —, causandum, non tamen oportet
quod concurrat tamquam obiectum; sicut apprehensio obiecti et
Deus concurrunt sicut causae partiales ad causandum actum virtuosum, non tamen sunt obiecta:

C o n t r a, si recta ratio solum requireretur sicut causa   435
partialis et essentialis modo praedicto, — cum Deus omnem causalitatem causae secundae possit supplere —, si Deus suppleret
causalitatem rectae rationis, stante causalitate voluntatis et apprehensionis, posset ille actus esse perfecte virtuosus sine actu prudentiae; quod est manifeste falsum, quia stante ordinatione quae   440
nunc est, nullus actus est perfecte virtuosus nisi eliciatur conformiter rectae rationi actualiter inhaerenti.

Ideo dico quod recta ratio est obiectum actus virtuosi; et ex
hoc quod requiritur ad actum virtuosum tamquam obiectum in
esse reali, sequitur quod habet causalitatem effectivam respectu   445
actus virtuosi secundum principium frequenter allegatum 'effectus
sufficienter dependet' etc.,[63] quia si non requireretur in esse reali
tamquam obiectum, tunc videtur quod sola eius apprehensio et
obiecti actus virtuosi cum voluntate posset causare actum virtuosum, sicut quemcumque alium actum potest causare.   450

Confirmatur, quia[64] nullus actus est perfecte virtuosus, nisi
voluntas per illum actum velit dictatum a recta ratione propter
hoc quod est dictatum a recta ratione, quia si vellet dictatum a
ratione, non quia dictatum, sed quia delectabile vel propter aliam
causam, iam vellet illud dictatum si solum esset ostensum per ap-   455
prehensionem sine recta ratione; et per consequens ille actus non
esset virtuosus, quia non eliceretur conformiter rationi rectae,
quia hoc est elicere conformiter rectae rationi: velle dictatum a
ratione propter hoc quod est dictatum. Nunc autem est impossibile quod aliquis velit aliquid propter aliud, nisi velit illud aliud,   460
quia si nolit vel non velit illud aliud, iam vult primum magis
propter se quam propter illud aliud. Igitur ad hoc quod virtuose
velim dictatum a ratione recta, oportet necessario quod velim rectam rationem per eundem actum, non per alium, quia si per alium,
iam ille actus quo volo dictatum a ratione non esset virtuosus,   465
quia non est virtuosus nisi propter hoc quod per illum volo dictatum a ratione propter hoc quod ratio sic dictat. Erit igitur per

---

62. Cf. Scotus, *Ord.* I d.17 p.1 q.1–2 n.92.94, V: 184–85; Ockham, a.3
492–518 above; OTh VI, 372, 389–90; OTh VII, 49–50.
63. Cf. Scotus, *Ord.* I d.3 p.3 q.2 n.414, III: 251; OTh V, 269.
64. Cf. a.2 134–36.

quired as an essential and partial cause of a virtuous act, although the act of prudence need not concur as an object of a virtuous act. Similarly, the apprehension of an object and God concur as partial causes in producing a virtuous act, although they are not objects:

435. On the contrary, if right reason were required only as an essential and partial cause in the manner described, then, since God can supply all the causality of a second cause, if God were to supply the causality of right reason, and the causality of the willing and apprehension remained, that act could be perfectly virtuous without an act of prudence. That is manifestly false, since given the present divine ordination, no act is perfectly virtuous unless elicited in conformity with right reason actually inhering [in the will].

443. Therefore, I hold that right reason is an object of a virtuous act. And since its real existence as an object is required for a virtuous act, it follows that its causality in respect to a virtuous act is effective, according to the principle frequently alleged— [namely, that] "an effect sufficiently depends," etc.[63] For if the real existence of right reason as an object were not required, it appears that merely the apprehension of right reason and the object of a virtuous act, together with the will, could cause a virtuous act, just as it can cause any other act.

451. Confirmation:[64] No act is perfectly virtuous unless by that act the will wills a dictate of right reason on account of its being a dictate of right reason. For if the will were to will a dictate of reason, not because it was a dictate, but because it was enjoyable or on account of some other reason, then the will would will that dictate if it were merely manifested by way of apprehension, [even] in the absence of right reason; and consequently that act would not be virtuous because it would not have been elicited in conformity with right reason. For to elicit [an act] in conformity with right reason is to will a dictate of reason on account of its being a dictate. In the present state of affairs, however, it is impossible that someone should will one thing on account of another, second thing, unless that person wills that second thing; for if he rejects or does not will the second thing, then he wills the first thing more for its own sake than for the sake of the second thing. Therefore, in order that I virtuously will a dictate of right reason, I must necessarily will right reason by the same act, and not by another. For if I will right reason by another act, then that act by which I will a dictate of reason would not be virtuous, since an act is not virtuous, unless because by that act I will what reason dictates on account of its being a dictate of reason. Therefore

eundem actum, sicut[65] per eundem actum utor creatura et diligo
Deum, propter quem diligo creaturam.

[Finis]   470

Et eodem modo potest probari quod finis, qui est una circumstantia, sit obiectum actus virtuosi; quia volo tale dictatum propter talem finem, igitur per illum actum volo finem, quia propter
quod unumquodque, et illud magis.[66]

[Locus et tempus]   475

Similiter potest probari quod locus et tempus, quae sunt circumstantiae, sunt obiecta partialia actus virtuosi, quia aliter sequeretur quod actus esset perfecte virtuosus sine illis circumstantiis
sicut cum illis, quod est manifeste falsum. Patet enim quod velle
coire est actus virtuosus si velit loco et tempore, et aliter non,   480
sed magis vitiosus.

Assumptum patet, quia positis causis sufficientibus ad actum
virtuosum, sive obiectis sufficientibus apprehensis et dictatis, potest poni ille actus; sed apprehensio actus carnalis propter Deum et
ratio dictans talem actum carnalem esse volendum propter Deum,   485
ita quod nec apprehendatur nec dictetur de loco et tempore, cum
Deo et voluntate sufficiunt ad causandum velle virtuosum respectu
illius actus, et hoc dico si locus et tempus non sint obiecta actus
virtuosi; igitur illud velle esset perfecte virtuosum sine talibus
circumstantiis.   490

S i   d i c a s quod requiritur ad actum virtuosum quod locus
et tempus apprehendantur et dictentur a ratione, sicut finis, et
aliter non potest ratio causare actum virtuosum; et per consequens
tam locus quam tempus sunt obiecta partialia apprehensionis et
actus dictandi, non tamen sunt obiecta volitionis virtuosae: 495

C o n t r a, volitio dicitur perfecte virtuosa quia in omnibus
conformiter elicitur rationi rectae, quia si in aliquo conformiter
eliceretur et in aliquo non, iam non esset perfecte virtuosa. Exemplum: si aliquis vellet actum carnalem propter talem finem dictatum a ratione recta, et nullum actum volendi haberet respectu   500

---

65. Cf. Ockham, OTh VIII, 138.
66. Cf. Aristotle, *Anal. Poster.* 1.2.72a 29–30.

it will [be virtuous] by the same act,[65] just as by the same act I use a creature and I love God, on account of whom I love the creature.

[The End]

471. In the same manner, we can prove that the end [for the sake of which an act is performed], which is one circumstance, is an object of a virtuous act. Because I will such a dictate on account of such an end, I will that end by means of that act, since "that on account of which [we love] each thing is better loved."[66]

[Time and Place]

476. Similarly, we can prove that place and time, which are circumstances [of an act] are partial objects of a virtuous act. Otherwise it would follow that an act would be perfectly virtuous without those circumstances, as it would be with them, which is manifestly false. For it is evident that willing coition is a virtuous act if willed in [the proper] place and time; otherwise it is not virtuous; instead, it is rather vicious.

482. The assumption is evident, since when we posit causes sufficient for a virtuous act, or sufficient objects apprehended and dictated, we can posit that act. But when we apprehend a carnal act performed on account of God, and reason dictates that such a carnal should be willed on account of God, in such a manner that the time and place of the act are neither apprehended nor dictated, these [objects], together with God and the will, suffice to cause a virtuous volition in respect to that act; I hold that this would be the case if time and place were not objects of a virtuous act. Therefore, that volition would be perfectly virtuous without such circumstances.

491. Someone might say that reason must apprehend and dictate the time and place, just as it dictates the end. Otherwise reason cannot cause a virtuous act; and consequently both place and time are partial objects of acts of apprehension and dictation, although they are not objects of a virtuous volition.

496. On the contrary, a volition is called perfectly virtuous because it conforms to right reason in every respect, since if it conformed in some respect and not in another, then it would not be perfectly virtuous. For example, suppose someone were to will a certain carnal act on account of an end dictated by right reason,

loci et temporis, quamquam ista dictentur a ratione, ista volitio
non est perfecte virtuosa sed potius vitiosa vel indifferens; igitur
ad hoc quod sit perfecte virtuosa, oportet quod conformetur rationi rectae et omnibus dictatis a ratione recta sibi debere competere;
igitur si recta ratio dictet quod talis actus sit volendus loco et   505
tempore, voluntas perfecte virtuosa debet velle talem actum in
loco et tempore; et per consequens quidquid est obiectum actus
dictandi recte, erit obiectum actus perfecte virtuosi.

S i d i c i s quod prima probatio[67] qua probatur quod recta
ratio est obiectum, — quae fuit, quia non requiritur solum sicut   510
causa partialis, quia Deus potest illam causalitatem supplere, igitur
etc. —, non valet, quia secundum istam viam, si Deus suppleret
causalitatem voluntatis in causando illum actum qui dicitur virtuosus, tunc non diceretur virtuosus, quia virtuosum connotat
activitatem voluntatis,[68] et tamen voluntas non est obiectum talis   515
actus, sed potentia et causa partialis. Eodem modo in proposito
virtuosum connotat activitatem prudentiae respectu actus virtuosi,
et quando illa activitas suppletur aliunde, non est actus virtuosus;
igitur propter illam suppletionem, non oportet ponere prudentiam
esse obiectum actus virtuosi: 520

R e s p o n d e o: potest dici quod melior et fortior ratio ad
probandum rationem rectam sive prudentiam esse obiectum actus
virtuosi est haec: quia aliter sequerentur duo inconvenientia. P r i-
m u m est quod nullus actus esset intrinsece et necessario virtuosus sed solum contingenter, cuius oppositum prius probatum   525
est.[69] S e c u n d u m, quod de actu non virtuoso fieret virtuosus
per aliquid mere naturale quod non est in potestate nostra; et
eodem modo, de non meritorio fieret meritorium per aliquid mere
naturale. Sed oppositum utriusque probatum est prius.[70]

P r i m u m probatur sic, quia quemcumque actum respectu   530
quorumcumque obiectorum, excepta ratione recta in ratione obiecti, potest voluntas elicere mediante ratione recta, potest elicere
sine ea et cum sola apprehensione illorum obiectorum; patet enim

---

67. Lines 435–40 above.
68. Cf. a.3 515–18.
69. See note 60.
70. Lines 96–104, 129–50 above.

and suppose that person elicits no act of will in respect of time and place, although these were dictated by reason; that volition would not be perfectly virtuous, but rather vicious or indifferent. Therefore, in order that it be perfectly virtuous, the volition must conform to right reason and to all things dictated by right reason; if right reason dictates that such an act should be willed at such a time in such a place, a perfectly virtuous will ought to will such an act at [that] time and place. Consequently whatever is an object of a rightly dictating act will be an object of a perfectly virtuous act.

509. Someone might say that the first proof,[67] in which we proved that right reason is an object [of virtuous acts], is not valid. That is the proof which showed that right reason is not required solely as a partial cause: for God can supply that causality, and therefore [right reason must also be an object]. The objection would be that according to the view presented here, if God supplied the causality of the will in causing that act which we call virtuous, then it would not be called virtuous, since [the term] 'virtuous' connotes the activity of the will,[68] and yet the will is not the object of such an act; rather, it is the faculty [eliciting the act] and a partial cause [of the act]. In the same way, in the case under consideration, 'virtuous' connotes the activity of prudence in respect to a virtuous act, and when that activity is supplied from elsewhere, the act is not virtuous. Therefore, we need not posit prudence as an object of a virtuous act on account of that [possibility that God could] supply [the causal efficacy of right reason].

521. I reply that a better and stronger argument proving that right reason or prudence is an object of a virtuous act can be advanced—namely, because otherwise two absurdities would follow. First, no act would be intrinsically and necessarily virtuous, but only contingently virtuous; the opposite has previously been proved.[69] Second, an act that was not virtuous would be rendered virtuous by means of something merely natural that is not in our power; in the same way, an act that was not meritorious would be rendered meritorious by means of something merely natural; but each of these [consequences] has been previously disproved.[70]

530. That the first absurdity is a consequence can be proved as follows: With the exception of right reason considered as an object, whatever act in respect to whichever objects the will can elicit by means of right reason, it can elicit without right reason,

quod sicut voluntas potest velle abstinere propter Deum loco et
tempore, et sic de aliis circumstantiis, mediante actu dictativo   535
intellectus, ita potest velle abstinere propter Deum loco et tempore etc., si solum intellectus apprehendit istam propositionem
'volendum est abstinere propter Deum' etc., et si intellectus nullo
modo assentiat illi complexo. Tunc quaero si illa volitio sit virtuosa intrinsece vel non. Non potest dici quod sic, quia non elici-   540
tur conformiter rationi rectae secundum praedicta,[71] quod necessario requiritur ad actum virtuosum.

S i d i c i s quod sic, quia talis actus elicitur sicut recta
ratio dictaret, et ideo licet actualiter non conformetur rationi rectae, tamen conformatur aptitudinaliter, et hoc sufficit: c o n t r a,   545
recta ratio dictaret quod volendum est abstinere propter Deum
etc., et hoc conformiter rationi rectae, hoc est, quia sic dictatum
est a ratione recta,[72] aliter non esset recta sed erronea; sed volitio
habens Deum et alias circumstantias pro obiecto praeter rationem,
non est eadem numero nec specie cum volitione quae eliceretur   550
quia sic esset dictatum a ratione recta, propter variationem obiecti,
puta rationis rectae; igitur ille qui non habet rationem pro obiecto,
non est natus conformiter elici rationi rectae, quia ratio recta non
eliceret illum, sed unum alium qui haberet rationem pro obiecto.

S i d i c a s quod non est iste virtuosus propter defectum   555
prudentiae: t u n c pono quod coexsistat actus prudentiae, et
quaero utrum tunc ille actus volendi sit virtuosus vel non. Si non,
patet tunc, discurrendo per singulas causas huius, quod nulla erit
causa huius nisi quia illa volitio non habet rectam rationem pro
obiecto, quia per hypothesim nullum aliud obiectum requisitum   560
deficit: et ratio recta coexsistit et omnia alia. Unde igitur est quod
non est talis actus virtuosus?

Si sit virtuosus coexsistente actu prudentiae, igitur sequitur
quod actus prius non virtuosus intrinsece nec extrinsece, modo
sit virtuosus intrinsece per solam coexsistentiam prudentiae. Et   565

---

71. Lines 410–69 above.
72. Cf. lines 458–59 above.

assuming only the apprehension of those objects. For it is evident that just as the will can will to abstain by means of a dictative, intellective act (for God's sake, in the [proper] time and place, and so on concerning other circumstances), the will can also will to abstain (for God's sake in the [proper] time and place, etc.), granted only that the intellect apprehends this proposition 'we should will abstinence for God's sake,' etc., even if the intellect in no sense assents to that proposition. Accordingly, I ask whether that volition [which presupposes only intellectual apprehension] is intrinsically virtuous or not. It cannot be said that it is virtuous, since it is not elicited in conformity with right reason, which is necessarily required for a virtuous act, as was discussed above.[71]

543. Someone might object that such an act is virtuous, since such an act is elicited as right reason would dictate. Therefore, although it does not actually conform to right reason, nonetheless it does conform aptitudinally, and that suffices.

545. On the contrary: Right reason would dictate that we should will to abstain for God's sake, etc., and that in conformity with right reason—that is, because it is so dictated by right reason; otherwise it would be erring reason, not right reason. But the volition that has God and [all] other circumstances except for reason as its object is neither numerically nor specifically the same as the volition that would be elicited because it was dictated by right reason,[72] since the object varies—namely, right reason. Therefore, the act that does not have reason as its object is not designed to be elicited in conformity with right reason, since right reason would not elicit that act, but rather another act, which would have reason as an object.

555. Someone might hold that that act would not be virtuous on account of a defect in prudence. In that case, I posit the coexistence of an act of prudence and ask whether that volitional act is virtuous then or not. If not, then by listing the [possible] single causes, it will be evident that the only cause that could account for this will be that right reason is not an object of that volition. On the hypothesis no other requisite object is missing; right reason coexists, as do all the other [objects]. So how is it that the act posited is not virtuous?

563. If an act would be virtuous given the coexistence of an act of prudence, it would follow that an act that was previously not virtuous, either intrinsically or extrinsically, is now rendered intrinsically virtuous by means of the coexistence of prudence

cum voluntas posset conservare eundem actum, stante prima apprehensione illius complexi, destructo illo actu prudentiae propter
aliquod aliud medium sibi apparens, sequitur quod idem actus
numero fieret iterum non virtuosus, quia non coexsistit prudentia,
et sic quilibet actus esset contingenter virtuosus. Igitur oportet   570
necessario quod actus qui est intrinsece et necessario virtuosus,
sic quod non potest fieri indifferens vel vitiosus, quod habeat non
tantum alias circumstantias sed etiam rationem rectam pro obiecto; et ille solus est sic virtuosus, et quilibet alius solum contingenter et extrinsece.   575

Et eodem modo potest argui, si ponatur quod actus dictativus
illius complexi simul ponatur cum actu apprehensivo eiusdem et
actu volendi praedicto, quia sicut actus ille volendi abstinere propter Deum etc., excepta ratione pro obiecto, potest causari sine
actu dictativo secundum casum prius positum,[73] ita potest conser-   580
vari sine eodem, quantumcumque simul causentur, quia non plus
dependet actus volendi ab eo in conservando quam in causando.
Et sic patet primum inconveniens.

S e c u n d u m[74] sequitur ex primo, quia per solam positio-
nem actus prudentiae fieret actus voluntatis praeexsistens virtuosus   585
vel meritorius, qui prius non esset meritorius propter defectum
rationis rectae secundum primum casum praedictum,[75] quia cum
actus prudentiae sit mere naturale et nullo modo in potestate nostra, sequitur quod de non meritorio nec virtuoso fieret virtuosum
et meritorium per aliquid quod nullo modo est in potestate nostra;   590
et sic de non digno vita aeterna fieret dignus per aliquid quod nullo
modo est in potestate nostra, quod est absurdum.

Eodem modo, si propter solam destructionem actus prudentiae
de actu virtuoso et meritorio fieret non virtuosus et non meritorius secundum alium casum,[76] cum actus ille prudentiae sit mere   595
naturale sicut prius, sequitur quod virtuosus et dignus vita aeterna
fieret non virtuosus et indignus per aliquid quod nullo modo esset
in potestate sua, quod est absurdum. Et ista inconvenientia possunt vitari ponendo quod recta ratio sit obiectum actus virtuosi,
et non aliter, ut videtur.   600

---

73. Lines 530–39 above.
74. Lines 526–29 above; cf. OTh VI, 389–90; OTh VIII, 414–15.
75. Lines 563–65 above.
76. Lines 566–69 above.

alone. And the will could preserve the same act after the destruction of that act of prudence on account of some other specious argument. So as long as the first apprehension of that complex expression lasts, it follows that numerically the same act would again be rendered not virtuous, since prudence would not coexist. Thus any sort of act would be contingently virtuous. Therefore, an intrinsically and necessarily virtuous act, which cannot be rendered indifferent or vicious, must necessarily have as its object not only other circumstances but also right reason. Only that act is virtuous intrinsically and necessarily; any other act is virtuous only contingently and extrinsically.

576. It can be argued in the same way if we posit a dictative act regarding a proposition and simultaneously posit apprehensive and volitional acts in regard to that same proposition. For in the case posited previously,[73] with the exception of an act regarding right reason considered as an object, just as that act of willing abstention for God's sake, etc., can be caused without the dictative act, in the same way that act can be preserved without the dictative act, however simultaneously they are caused. For the volitional act no more depends on the [dictative act] for its preservation than for its causation. Thus the first absurdity is evident.

584. The second[74] absurd consequence [of not positing that right reason is an object of any virtuous act] follows from the first. According to the first case posited above,[75] the positing of an act of prudence alone would render a preexisting act of will virtuous or meritorious, an act that previously was not meritorious on account of a defect of right reason. For since an act of prudence is merely natural and in no sense in our power, it follows that an act that is neither meritorious nor virtuous would be rendered virtuous and meritorious by means of something that is in no sense in our power. Thus we who were not worthy of eternal life would be rendered worthy by means of something that was in no sense in our power, which is absurd.

593. In the same way, in the other case described,[76] since that act of prudence is merely natural, as was indicated above, if a virtuous and meritorious act were rendered neither virtuous nor meritorious on account of the destruction of an act of prudence alone, it would follow that someone virtuous and worthy of eternal life would be rendered unworthy and cease to be virtuous by means of something that would in no sense be in her power, which is absurd. These absurdities can be avoided by positing that right reason is an object of a virtuous act and not in any other way, as is apparent.

Ad p r i m u m argumentum secundae dubitationis[77] dico
quod non sunt circumstantiae respectu actus intrinsece et necessario virtuosi, sed sunt obiecta secundaria respectu illius actus.
Sed sunt circumstantiae respectu aliorum actuum, sive sint actus
voluntatis sive intellectus sive cuiuscumque alterius potentiae, qui   605
solum sunt virtuosi extrinsece secundum quandam denominatio-
nem extrinsecam per conformitatem ad actum aliquem intrinsece
virtuosum, quia tales actus possunt semper idem remanere et circumstantiae variari, sicut idem potest esse actus volendi aliquid
et intelligendi et ambulandi propter bonum finem et malum, et   610
cum recta ratione et contra rectam rationem; et ideo respectu
talium dicuntur proprie esse circumstantiae. Sed actus qui est intrinsece et necessario bonus, non esset idem variata quacumque
circumstantia, quia variato obiecto, non potest actus esse idem
propter transitum a contradictorio in contradictorium; et ideo   615
respectu talis actus non sunt proprie circumstantiae. Vel si dicatur
omnino quod sic, tunc dicuntur circumstantiae quia non sunt
obiecta principalia sed secundaria, saltem aliquae, licet finis sit
obiectum principale.

Ad a l i u d[78] dico quod idem actus potest habere diversas   620
denominationes, ut terminatur ad diversa obiecta. De hoc quaere
in quarto O c k h a m, quaestione de poenitentia.[79]

[Solutio dubii tertii]

Ad tertium dubium[80] dico quod actus exterior non habet propriam bonitatem, sicut imaginatur I o a n n e s. De hoc quaere   625
in *Quolibet* Ioannis, et responsionem O c k h a m ad argumenta
Ioannis in tertio, in materia de virtutibus moralibus.[81]

[Solutio dubii quarti]

Ad quartum dubium dico quod P h i l o s o p h u s intel-
ligit quod in parte sensitiva sunt aliqui habitus ponendi, qui in-   630
clinat ad actus virtuosus, non intrinsece, sed solum extrinsece,
sicut prius dictum est.[82]

---

77. Lines 20–22 above.
78. Lines 22–28 above.
79. Cf. OTh VII, 229; OTh VIII, 139.
80. Lines 30–34 above.
81. Cf. Scotus, *Quodl.* q.18 n.12, XXVI: 246–47; Ockham, OTh VI,
370, 375–80.
82. Cf. a.3 478–89; a.1 145–50; OTh VI, 368–69; Scotus, *Sent.* III
d.33 n.13, XV: 47–48.

601. In reply to the first argument of the second doubt,[77] I hold that these things are not circumstances but secondary objects of an intrinsically and necessarily virtuous act. They are, however, circumstances in respect to other acts, whether they are acts of will, of intellect, or of any other faculty whatever; they are circumstances in respect to acts that are extrinsically virtuous according to some extrinsic denomination by way of conformity to some intrinsically virtuous act. For such acts can always remain the same when circumstances vary. For example, the same act can will something or understand something on account of a good end and on account of a wicked end, both with right reason and contrary to right reason (the same thing can be said about an act like walking). Therefore, in respect to such acts, these are properly called circumstances. But an act that is intrinsically and necessarily good would not remain the same when any circumstance varied. For once the object varies, it cannot be the same act on account of the transition from one contradictory to another. Therefore, in respect to such an [intrinsically good] act, these are not properly called circumstances. Or if someone is determined to say that they are, then they are circumstances because they are not principle but secondary objects; at least some of them are, although the end [for the sake of which an act is performed] is the principal object.

620. In reply to the other argument,[78] I hold that the same act can have different denominations, insofar as it terminates at different objects. On this question, see Ockham's commentary on book 4, the question on penitence.[79]

[Reply to the Third Doubt]

624. In reply to the third doubt,[80] I hold that an exterior act does not have its own goodness, as John imagines. Concerning this, see John's *Quodlibet* and Ockham's reply to John's arguments in the commentary on book 3, the material on moral virtues.[81]

[Reply to the Fourth Doubt]

629. In reply to the fourth doubt, I say that the Philosopher understood that some habits belong to the sensitive faculty, habits that incline us not to intrinsically virtuous acts but only to extrinsically virtuous acts, as was indicated previously.[82]

[Solutio dubii quinti]

Ad quintum dico quod respectu obiecti supernaturalis potest
esse virtus moralis, immo nulla est perfecta virtus nisi inclinet ad   635
actum respectu obiecti supernaturalis, sicut prius ostensum est.[83]
Philosophus tamen non poneret virtutem moralem esse respectu
obiecti supernaturalis sicut nos ponimus, quia non ponit quod
abstinentia vel continentia sit volenda propter honorem divinum
tamquam propter finem, — nec talia et similia sunt praecepta a   640
Deo —, quo modo bonus christianus vult talia, sed tantum ponit[84]
talia esse volenda quia honesta vel conservativa naturae vel aliquid
aliud mere naturale.

Et ex hoc sequitur quod virtus moralis quam poneret philosophus et bonus christianus differunt specie, non solum numero,   645
secundum praedicta,[85] quia universaliter quorum obiecta totalia
vel partialia differunt specie, illorum actus et habitus differunt
specie; sed Deus non est eiusdem speciei cum quacumque creatura;
cum igitur Deus sit obiectum cuiuscumque actus perfecte virtuosi
quem eliceret bonus christianus, et non sit obiectum alicuius actus   650
virtuosi quem eliceret philosophus vel paganus, sequitur quod illi
actus et habitus differunt specie.

[Solutio dubii sexti]

Ad sextum dico[86] quod illa probatio non est universalis, nec
probat universaliter quod notitia principii et conclusionis et noti-   655
tiae quarumcumque conclusionum differunt specie. Sed bene probat quod notitiae aliquarum conclusionum differunt specie, quia
notitiae conclusionum contrariarum necessario differunt specie,
puta notitiae istarum 'omnis triangulus habet tres', 'nullus triangulus habet tres' vel similium, quia error istius 'omnis triangulus'   660
etc. bene stat cum scientia istius 'nullus triangulus' etc., sed non
stat cum notitia istius 'omnis triangulus' etc. Sed ad hoc oportet
plus addere antequam inferatur distinctio specifica inter notitias,
scilicet quod isti errores differant specie, quod potest inferri ex
hoc q u o d isti errores sunt contrarii, v e l habent obiecta   665
distincta specie.

---

83. A.2 137–51.
84. Cf. a.2 155–56, 116–23.
85. A.1 60–97; a.3 337–41; cf. OTh VII, 58.
86. Cf. Scotus, *In Metaph.* VI q.1 n.4, VII: 305; ed. St. Bonaventure
n.20–21; Ockham, OTh I, 215–17; OTh VI, 287–89.

[Reply to the Fifth Doubt]

634. In reply to the fifth doubt, I hold that there can be moral virtue in respect to a supernatural object. Indeed, no virtue is perfect unless it inclines us to an act in respect to a supernatural object, as was shown above.[83] The Philosopher, however, would not posit moral virtue in respect to a supernatural object as we do, since he does not suppose that the end of an act of willing abstinence or continence should be God's honor as does a good Christian, who wills such acts. Nor does the Philosopher[84] suppose that these and similar [ethical precepts] are commanded by God. Instead, he supposes that such acts should be willed simply because they are worthy or preserve [human] nature or for some other merely natural end.

644. From this it follows that moral virtue as posited by the Philosopher and by a good Christian differ specifically, not just numerically, as has been indicated.[85] For it is universally true that whenever total or partial objects are specifically distinct, the corresponding acts and habits differ specifically. But God is not specifically the same as any creature whatever. Since, therefore, God is the object of any perfectly virtuous act elicited by a good Christian, and he is not the object of any virtuous act a philosopher or a pagan might elicit, it follows that those acts and habits differ specifically.

[Reply to the Sixth Doubt]

654. In reply to the sixth doubt,[86] I hold that that proof is not universal, it does not universally prove that knowledge of a principle differs specifically from knowledge of the conclusion; nor does it prove that knowledges of any conclusions whatever differ specifically. But it does satisfactorily prove that knowledges of some conclusions differ specifically, since knowledges of contrary conclusions necessarily differ specifically—for example, knowledges of these propositions 'every triangle has three [sides],' 'no triangle has three [sides],' or of similar propositions. For error in regard to the proposition 'every triangle,' etc., is quite compatible with scientific knowledge of the proposition 'no triangle,' etc., but not with knowledge of the proposition 'every triangle,' etc. But we must add more before we infer a specific distinction between knowledges—namely, that these errors differ specifically, and this can be inferred from the fact that these errors are contraries, or have specifically distinct objects.

Exemplum p r i m i[87] in proposito: errores istarum duarum
conclusionum 'omnis triangulus' etc. et 'nullus triangulus' etc.
differunt specie, quia contrariantur; quia impossibile est quod aliquis habeat habitum erroris quo firmiter assentiat quod omnis   670
triangulus etc., et habitum erroris quo firmiter assentiat quod
nullus triangulus etc., quia isti assensus formaliter repugnant.

Exemplum s e c u n d i:[88] error circa principium et conclusionem, et circa duas conclusiones disparatas omnino vel quantum
ad aliquem terminum subiectum vel praedicatum, sic sunt alterius   675
speciei, non propter repugnantiam formalem, quia simul stant,
sed quia unus error habet obiectum totale vel partiale distinctum
specie ab obiecto alterius erroris, quia in quolibet principio accipitur ad minus aliquis terminus distinctus specie ab aliquo termino
conclusionis, et eodem modo de conclusionibus disparatis totaliter   680
vel partialiter.

Et tunc, habito quod errores distinguuntur specie, sequitur
necessario quod notitiae eorundem obiectorum, respectu quorum
sunt errores, distinguuntur specie. Et per istam viam potest probari quod notitia principii et conclusionis distinguuntur specie,   685
quia obiecta, quia errores, distinguuntur specie, — quia universaliter quorum obiecta distinguuntur specie, ipsa inter se distinguuntur specie —, et similiter, quia obiecta istarum notitiarum distinguuntur specie. Et ita tenet ratio I o a n n i s.

Et eodem modo potest[89] probari distinctio specifica inter duas   690
virtutes, quia vitia contraria distinguuntur specie. Et hoc probatur
vel per repugnantiam formalem vitiorum, si aliqua talis sit, vel
propter distinctionem specificam obiectorum vitiorum vel virtutum. Sed odium Sortis et Platonis nec distinguuntur specie uno
modo nec alio, ideo nec istae dilectiones distinguuntur specie. Et   695
sic patet ad illud.

S e d s e m p e r remanet dubium, si ista odia sint eiusdem speciei, quomodo unum odium plus repugnat dilectioni Sortis
quam aliud, ex quo omnino sunt eiusdem speciei. R e s p o n-
d e o[90] . . .   700

---

87. That is, an example of contrary errors.
88. Namely, errors whose objects are specifically distinct.
89. Lines 52–56 above.
90. The reply is missing.

667. An example of the first kind[87] considered here follows: Errors in regard to these two conclusions—'every triangle,' etc., and 'no triangle,' etc.—differ specifically because they are contraries. For it is impossible for someone to have an erring habit by virtue of which he firmly assents to the proposition that 'every triangle,' etc., and [also] an erring habit by which he firmly assents that 'no triangle,' etc., since these assents are formally incompatible.

673. Example of the second kind:[88] Error concerning a principle and a conclusion, and error concerning two entirely disparate conclusions, or conclusions disparate as to some subject or predicate term. Such errors of different species are thus compatible; they are not specifically distinct on account of formal incompatibility because they are compatible. Instead, they are specifically distinct, because one error has a total or partial object that is specifically distinct from the object of the other. For any principle includes at least one term that is specifically distinct from some term in the conclusion; and the same can be said about totally or partially disparate conclusions.

682. Accordingly, given that the errors are specifically distinct, it necessarily follows that the knowledges of the objects in respect to which they are errors are specifically distinct. And in this way we can prove that knowledges of the principle and the conclusion are specifically distinct. They are distinct because the objects—[that is], because the errors—are specifically distinct (for it is universally true that things whose objects are specifically distinct are themselves specifically distinct), and similarly because the objects of these knowledges are specifically distinct. Thus John's argument holds.

690. In the same manner, a specific distinction between two virtues[89] can be proven, since their contrary vices are specifically distinct. This is proved either by virtue of the formal incompatibility of the vices (if there is that sort of incompatibility), or on account of the specific distinction of the objects of vices and virtues. But hatred of Socrates and of Plato are not specifically distinct in one way or the other, therefore neither are these loves specifically distinguished. The reply to that doubt is evident accordingly.

697. But the doubt always remains: If these hatreds are specifically the same, how is one hatred more incompatible with love of Socrates than the other, since they are altogether the same species? I reply[90] . . .

[Solutio dubii septimi]

Ad septimum[91] dico, sicut supra patet in quibusdam dubitationibus de ista materia,[92] quod perseverantia non dicit distinctum
gradum virtutis a continentia et temperantia. Quaere ibi.

S e d q u o m o d o continentia et temperantia continentur   705
sub gradibus virtutum prius assignatis? R e s p o n d e o quod
continentur necessario sub illis ut sunt actus virtuosi, quia si aliquis est continens vel temperatus virtuose, vel est continens conformiter secundum rectam rationem et propter honestatem, vel
sic quod non vult dimittere continentiam pro quocumque quod est   710
contra rectam rationem, vel praecise quia sic dictatur a ratione,
vel propter honorem Dei cum aliis circumstantiis, vel habet continentiam generatam ex actibus imperativis exsecutionum quae
excedunt communem naturam hominum; et sive sic sive sic, semper continetur sub gradibus praedictis.   715

Tamen aliquis potest habere continentiam et temperantiam
quae nullo modo continentur sub gradibus praedictis, puta si aliquis velit continere vel esse temperatus propter nullam circumstantiam bonam vel malam, v e l si velit continere propter malam circumstantiam. Primus non continetur sub praedictis, quia   720
est actus indifferens, nec bonus nec malus moraliter, modo prius
dicto.[93] Secundus non continetur, quia est actus vitiosus, et prae-
dicti sunt actus virtuosi.

[Solutio dubii octavi]

Ad ultimum dico quod in omni genere virtutis contingit repe-   725
rire virtutem heroicam, quia propter actum cuiuslibet generis virtutis potest quis imperare formaliter exsecutionem alicuius actus
qui est contra inclinationem naturae. Sed aliquis potest imperare
exsecutionem actus v e l sic quod imperet exsecutionem actus
causati a seipso vel in se sine aliqua violentia vel molestia sibi il-   730
lata ab aliquo alio homine extrinseco, sicut quidam imperator[94]
propter iustitiam servandam et legem, quam statuerat in aliis,
eruit sibi oculum. Iste actus, quo imperavit exsecutionem illius
actus, non est actus fortitudinis nec generativus fortitudinis, sed
solum est actus generativus iustitiae heroicae. Similiter aliquis   735
propter castitatem servandam, semper abstinet a vino et carnibus,

---

91. Lines 58–62 above.
92. Cf. Ockham, OTh VIII, 275.
93. A.2 200–210.
94. Cf. Vincentius Bellovacensis, *Speculum Doct.* IV c.66 (Douai,
1624), col. 337 E.

[Reply to the Seventh Doubt]

702. In reply to the seventh doubt,[91] I hold that perseverance does not indicate a degree of virtue distinct from continence and temperance, as was evident in certain doubts concerning this subject.[92] See the discussion there.

705. But how are continence and temperance contained within the degrees of virtues previously assigned? I reply that they are necessarily contained within those degrees, insofar as they are virtuous acts. For if someone is continent and temperate virtuously, he is either (1) continent in conformity with right reason and on account of worthiness; or (2) in such a way that he does not intend to give up continence for anything whatever that is contrary to right reason; or (3) precisely because it is dictated by reason; or (4) on account of God's honor together with other circumstances; or (5) his continence is generated by imperative, executive acts that exceed common human nature. Whatever the case, it is always contained within the aforesaid degrees.

716. Yet someone could be continent and temperate in a manner that is in no way be contained within the aforesaid degrees. For example, someone might will continence or temperance on account of no circumstance, good or bad, or on account of a wicked circumstance. The first act is not contained within the aforesaid degrees, since it is an indifferent act, neither morally good nor morally bad, in the manner previously described.[93] The second act is not contained, since it is a vicious act, and the aforesaid degrees pertain to virtuous acts.

[Reply to the Eighth Doubt]

725. In reply to the last doubt, I hold that heroic virtue may be found in every genus of virtue. For one can direct the formal execution of any act that is contrary to a natural inclination for the sake of an act in any genus of virtue. But someone can direct the execution of such an act [in more than one circumstance]. In one sense, a person could direct the execution of an act caused by herself against her own person without any violence or any harm inflicted on her by someone else, an external agent. For example, a certain emperor[94] tore out his own eye in order to preserve justice and maintain the law that he had established for others. The act in which he directed the execution of that act is not an act of courage, nor does it generate courage. Instead, it is an act that generates only heroic justice. Similarly, one person always abstains from wine and meat in order to preserve chastity, while

et aliquis[95] abscindit sibi verenda; et actus imperativi istarum exsecutionum non sunt actus fortitudinis, sed sunt actus temperantiae heroicae; et sic de aliis.

    A l i o m o d o, potest imperare exsecutionem actus causati   740
ab alio vel a se propter aliquam molestiam sibi illatam ab alio
propter actum virtutis, sicut sustinere vulnera nisi dimittat actum
iustitiae, et carcerem nisi dimittat actum temperantiae; et tales
sunt actus fortitudinis heroicae, et ad illos inclinant iustitia et
temperantia modo supradicto. Cetera quaere alibi, de materia mo-   745
rali.[96]

---

95. For example, regarding Origen, cf. Vincentius Bellovacensis,
Speculum Hist. XI c.9 (Douai, 1624), col. 415b.
    96. Cf. Ockham, OTh VIII, 275–76, 285–86.

another person castrates himself;[95] the acts directing the execution of these acts are not acts of courage; instead, they are acts of heroic temperance. And the same can be said in other cases.

740. In another sense, a person can direct the execution of an act caused by himself or someone else on account of some harm inflicted on him by another person for the sake of a virtuous act. For example, [a person wills] to sustain injuries unless she discharges an act of justice, and to undergo imprisonment unless she discharges an act of temperance. Such acts are acts of heroic courage; justice and temperance incline us to perform them in the manner described above. For all other questions, see [the treatment] elsewhere, on morality.[96]

P A R T
T H R E E

Commentary

On Medieval Psychology

Ockham begins by establishing six basic conclusions regarding virtuous acts. A medieval Aristotelian, he assumes that virtues are states or habits; he distinguishes between acts and habits of virtue. Ockham speaks of eliciting acts and producing habits. Habits are modifications in a subject produced naturally by acts; they are the effects of acts on the soul. But habits are also dispositions that act as causes; they incline the soul to elicit the same kind of acts that originally produced the habits in question. 'Habit' can refer to any modification of a faculty, including the behavioral dispositions of athletes. In moral theory, however, we are concerned with volitional and/or intellectual habits—with the sort of habits that prompt us to act worthily or unworthily.

Modern English distinguishes sharply between character (the state resulting from habituation) and training (the process of habituation). By contrast, medievals, following Aristotle's example, use forms of the same word to describe moral development; they translate the terms 'êthos' and 'ethismos' with the noun (*habitus*) and the verb (*habituare*).[1] Unlike classical Aristotelians, however, medievals also allow for habits produced

---

1. C. Kalinowski discusses the ambiguities of Aristotle's usage of the term translated as habit in "La Théorie aristotélicienne des habitus intellectuels," *Revue des sciences philosophiques et théologiques* 43 (1959): 248–60.

For a discussion of medieval Aristotelian views on habits current before Aristotle's ethical works themselves were available, see C. Nederman, "Nature, Ethics, and the Doctrine of 'Habitus': Aristotelian Moral Psychology in the Twelfth Century," *Traditio* 45 (1989–90): 87–110; and M. Colish, "*Habitus* Revised: A Reply to Cary Nederman," *Traditio* 48 (1993): 77–92.

not naturally by training but supernaturally by grace; they reserve the term 'character' for indelible, supernaturally infused habits. Aquinas refers to the characters of baptism, confirmation, and ordination. Nonetheless, the resemblances between medieval Scholastics and Aristotle are more important than the differences. Like Aristotle, medieval Aristotelians emphasize the role of stable states (habits) of the soul in understanding moral questions. And what we call character is the product of habits in their view.

Talk of habits and acts is just as relevant to the theoretical as to the practical realm of morals. Knowledge, doubt, and opinion are habits of the soul in just the same way as moral and theological virtues—such as justice and charity. For this reason, when discussing habits and acts generally, arguments about cognitive habits and acts are just as appropriate as arguments about appetitive habits and acts. Indeed, Ockham more frequently uses cognitive than appetitive habits as examples.

To a person accustomed to modern psychological theory, the terminology of Aristotelian habit-based moral theory may sound arcane, but in fact commonsense moral discourse frequently assumes the existence of virtuous dispositions—that is, Aristotelian habits. When we speak of an honest person, we are not referring simply to a person who has acted honestly at least once in the past; we are also expressing a belief that that person has a propensity to honest actions and can be expected to continue acting honestly in the future. Virtues are not mere behavioral tropisms, either. They involve judgment and considered values, and they are produced in certain characteristic ways. We presume that honesty is ordinarily the result of training and part of an established pattern of behavior, a disposition that will normally reveal itself in the appropriate circumstances.[2]

If we are to consider the virtues of prudence, courage, justice, and temperance in terms of habits, we must establish what kind of habit we are dealing with and what makes one habit different from another. Since this is a treatise about the connection of the virtues, Ockham also has to consider whether and how the possession and practice of one virtue strengthens another. He assumes that his readers will agree that prudence is an intellectual virtue produced by the exercise of right reason, while justice, courage, and temperance are volitional, moral virtues.

---

2. A good discussion of the Aristotelian theory of habits is provided in Myles Burnyeat's "Aristotle on Learning to Be Good," in *Essays on Aristotle's Ethics,* ed. A. Rorty (Berkeley-Los Angeles, 1980), 69–92.

Ockham's initial conclusion is that moral virtues are independent at the level of ordinary virtue. Ordinary justice and temperance are essentially distinct and unrelated virtues, not produced by specifically the same acts. Also, prudence without moral virtue is possible, supposing we do not will in accordance with the dictates of prudence. But moral virtue without prudence would be a contradiction in terms, since following the dictates of right reason is part of the definition of moral virtue. Ockham denies that justice and temperance are part of a single unified habit of moral virtue; rather, there are many kind of moral knowledge or prudences and correspondingly many virtues. For example, because the virtues are not necessarily connected, we find honest people who cannot control a drinking problem. Exercising the habit of justice by always giving correct change at the cash register does not produce temperance, the habit of eating and drinking in moderation. There are only coincidental connections between ordinary virtues—as, for example, when a cashier finds that drinking on the job often leads to mistakes in calculating the correct change.

On the other hand, extraordinary virtues, those of the philosopher as well as the Christian, are connected. That is because the total object of true virtue as practiced by philosophers includes not just conformity with right reason, but also willing virtuous acts precisely because they conform with right reason. Similarly, perfect Christian virtuous acts are performed precisely for the sake of the love of God. Take the cashier: if she tries to give correct change because she is determined to follow the dictates of right reason, then, even if drinking does not interfere with her work, she will find that she is inclined to follow right reason when it dictates temperance. If her primary motivation for being just is commitment to follow right reason, then she can be expected to follow the dictates of right reason wherever she encounters them.

| Prefatory Conclusions

| First Conclusion

9. Ockham's first conclusion establishes his basic principle: Different acts produce different habits. But where the effects are different, their causes must be different. On this basis he will argue that each of the different degrees of virtuous acts that he posits is specifically different from the others.

Ockham proves inductively that habits in regard to intellectual objects differ.[1] Everyone acknowledges that a simple, abstract intellectual apprehension of an individual donkey differs from knowledge of complex general conclusions about donkeys — such as 'donkeys are mammals.' Here the word 'complex' does not mean "complicated"; it refers to mental constructs, produced by combining simple terms. Strictly speaking, 'incomplex' refers to single terms — either spoken, written, or mentally grasped; 'complex' refers to combinations of terms. Speaking more broadly, as Ockham usually does, 'incomplex' can also refer to combinations of terms — such as 'white musician' or 'this science,' while 'complex' refers to a combination of a noun and a verb that produces understanding (OTh II, 148–50). Accordingly, incomplex knowledge is an act by which someone apprehends a single object — or objects — but forms no propositions (OTh V, 280–81). By contrast, complex knowledge ordinarily refers to knowledge of a proposi-

---

1. The best recent work on Ockham's views on thought and its objects is by Elizabeth Karger. In addition to articles listed in Beckmann's bibliography, see, for example, "Théories de la pensée, de ses objets et son discours chez Guillaume d'Occam," *Dialogue* 33 (1994): 437–56.

tion. I have translated 'complexum' as 'propositional knowledge,' since Ockham's examples are propositions—such as 'Socrates is a man.' But a combination of words (what is called an enunciable in medieval logic and semantics), such as 'that Socrates is a man,' can function as a term in a proposition. For example, 'I know that Socrates is a man' also counts as *complexum* (OTh I, 7–10). For the point he is making here, Ockham only needs to establish that the cognitive habit that results from abstractly apprehending donkeys is specifically different from the habitual knowledge that arises from assenting to the proposition, 'donkeys are mammals.'

41. Ockham strengthens the first conclusion with an argument from Scotus about the difference between the habits by virtue of which we know premises and conclusions. A person can know geometrical premises without realizing what conclusions can be deduced from those premises.[2] Knowing the premise is not the same as knowing the conclusion. This is contrasted with acts regarding the same object. A person cannot know a premise and be ignorant of it at the same time, from which it follows that numerically different acts of knowing a given premise are specifically the same, unlike the different acts by which we know the premise and the conclusion. In ethics, a parallel argument might be based on the fact that knowing generally that we should love our neighbors is not the same as knowing that we should financially support shelters for street people.

Here the reader may be puzzled by the phrase 'dispositional ignorance,' a phrase that Ockham assumes his reader will understand. As is so often the case, a glance at Scotus clarifies what he has in mind. In his *Metaphysics* commentary (I q.4 n.80), Scotus distinguishes three kinds of ignorance: simple, dispositional, and negative. Negative ignorance is the most basic; it occurs when the terms of a judgment are not apprehended. Simple ignorance occurs when no judgment is based on apprehended terms, and dispositional ignorance is a false judgment. Ockham specifies dispositional ignorance because it has the same object as scientific knowledge; it is dissenting from a true proposition. Ultimately, this distinction comes from Aristotle, *Posterior Analytics* 1.16.79b23–28.

50. Ockham establishes in the first conclusion that the habits produced by different acts differ from each other. But Ockham

---

2. 'Know scientifically' (*scire*) refers to the Aristotelian concept of science in terms of logical demonstrations from first principles.

does not want to say that there are as many habits as there are acts. Rather, he claims that acts which are specifically the same produce specifically the same habits. If the subject and object are the same, specifically distinct acts can produce numerically the same habit; if the subjects are different, the habits can only be specifically the same. The knowledge that I acquire by apprehending a Euclidean axiom is specifically the same knowledge that you acquire when learning geometry; we have the same habit of knowledge. Similarly, Henry and Megan can both exercise specifically the same virtue when they give correct change at the cash register.

Moreover, not every difference in objects corresponds to a specific distinction in acts and habits. Here an incomplex act provides a good example. Knowing a conclusion may be specifically different from knowing a premise, but seeing three numerically distinct donkeys is not like knowing three different geometrical conclusions; it does not produce three specifically different, incomplex apprehensions of the terms 'animal' or 'donkey.' Stated precisely:

1. Specifically the same objects produce specifically the same acts.
2. Specifically the same acts produce numerically the same habit in numerically the same subject.
3. Specifically the same acts produce specifically the same, but numerically distinct, habits in numerically distinct subjects.
4. But specifically distinct acts produce specifically distinct habits.

Four is Ockham's main point.

I Second Conclusion

60. Having established in the first conclusion that specific differences between habits result from specifically distinct acts, Ockham establishes in the second conclusion how acts differ specifically. His basic intuition is that acts differ primarily in terms of their objects. But as we saw above, the same act can have different partial objects, and a person can even apprehend more than one object in a single incomplex act of knowledge (OTh V, 280–81), as, for example, when I look out my window and see both a dog and a cat. For Ockham, acts often have very complex objects, and it might have been helpful if at this point he had begun a discussion of partial and total acts, as he will subsequently do in reply to the sixth doubt (a.4 677). The claim would then be that acts are specifically distinct if they have different partial objects or if their total objects are specifically distinct. Instead,

Ockham presents an a fortiori argument: Acts are in fact distinct; but if acts with specifically distinct objects belonged to the same species, there would be no basis at all for distinguishing acts specifically; therefore acts with specifically distinct objects must be specifically distinct. This is an argument from experience. Knowing how to cook does not make it easier to do astronomy, and the converse is also true.

Here Ockham establishes that even acts with specifically the same total objects can be specifically distinct, an argument based on cognitive acts. He treats complex and incomplex acts separately. Ockham contrasts abstractive and intuitive cognition of the same incomplex object. He distinguishes between intuitive cognition and abstract cognition in terms of their results. Intuitive cognition is the immediate apprehension by virtue of which we know evidently that a thing exists; abstract cognition does not produce a judgment about existence (OTh I, 30–38). My knowledge of a cat who is present now is different from my knowledge of the same cat when she is absent. Ockham's example of different acts in regard to the same complex object involves knowing and doubting. Doubting the truth of a Euclidean proposition differs from knowing its truth on the basis of a geometric demonstration. A complex object from ethical theory might be the proposition that 'abortion should be prohibited by the state, for sake of the life of the fetus at all stages of pregnancy, without regard to the circumstances of conception or the pregnant woman's life situation.' Though they have the same partial object, the assent of a priest and the dissent of a women's rights advocate are not specifically the same act, though they would be specifically (though not numerically) the same act if the two agreed on the purpose and extent of the prohibition.

I Third Conclusion

99. His discussion about the relation of acts and habits completed, Ockham begins his discussion of imputability. Conclusions 3 to 6 discuss what makes acts virtuous or praiseworthy. The third conclusion states Ockham's central thesis: There is some act that is necessarily and intrinsically virtuous. He argues that contingently virtuous acts presuppose the existence of necessarily virtuous acts, and similarly there can be no extrinsically virtuous acts without intrinsically virtuous acts. In fact, only an argument for a necessarily virtuous act (or acts) is presented, but the argument for an intrinsically virtuous act would have the same form; such an argument is presented in Ockham's commentary on book 3 of

Lombard's *Sentences* (OTh VI, 383–87), where examples of intrinsically virtuous and vicious acts are provided. Both arguments are analogous with the cosmological argument for the existence of God,[3] which in its most simplified form shows that if there are secondary causes, there must be a first cause. There is a considerable body of literature about the same strengths and weaknesses of such arguments based on the impossibility of an infinite regress, which the reader may wish to consult.

As Ockham states the conclusion, it is an argument for the actual existence of such a necessarily virtuous act, and that means he assumes the actual existence of contingently virtuous acts. He could have, but has not, restricted himself to a conditional argument: If there are contingently virtuous acts, then there must be necessarily virtuous acts. But though Ockham is committed to the assumption that some contingently virtuous act exists, he need not claim that any given act necessarily exists. So this assumption is consistent with Ockham's claim that no creaturely act exists necessarily.

According to Ockham, contingently virtuous acts are morally neutral or indifferent acts performed in conformity with necessarily virtuous acts. We could not say that such acts are virtuous because they conform to other contingently virtuous acts, because that would produce an infinite regress. Cutting someone's hair is an example of an indifferent or contingently virtuous act that Ockham might have used. Suppose Cynthia cuts hair. If she cuts hair to obtain money and she uses the money to buy extra clothes, her action is morally indifferent. But if she needs the clothes to stage a benefit for the homeless, she is acting virtuously. By itself, cutting hair is neither virtuous nor vicious. If done for the sake of a morally indifferent end, or even a series of morally indifferent ends, we would not call it virtuous; only Cynthia's virtuous resolution to be charitable makes cutting hair virtuous. No description of the act in terms of other indifferent acts (even infinitely many indifferent acts) would justify calling it virtuous. But we would call the act virtuous if it were done for the sake of being worthy, or in conformity with a necessarily virtuous act. We do correctly describe some indifferent acts as virtuous, therefore there must be necessarily virtuous acts.

113. Neither Ockham nor any other member of the philosophical tradition to which he belongs considers it appropriate to demonstrate the existence of virtuous acts. What Ockham proves

---

3. I owe this point to Marilyn McCord Adams.

instead is the existence of indifferent acts, interior and exterior. Going to church is a virtuous exterior act if it is done for a proper end. It is virtuous only contingently because it is possible to go to church for wicked purposes; indeed, someone could start for church for the sake of prayer and decide on the way to use the occasion of church attendance not for prayer, but to vilify the neighbors. The same external act could start as a virtuous act and finish as a vicious one. Ockham's example of an indifferent internal act is similar: philosophical speculation that is begun for a virtuous end and continued for an improper purpose.

124. The conclusion justified by this argument is that there is some necessarily virtuous act; the more ambitious conclusion that Ockham actually states introduces a number of new concepts—"primarily virtuous," "primarily praiseworthy," and "in perfect circumstances." Essential to his definition of a necessarily virtuous act, most of the new concepts are explained subsequently. An exception is the use of the term 'primarily.' The meaning of "primarily virtuous" must be inferred from the example that Ockham provides: willing to do something because it is divinely commanded. Willing to obey the creator is the chief worthy act, the most proper act a creature can perform. In our haircutting example, we were satisfied that the act was virtuous when it was described as an act performed for a worthy purpose. And that was correct, but willing worthy ends is not the primary virtuous act for Ockham; the primary virtuous act is willing the highest good—or its equivalents, loving God or willing obedience to divine precept.

There are also some important stipulations about what 'necessarily virtuous' implies. According to Ockham, this concept refers to acts that cannot be vicious. Such acts produce habits or capacities that cannot be abused, cannot produce vicious acts. Ockham cites the authority of Augustine in support of the view that there are such virtues. Cited implicitly is Lombard's famous definition of virtue, a good quality of the mind that no one can misuse, since it is God acting in us.[4] Absent is Lombard's positive claim that virtue is the means by which we live rightly. The other half of the definition may be reflected in a second condition for necessarily virtuous acts, which Ockham states elsewhere: "They cannot be caused by the will except virtuously" (OTh IX, 255).

Both conditions are stated using negatives—'cannot be willed except virtuously,' 'cannot be used viciously'—because

---

4. Lombard, *Sent.* II d.27 c.1 n.1, I: 480.

Ockham qualifies the claim that there are necessarily virtuous acts. According to Ockham, absolutely speaking, no act is necessarily virtuous, for two reasons: First, because no creaturely act exists necessarily; there is no necessarily virtuous act, since the existence of all creaturely acts is contingent. Second, because of Ockham's imputability theory; he believes that no one can be praised or blamed for actions they do not control, and he also believes that it is logically possible for creaturely acts to be caused and controlled by God in a manner that would exclude their control by the creature involved (OTh VI, 389; VII, 225). In this situation, we would merely be instruments, not moral agents; even our acts of will would be morally indifferent. But the reader should note that Ockham believes that this situation does not obtain; we know from experience that God does not control us, that our wills are free (OTh IX, 88).

Unfortunately, Ockham also introduces a qualification that is incompatible with the concept of "necessarily virtuous" acts or habits: "given divine precept." It is a short, throw-away phrase that might have been added inadvertently, but it is found on more than one occasion (e.g., OTh IX, 255), and it is a potentially important mistake. If an act is virtuous only given divine precept, it is not necessarily virtuous; whether it is virtuous is contingent on divine command. As Adams has shown, understood in the most straightforward way, this qualification means that Ockham's "Intrinsic-Imputability theory is untenable" (Adams 1981, 30); the same act cannot be both necessarily and contingently virtuous.

Fortunately, another interpretation is possible. First, Ockham may not have finally intended the qualification. Dealing with precisely this sort of case, an act of some duration that can be rendered successively correct and faulty (*deformis*), Ockham says that the primary virtuous act, loving God above all, cannot be a faulty act (OTh IX, 260). Second, it seems likely that Ockham blurs the picture here, because he starts out thinking in terms of a number of intrinsically virtuous acts—acts such as willing justice or courage. He presents the act of willing something because of divine precept just as an example—presumably one among many. But in fact it will turn out to be the only necessarily virtuous act, strictly speaking. It is, as Ockham says, the primary virtuous act.

As Ockham develops the theory, the virtue of all other acts—even acts of willing worthiness—are contingent on divine command. Ockham establishes that there is only one kind of necessarily virtuous act, a primary virtuous act—willing something because God wills it—such that if a creature elicits it, it is necessarily virtuous; there are no circumstances in which it could be vicious. The other acts that Ockham, like the rest of us, normally considers necessarily virtuous are only necessarily virtuous given divine command. But since divine precept is fixed and immutable, and God eternally wills us to follow the dictates of right reason (OTh VIII, 428–31) and be worthy, there is still an important sense in which willing worthiness is necessarily virtuous, and any act in accord with the will to be worthy is so virtuous that it could not be abused.

∎ Fourth Conclusion

132. The fourth conclusion states that the primary, necessarily virtuous act must be an act of will.[5] In his first argument, Ockham introduces explicitly for the first time the distinction between intrinsically and extrinsically virtuous acts, which he defines in terms of the distinction between primary and secondary imputability. Kneeling in prayer is only secondarily praiseworthy—that is, praiseworthy only if undertaken in conformity with the will to worship. Adverting to his discussion of contingently virtuous acts in the third conclusion, Ockham concludes that only acts of will can be necessarily virtuous. All other acts could be made vicious without changing their nature in any way.

Ockham's final argument is based on the authority of the saints. Here Ockham's editor, Joseph Wey, cites Aquinas and Lombard in support of the view that no act is praised or blamed except on account of a good or bad intention. Strictly speaking, according to Aquinas, intentions are acts of will that aim at an end (ST I-II q.12 a.1), and so Ockham's conclusion that only acts of will are intrinsically virtuous can be justified from authority. But the reader should note that relatively few authorities agree with Abelard, Anselm, and Ockham that only the will sins.

By contrast, ancient moral thought emphasizes the connection between virtue and knowledge. In evaluating the roles of will and intellect in moral action, Ockham and other Franciscans assign primacy to will. Ockham's great Franciscan predecessor, Scotus, argues that will, not intellect, is the rational faculty of

---

5. Ockham's insistence that primary, necessarily and intrinsically virtuous acts must be acts of will anticipates Kant's claim that the only unqualified good is a good will. For an exciting account of medieval developments in the transformation of Aristotelian ethics in the direction of an ethics of good will, see B. Kent, *Virtues of the Will* (Washington, D.C., 1995).

the soul. The intellect is a natural faculty—that is, a faculty that is determined, not free but compelled by the evidence (Scotus, *Sent.* II d.7, XII: 407–8; Wodeham, *L. sec.* prol. q.6, I: 163). By contrast, the will is free; it fits the Aristotelian definition of a rational faculty, since it is capable of contrary effects (OTh VII: 358; Scotus, *In Metaph.* IX.15; *Quodl.* XVIII n.9, XXVI: 241–42, Alluntis a.2 n.24, 643; Aristotle, *Metaph.* 9.2.1046b4–6; but see also Scotus, *Sent.* III d.33 n.4, XV: 441). Going a step further, Ockham holds that only acts of will can be sinful or meritorious, virtuous or vicious.

Here Ockham's position is qualified in some ways, first because he maintains that will and intellect are not distinct; will is the soul willing and the intellect is the soul comprehending (OTh I, 396; VI, 368). So, strictly speaking, the last sentence, "only the will sins," may mislead. Also, though Ockham agrees that our intellective faculty is natural or determined while our volitional faculty is free, he allows that the intellect is free, in that acts of intellect are not coerced (OTh I, 501). Here Ockham stipulates that this is an improper sense of the term 'free.' The intellect is moved or acted on (OTh VI, 65), but only by its natural objects, which effectively cause intellection. Ordinarily, Ockham, like his Franciscan confreres, contrasts will and intellect as the free as opposed to the determined faculty (OTh VI, 356).

Ockham maintains the fourth conclusion not only against contemporaries who were more intellect-oriented than the Franciscans, but also against Scotus. Scotus argues that external acts as well as acts of will could be virtuous or vicious. He holds that going to church consists of two acts: one interior and the other exterior. Both can be virtuous, and the virtue associated with the external act is distinct from that associated with the internal act. Attendance at church is commanded, and it is within our control; therefore it is praiseworthy. By contrast, Ockham argues that the external act is not praiseworthy except by virtue of a praiseworthy internal act; going to church is praiseworthy only if we go for the purpose of obeying God. Church attendance for the sake of gossip is specifically different from the act of going to church to honor God. Both Scotus and Ockham agree that only voluntary acts can be virtuous, and both distinguish between different acts. But where Scotus distinguishes between internal and external acts and argues that both are morally significant, Ockham distinguishes between acts performed for different purposes and argues that the external act is an automatic, if not an unobstructable, consequence of the executive interior act and hence in itself morally indifferent. Going to church for gossip does not incline us to attend church for the purpose of worship. Only going to church for God's sake is virtuous. Attendance is virtuous only if we intend to worship; in itself, the external act is neither virtuous nor vicious; it is virtuous only if it is dictated by our intention to worship. External acts are virtuous only as manifestations of internal acts. Contrary to Scotus, Ockham holds that external acts cannot be intrinsically virtuous.

| Fifth Conclusion

145. The fifth conclusion supports the claim that only acts of will are necessarily (conclusion 3) and intrinsically (conclusion 4) praiseworthy or blameworthy, a conclusion for which Ockham has already argued in the fourth conclusion. The first argument restates the third conclusion, this time using a phrase characteristic of Ockham and Scotus, 'right will.' The walk to church can first be virtuous and then vicious if it is elicited first in conformity with right will and later in conformity with vicious will. Here we would expect to read 'virtuous will,' reserving the adjective 'right' to modify reason or judgment; using 'right' to modify 'will' is in keeping with the Franciscan move away from reason as a moral faculty. But elsewhere Ockham frequently uses the conventional Aristotelian phrase 'right reason' (e.g., a.3 495; OTh VI, 359).

The second argument is new and crucial in this context. The major premise includes a verbatim quotation from Augustine in support of the claim that we can only be praised or blamed for voluntary acts. Elsewhere, in defending the view that only voluntary acts are praiseworthy or blameworthy, Ockham can and does appeal to the authority of Aristotle as well as Augustine and Anselm (OTh VI, 366), citing book 3 of the *Nicomachean Ethics* (1.1109b30–31; 5.1114a26–27).

The thesis that only voluntary acts are imputable is not controversial; what is controversial is Ockham's further claim that all acts other than acts of will can be indifferently praised or blamed (158). External acts and acts of intellect are indifferent acts, according to Ockham, because they can be successively virtuous and vicious if performed first in conformity with a virtuous act of will and then in conformity with a vicious act of will. Moreover, the same act can first be voluntary and then involuntary. By contrast, acts of will are necessarily voluntary. Ockham concludes on this basis that only acts of will are intrinsically imputable—that is, without reference to another act.

Ockham claims that all acts other than acts of will are called virtuous only by reference to the acts of will that give rise to them—that is, by extrinsic denomination. The walk to church can start as a display of rich and opulent wardrobe and finish as the path to worship. It is virtuous only if our intentions are virtuous; the walk itself is only contingently virtuous. The same is true of intellectual acts: studying biology for the glory of God is virtuous; for the sake of vainglory, vicious. Viewed in abstraction from the purposes for which it is undertaken, the study of biology is neither virtuous nor vicious.

Prefatory Distinctions

First Distinction

2. Article 2 is a second beginning to *De connexione*. Ockham defines degrees of virtue and distinguishes the different meanings of prudence and moral science. He also distinguishes efficacious acts of will from good intentions. Finally, in the last three distinctions, he argues again for the same theses established in conclusions 3–6 of article 1.

Most generally understood, 'prudence' refers to any and all practical moral knowledge. Ockham distinguishes different definitions or modes of prudence in terms of its causes or its results. Does it proceed from our understanding of universal self-evident propositions or from particular experiences? Does it result in general practical knowledge or in moral knowledge with immediate application? Notice that when Ockham speaks of prudence as deduced from self-evident universal principles, he does not imply that we will learn virtues on our own, but rather that we will be taught to make these inferences (cf. also OTh VIII, 281, 283).

Ockham associates the first and most general definition of prudence with Augustine.[1] It includes universal self-evident propositions that we are taught as well as universal propositions evident from experience. It is the only definition of prudence that includes universal propositions with no immediate application. It

---

1. A tabular presentation of the the four different modes of prudence that Ockham describes here is presented below at the third distinction, where it is combined with the five degrees of virtue Ockham postulates. Thoughout *De connexione virtutum* Ockham returns repeatedly to these distinctions, so the reader may want to photocopy the table for use as a bookmark.

is mediately as well as immediately directive, comprised of immediately directive particular propositions, as well as mediately directive universal propositions. True, Ockham only gives examples of universal propositions, but that is because he will be giving examples of particular propositions when he discusses the next three definitions.

The second, third, and fourth definitions of prudence include only particular knowledge. Prudence 2 consists in conclusions which follow from self-evident universal propositions. Prudence 3 is evident from experience. Prudence 4 is the aggregate of 2 and 3 but does not include universal propositions, which are only mediately directive. Ockham's example of particular prudence—which is also moral science, strictly speaking—starts with what he takes to be a self-evident major premise: 'people who act generously deserve to be treated generously,' from which we could conclude that if Marilyn acts generously, she should be treated generously. Notice that 'people who act generously deserve to be treated generously' counts as part of prudence 1, but not prudence 2.

20. Prudence 3 is Aristotelian prudence (*phronesis*); it is quite different from Augustinian prudence, since it includes only immediately directive particular propositions evident from experience. Ockham contrasts *phronesis* strictly speaking with moral science strictly speaking.[2] Augustinian moral science includes *phronesis*. But there is no overlap between moral science strictly speaking and *phronesis*. Moral science strictly speaking must be based on self-evident propositions and can be universal; *phronesis* is particular and must be evident from experience. Ockham distinguishes "prudence" as the capacity to judge and respond rightly in particular cases from moral science as a deduction from general principles.

Here Ockham is consciously departing from Scotus (OTh VIII, 283–84), who simply contrasts universal moral science with particular prudence (*Ord.* I prol. p.5 q.1–2 n.351, I: 238). Ockham disagrees with Scotus, because he holds both that experience can result in knowledge of general principles and that particular directives follow from deductive moral science as well as from experience.

27. Prudence 4 is the aggregate of particular directives, whether derived from experience or general principles. Ockham's use of the word 'aggregate' reflects his disagreement with Aquinas, who holds that virtues form a unified whole rather than

---

2. Note that elsewhere Ockham makes other distinctions regarding science, most notably at OTh I, 76–87 and OPh IV, 6–10.

a mere aggregate. The virtues are unified because they proceed from a single habit of prudence. Disagreeing with Thomas, Henry held that there were many different kinds of prudence; he spoke of 'prudences,' a practice followed by Ockham. Awkward as it sounds, the translation follows Ockham's usage because it reflects his disagreement with Aquinas. According to Ockham, the accumulation of virtues is an aggregate whole, like the seven courses of a gourmet dinner, where one course is simply added on to the next without any of them depending on the others. Though they regulate every aspect of human life, the virtues do not themselves form a unified whole, like the biological organs that constitute a single living animal. Ockham argues that if the virtues were specifically the same, the virtue of temperance could not be present in the absence of the virtue of courage. But in fact the practice of temperance is compatible with a lack of courage in defense of the faith.

In holding that the virtues do not form a unified whole, Ockham is following Henry and Scotus, both of whom nonetheless followed Aristotle's commentator, Eustratius of Nicea, in characterizing the virtues as sisters who help each other (a.3 63; Scotus, *Ord.* III d.36 n.10, XV: 622, Wolter 392). Ockham does not employ this analogy, perhaps because he would not have agreed that all the sisters had the same parent. Had he accepted the analogy, he would have added that not every family has the same number of daughters; some people have faith without charity. For Ockham, the virtues are specifically distinct. They are compatible with each other, like whiteness and sweetness, but they do not have their source in the same prudence.

| Second Distinction

76. The second distinction helps Ockham defend his thesis that only acts of will, not external acts, can be intrinsically virtuous. Against Ockham's position, Scotus could argue that we value deeds themselves, not just the intention to do them; actually giving money to the poor is more valuable than the mere intention to be charitable. Ockham's distinction between equivalently imperative and formally imperative executive acts of will allows him to reply. He contrasts acts of will that actually determine action and acts of will that express only resolution.

In one sense, equivalently imperative and formally imperative acts of will have the same object (78)—for example, giving money to charity. But in another sense, they have different objects

(102). The presence of an obstacle makes it impossible rationally to will as if there were no obstacle. If you have no money, you cannot rationally intend to give a million dollars to charity, but only to give money if you have it. Suppose Jan vows to assist the homeless if she wins the lottery. That act is specifically distinct from her act of will when she is actually writing a check for a million dollars to Annunciation House. And as Ockham might say to Scotus, once she wins the lottery, if she sits down and writes that check and puts it in the mail, Jan's act of charity is no less valuable morally if the post office loses her check, provided she has no reason to believe that her check will be lost.

I Third Distinction

111. Here Ockham distinguishes five degrees of virtue—proceeding from ordinary virtuous acts to heroically virtuous acts. The first degree (116) has everything requisite to virtue: proper circumstances, a worthy act in conformity with right reason, and a good end. To will the performance of a just act in conformity with right reason for the sake of civic pride is such an act. The second degree of virtue is like the first, but in addition it requires the intention to persevere even if death is imminent. Here the reader should note that death is not actually imminent; the second degree of virtue requires only the conditional intention not to abandon justice regardless of consequences. It includes the same partial objects as first-degree virtue, and it adds a partial object—the conditional (or equivalently imperative) intention to overcome all possible obstacles. Second-degree virtue also begins the process of generalizing the commitment to right reason: it is unwillingness to give up willing a specific virtue for anything contrary to right reason.

132. The third and fourth degrees of virtue specify the end for which the virtuous act is performed. Third-degree virtue is the philosopher's virtue: the will to perform a just act, in the proper circumstances, for the sake of right reason. It is an act performed precisely because it is dictated by right reason. Fourth-degree virtue (137) is Christian virtue; fourth-degree virtues are performed precisely on account of love for God. Only fourth-degree virtue, Ockham says, is the perfect virtue, about which the saints speak. Fifth-degree virtue is heroic virtue (152). Like second-degree virtue, it differs from an earlier degree by requiring the resolve to persist in the face of adversity, but where the resolve required by second-degree virtue is conditional, since there is no actual danger, with fifth-degree virtue the resolve is actual (executive), since adversity is present. Since heroic virtue is possible for pagans, it is a higher degree of third-degree virtue (acts performed precisely for the sake of right reason) as well as a higher degree of fourth-degree virtue (acts performed precisely for love of God).

Mode 1	Mediate and immediately directive (universal or particular)	Self-evident propositions and propositions evident from experience and conclusions based on such propositions
Mode 2	Immediately directive	Taught by self-evident universal propositions
Mode 3	Immediately directive	Evident from experience
Mode 4	Immediately directive	Evident from experience and from self-evident propositions

THE FOUR MODES OF PRUDENCE

Degree 1	Willing the performance of a just work **1.** in conformity with right reason, **2.** in the proper circumstance respecting precisely this work, **3.** for the sake of the worthiness of the work as an end
Degree 2	Degree 1, together with the intention not to give up such a work for anything contrary to right reason, even to avoid death, if right reason tells us not to give up the work to avoid death, an equivalently imperative act of will
Degree 3	Degree 2, undertaken precisely and solely because it is so dictated by right reason
Degree 4	Degree 2 or 3, undertaken precisely and solely for the sake of love of God
Degree 5	Degree 2, 3, or 4, by a formally imperative act of will when such an act of will exceeds the common human state or is contrary to natural inclination

THE FIVE DEGREES OF VIRTUE

Ockham indicates explicitly that this is not a hierarchy of virtues in which the lower virtues are necessarily subsumed in the higher virtues. Using his terminology, the objects of the lower degrees need not be part of the total object of the higher degrees. Rather, as he says a little later (187–88), each higher degree has an object and/or a circumstance different from a lower degree. First-degree virtue is a partial object of every other degree of virtue; and second-, third-, or fourth-degree virtue is subsumed in fifth-degree virtue. But fourth-degree virtue need not be a partial object of fifth-degree virtue.

Moreover, though Ockham says that the intention to persist in the face of death characteristic of second-degree virtue is a partial object of third- or fourth-degree virtue, there seems to be no reason why this has to be the case. The object of first-degree virtue is a deed dictated by reason; the object of third-degree virtue, conformity with right reason. It is the difference between my not stealing Allen's Honda because I want be fair to him and not stealing because I want to obey the law. In the first case, I know the law prohibits theft, but fairness, not following the law, is my object. If I were virtuous in the second degree, as Ockham defines it, I would have to resolve not to steal even if threatened by death (supposing, as seems unlikely, that right reason would dictate that I should face death rather than steal a car). To achieve third-degree, I would make following the law, or rather the dictates of right reason, my principal aim; it seems I could do that without also resolving to make every sacrifice that right reason might require of me toward this end. But probably Ockham would disagree. He might say that if willing conformity with right reason were precisely why I refrained from stealing, then I would at least want to do whatever right reason dictated regardless of the consequences.

The juxtaposition of two ranking criteria—according to how much perseverance is required and according to the intrinsic value of the end—makes the hierarchy awkward. Perhaps Ockham should have defined two sets of degrees. As it presently stands, first-degree virtue is virtue properly speaking. Second- and fifth-degree virtue require supererogatory fortitude, either conditionally or actually. In third- and fourth-degree virtue, it is not enough for the end to be worthy; the end must be conformity with right reason or the will of God.

137. Ockham identifies fourth-degree virtue with necessary virtue, the virtue described by the saints, which cannot be abused (a.1 124–30)—that is, when elicited it cannot be vicious, since it is an act of loving God; its purpose is obedience to divine precept. Of course, fourth-degree virtue is also intrinsically virtuous—or virtuous by intrinsic denomination—but that is a characterization that Ockham would probably identify with third-degree virtue as well.

In his discussion of fourth-degree virtue, there is some imprecision in terminology (141), which may come from the reporter. What should be said is that only fourth-degree virtue is perfect. What is reported in the text is that only fourth-degree virtue is perfect and true, whereas Ockham in fact maintains that third-degree virtues are also true. A complementary misstatement occurs later (a.3 157), where Ockham says that both third- and fourth-degree virtues are perfect, when he means that both third- and fourth-degree virtues are true.

The two distinctions (between perfect and imperfect virtue and between true virtue and lesser degrees of virtue) are stated more clearly in Ockham's *Dialogus*. What makes virtues true are the ends at which they aim: true virtue is for the sake of right reason, or for the love of God. By contrast, perfect virtue is necessary virtue. Only virtuous acts performed for the love of God are perfectly or necessarily virtuous.

In his *Dialogus,* Ockham contrasts *true* pagan virtue with *perfect* Christian virtue. Both virtues have partial ends—love for God and the desire to conform to right reason—with universal moral significance that incline the soul to elicit other virtues in the appropriate circumstances. The difference between the two is that love of God is nobler than love of right reason. And more importantly, the will to obey God cannot be abused; while the desire to conform to right reason is not necessarily a reliable guide to virtue, since reason is fallible. The sanity of faith protects against ignorance, as the desire to conform to right reason cannot do (*Dial.* 1.VI.77, fol. 90r–v).

If the terminological imprecision at line 141 comes from Ockham himself, it may be because he develops the distinction between perfect and true virtues quite late. Earlier he followed Henry in identifying perfect virtue with heroic fifth-degree virtue (OTh VIII, 285). Or alternatively, the imprecision may also be occasioned by his appeal to the saints. The editor quite correctly refers to passages from *De civitate Dei* and *De Trinitate* in which Augustine claims that only truly virtuous acts are performed for the love of God. But Ockham is also implicitly referring to his earlier appeal to the authority of the saints on the subject of perfect virtue, which cannot be abused. Cited earlier in article 1 at the end of the third conclusion (129–30), this implicit reference is to *De libero arbitrio* on the subject of virtues that cannot be abused. The claim that there are perfect or necessarily virtuous acts is crucial to Ockham's central argument that the only morally significant acts are acts of will, and it is based on the appeal to the authority of the saints (a.1 129).

Ockham does not, however, follow Augustine in contrasting true Christian virtue with false pagan virtue. Rather, he contrasts necessarily virtuous Christian morality with contingently virtuous pagan morality. Ockham allows that simple pagans can act according to right reason without having a proper concept of the final end (a.3 339–41; OTh VII, 58). Here Ockham differs from a number of his Franciscan predecessors—such as Matthew of Aquasparta (fl. 1270–88; see BFS 1 [1957]: 96)—who simply deny that pagans can be virtuous. The difference should not be exaggerated, however, since according to Ockham only pagans who eschew idolatry can be virtuous (*Dial.* 1.VI.77, fols. 90v–91r).

143. As was indicated in the introduction, there is a great variety in the definitions of "perfect" virtue among Scholastics. For the most part, Scotus identifies perfection simply with intensity. For Henry, perfect virtue is identified with the higher degrees of temperance and with heroic virtue; imperfect virtue, with persistence and continence. Here Ockham appears to be reacting against Henry. Earlier Ockham had tried, like Henry, to map all the virtues onto an Aristotelian scheme (OTh VIII, 272–80). This not very successful scheme starts with continence, distinguishes grades of temperance, as Henry does, and speaks of persistence in connection with heroic virtue. Intended only as an interpretation of Aristotle, this scheme had no place for Christian virtue.

In *De connexione,* Ockham puts Christianity in the picture. And that is a step he has to justify. After all, someone might argue that acts of obedience to divine precept are not virtuous, since they are not acts performed for the sake of right reason, even if they happen to conform with what right reason dictates. The five degrees described here allow him to do so, since first-degree virtue includes all acts performed for a worthy purpose and dictated by right reason, whether willing conformity to right reason is the goal or not.

Whether Ockham intends to claim that third-degree virtue is subsumed in fourth-degree virtue is not clear. Suppose (because Ockham says that fourth-degree virtue includes all the conditions previously stated) that it is, then what Ockham calls Christian virtue includes the will to obey right reason as well as the will to obey God. That is consistent with what Ockham says elsewhere—namely, that God wills us to obey right reason (OTh VIII,

428–29, 436). Since Ockham also holds that right reason dictates that we should will what God wills because God wills it (OTh IV, 610), he may hold that obedience to God and right reason constitute a single purpose.

What makes this assumption problematic is that it is hard to see how third-degree virtue, which is motivated solely by the will to conform to right reason, could be part of a virtue whose only end is to obey God. So suppose, alternately, that Ockham means only that all of the conditions stipulated in first-, or more likely second-, degree virtue are included. Then Ockham needs to show that acts motivated solely by love of God are virtuous. Here he argues that Christian practice counts as virtuous because (1) it generates habits that elicit similar acts dictated by right reason in regard to the same objects; because (2) the only difference between it and other virtues is a difference in purpose, and a shift from one worthy purpose to another does not affect whether the act is moral or not; and because, (3) like all the other virtues, the opposite of Christian virtue is vice.

What Ockham actually seems to say when presenting the second argument is that varying the end of an act does not affect whether an act is or is not virtuous, and that is contrary to what he has established above—that, for example, church attendance for the sake of vainglory is vicious. What he must be referring to are changes from one worthy purpose to another. That variation affects the degree of virtue, but not whether or not the act is virtuous at all. Thus temperance for the sake of peace is not the opposite of temperance for the sake of love of God; it is merely a lower form of temperance.

In presenting the third argument, Ockham claims that the opposite of Christian virtue is vice, strictly speaking. Here "strictly speaking" may just mean that it would be an act in defiance of right reason. Or it may mean that it is necessarily vicious, since the opposite of Christian virtue would be an act in defiance of right reason, the purpose of which is to disobey right reason on account of hatred for God. Such an act could not be virtuous under any circumstances.

152. Fifth-degree virtue is heroic virtue, which Ockham takes pains to describe in a manner that allows for non-Christian as well as Christian heroism. Like second-degree virtue, it differs from an earlier degree by requiring persistence in the face of adversity. Since heroic virtue is possible for pagans, it is a higher degree of second-degree virtue (acts in accordance with right reason) or third-degree virtue (acts performed precisely for the sake of right reason) as well as a higher degree of fourth-degree virtue (acts performed precisely for love of God). Here Ockham is thinking primarily of the virtuous philosophers of antiquity; that is why he refers to philosophical virtue rather than pagan virtue.

This does not mean that heroic Christian virtue is not higher than heroic pagan virtue. In *De connexione virtutum*, Ockham makes fewer concessions to pagan virtue than in the *Dialogus*. He implies that pagan heroic virtue, unlike Christian heroism, is compatible with vice (a.3 322–29). By contrast, in the *Dialogus*, he argues that both pagan and Christian virtue are incompatible with vice—acts motivated by hatred of God and rebellion against right reason (1.VI.77, fols. 90v–91r). It may be that further reflection persuaded Ockham to adopt the view that all the higher degrees of pagan virtue were incompatible with vice. For Ockham, pagan unbelief is a product of ignorance. But ignorance is only culpable if it can be overcome using right reason; if it is invincible, it is not vicious. So suppose that it can be overcome. If that is so, unbelief is a product of not following right reason, and the pagan is not practicing third-degree virtue. On this reasoning, pagan heroic virtue would be incompatible with vice, but in comparison with Christian virtue it would still be a state of deprivation.

In defining heroic virtue, Ockham deploys his second distinction, the distinction between equivalently and formally executive imperative acts (101). Formally executive acts regard circumstances as they actually obtain; equivalently imperative acts presuppose a different set of circumstances. He combines this distinction with another distinction, between acts that do not exceed the common state of humanity and are in accordance with natural inclination and acts that exceed the common state and are contrary to natural inclination. If the work willed—either in itself or in the circumstances—exceeds the common state of humanity and is contrary to natural inclination, and someone actually wills it executively, then it is heroic.

It would appear that heroic virtue must include not one but three additional partial objects: exceeding the common state, acting contrary to natural inclination, and acting altruistically. But it turns out that the common state has already been exceeded in second-degree virtue (176). Ockham's examples often suggest that altruism is necessary, since he usually describes cases of defending the faith or its pagan equivalent, acting for the common good (OTh VIII, 275, 447). Those may be the actions he primarily has in mind, and it may be that he thinks right reason requires extreme sacrifice only for the sake of the faith or the common good, but he also includes heroic virtue for the sake of individual temperance (a.4 740). So the only really new condition to be met is acting contrary to natural inclination. Ockham holds that as a matter of experience, it always exceeds the common state to act contrary to our natural inclination for sensory enjoyment (OTh VIII, 275–77, 446–47). So what Ockham means by heroic virtue is persevering in an act undertaken for the sake of a worthy goal when perseverance is dictated by right reason in circumstances that are actually, not conditionally, painful. Thus Norman's simple rejection of injustice does not count as heroism, but if, rather than commit injustice, he has go to prison in order not to be unjust, he is acting heroically.

168. "In accordance with universal right reason" is the phrase Ockham used in an earlier work when discussing what he here calls second-degree virtue (OTh VIII, 277). It indicates that although desire to conform to right reason need not be the precise goal of heroic action, the resolve not to depart from virtue for any reason contrary to right reason must be present. Note here that Ockham says that willing universally not to depart from the dictates of right reason in a particular circumstance exceeds the common state, whether that act of will is formally or only equivalently imperative, thereby restricting ordinary human virtue to first-degree virtue.

181. The final paragraph takes up again Ockham's discussion of how virtuous habits and acts differ from each other. Each degree of virtue is characterized by numerically and specifically distinct acts, which produce correspondingly distinct habits. This claim could be challenged; Scotus would say that only circumstances vary between different degrees, and changed circumstances do not produce specifically distinct acts (Adams 1981, 8). Ockham defends himself by explaining that what others characterize as the circumstances of acts he views as partial objects of acts. He argues for this view on the grounds that if these degrees of virtue belonged to the same species, then the intensification of first-degree virtue would produce second-degree virtue, and so on. Given his definitions of the degrees of virtue, he is, of course, correct to claim that this could not happen regardless of the intensity of the virtue. Assuming that Scotus would agree that intensified pagan virtue does not produce Christian virtue, this is a good argument for Ockham's claim that virtues with different ends differ specifically. Surely Scotus would not also want to claim that if Socrates pursued acts dictated by right reason more intensely, he would eventually achieve Christian virtue.

I Fourth Distinction

194. The fourth distinction introduces the three theological virtues—faith, hope, and charity. Ockham is not concerned with distinguishing between theological virtues and the natural or political virtues of temperance, courage, and justice, which we discussed in the introduction, but rather between the acquired and infused virtues. Acquired virtues are habits produced by repeated acts; infused virtues are dispositions to virtuous acts that are supernaturally produced. Both kinds of faith can be called theological, since both have God as the object; but one is naturally, the other supernaturally, produced.

I Fifth Distinction

200. A reintroduction of the distinction between good, bad, and indifferent acts, the fifth distinction appears to provide a definition of indifferent acts different from that of article 1, where it was established that only acts of will were intrinsically virtuous. In article 1, Ockham indicated that indifferent acts were simply acts that could be successively virtuous and vicious as the purpose for which they were performed changed. Here Ockham suggests that indifferent acts are defective or unmotivated, rather than simply performed for an indifferent purpose. As before, Ockham indicates that indifferent acts can be called good only by reference to an act of will with a worthy purpose.

I Sixth Distinction

212. Here we are introduced to generically good acts, circumstantially good acts, and meritorious acts. Generically vicious acts cannot be good; their names implies vice. The names of these acts are connotative terms and have two parts. Theft, for example, is taking something one is prohibited to take. What is absolute in the definition of theft, taking something, is generically good—that is, it is an act that is good in some circumstances. What are called generically vicious acts are described in terms of an improper circumstance—such as the obligation not to take. If we say that George stole something, no further examination of the circumstances is necessary in order to determine that his act is vicious.

Ockham's example of a generically good act, prayer—or the expression of reverence for the divine—might seem to be a case where no further inspection of the circumstances would be necessary to conclude that it is virtuous. But that is not the case. To say the Lord's Prayer solely to impress somebody would be to perform a generically good action in vicious circumstances. As Ockham indicates with his example of abstinence, virtue requires appropriate circumstances, the most important of which is a worthy purpose. Unfortunately, Ockham's example of circumstantial vice is fornication, which is a generic vice, since its definition implies wrongdoing. What is intended here is sexual connection, which, like prayer, is vicious if undertaken at the wrong time and place, contrary to the dictates right reason, or for an unworthy purpose.

Meritorious acts aim at conformity with divine will; God has ordained that they will be accepted or rewarded with eternal life.

Note that in the sixth distinction, Ockham departs from his own terminology (181) and adopts common usage. For Ockham, generic acts are specifically distinguished in terms of their partial objects, not by circumstances. Thus Ockham holds that what I intend when I pray is just as much a part of that action as what I say. What others call circumstances, Ockham handles as partial objects. He will return to make this point most forcefully with regard to time and place, purpose, and conformity with right reason in article 4, reply to doubt 2 (a.4 401–602).

| Seventh Distinction

231. Ockham introduces the distinction between habits of the sensitive soul and habits of the will, since he is concerned with actions that appear to be virtuous actions, but are elicited by people who act involuntarily on account of mental illness. He is thinking of people whose habits of temperance in eating and drinking persist when there is no reason to think that they are in control of their actions. He argues for the existence of both sensitive habits (what we might call physical habits) and volitional habits. Note that both kinds of habits act as natural causes (257)—that is, always or for the most part they incline us to perform specifically the same actions.

248. The argument for volitional habits is complicated but important, because it is an argument for the thesis that there is a primarily virtuous habit. The first argument simply appeals to the conclusion that a primarily virtuous act must exist. The second breaks new ground. Ockham argues that there must be a primarily virtuous habit because an objection to this conclusion would have to be based on the freedom of the will or its conformity to right reason. In other words, someone might argue (1) that there are no habits of the will, because the will acts freely; its actions are not determined by a habit. Ockham's reply to this objection is based on the theology of merit. Theologians agree that merit without the habit of infused charity is impossible; but involuntary merit would be a contradiction in terms; hence volitional habits are not incompatible with the freedom of the will. Or someone might argue (2) that the will cannot fail to chose in conformity with right reason; hence virtue is a habit of the intellect, not a habit of the will. Ockham rejects the assumption on which this objection is based—namely, that the intellectual virtue of prudence is incompatible with a vicious act of will (see article 3, principally lines 520–32).

ARTICLE III | **Reply to the Question**

| Opinions Concerning the
| Connection of Moral Virtues

| Thomas Aquinas's
| Opinion Considered

2. Ockham divides the third article into four subordinate articles. The first sets out seven conclusions about the relation of the moral virtues to each other after presenting the opinions that Ockham sets out to refute; the second article lists eight conclusions dealing with the special problems introduced by theological virtues; the third article argues briefly for the almost total independence of virtues from sensitive habits; the last article, which deals with the relation between prudence and the moral virtues, is the longest. It includes seven proofs of the second of six conclusions in support of view that prudence without virtue is possible. Ockham's reply to the second part of Aquinas's opinion, as he presents it, appears in the last of the subordinate articles.

9. Ockham begins by summarizing the views that Aquinas presents in the *Summa theologica*. The four cardinal virtues are connected: prudence is a necessary prerequisite for justice, courage, and temperance; and at the same time, prudence is inconceivable in the absence of justice, courage, and temperance. Missing from Ockham's summary of the *Summa,* I-II q.65 a.1, is the first part of Aquinas's reply, in which he acknowledges that imperfect virtues are not connected. Ockham appears to think that this concession is unimportant, probably because Aquinas understood imperfect virtues as inclinations prior to virtue, as was noted in chapter 4 of the introduction; in the unqualified sense of the term, they are not virtues at all.

Aquinas defines prudence as right reason regarding possible actions whose principles or aims are those that all morally upright people seek by the practice of justice, courage, and temperance. In addition to the four cardinal virtues, there are two virtues that are appropriate only to people in positions of power and dignity; common people lack the wealth required for magnificence and the greatness required for magnanimity. Since they have no immediate potential for these virtues, we must assume that their virtues can exist without magnanimity and magnificence. The designation of these four Platonic and Aristotelian virtues appropriate to everyone as the "cardinal" virtues comes from Ambrose.[1] But we owe to Aquinas the adaptation to Christian moral thought of the Aristotelian distinction between virtues appropriate to everyone and virtues appropriate to the great.

19. Ockham also presents here for the first time the ancient arguments for the incompatibility of prudence with vice. Vice corrupts the principle or cause of the virtues, but prudence is the cause of virtues, therefore vice cannot coexist with prudence. All wickedness proceeds from ignorance, so wickedness in the presence of moral science is impossible, a position attributed to Socrates in the *Nicomachean Ethics* (7.2.1145b22–32; 3.1147b15).

Note that as Ockham presents Aquinas, he is a proponent of the view that virtue is an intellectual or deliberative habit. A more careful reading of Aquinas reveals a subtle interplay between deliberation and will, as Mark Jordan has recently shown.[2]

Ockham sets out to refute here only the argument that virtues are connected. Rather than deal directly with the argument that Aquinas presented for the connection of the virtues, Ockham presents an *ad hominem* argument. Aquinas has conceded that not all virtues are connected; Ockham argues, by parity of reasoning, that no virtues need necessarily be connected. If prudence can exist apart from the virtues of magnificence and magnanimity, then it can exist apart from any given virtue. In reply, Aquinas might argue that there is no parity of reasoning here, because common people lack the occasion (or subject matter) for the vir-

---

1. "De excessu fratri sui Satyri" (PL 16, 1366), *Expositio Evangelii sec. Luc.* (CCL 14, 152; PL 15, 1734). Cf. a note by I. Brady, in Lombard, *Sent.* III d.33, II: 188.

2. Mark Jordan, "The Transcendentality of Goodness and the Human Will," in *Being and Goodness,* ed. S. MacDonald (Ithaca, N.Y., 1991), 145–49.

tues of the great. Ockham deals with this objection in the second refutation. He claims that just as no common people are in a position to practice magnanimity, some common people have no occasion to practice courage—no need for courage in defense of the faith, for example. Hence the case of the cardinal virtues does not differ from the virtues of the great; courage, like the magnificence, can exist without other virtues.

Henry of Ghent's Opinion Considered

45. When he comes to Henry's opinion, Ockham deals with the view that although imperfect degrees of virtue are unconnected, perfect virtues are necessarily connected. Henry posits four degrees of virtue, claiming that although virtues are unconnected at the start and in the period of their first development, no virtue can be complete without the support of the other virtues.

63. Ockham mentions that many arguments have been presented for the position that perfect virtues are connected—by Ockham's illustrious Franciscan predecessor, Bonaventure, among others, as we saw in chapter 4 of the introduction. But Ockham fails to warn the reader that he himself, unlike Scotus, allows that virtues willed precisely for the sake of conformity to right reason or conformity to divine precept do produce inclinations to other virtues if the occasion arises.

73. Ockham rejects Henry's opinion first as an interpretation of Aristotle. As Ockham points out, Aristotle does not posit a fourfold distinction. Ockham sees rather a threefold distinction: continence and incontinence, temperance and intemperance, heroism and bestiality. Ockham asks us to reject Henry because he misunderstands Aristotle and posits nonexistent degrees of virtue (106). Unfortunately, however, Ockham's own interpretation of Aristotle on intemperance is also open to criticism. Ockham is right to suggest that the continence/incontinence distinction pertains to pleasures, while perseverance and softness relate to pains. Moreover, he notices that for Aristotle, the intemperate person is not someone whose will is overcome by sensual desire (OTh VIII, 273). But he takes that to be a sign that for Aristotle temperance is a superior state of continence, which is not the case. Rather, Aristotle does not see incontinence as a vice or continence as a virtue. For though an incontinent person is overcome by his or her inclinations, no decision to disregard right reason is made (*Eth. Nic.* 7.8.1151a5). Aristotle then argues that intemperance, unlike incontinence, does involve such a decision, and hence corrupts the first principles of prudence or virtue; this can be a basis for an argument that vices and virtues are connected that Ockham does not address.

This criticism of Ockham, however, need not be taken too seriously for two reasons. First, the claim that 'continence is not a virtue' is one of the articles condemned at Paris in 1277.[3] So a straightforward literal interpretation was not an option for Ockham. Second, since he posits distinct prudences for each of the virtues, what corrupts one principle need not affect another.

For Ockham, incontinence is itself a vice, since it involves willing contrary to right reason. 'Temperance' has a variety of meanings. Often it just means restraint in eating and drinking (a.3 455, 473; a.4 420). As related to bodily pleasures in general, Ockham sees temperance as a superior degree of continence, either because inclinations for depraved pleasures are absent or because the person involved has taken steps to avoid temptation (a.4 745; OTh VIII, 273–75).

95. Perseverance, unlike continence, cannot be an independent virtue. It is rather a circumstance that determines the degree of virtue. It allows us to follow the dictates of right reason even when external circumstances make it difficult to do so. Ockham's example here is apt. Matins are the prayers said before dawn. Who can have failed sometimes to feel cold and sluggish at matins? Certainly, resolution would be required to persist in virtuous prayers when woken before dawn. This makes these prayers a common topic in the literature of virtues and vices (see, for example, William of Auxerre, *Summa aurea* II t.18 c.3 q.1 a.2 [Paris-Grottaferrata, 1982], 602–4).

106. Before stating his arguments for the independence of the virtues, Ockham reminds his audience that he and Henry disagree about how virtues are divided into species. Henry assumes that specifically the same virtue is present in beginners and in the proficient; by contrast, Ockham laid the basis for the claim that such virtues are specifically distinct in the first two conclusions of article 1. Ockham thinks that Henry's opinion that specifically the same virtue of courage is found in beginners and in heroes is particularly vulnerable to attack when we consider the extremes: weak ordinary people and extraordinary saints.

114. Ockham has in mind ordinary people who, though not without vice, continue to be capable of virtue. It is obvious from

---

3. *Chartularium Universitatis Parisiensis* a.168, ed. H. Denifle and A. Chatelain (Paris, 1889), I: 553; R. Hissette, *Enquête sur les 219 articles condamnés à Paris le 7 mars 1277* (Louvain-Paris, 1977), 297–98.

experience that intemperate people are capable of acts of justice. More importantly, this paragraph is the first sign that Ockham will concede that total vice (*vitium in complemento*) is incompatible with virtue of any kind. But we can already see how extreme Ockham's definition of complete or total vice is: it is vice chosen for the sake of vice and in order to avoid virtue. Its controlling principle is the desire to lead a life that does not conform to right reason.

128. An example of the extraordinary virtue that Ockham has in mind might be a desert saint who practiced heroic feats of prayer and endurance, but had no occasion to develop social virtues (107–14, 128–38). These cases show that even heroic degrees of virtue can exist in the absence of other virtues, since there is no occasion for the acts that would produce these habits.

132. An opponent might argue that the desert saints would have been prepared to govern well, and that they had considered the situations in which such justice would be required. A Thomist might say that they had the proximate potential for justice (ST I-II q.65 a.1). Ockham replies that nothing requires us to suppose that these saints had contemplated the specific actions that would have been required by justice. Unlike abstract speculation, moral science focuses on practice, and no acquired virtue is possible without particular prudence, as Ockham established in distinction 2.

Conclusions about the Connection of the Moral Virtues

In stating his own opinion, Ockham begins by stating a trivial sense in which the virtues are often connected. They may be connected because they are produced by acts elicited as the result of practical syllogisms that share some of the same premises. All virtuous acts are dictated by three universals. Ockham lists them as if they were haphazard examples; indeed, he says elsewhere that many others could be listed (OTh VI, 425). But in fact these and only these universals are intrinsic to natural virtue. They tell us in the most general terms what we should do, what we should value, and what rule we should follow:

> Everything worthy [here a synonym of 'virtuous'] should be done.
>
> Everything good [where goodness is the end of virtue] should be loved.
>
> Everything dictated by right reason [the principle that determines what is virtuous] should be done.

As Ockham puts it elsewhere, these are *sine qua non* conditions of virtue (OTh VI, 425). Moreover, each universal implies the others: worthiness requires conformity with right reason; right reason dictates the pursuit of goodness; goodness is the aim of worthiness. Since by definition virtuous acts are dictated by right reason for the sake of good ends, this concession to the view that the virtues are connected is trivial.

154. Ockham's second conclusion makes a more substantial concession: third- and fourth-degree virtues incline us to acts of other virtues. Here both third- and fourth-degree virtues are called 'perfect' virtues, probably a mistake for 'true' virtues, as was mentioned in the discussion of distinction 3, where third- and fourth-degree virtues are defined (a.2 141). The concession that Ockham makes here is dictated by the definitions of third- and fourth-degree virtues: the third degree refers to acts undertaken precisely because they are dictated by right reason; the fourth degree, to acts done for the love of God. As Ockham puts it, if we do one thing solely because it is dictated by right reason, we will undertake every other act dictated by right reason. There is no reason to suppose we would perform one act dictated by right reason and not another if our only motivation is conformity with right reason. Here, despite the use of the simple indicative, the conclusion that Ockham intends is conditional, as will be evident in the third conclusion.

167. But before stating the condition, Ockham takes up first-, second-, and fifth-degree virtues. The most interesting case he deals with is second-degree virtue, a resolute virtuous act that we intend to persist in at all costs. Here circumstances alter cases. If the circumstances we face require us to practice a different virtue in order to persist in the first, then second-degree virtue will incline us to acts that can produce a virtue different from the original virtue; this is what Ockham calls a pertinent circumstance. He discusses, first, cases in which second-degree virtue does prompt initial acts of other virtues, and then cases in which it does not do so. Of course, Ockham is not asserting that we will necessarily follow the promptings of virtue; rather, he is suggesting that one stable virtuous habit will sometimes motivate us to other, unrelated acts of virtue. If, rather than commit injustice, we conditionally resolve to face death, then perseverance in justice will produce courage. Since second-degree virtue is defined in terms of the resolve to persevere in the face of the threat of death, any external threat to second-degree virtue will incline us to acts of courage. By contrast, intemperance—here understood as weaknesses of the flesh—is not incompatible with justice, and so a threat to second-degree justice will not produce acts of temperance. Had Ockham defined intemperance as Aristotle does, in terms of a decision to disregard the dictates of right reason about pleasures, then threats to temperance would be pertinent, not impertinent, to the development of other virtues.

188. The case of first-degree virtue is easily disposed of. The habits are independent, and the circumstances are irrelevant, so one habit will not prompt acts related to another habit.

197. Building toward the condition that he will state in the third conclusion, Ockham's discussion of fifth-degree virtue is qualified. Fifth-degree virtue inclines us to other virtues only if the circumstances in which we practice fifth-degree virtue present an occasion that requires the practice of another virtue. The case is the same as with second-degree virtue, and the same examples are presented, the difference being that in fifth-degree virtue the will to face death is actual rather than conditional.

207. Ockham completes the picture by discussing whether different degrees of one virtue will prompt us to elicit other degrees of that same virtue. This is a relevant question for Ockham, because he holds that the different degrees of the same virtue are not specifically identical. His answer is dictated by what has already been said. Thus, first-degree virtue does not prompt us to second-degree virtue; but second-, third-, and fourth-degree virtues all incline us toward acts of fifth-degree virtue. Suppose, for example, second-degree continence is actually threatened with a punishment more severe than the common human state can withstand—that is, someone tells us to fornicate or go to prison; we will be inclined to persist in chastity, and if we follow that inclination, we will have elicited an act of heroic virtue. But first-degree virtue will not necessarily incline us to heroic virtue, because it is not dictated by allegiance to right reason for its own sake and because it is not accompanied by a resolve to maintain that virtue in the presence of obstacles.

Here the reader should note that Ockham is not committed to a morality that dictates heroic sacrifices for unimportant matters. Second-degree virtue requires the resolve to persist in virtue and not to depart from it for the sake of anything contrary to right reason. It does not require that we simply persist at all costs. So if we suppose that right reason dictates that fornication is to be preferred to loss of life, then vowing to choose death rather than fornication is foolish and imprudent, and keeping that vow is not heroic chastity.

❙ Third Conclusion

215. A important conclusion, conclusion 3 indicates that no moral virtue necessarily requires another virtue. The virtues are independent because of what has been termed the "independence of act-opportunity": "habits are caused by corresponding acts, while acts require a relevant opportunity, . . . [so] that agent could have occasion to perform acts of temperance while no opportunity for courage presented itself or vice versa."[4] Isolated saints, for example, lacking human contact, have no occasion for courage, which, as we will see, cannot be a solitary virtue as Ockham defines it (a.4 725). Thus, whether the practice of one virtue will prompt us to elicit acts of another virtue depends on our circumstances. Connections between the virtues depend on the kind of circumstances we confront. Therefore they are contingent.

❙ Fourth to Seventh Conclusions

Conclusions 4 to 7 deal with the compatibility of different degrees of virtue with vice. In general these conclusions complement those stated above. Having stated that first-degree justice is independent of first-degree temperance, Ockham must also say that first-degree temperance is compatible with injustice. It also follows from what Ockham has already said that third- and fourth-degree justice are incompatible with cowardice. But there are some surprises, as when Ockham maintains that all second-degree virtue is compatible with vice, although he maintained in conclusion 2 that second-degree virtue sometimes prompts us to other virtues. It turns out that Ockham states a stronger conclusion about the compatibility of the vice of injustice with second-degree temperance, because he stipulates cases in which pertinent circumstances are not present—that is, no circumstances in which it would be impossible to maintain one virtue without practicing another.

225. Ockham states the fourth conclusion in two parts, according to whether reason functions properly or not. In the first part, he maintains the view that even when reason judges rightly, the first two degrees of one virtue are compatible with other vices. He devotes very little attention (266) to the much easier task of defending the proposition that when reason errs,

---

4. This point is made by Adams in "Scotus and Ockham on the Connection of the Virtues," in *John Duns Scotus: Metaphysics and Ethics,* ed. L. Honnefelder, R. Wood, and M. Dreyer, Studien und Texte zur Geistesgeschichte des Mittelalters (Leiden, 1996), 502, 504, 514.

different second-degree virtues and vices are compatible. His basic example is of a temperate person who is capable of acts of injustice even when right reason judges correctly both about temperance and about justice.

239. After presenting an argument from experience (231), Ockham now presents a demonstration. The major premise is conditional: If one act is compatible with another act in the absence of pertinent circumstances, it is compatible in the presence of irrelevant circumstances. Ockham argues that this must be so, since incompatibility could only result from a pertinent circumstance.

The remainder of the paragraph introduces a qualification of the fourth conclusion: First- and second-degree virtues are not compatible with every degree of vice. Ockham does not define degrees of vice, but he now mentions what would be third-degree vice — actions willed because they are contrary to right reason. Presuming that he would define vices as he defines virtues, Ockham's reasoning implies that first- and second-degree virtues are not compatible with third- or fourth-degree vice but might be compatible with fifth-degree vice — a heroic act contrary to our inclinations undertaken for an unworthy goal. Instead of developing this line of reasoning, Ockham points out instead that this incompatibility is the result of an incompatible circumstance — namely, the goal of willing not merely actions contrary to right reason's dictates but acts chosen for the sake of their departure from those dictates.

The reader should note that the remark here about 'generically' and 'numerically' the same acts may be misreported. The presence or absence of such circumstances should make for a specific as well as a numerical distinction. Showing temperance by refusing fruitcake on Monday and shortcake on Tuesday may be acts that are only numerically distinct. But according to Ockham, refraining from dessert so that others will not be deprived is specifically as well as numerically distinct from temperance dictated by regard for right reason. Note, too, that when Ockham says that acts of first- and second-degree virtues are performed because they conform to right reason, he does not mean that they result from a generalized commitment to right reason; for that would be third-degree virtue.

At the close of the paragraph, Ockham says that he has established the major and proceeds to prove the minor in the next paragraph. Here the minor is stated in terms of temperance and justice. Instead of 'one act of virtue is compatible with the vice corresponding to a different virtue in the absence of circumstances,' we find the claim that temperance is compatible with injustice in the absence of any circumstance at all (257). Ockham's proof of the minor is from experience. So ultimately both proofs for the compatibility of virtue and vice are based on experience.

272. Conclusion 5 more smoothly establishes the incompatibility of third-degree virtues with unrelated vices. Once again, the second part of the conclusion (306) deals very briefly with the case of erring reason, allowing the compatibility of third-degree virtue with vice when reason errs.

The basic argument in conclusion 5 is that if I will one thing because it is dictated by right reason, there is no reason to suppose I would fail to will other things dictated by right reason. Given that I am motivated by the desire to obey right reason, there is no difference between choosing justice because it is dictated by right reason and choosing temperance under the same description. The two objects are indistinguishable objects of our wills, given that description of those acts and the determination of our wills to obey right reason.

287. Ockham considers two objections. The first objector holds that even if we continue to will conformity with right reason, we could still will an act that does not conform. The question is whether I can act inconsistently. The objector says yes, even after deciding to make right reason the arbiter of my actions, I can steal an apple. The object of my will is the apple, not disobedience to the dictates of right reason. And if I do take the apple and then also take bananas and persimmons without paying, I will acquire the habit of stealing fruit.

293. Ockham replies by rejecting the suggestion that someone temperate in the third degree could want to perform an unjust act. The dictates of right reason are evident. I cannot fail to know that taking the apple is contrary to right reason, so if I take the apple, I am not willing conformity with right reason. And as long as I do really will conformity, I will not engage in theft. Here Ockham is rejecting the sort of "bad faith" explanation of vice that might be presented by Existentialists. He does not see people deceiving themselves, knowing at one level and not knowing at another level whether an act is in conformity with, or contrary to, right reason. Or rather, Ockham thinks that the relevant level on which to consider the act, from the standpoint of judging the agent's virtue, is the level on which the agent evidently knows it to be contrary to right reason. Self-deception should not allow an agent to claim virtues that are not exhibited in conduct.

302. This reply leaves Ockham open to the second objection, which claims that my inability to will the act of theft does not count as virtue. It is not virtuous, since, given my third-degree temperance, I am incapable of injustice. Since Ockham is committed to a very strong form of the view that only voluntary acts are virtuous (a.1 145), this is a serious objection. He replies that the second act is virtuous insofar as the first act is virtuous. Both acts count as voluntary because I can stop willing the first act.

Unlike third-degree virtue, fourth-degree virtue is not compatible with vice, even when reason errs. Ockham's grounds for this conclusion are his views about culpability, which has three possible causes, according to Ockham: ignorance, malice, and passion. Passion and malice can be discounted because they are incompatible with ordinate love of God—namely, love of God above all else; passion and malice can arise only in inordinate love—that is, when we prefer some other end to God's honor. Ignorance is the more complicated case, since ignorance is compatible with ordinate love of God, and Ockham holds that not all ignorance excuses. Ockham eliminates the possibility of ignorance leading to vice in combination with fourth-degree virtue by distinguishing between vincible and invincible ignorance. He holds that invincible ignorance excuses, and ignorance that can be overcome will be overcome if we love God ordinately.

Here we have Ockham's justification for claiming that Christian virtue is morally preferable to pagan virtue, not just more acceptable to God. Reason can err, divine precepts do not. Few dispute that we can be mistaken about how we should regulate our behavior in regard to the sensual pleasures or the desire to avoid pain. But many claim that we are just as likely to be wrong about what God requires of us (though medievals would be less likely to entertain this view). Before accepting that criticism, the reader should note that ordinate love of God, as Ockham understands it, is an extraordinary commitment—it requires the Christian to sacrifice everything else.

Conclusion 7 reiterates what was said in conclusions 5 and 6. Having taken great trouble to define heroic virtue so that it could apply to all cases of superhuman perseverance, both in Christian virtue and in the virtues of the philosophers, Ockham has to deal with them differently here. Fifth-degree philosophical virtue, like third-degree virtue, is compatible with vice, provided that reason errs; fifth-degree Christian virtue is not. The degree of perseverance does not affect whether one virtue prompts another; only acting for the right end establishes a propensity for all virtues.

As we noted above (a.2 152), Ockham subsequently changed his mind about heroic virtue. He came to believe that someone willing to go to prison rather than commit injustice would be incapable of vice.

Conclusions about the Connection of the Moral Virtues with the Theological Virtues

331. The second part of the third article deals with the special problems presented by the theological virtues. The principal object and end of the theological virtues is God—faith in God, hope for beatific vision of God, and love of God. Ockham asks first how each degree of moral virtue is related to the theological virtues. Then he takes up theological virtue and its relation to the problematic cases: the absence of moral virtue and the presence of moral vice.

I First to Third Conclusions

In one sense, moral and theological virtues have the same end, goodness. Since the highest good is God, it might appear that they would always occur together. If that were so, no further discussion would be required. Ockham's first conclusion rejects this view. He holds that only a general grasp of the nature of goodness is required for the moral virtues. By contrast, the theological virtues are not possible without some particular knowledge of God. Since the moral virtues do not require the same knowledge as the theological virtues, they can exist apart from the theological virtues. Pagans are capable of virtue, since they can do what right reason requires without a proper concept of the end that is God.

Note that Ockham distinguishes between complex and simple concepts of God, as well as between common and proper concepts of God. Though the concept requisite to theological virtue is proper, it is not simple. No simple concept proper to God is attainable in this life. The complex proper concept about which Ockham speaks is a composite concept combining the simple concept of being with a variety of connotative and negative terms— for example, first being, creative being, and immortal and ingenerable being (OTh II, 402–5).

343. Ockham's second conclusion argues that both first- and second-degree virtues are compatible with theological vice. A pagan can perform just acts even if he rejects Christianity. This conclusion is a consequence of Ockham's views on the limits of human reason. Ockham holds that no creaturely cause produces any effect without God's cooperation. But he also holds that human reason is incapable of demonstrating that creaturely causes by themselves cannot be total causes (OTh V, 91). Consequently, pagans can reason correctly and yet fail to believe what Christianity teaches about the dependence of the world on God. If human reason were less restricted, and pagans could know naturally everything that Christianity teaches, then right reason would be incompatible with error concerning the truths of the Christian faith.

Note that desperation is the vice corresponding to hope; it is the failure to hope for what we should hope for, beatitude or enjoyment of the vision of God.

349. Ockham's second argument for the second conclusion follows a different strategy, one that allows him to refer the reader to his conclusions about the relations of the moral virtues to each other for proof of the conclusions that he states regarding the relations of the theological virtues to the moral virtues. Here Ockham's major premise is that there is no greater connection between the theological virtues and moral virtues than between one moral virtue and another. No argument is presented for this premise.

357. The third conclusion states that third-degree moral virtue is not compatible with theological vice, except on account of a defect of reason. It is like the fifth conclusion concerning the moral virtues (271): If human reason were reliable, third-degree virtue would protect against vice.

Formally the second conclusion denies, and the third conclusion asserts, a connection with theological virtue. The second conclusion draws attention to such theological vices as have earned the philosophers eternal damnation (OTh VI, 280). The third conclusion allows that commitment to right reason might help one avoid theological vice. But key to both is the inadequacy of human reason as a protection against error in the theological realm.

| Fourth to Fifth Conclusions

362. Fourth-degree or Christian moral virtue is impossible in the absence of theological virtue. Here Ockham specifies that he means both infused and acquired theological virtue. As the reader will recall, strictly speaking the phrase 'theological virtues' refers to divinely infused virtues (a.2 194–98). Only loosely speaking does the phrase 'theological virtue' refer to the habits of faith, hope, and charity, which result from repeated acts of believing in, longing for, and loving God.

The argument is based on the definition of fourth-degree virtue, willing virtue for the sake of God. But it is an Aristotelian logical principle that you cannot love one thing for the sake of the another unless you love the second thing better than the first. Thus I cannot love dinner for the sake of dessert unless, for example, I prefer triple fudge sundaes to steak. Similarly, I cannot love virtue for the sake of God unless I love God. But loving God ordinately is impossible in the absence of theological virtue, since by definition loving God ordinately is charity, the principal theological virtue.

Regarding the infused theological virtues, the argument is problematic. According to Ockham, our experience of pagans raised among Christians shows that unbaptized humans in their natural state are capable of acts of loving God; Ockham even claims that a pagan can love God above all without supernatural virtue (OTh III, 451; OTh VI, 281–82). Such statements are found in arguments for the claim that acquired and infused theological habits are distinct; they relate to cases of pagans educated among Christians and sharing the same beliefs; on the hypothesis, baptism is the only difference between believing pagans and Christians. Do such statements imply that pagans can love God ordinately? Ockham evidently believes that they cannot (cf. also OTh VI, 312). Indeed, his argument succeeds only if ordinate love of God in the absence of infused charity is impossible, a thesis that echoes the decrees of the Council of Orange, "no one can love God as he ought . . . or believe in God, or act for God's sake . . . unless by divine grace,"[5] where reference is to grace infused at baptism. Presumably, then, Ockham was aware of this doctrine and believed that his other statements could be reconciled with it. So though it is humanly possible to love God above all, what is humanly possible is neither adequate nor ordinate.

370. Both the fourth and the fifth conclusion mention God's ordained power. Distinguishing between what is possible by virtue of God's ordained and absolute power is characteristic of Ockham's philosophical method; the meaning of this distinction is discussed in chapter 3 of the introduction. Here Ockham is adverting to his belief that God need not have ordained the infusion of a supernatural habit in baptism as a prerequisite for acts in which people love ordinately. Absolutely speaking—that is, con-

---

5. Councilium Arausicanum (Orange) II 529, *Enchiridion Symbolorum* n.396, ed. H. Denzinger and A. Schönmetzer, 36th ed. (Barcelona, 1976), 136.

sidering his power in abstraction from anything else—it would have been logically possible for God to have ordained otherwise.

| Sixth to Eighth Conclusions

378. The sixth conclusion claims that the relationship between moral and theological virtues is not symmetrical. Moral virtue does not produce theological virtue, but theological virtue can cause moral virtue. This discussion shows the orthodoxy of Ockham's views on the independence of the moral virtues and infused theological virtues. Infused virtues are possible in the absence of some moral virtues; people with habits of moral vice can be baptized. Taken together with right reason, infused virtues are sufficient principles for virtuous actions, and yet, unlike acquired virtues, they are not reliable dispositions for virtuous actions. They are undeveloped powers. By themselves they do not produce facility in virtuous action, and they do not remove vicious habits produced by past acts. Here the conditions stipulated are important: infused virtues act only together with acquired virtues and in the appropriate situation. As Ockham explains in the third book of his *Sentences* commentary, infused virtues cannot act alone; they act as partial causes in conjunction with acquired theological acts or habits (OTh VI, 291–92). Ockham's book 3 example is of a baptized infant who cannot actually believe what is revealed in Scripture unless she knows its contents—that is, she must have the acquired habit of faith. Ockham is careful to point out that though infused virtues are sufficient principles for virtuous actions, they will not produce acquired virtue except in situations that require those virtues. The reader will remember Ockham's argument against Aquinas, that even the most saintly of hermits does not have the virtue of ruling well.

384. The first part of the sixth conclusion establishes the possibility of theological virtue in the absence of first-, second-, or third-degree moral virtues, but not in the absence of fourth-degree moral virtue. The proof of the independence of the first three degrees is based on the case of adults with moral shortcomings who seek baptism. This could have been an argument from experience; people's characters do not change overnight when they are baptized. Instead, Ockham presents a syllogism that does not appeal to experience: Faith in, hope for, and love of God are all possible in the absence of actions in regard to creatures, and hence without moral virtue; first-, second-, and third-degree moral virtues concern our behavior toward creatures; therefore there can be theological virtue without moral virtue in the first three degrees.

The claim that theological virtue requires fourth-degree moral virtue is based on authority. The medieval church taught that grace was first conveyed in baptism and that no adult received baptism without previously eliciting a good act. Ockham assented without prejudice to this doctrine: for someone who can exercise free will, a good act must precede baptism. From this it follows generally that some good acts can be elicited without grace. Not only does Ockham adhere to the view that good acts are possible in the state of mortal sin, but he also holds that in some sense they can be a reason why God confers grace (OTh IV, 600; OTh VII, 218–21). In the controversy regarding Ockham's alleged Pelagianism, this is the strongest evidence that his detractors can present. It might be taken as a form of semi-Pelagianism that questions predestination and affirms that human free will can take some initiative in faith. By contrast, the Council of Orange affirms that the "beginnings of faith are always due to the inspiration of the Holy Spirit."[6]

Despite these views, it is incorrect to call Ockham a Pelagian or a semi-Pelagian. It is incorrect because Ockham accepts predestination and because he qualifies the sixth conclusion radically. Properly speaking, these good works do not cause grace; rather, they produce a disposition for grace in the sinners. Even loosely speaking, they do not render sinners acceptable to God; they are not meritorious. Finally, it is incorrect because adhering to this tenet is not optional for Ockham. He is assenting to an ecclesiastical doctrine on the actual order of salvation; he is not describing a necessary relation between works and grace based on human and divine nature. Ockham makes this clear when he says that the first part of the sixth conclusion is true *de potentia ordinata;* it is a result of the actual order of salvation established by God and taught by the church.

Though many theologians today would deny this medieval doctrine about a prior disposition to grace, the medieval church claimed for this position the support of the saints and the doctors. Ockham quotes the words of Augustine (from a sermon whose authenticity is questioned today) in addition to the authorities adduced by Lombard (OTh VII, 218–20). Matthew of Aquasparta, too, cites Augustine, as well as Dionysius and John Damascene, in favor of the view that a disposition to grace was necessary prior to

---

6. Pelikan, *The Emergence of the Catholic Tradition* (Chicago, 1984), 318–31; Concilium Arausicanum (Orange) II 529, *Enchiridion Symbolorum* n.371–78, pp. 132–33.

baptism.[7] Aquinas, against whom Ockham is arguing in this passage, also held that a prior disposition was required in adults seeking baptism—namely, free will (ST I-II q.113 a.3 ad 1). Among the many other medieval theologians with views similar to Ockham's are Bonaventure[8] and Scotus (*Sent.* III d.19 n.8, XV: 719). As Victorin Doucet indicates in his edition of Aquasparta, this was the common view among medieval theologians.

Like his contemporaries, Ockham allows a humanly achievable "disposition" to grace. However, this is not tantamount to maintaining that people can take an initial step toward meriting salvation. The step taken merits only a temporal, not an eternal, reward. Here Ockham takes 'temporal' quite literally. Whether we receive grace is, of course, predestined, but how soon we receive grace has something to do with our actions (OTh IV, 600). More importantly, though it is required from penitents in the state of mortal sin, a disposition to grace cannot earn an eternal reward; only grace suffices for merit.

393. The first part of conclusion 6 agrees with Scotus—ordinate love of God without any social virtue is possible. The second claim—that theological virtue is a sufficient cause of moral virtue in the appropriate circumstances—is a step away from Scotus, who maintains that moral and theological virtues are unconnected (*Sent.* III d.36 n.29, XV: 726). Here the connection claimed is that love of God immediately and sufficiently inclines to obedience to divine precept. The quotation from Gregory supporting the claim that love of God produces obedience to divine precept is based itself on Jesus' reply to Judas: "Anyone who loves me will keep my word" (John 14:23). For Ockham, love of God inevitably results in obedience to divine precept: love of God means loving what God wills that we love; acts inevitably follow, because the inclination is sufficient.

So closely connected are the theological virtues with moral virtue that they cannot long survive its absence. Failure to elicit a morally virtuous act in the appropriate circumstances results in the loss of the theological virtues.

405. While the sixth conclusion proved that the theological virtues were compatible with the absence of moral virtues, at least for a little while, the seventh conclusion demonstrates that they are incompatible with moral vice. The proofs are closely

---

7. Mattheus ab Aquasparta, *Quaestiones disputatae de gratia* q.3, BFS 11 (1935): 61–72.

8. Bonaventure, *Sent.,* IV d.14 p.1 a.2 q.3 (Quaracchi, 1889), IV: 327.

related. The proof of the sixth conclusion begins: "Rectitude concerning the end can exist *without rectitude* concerning those things that pertain to the end"; for someone can love God without loving creatures. By contrast the major premise of the seventh claims that rectitude concerning the final end is incompatible with improbity concerning those thing which pertain to the end; no one who loves God will neglect or disregard his commands about loving creatures. As before, the apparent contradiction can be resolved. The difference between the sixth and seventh conclusions is the difference between the presence of moral vice and the absence of moral virtue.

413. This proof is, in effect, a repetition of Ockham's earlier conclusion that fourth-degree or Christian virtue is incompatible with vice (312). The theological virtue of charity, love of God, above all prevents vice, since it rules out inordinate love of creatures. Like adultery, avarice and gluttony can be seen as inordinate attachment to creatures.

417. As Ockham subsequently remarks (436), this argument is intended to establish that you cannot will the end without willing the means to that end. Here the end of the theological virtues is love of God, or willing what God wills. But engaging in any act of vice requires willing what God decrees that we should not will. Willing what God wills and not willing what God wills are formally incompatible; one destroys the other.

422. Here and at 408–11 Ockham lists the possible causes of improbity: ignorance, malice, and passion. As he does earlier (314), Ockham distinguishes between vincible and invincible ignorance. Invincible ignorance excuses; vincible ignorance will be overcome if theological virtue is present.

425. Ockham formulates the eighth conclusion to take habitual moral vice into account: infused theological virtues are, and acquired theological virtues are not, compatible with habitual vice. For the argument in regard to actual vice, the reader is referred back to the seventh conclusion (437).

Infused theological virtue is incompatible with morally vicious acts, but not with the habitual vice produced by past acts of vice. The incompatibility between theological virtue and morally vicious acts is not formal—that is, they are not related as two contradictories that cannot inhere in the same subject (OTh VII, 316–17). Rather, because a vicious act is discreditable (*demeritorius*), it destroys theological virtue. Elsewhere Ockham argues that this may be a consequence of divine ordination (OTh VII, 60).

438. The case regarding acquired theological virtues is different. Unlike infused theological virtue, acquired theological virtue is produced by acts. Since acts of theological virtue are incompatible with acts of moral vice, the habits thereby produced are formally incompatible. The difference between the case of acquired and infused theological virtue is a result of the fact that infused virtues are neither acquired nor augmented by human acts (OTh VII, 52).

Conclusions Concerning the Connection of Moral Virtues with Habits of the Sensitive Soul

447. These two conclusions establish the independence of the moral faculty from bodily habits. Ockham holds that although the will can produce bodily habits, bodily habits can neither produce nor completely impede the voluntary habits of moral virtue.

Key to understanding this set of conclusions is Ockham's understanding of temperance. As we mentioned earlier, there is ambiguity. As it is actually used here and elsewhere (a.4 420), the term ordinarily refers to restraint in eating and drinking. When related more generally to all bodily pleasures, in a technical Aristotelian sense, it is as a superior degree of continence, characterized by the absence of temptation, that obtains when either the inclination for depraved pleasures is simply absent, or the person involved has taken steps to avoid temptation (a.4 745; OTh VIII, 273–75).

Ordinarily, following the dictates of right reason to eat temperately produces bodily habits that facilitate the practice of the virtue of temperance; a physical as well as a moral habit is produced. But this is not necessarily the case. In the case of temperance in its technical sense, virtuous acts of will produce physical habits, which weaken fleshly inclinations to excessive eating or drinking or sexual improprieties to such an extent that temperate people can enjoy and perfect virtue. By contrast, with continence the inclination to excess remains strong, so that virtue is difficult and/or imperfect (OTh VI, 417–19). The basis for the distinction between temperance and continence is the view that while exterior acts can be controlled by the will, no such control is possible in the case of passions such as wrath and lust (OTh VI, 368).

Ockham's chief example of continence is the apostle Paul, whom he sees as someone who practiced continence despite strong sensual inclinations. Paul's case is Ockham's proof for the claim that bodily habits cannot impede virtue. One of the few references to Scripture in Ockham's introductory lecture on the

Bible, this is a citation of 2 Cor. 12:7, a text whose modern scholarly interpretation differs sharply from medieval exegesis. The disagreement is about whether Paul had a problem with fleshly pains or pleasures. Most modern authorities read this verse as a reference to a physical pain, a thorn in the flesh; following Gregory, the medievals understood it as a reference to sensual temptations, basing their views on the Vulgate translation of '*skolops*' as a fleshly *stimulus*.[9]

456. The capacity of the will to cause habits in the sensitive faculty depends on the force of the passions in the sensitive faculty, according to Ockham. As long as there are no strong natural inclinations contrary to the dictates of the will, the will can produce habits in the sensitive soul. But this is not the case where contrary inclinations are strong. Ockham suggests that when passions are strong, the will can continue to act, but its efficacy is limited, and it does not produce habits in the sensitive soul.

471. The second conclusion denies that habits in the sensitive soul can produce virtue, it having already been shown that it cannot produce vice, since the will can resist. Ockham shows first that generically good sensitive habits are compatible with disparate vice—for example, dietary moderation and intellectual pride can coexist. The more difficult case for which he argues is the compatibility of dietary moderation and gluttony in the will.

Ockham's example here is temperate eating. Suppose that Deedee habitually eats oatmeal bread because she wants to live modestly, not consuming more than her share of the world's food resources. Suppose further that she discovers on Sunday that anyone found eating oatmeal bread will be awarded a magnificent ten-course dinner. Once she is used to eating oatmeal bread for breakfast, she will be habituated to continue that practice. Physically, she will want to continue, but if she does so on Sunday, it will be for the sake of gluttony, not modest use. Here Ockham's point is that physical inclinations by themselves have no moral significance. He supports that conclusion by claiming that all sensitive habits are compatible both with moral virtue and moral vice. Elsewhere Ockham uses as an example the prowess of the courageous military man, which can serve virtuously to preserve justice or viciously to attract attention (OTh VI, 361–62).

---

9. H. R. Minn, *The Thorn That Remained* (Auckland, 1972), 24–31; F. Bruce, *I & II Corinthians* (London-Grand Rapids, 1982), 248; V. Furnish, *II Corinthians* (Garden City, N.Y., 1984), 548–50.

On the Connection between Virtue and Prudence

First Conclusion

492. Virtue necessarily requires prudence, or the science of right reason. Ockham repeatedly reaffirms this conclusion (OTh VI, 421–22), which, as he points out, was uniformly conceded by all Scholastics (OTh VIII, 409–13). Following right reason is part of the definition of virtue. At issue is only the question whether actual or only habitual prudence is required. The case considered by Ockham is that of someone insane, here called *fatuus,* but elsewhere described as *furiosus* (OTh VI, 356); *fatuitas* refers to stupidity but also to insanity; like its modern cognate, it is associated most strongly with speech. Here the person has lost control of his actions, but the strength of past habits will prompt him to continue as he did when his will was in control. Aristotle's example is of a drunkard reciting the verses of Empedocles (*Eth. Nic.* 7.3.1147b12). Perhaps Ockham is thinking of a psychotic muttering "nice boy, that's a good boy" to a hospital orderly, since soothing the irate with soft words is his favorite example of a prudent dictate derived from experience. Would the acts of such a babbler count as virtuous? Not if he is just repeating words heard from his mother. More generally, not if his present actions result from virtuous habits established in the past rather than the dictates of right reason, according to Ockham. By parity of reasoning, no unconsidered actions are virtuous, in Ockham's view, and habitual prudence does not suffice for virtue.

510. As a necessary prerequisite to virtue, prudence must be a cause. Here Ockham asks what kind of cause: formal, final, material, or efficient? Ockham replies that prudence is an efficient cause. There is some difficulty with the report as we presently have it. Ockham is thinking here of a famous definition of a cause that he frequently uses himself, usually remembering to attribute it to Scotus (OTh V, 257–58). But as it presently stands, what is associated with Scotus is not his definition of cause, but the universally held view that prudence is necessarily required for virtue. Presumably what happened is that the word 'and' (*et*) was transposed; it should go after the phrase '*per se.*' If we correct the likely manuscript error, transposing the stenographic symbols for '*et*' and '*per se,*' the reading of lines 511–12 would be: "Since prudence is necessarily required, and in your view an effect sufficiently depends on its essential causes, etc., I reply that prudence is a necessary cause requisite to a moral act . . ." This minor correction would result in a Scotus citation that makes more sense. The major change is a question of punctuation: do we read the 'since' (*ex quo*) forward or backward? Unlike Wey, I have read it forward: "Since . . . I reply," rather than "someone might ask . . . since."

Another problem is the phrase 'according to the present divine ordination.' Does Ockham mean to suggest that God could have ordained that prudence be a formal or material rather than an efficient cause of virtue? Is he retracting what he has just established, so that habitual prudence would suffice for virtue? Might he even be claiming that virtue was possible without prudence? There is no support for any of these alternatives elsewhere in Ockham's writings. What is found elsewhere is a suggestion based on the thesis defined in article 63 of the Condemnations of 1277 and discussed in chapter 3 of the introduction (in the section on the principle of abstract divine power), namely, that God could produce any act without any creaturely cooperation whatsoever. God could produce in us the same acts we normally consider virtuous—justice, temperance, and courage—without our cooperation (OTh XI, 245–55).

Suppose, then, that I virtuously render justice to a neighbor. God could cause me to continue that action without the assent of my will and without my understanding that rendering justice is right. Ockham is committed to saying that it is the same act, but it is not clear that he wants to claim further that it would be virtuous. To do so would appear to be tantamount to claiming that an act is and is not virtuous; it does not fit the definition of virtue, and yet it is a continuation of the same act that was originally virtuous. Normally, Ockham deals with this problem simply by saying that no act is necessarily virtuous (OTh IX, 245–55). 'Virtue' is a connotative term—that is, its definition signifies one thing primarily and another secondarily (OPh I, 35–38). In this case, it signifies primarily the act of rendering justice and secondarily the will that elicits the act and prudence in accordance with which the act is elicited. When we say that God can produce the same act, we are referring only to the primary significate, the act, which by itself is neither good nor bad. Goodness or virtue is a function of the secondary significate (OTh VI, 388–89).

I Second Conclusion

521. Having demonstrated the uncontroversial conclusion that prudence is a necessary condition of virtue, Ockham devotes most of the rest of article 3 (conclusions 2–5) to a demonstration that prudence is not a sufficient condition for virtue. Reminding the reader of the definitions of prudence provided at the beginning of the second article, Ockham devotes a conclusion to each of the four definitions provided there (a.2 2–34). The first definition of prudence refers generally to all normative or directive knowledge; the second derives particular propositions from universal norms; the third is particular knowledge based on experience rather than demonstration; the fourth refers to an aggregate of all immediately directive (particular) knowledge.

Here Ockham is following Scotus and arguing against Aquinas and Godfrey of Fontaines. Ockham holds that the will can choose contrary to right reason. Wey provides references in the notes of his edition to the history of the controversy about the freedom of the will to choose contrary to right reason.

The basic assumption behind the six proofs of conclusion 2 is the thesis that the primary virtuous faculty is the will, not the intellect, a thesis established in article 1 (132–56). Ockham's first proof is based on the assumption that only free acts are imputable. But if prudence necessitates the corresponding act of will, then the will is not free, and hence praise or blame cannot be imputed to it. His analogy is with sensory experience. He claims that people are neither praised nor blamed for their appetites, and that this is because they follow necessarily from sensory apprehension. Having seen an apple, I cannot fail to find it appetizing. No one blames me for this, even if I know I should not eat the apple, because appetite is the inevitable consequence of the apprehension of so tantalizing a fruit. Blame is attached only to what can be controlled—to my stealing the apple, for example. By parity of reasoning, if acts of will were the inevitable consequence of prudence, no one would be praised for willing to follow right reason, which is absurd.

534. The second proof is based on the claim that acts of will cannot be involuntary. Ockham argues that if there were no prudence not followed by virtue, virtuous acts of will would be involuntary, or rather they would be in the power of the will only to the extent that acts of intellect are voluntary. In the course of the argument, the reporter moved to the subjunctive when he should, but then returned to the indicative much too soon. The translation has been altered to read in the subjunctive as long as Ockham is talking about counterfactuals. Suppose we call the major premise CA: if one act is a necessary consequence of another, we control the consequent act only to the extent that the antecedent act is in our power. This is a thesis about essentially ordered causes, a concept that Ockham owes to Scotus (OTh V, 257–58). Essentially ordered causes are a series of causes each of which necessarily follows from the other; they act simultaneously. They contrast with accidentally ordered causes, which act successively; one cause follows another contingently, not necessarily. The minor premise states that if prudence is a sufficient cause of virtue, then acts of intellect and will are related as essentially ordered causes.

Ockham asks us to reject the conclusion that acts of will are only in our power to the extent that intellectual acts are within our power, because the will, not the intellect, is the primary moral faculty. Here the suppressed premise is that since the will is the primary moral faculty, it must be the primary locus of control, since only acts within our power are imputable. Ockham argues for the claim that the will is the primary moral faculty on the ground that acts of intellect are not primarily virtuous. They cannot be primarily virtuous, since the same act of apprehension can coincide successively with virtuous and vicious acts of will. My apprehension of a man struck down on the road does not change as I decide first to rob him and then to take him to the hospital. This is little more than a repetition of the earlier argument, that will is the primary moral faculty (a.1 132–56).

Instead of arguing that the will is the primary faculty within our control, Ockham might have done better to argue as he does later (673–89) and did elsewhere (OTh VII, 358–59), and as Scotus did (*In Metaph.* IX q.15), that intellectual acts are not within our power, since intellect is a natural, not a voluntary, faculty. Given CA, from 'there is no prudence not followed by virtue,' which implies that some volitional acts are necessary consequents of intellectual acts, it would follow that some acts of will are involuntary consequences of intellectual acts, which are themselves determined by their objects, a more obviously absurd conclusion.

549. Here Ockham deals with an important objection from Albert and Thomas that suggests that the ignorance which accounts for wickedness is ignorance of the particular.[10] The suggestion is that the wicked cannot scientifically know a particular moral dictate, since the certainty of that knowledge, based as it is on evident principles, would sufficiently incline them to act accordingly. This appears to be a version of the thesis that vice

---

10. For an excellent account of a number of medieval treatments of weakness of will, see R. Saarinen, *Weakness of the Will in Medieval Thought* (Leiden, 1994).

must proceed from ignorance that would appeal to Ockham, since he has such strong views about incompatible acts. Consider the example of a televangelist who knows he should assist the weak. Perhaps the reason he sends out appeals to the elderly poor, asking them to make great sacrifices so that he can live in luxury, is that he has not realized the elderly belong to class of people he should protect. But Ockham dispatches the objection promptly. The rectitude of the universal principle is just as great as the particular dictate that follows from it. Consequently, there is no more reason to deny that our villain evidently knows the particular dictate than there is regarding the general principle.

555. The third proof is a second reply to the objection in 549, in defense of the thesis that particular prudent dictates derived from evident moral principles are compatible with moral vice. The wording is awkward, owing to defects in the report, which Ockham's twentieth-century and fifteenth-century editors—Wey and Augustinus de Ratisbona—have intelligently emended (561, 568). Nonetheless, the argument is effective. Everyone admits that malicious sins are different from sins arising from ignorance. But if, when a particular situation is understood, the will is bound to react in the morally appropriate manner, then the distinction will be obliterated. Malice consists in doing the wrong thing knowingly. Ockham takes it to be evident that everyone knows universal moral principles, simply reminding his listeners of some such principles. He then asks whether the malicious sinner does or does not know the particular precept she disobeys. If she does, then the will is free to choose against the dictate of right reason. If she does not, then her situation is no different from those who act in ignorance.

569. Someone objects that the malicious differ from the ignorant in the degree of their universal knowledge; the suggestion is that the televangelist does not really know or fully appreciate the significance of the dictate: Do not victimize the weak. What difference could there be? Ockham asks in reply. It must relate either to the same or to different propositions. If no different proposition is known more intensely, then the degree is irrelevant. If different propositions are known, then the argument made in the previous paragraph applies, and the distinction between ignorance and malice will be destroyed.

580. The fourth proof, too, deals with cases of particular prudence based on universal moral principles. It is an argument based on the church's teaching with regard to demonic temptation. Catholic doctrine holds that the fallen angels cannot repent and return to beatific vision; they remain obstinate in their error. Aquinas (ST I q.64 a.2), and the other authors mentioned in Wey's notes, explained this doctrine in terms of the immutability of angelic cognition, which apprehends intuitively what humans know discursively. Following Scotus (*Sent.* II d.7 n.7, XII: 381), Ockham uses this argument against the view that prudence is a sufficient cause of virtue. If we suppose both that angelic cognition is immutable and that the will cannot choose contrary to the dictates of right reason, we will not be able to explain how fallen angels can induce people to sin. For the relevant universal proposition—no one should be induced to act contrary to divine precept—is self-evident, and the minor is known to humans, and therefore better known to angels. Ockham concludes that his opponents are committed to the conclusion that these angels must be both prudent and vicious, which is impossible.

590. An objection based on the distinction between speculative and practical knowledge is raised. Ockham argues in response that angels originally possessed practical as well as speculative knowledge. If Beelzebub lacked practical knowledge at the time of the fall, what destroyed it? Ockham asks. The reader will remember that there are three possible causes that can corrupt prudence or virtue—ignorance, malice, and passion (408–11). Ignorance need not be considered in the case of angels, since their knowledge is immutable and direct; neither need we consider the case for passion, given angelic nature as posited by the medievals. Therefore, the sin of the fallen angels was malice. But malice presupposes choices contrary to the dictates of right reason.

596. While the third and fourth proofs are based on the existence of malice, the fifth proof of the freedom of the will to choose against right reason is based on the existence of incontinence. Again, we have sin that is not based on ignorance; in this case it is caused by passion rather than malice. The powers of the intellect are undiminished. A modern example of what Ockham has in mind can be taken from dietary practice. Most people agree that one is obligated to maintain good health. Today they also know that it is bad for their health to consume food that contains sugar or sugar substitutes in the absence of other nutrients, and that soft drinks fit this description. Nonetheless, many people today drink soft drinks more frequently than any other beverage. In medieval moral theory, such behavior would be described as incontinent. Such examples seem to show that prudent knowledge, even particular practical knowledge, is not sufficient to produce virtue. Alternatively, Ockham might have argued—as he did previously in regard to malice (569)—that to deny that vice is compatible with prudence is to destroy the distinction between vice resulting from ignorance and vice resulting from passion.

604. This objection comes from Aquinas. For Aquinas, as for most medievals, the question with which we are dealing here, the reciprocal causality of will and intellect, is a complicated and important problem. For a more sympathetic and thorough examination of Aquinas's views, see Jordan's account.[11]

This particular attempt to explain incontinence in terms of ignorance suggests that incontinence is the result of assenting to different universals with contrary implications. The argument is that passion is like ignorance; it blinds the incontinent to consequences that follow from normative universals. Stephen might provide an example illustrating this argument. He knows that he should try to stay in good health and avoid eating lots of food with empty calories. But his passion for root beer blinds him to fact that its chemical content makes drinking root beer an unsound dietary practice. His continued consumption of root beer indicates that he is not paying attention to the normative universal, but only to another universal proposition: Have fun, grab for the gusto. Ockham's first impulse is simply to deny that anyone can assent to propositions with contradictory implications. It makes no sense to say that Stephen assents to the universal proposition about empty calories if he rejects its consequences. If that argument is rejected, Ockham returns to his former argument: It is evident from experience that Stephen will choose to drink root beer, even if he is reminded of both the major and minor propositions.

614. The long, sixth proof claims that acceptance of the view that prudence is a sufficient condition for virtue implies that the will is no more capable of self-regulation than is the sensitive soul with its uncontrollable appetites. It is agreed that in the sensory soul, apprehension is immediately followed by appetites for pursuit or avoidance. Ockham's controversial further claim is that if comprehension of the dictates of right reason in the intellectual soul is immediately followed by the will to conform, then the will is no freer than our sensory appetites, an absurdity that his opponents would reject.

627. Ockham's opponents must have a theory that allows them to posit a free will. All Scholastics agree that the will is a locus of freedom; Aquinas, for example, says that the will is the root of our liberty (ST I-II q.17 a.1 ad 2). This objection to the

---

11. Mark Jordan, "Goodness and the Human Will," in *Being and Goodness,* ed. S. MacDonald (Ithaca, N.Y., 1991), 137–49.

sixth proof is an attempt to avoid the conclusion to which Ockham believes his opponents are committed—namely, that the will is not free. In the *Summa theologica* I-II q.10 a.2, Aquinas advances the suggestion that the will is free, because it need not consider the dictates of right reason. What we think about is determined by the will. We may not be able to avoid compassion for a frightened child trapped in the violence of Haitian society, but we can ignore the problem and busy ourselves instead with thoughts about fancy dresses and fine foods.

631. Ockham replies by trying to show that his opponents have not really resolved the problem, but rather taken the first of a series of steps that will constitute an infinite regress. Take the command to avert the intellect. Acknowledging that it is an act of will, he asks whether that command is or is not in accordance with the dictates of intellect. If it is not, he has proven what he set out to prove—that there can be acts of will independent of, or contrary to, the intellect. If it is in accordance with a dictate of the intellect, then the will's avoidance command is determined by intellect, and the will is not free.

636. In a more radical approach, Ockham argues that there can be acts of will in the absence of such practical dictates as prudence provides. He claims that if the sensory soul can be repelled by the sight of a hideous object without our understanding what we are seeing, then the will, which is a higher faculty, can also reject that object. The argument depends on theses from medieval psychology and logic. There is the psychological thesis that sensory apprehension is independent of, and prior to, intellectual comprehension. Logic and psychology supply a hierarchical principle: If something can be shown to be possible for a lower faculty, then a fortiori it is within the capacity of the higher faculty.

640. The next reply to the objection, which begins at line 627, is flawed. It is based on the same thesis regarding the relation of causes stated in the second proof. For the purposes of this reply, Ockham assumes that the act of will averting the intellect has itself been elicited in conformity with an act of intellect. The argument is about that putative original act of intellect. For example, it might be that a decent regard for my own family dictates that I not spend a lot of time considering the needs of distant, unrelated children who are in jeopardy. Ockham asks whether that conclusion is or is not necessarily elicited. If it is, then neither the act of averting intellect nor the subsequent attention to my family is voluntary or imputable. If the act of averting the intellect is free, which is what Ockham's opponents claim, then it is not clear what follows. If Ockham's argument is to work, what has to follow is that even so, my attention to my family is not voluntary and hence not virtuous. But his opponents have suggested that it is voluntary, because the decision to avert the intellect is free. Here it seems safest simply to conclude that there is something wrong with the report we are examining; something was lost.

649. A somewhat less confusing reply to the objection at line 627, this argument plausibly assumes that Ockham's opponents are committed to the view that an averting act of will must be elicited in response to a dictate of right reason. Ockham aims to show again that his opponent is committed to an infinite regress. The strategy is to show that if the will averts the intellect from the plight of suffering children, this must be in response to a contrary dictate. But if it is a contrary dictate, then it cannot be the same dictate, which takes us a step further in the regress. Each time his opponent claims that the will is free because it could avert the intellect, Ockham replies that this could only be in response to another act of intellect. The regress can only be halted, according to Ockham, if we admit that the will can act without a prior act of intellect. Instead of an intellectually understood object, its object could be grasped by the senses alone; an object of the will may be a bare manifestation. Ockham's aim in using the phrase 'bare manifestation' is to contrast 'being shown' an incomplex object with propositional knowledge or understanding. It is constructed by analogy with simple sensory apprehension at line 638. Like that reply, it presents Ockham's solution to the problem of the mutual causality of will and intellect: the will is prior to the intellect.

665. The analogy between will and sensory appetite also forms the basis for the next reply. The objection claims that the will is free, since it can avert the intellect (627). Passions can also impede the intellect, and we do not for that reason infer that our sensitive appetites are free, Ockham replies. He concludes that the ability to avert the intellect is no grounds for saying that a faculty is free.

669. With this confirmation, Ockham begins an intricate dialogue with Godfrey about cases in which the intellect errs. In the passages cited in Wey's notes, Godfrey maintains that freedom requires both will and intellect, from which it seems to follow that sin is as much a matter of intellect as of will. He also holds that both the will and the intellect are to some extent necessitated by their objects. It is no derogation of liberty, he holds, to be determined by the highest good. Godfrey also maintains that vice really blinds the intellect, so that it does not function accurately regarding our moral duties. The vicious really do not know what they should do.

Ockham's first response to Godfrey is to present a dilemma: When reason errs, is this within the power of the will or not? If it is not, this error is the result of invincible ignorance and is not sinful. Ockham is saying that if there is real blindness, then there is no sin, even if this blindness is the result of past sin—a conclusion Godfrey would reject. The other alternative is the traditional view accepted by Ockham: the will is the primary moral faculty; sin is a question of will alone.

673. Here Ockham argues, contrary to Godfrey, that the intellect is not free. Intellectual adherence is the result of one of three things: evidence (either of reason or experience), authority, or will. Given what has gone before (665), Ockham should probably have added sensory appetites to the list. Our passions, like authority and will, can move the intellect in the absence of evidence. Godfrey agrees that the intellect is not always free—it cannot dissent from first principles—but he claims that sometimes in the course of investigation the intellect is free. By contrast, Ockham claims that the intellect is always necessitated—whether by the force of evidence or by the force of will, authority, or sensory appetites.

Like the first proof, this argument shows that prudence cannot be a sufficient cause of virtue. Virtue must be voluntary, and prudence, like other acts of intellect, is necessitated, not voluntary.

680. The next argument aims to show that if his opponents' views are conceded, it follows that the first sin was intellectual, which contradicts Augustine. Suppose in considering the question of the mutual causality of will and intellect, you decide that the regress halts at an act of intellect. On Ockham's opponents' view, when intellect errs, the will necessarily assents unless the intellect presents another dictate. According to Ockham, it follows from this that if there is no other dictate, there is sin in the absence of free will. Furthermore (685), in a case where God interfered in the causal chain, so that the will did not assent, the intellect would sin by adhering to the false dictate without there being any act of will.

I Third to Fifth Conclusions

691. Conclusions 3 to 5 argue that in the second, third, and fourth senses of the term, prudence is not a sufficient cause of virtue. In the second definition, prudence refers to particular dictates of right reason derived from universal dictates. Ockham points out that the arguments in support of conclusion 2 will work in that case, too.

696. Here Ockham resumes his argument with Godfrey. Godfrey holds that though the will is moved by its object, our judgment is nonetheless free for four reasons: the universality of the objects considered, the immateriality of our faculties, the freedom of the will in executing acts, and the capacity to choose contraries. Here Ockham takes up the third reason. The will is free because it controls our external activities. According to Godfrey, although the root of free judgment (*arbitrium*) is in the intellect, it is completed by the will.

702. Ockham's counterargument begins with the rule about essentially ordered causes adduced earlier (CA, 535, 641); they are in the power of the will only to the extent that the first member of the chain is in the power of the will. Here, instead of being concerned with the relation of will and intellect, Ockham is concerned with the relation of both to the exterior act. If the intellect dictates without qualification, and the will wills efficaciously, only an external obstacle can prevent the act. Ockham rejects the possibility of efficacious internal acts that do not produce corresponding external acts. As he did earlier, Ockham quotes Gregory: If there is love, it will show itself in works. Suppose, for example, that Forrest knows that you need a coat because it is ten degrees below zero, and you are in a swimsuit. Forrest has an extra coat, and he tells you that he loves you and has decided to help you by giving you a coat. Here there is no external obstacle, since Forrest has the extra coat. What can you conclude if he does not hand you the coat? Would you conclude that he does want to help, but just does not happen to do so? If you conclude instead that Forrest either does not want to help or does not understand, you have conceded Ockham's point: action follows necessarily from what he calls a formally imperative, executive act of will. Ockham maintains that exterior acts follow formally imperative, executive acts of will necessarily. Hence, the link between will and action is necessary, and the execution of exterior acts is no proof of the freedom of the will.

After citing Gregory, Ockham adduces Aristotle's authority in defining rationality: a rational faculty can choose contraries. This is relevant, because Ockham (OTh VII, 358–59), like Scotus (*In Metaph.* IX q.15), argues that the will, not the intellect, is the true rational faculty; it is the will, not the intellect, that is free to opt for contraries.

720. Having argued that willing something efficaciously is the same as doing it in the absence of unanticipated obstacles, Ockham now considers whether there is any difference between willing conformity with a dictate and willing the exterior act that conforms efficaciously. His answer is based on the distinction that he drew earlier between acts of second-degree virtue (fortitude) and acts of heroic virtue. In Ockham's scheme, the resolve to persevere is a conditional act of second-degree virtue. An example similar to one of his earlier examples pertains to Franciscans like himself (a.2 87). Suppose Fr. Conrad, a Franciscan without substantial personal possessions, wishes to support a university and vows to do so if he can, even at great personal cost. That is virtuous, but it is different from the actions of a millionaire who endows the library, even at the cost of ending his days in the county nursing home. The difference between equivalently imperative acts of fortitude and formally imperative acts of heroism is the difference between pious resolves and real sacrifice beyond our natural human capacity. Ockham replies that there is no difference between willing conformity and willing the deed in the case of formally imperative acts of will. But there is a difference in the case of equivalently imperative acts of will. Suppose that Conrad inherited wealth unexpectedly as an old man and was permitted to dispose of it himself. If he gave it all to Saint Bonaventure University's Friedsam library, his action would be heroic, and it would be a different act from the act of the young man with no fortune to give.

736. Ockham's fourth conclusion covers the case of immediately directive particular prudence that which results from experience, prudence 3. Here he comes closest to allowing that some prudence is necessarily connected with virtue. But first he provides instances of prudence acquired by experience that can exist in the absence of virtue. Watching other people, we can learn what should be done without engaging in those practices ourselves.

748. In this paragraph, Ockham holds that some prudence is inseparable from virtue. An important example is the proposition that 'someone who loves God finds more enjoyment in temporal things.' Here he is thinking of the mystic who finds that the world is lovelier after meditation. Ockham holds that because only experience could provide evidence of this proposition, and because such experiences are essentially private, this prudent true belief cannot exist without virtue. But the reader should note that this is not the same as saying that prudence is a sufficient cause of virtue; rather, it is an effect of virtue, one of the few kinds of prudence that could only be produced by virtue and cannot be learned without practicing virtue.

768. In the next two paragraphs, Ockham drives home the qualification. Strictly speaking, it is only at the time when experience is actually producing prudence that virtue and prudence need coincide. At all other times, it is logically possible for there to be prudence in the absence of virtue. Ockham emphasizes that the causation is not mutual (782).

| Sixth Conclusion

800. In the sixth conclusion Ockham qualifies what he has said in the first conclusion—that prudence is a necessary cause of virtue—in some relatively minor ways. Prudence is a necessary cause of virtue, because conformity with right reason is part of the definition of virtue. But the second mode of prudence is identified not just with particular dictates of right reason, but also with understanding the universal, self-evident propositions from which they follow. Since we can acquire knowledge of particular normative propositions from experience, rather than deductively, this form of prudence is not necessary for virtue.

Regarding the first mode of prudence, there is confusion, and it appears to come from Ockham himself. In article 2, where he distinguishes the various possible meanings of 'prudence,' the first mode that Ockham defines refers to all directive knowledge, universal or particular. But here Ockham seems to restrict the first mode of prudence to *universal* practical knowledge, acquired by reason or experience. And as Ockham argues here, no universal knowledge is necessary for virtue. That is, a sense of gratitude might prompt Barbara to do something nice for a generous friend, even if she did not know the general rule that we should do nice things for generous people.

810. Though virtue does not require universal moral knowledge, it does require particular knowledge, whether acquired by reason (mode 2) or experience (mode 3). There is no virtue without prudence, and it must be specific. If reason fails, experience is necessary; in the absence of experience, reason is required. Elsewhere, Ockham suggests that some degree of prudence in the third mode really is necessary. He says that though it is theoretically possible to lead a virtuous life solely on the basis of particular principles rationally derived from universal principles, in fact there is no substitute for experience (OTh I, 320).

Doubts

Here there are eight doubts, or rather eight objections against Ockham's position. Only the first two get significant'treatment, though a number of the other doubts are answered implicitly in the course of the reply to doubt 1. A rather miscellaneous list, these eight doubts probably represent objections actually raised at Oxford when Ockham was speaking. Doubt 1 raises objections against Ockham's position that would be raised by a Scotist. Scotus believed that moral virtue depended on appropriate external circumstances, and he regarded time, place, and purpose as external circumstances; an act is virtuous if it is done for the right reason at the right time. Ockham agrees, of course, but argues that time, place, and purpose are intrinsic to virtuous acts; they are not external circumstances. Instead of speaking about circumstances, he speaks of secondary partial objects (a.2 185), and he argues further that acts with different partial objects are specifically distinct. Going to church to worship is specifically distinct from going to church to gossip. The purpose of the action is essential to its description; it is not an external circumstance.

3. Both Ockham and Scotus posit indifferent acts. But for Ockham, there are also intrinsically virtuous acts. The first doubt challenges Ockham to explain how an act can first be morally indifferent and subsequently be morally virtuous, or how it can even go from being virtuous to being vicious. In answer to the first doubt, Ockham sets out the differences between his and Scotus's positions.

18. The second doubt also pertains directly to Ockham's dispute with Scotus. It suggests that an act's purpose, its time, its place, and whether it conforms to right reason should be described as the circumstances of that act, not as partial objects. Less importantly, it raises the question of how the same act can be described as an act of love and as an act of hate—a problem that arises when we hate sin for the sake of God because we love God.

30. Doubt 3 again raises Scotistic objections to Ockham. If exterior acts are no more than automatic consequences of unimpeded internal acts, why are they separately prohibited in the Decalogue and other legal systems? Why is it worse actually to commit a crime than merely to contemplate it?

36. Doubt 4 points out a respect in which Ockham's account of moral virtue differs from that of Aristotle, who believed that we could describe irrational as well as rational excellences. In medieval terms, he held that there were virtues in the sensitive as well as the intellectual soul. Ockham does, of course, allow that there are habits in other faculties, rational and irrational. But he denies that they have moral significance, and he opposes Aristotle's views more than other Scholastics, since he holds that moral virtues pertain only to the will.

40. The fifth doubt asks for a defense of Ockham's distinction between third- and fourth-degree virtues, between pagan virtue and Christian virtue. It suggests that since moral virtue deals with people and things encountered on earth and in this life—as Ockham himself concedes for the first three degrees of virtue (a.3 388–89)—mention of a supernatural deity is inappropriate in discussing morality. This doubt forces Ockham once more (a.2 143) to defend the claim that Christian virtue is moral virtue properly speaking. It suggests that Christian virtue is supernatural, not moral.

48. Doubt 6 returns to the dispute with Scotus. It challenges Ockham's claim that acts with different partial objects differ specifically. A counterexample similar to Ockham's argument for specific distinctions is suggested: loving Plato does not differ specifically from loving Socrates, and yet love of Plato is compatible with hatred of Socrates.

58. The seventh doubt asks Ockham to explain why the distinctions that he draws between the virtues are different from those of Aristotle. Unlike the grades of virtue posited by Henry of Ghent, Ockham's degrees of virtue do not correspond to the distinctions drawn by Aristotle. In reply to doubt 7, Ockham will have to clarify his understanding of temperance, perseverance, and continence.

64. Again a challenge to Ockham's departures from Aristotle, the eighth doubt objects to the second and fifth degrees of virtue as defined by Ockham. Why should we allow resolute or heroic degrees of honesty? The claim is that heroism pertains only to one virtue, courage. So take the case where Norman chooses to go to prison rather than commit an act of injustice. The objector claims that this action is not properly described as an instance of heroic justice, but rather of two connected virtues, justice and courage. The objection suggests that Ockham has confused a virtue with a degree of virtue, that he has committed a category mistake. Henry would be making a similar mistake at the supermarket if he said to a customer, "What you have here is a very juicy apple and a drier apple," not an orange and an apple.

A summary of the doubts in tabular form, distinguishing between two broad classes of objections that challenge Ockham's departures from Scotus's views and those of Aristotle, may be helpful:

Doubt (line number)	Topic	Reply line
One (3)	Indifferent acts (Scotist challenge)	72
Two (18)	Object of virtuous acts (Scotist)	401
Three (30)	Exterior acts (Scotist)	624
Four (36)	Sensitive acts (Aristotelian challenge)	629
Five (40)	Supernatural object (Aristotelian)	634
Six (48)	Specific distinction (Scotist)	654
Seven (58)	Continence, Temperance, & Perseverance (Aristotelian)	702
Eight (64)	Heroism (Aristotelian)	725

Of course, many of these doubts raise problems as much or more for the internal consistency of Ockham's views as for his departures from the views of his predecessors. Moreover, medieval authors will have raised the Aristotelian objections, and some of the Scotistic objections might just as well have been raised by earlier authors. To do justice to the complexity of the situation, one would have to explain that students of Henry of Ghent would have raised doubt 6, and that (like Ockham) they would have had to reply to doubt 8, but we cannot discuss these complicated interactions here. The reader may, however, be interested in distinguishing the more ancient from the Scholastic objections considered by Ockham; certainly it is instructive to see how much more weight Ockham gives to the Scotistic objections than to the others.

| Reply to the First Doubt

| Summary and Refutation of Scotus's Opinion

72. Ockham starts by summarizing Scotus's reply to the first doubt. The subject of the first doubt, "indifferent acts" comes from Scotus, who uses the phrase somewhat hesitatingly. Though positing such acts is basic to his position, he concludes at one point only that it is probable that there are morally indifferent acts (*Sent.* II d.41 n.4, XIII: 435). By contrast, though Ockham challenges many of Scotus's other views, he takes the existence of indifferent acts more or less for granted. His proof of their existence is very brief (a.1 113). But though Ockham assumes the existence of indifferent acts—which he also calls extrinsically virtuous acts—he challenges the view that an intrinsically virtuous act of will can be successively indifferent and virtuous. An intrinsically virtuous act of will is an act that aims at conformity with right reason or obedience to God—that is, all acts of third- and fourth-degree virtues and most acts of fifth-degree virtue, as was mentioned earlier in the commentary (a.2 137).

In general, Ockham's summary of Scotus is accurate, but Ockham's mention of numerical identity (81) is doubtful. In the passages cited by Ockham, Scotus does not say explicitly that numerically the same act is successively indifferent and then meritorious; Scotus is concerned rather with specific identity. Moreover, so brief a summary could not do justice to the complexity of Scotus's position. For a fuller account of Scotus's position, including a discussion of the analogy that Scotus draws between virtue and beauty (*Ord.* I d.17 p.1 q.1–2 n.62, V: 163) in terms of the appropriateness of a thing to its function and setting, see Adams 1981 (p. 17) and Wolter (pp. 84–89).

80. Here Ockham is reciting Scotus's replies to some interesting objections. Someone might argue that since virtue is specifically distinct from merit, virtuous acts must be specifically distinct from meritorious acts (*Quodl.* q.17 n.6–7.13, XXVI: 211–12.224–25; Alluntis a.3 n.13–17.34, 617–20.628). Again, meritorious acts differ from acts that are not meritorious, because they are caused by charity; how can acts with different causes be specifically identical? (n.13, XXVI: 224–25; n.34, 627–28). Furthermore, Aristotle defines goodness as a quality, so it must be a mistake to define goodness as a relation (*Quodl.* q.18 n.7, XXVI: 237–38; Alluntis a.1 n.17–19, 638–39).

89. Ockham touches here on the core of his disagreement with Scotus. Following Anselm, Ockham holds that virtue is in the will. Scotus disagrees: virtue is caused by the will, but it does not inhere in the will (*Quodl.* q.18 n.16, XXVI: 249; Alluntis a.3 n.42, 653). Rectitude is not a quality of the will; rectitude consists in the will's conformity with prudence.

96. Ockham believes that Scotus has not adequately answered the objections against his opinion. As good Aristotelians, both agree that only acts in the power of the will can be virtuous. But Scotus is committed to saying that if Marilyn starts out abstaining from eating grasshoppers because she hates the taste, and later learns that it is wrong to eat grasshoppers because they are an endangered species, her continued abstention is first morally indifferent and subsequently morally virtuous. And yet the only thing that has changed is that she has gained practical knowledge — an act of prudence that Scotus and Ockham both agree is not voluntary. If we are presented with the evidence, learning, like seeing, is an involuntary act in all relevant respects. Scotus agrees that acquiring the new information about endangered species is not virtuous, but holds that the change in the relation of Marilyn's will to that knowledge is. Ockham disagrees: the act of prudence as related to the act of abstention does not suffice; there must be a new act of will — in this case, the will to protect endangered species.

105. Both the major (105) and the minor (108) premises of this disproof were established in the first article. Necessarily virtuous acts are acts undertaken for the sake of love of God — fourth-degree, perfect acts of virtue (634; a.3 312). Acts of third-degree virtue, though intrinsically virtuous, are not necessarily virtuous (a.3 272). Since the aim of this proof is to show that only acts of will are intrinsically virtuous, mention of the necessarily/contingent distinction is inappropriate here. Strictly speaking, the argument should read:

> No indifferent act can be rendered virtuous by an extrinsically virtuous act.
>
> But only an act of will is intrinsically virtuous or vicious, since exterior acts and intellectual acts can only be virtuous by extrinsic denomination.
>
> Therefore prudence, an act of intellect, cannot render extrinsically virtuous acts virtuous.

Ockham concludes that the mere coexistence of an act of prudence cannot by itself render an indifferent act virtuous.

116. Here Ockham tries a different strategy against Scotus. He suggests that we reject the view that virtuous acts are complex.

123. It is Scotus, of course, who holds that apart from the substance of an act, a virtuous act includes a relation of conformity to prudence. Scotus says that it is the conformity of an act to right reason that is the moral goodness of that act. Like other relations, goodness does not have its own proper principle, but arises naturally once the extremes of the relation are posited (*Ord.* I d.17 p.1 q.1–2 n.62–63, V: 164). In Marilyn's case, the extremes are abstinence and her knowledge of the dictate 'protect endangered species.' The basis for this argument against Scotus is the claim that nothing can be rendered virtuous by something involuntary. But once the prudence is posited, the relation arises naturally and inevitably, as Scotus himself agrees.

129. Here Ockham argues, against Scotus, that nothing can go from being vicious or indifferent to being virtuous without one's positing a new act of will. Ockham presents an argument for the major premise: 'nothing can go from being morally good to not being morally good without one's adding or subtracting something.' He infers the major premise from two uncontroversial propositions: 'nothing can go from one contradictory to another without adding or subtracting something' and 'being morally good and not being morally good are contradictories.' To establish that we must posit an additional act, Ockham begins by eliminating the possibility that something could be subtracted, on the grounds that Scotus concedes the point. Ockham continues by suggesting that what is new must be either something absolute or something relative. He deals first with the possible absolutes: a habit, a species, or an act. Eliminating habit and species because they are compatible with vice, Ockham concludes that we must posit an additional act. It cannot be an act of intellect, since intellectual acts are involuntary; therefore it must be an act of will.

144. Here Ockham deals with the alternative to something absolute, something relative. But there are no new relations except as the result of new absolutes, as Ockham establishes from Scotus's own writing. So this alternative, too, yields the conclusion that a new absolute entity must account for the change. At this point, Ockham adds that the new absolute entity must be formally and intrinsically good, a claim that Scotus would reject.

Had Marilyn's case been described, Ockham might have said that "Marilyn does not act virtuously" and "Marilyn acts virtuously" are contradictories, so something must have changed. Something new must have been introduced. By itself, nothing relative would suffice, so it must be something absolute—either a habit, a species, or an act. No habit would suffice, because the habit of virtuous abstention is compatible with occasional acts gluttony; even people who habitually refrain from buying products made from the hides of endangered reptiles are capable of buying leopard-skin pillbox hats. So there must be a new act. It cannot be Marilyn's intellectual act—her learning that grasshoppers are an endangered species—since her friend Bob eats caribou even though he knows that naturalists have established that only a few remain in the wild. It cannot just be her failure to eat grasshoppers, since she might just as well refuse to eat them because she hates the taste. So it must that what makes her refusal virtuous is her determination not to eat the flesh of animals whose survival as a species is in danger. Scotus, on the other hand, might have said that though Marilyn's new information on the perils of grasshoppers is not virtuous, neither is her determination to refrain from eating grasshoppers new. It is the same act of abstention, whether performed for the sake of endangered species or simply to avoid nausea. What makes her action virtuous is the relation between that newly acquired knowledge and her continued determination not to eat grasshoppers.

Ockham's qualification at line 150—'if God were to accept an act of intellect, it could be called intrinsically good'—poses a problem. It shows him experimenting with a second definition of goodness. Following Aristotle, his primary definition is 'what is lovable,' which is divided into three goods: what is worthy (lovable for its own sake), what is useful, and what is pleasant (*Eth. Nic.* 6.2.1155b19). That is the definition from which the self-evident proposition, 'everything worthy should be done' is derived, and Ockham uses it consistently There is one point where Ockham might appear to define 'good' as that which is loved by God (OTh VI, 215). But that appearance is illusory. Ockham holds that when we say "God is good," the word 'good' signifies God as something to be loved. Similarly, if I say "this coat is good," that signifies that the coat is to be loved. Given the Aristotelian distinction, the difference between the two cases is that God is loved for his own sake; the coat, for its usefulness in keeping me warm. It is as well that Ockham does not entertain a "voluntarist" definition of goodness, since it would not be compatible with discursive moral science, with a sphere of nonpositive law regarding what is good apart from the dictates of an extrinsic cause (OTh IX, 177).

As Ockham correctly notes at the close of the paragraph, the qualification tentatively considered at line 150 would undermine the theory of intrinsically good acts of will (a.1 99–160) on which the *De connexione* is based. So the question is: Why, after repeatedly arguing that only an act of will can be intrinsically virtuous, because only acts of will are within our control, does Ockham imply here that acts of intellect, which are not within our control, could be intrinsically virtuous? Why does he say that God could make something that is extrinsically good intrinsically good? That seems to imply that God can cause something logically impossible, which Ockham, like virtually all his contemporaries, denies. It seems unlikely that Ockham means to suggest that God could make intellectual acts voluntary, since that, too, would be a contradiction in terms, given Ockham's understanding of intellectual acts in this context. The answer seems to be that the subject has changed. Ockham's reference to what "God accepts" suggests that he may be shifting to a consideration of merit, which necessarily depends on acceptance, rather than notions of intrinsic goodness. Merit, unlike virtue, is chiefly a matter of divine acceptance, so whatever God chooses to accept, things which meet that description count as meritorious, whether or not we have voluntary control over them. By contrast, virtue arises from the voluntary choice of goodness (a.1 131–60). Though it is logically impossible for intellectual acts to be voluntary, God could nonetheless ordain that we would be rewarded for them, in which case performing those acts would in some sense be meritorious, which is probably what Ockham has in mind here. It is probably part of the transition to a discussion to sin.

155. Ockham shifts in this paragraph to a discussion of rectitude, which is common both to the sphere of virtue/vice and to merit/sin. He is responding to Scotus's account of sin as a lack of rectitude. The first thing to note is that strictly speaking we should be discussing vice, not sin—offenses against right reason rather than offenses against God. In this case, however, the shift poses no special problems, since 'rectitude' is a term that refers generally to conformity with rules, either with the dictates of right reason (virtue/vice) or love of God (merit/sin) (Scotus, *Quodl.* q.17 n.9, XXVI: 213; Alluntis a.3 n.21, 622). Ockham begins by suggesting somewhat implausibly that Scotus understands by 'rectitude' failure to act properly—or rather the omission or commission of acts of will commanded by God. Suppose God commands Glenn not to eat pork, and Glenn does not eat pork, but his reason for not eating pork is that he is trying to lose weight, not that he is trying to obey God. Suppose further that Glenn subsequently decides that it is important not to eat pork because of divine command, not for dietary reasons. According to Ockham, the first and the second acts of will are not only numerically, but specifically distinct. Going on a pork-free diet to lose weight is specifically different from obeying biblical prohibitions against unclean food. What Scotus would describe as circumstances of the same act, Ockham describes as the objects of two distinct acts.

164. Having dealt with the issue of specific difference, Ockham now turns to theological issues. Ockham agrees, of course, with the Augustinian view that sin is nothing positive or absolute; rather, it is the absence of something to which divine command obligates us (OTh VII, 195–97). But what is that something? For Ockham, it is an act inhering in the will; for Scotus, something inhering in the act. Setting out to defeat the suggestion that rectitude inheres in acts, Ockham starts with a dichotomy: what inheres in an act must be either absolute or relative. As before, Ockham considers absolutes first and eliminates the possibility of species or habits. He also eliminates the possibility of acts, since acts do not inhere in acts and acts are not designed to perfect acts. Rectitude as a relation, Scotus's position, is considered last. This alternative is rejected because relations arise naturally, and nothing involuntary can cause sin.

Among the ontological possibilities, here and above Ockham lists species (135, 168). 'Species' has a variety of meanings for medievals; relevant here are sensible and intelligible species, which represent external objects in the soul. The trio, species, act, and habit, is essential to medieval psychology. Species are prior to acts; habits are subsequent. As Scotus explains, species are posited to explain the presence of objects to the mind, and because they are abstract, they also account for our ability to apprehend universals, such as humanity, as well as individuals, such as Socrates (*Ord.* d.3 p.3 q.1 n.351–70, III: 211–25). Without species the intellect could not act (n.339, III: 204). Ockham is famous for denying that we must posit sensible and intelligible species (OPh II, 31; OTh V, 268, 272–76), a view espoused earlier by Peter John Olivi,[1] Henry of Ghent (*Quodl.* V q.15, fols. 174–79), and Godfrey of Fontaines.[2] According to Ockham, the external objects suffice by themselves; few medievals agreed,[3] not even Adam de Wodeham (*L. sec.* prol. q.3; d.1 q.5, I: 81, 287).

---

1. *Quaestiones in II lib. Sent.* q.58, ed. B. Jansen, BFS 5 (1924): 470–74; q.73, BFS 6 (1926): 83–89.
2. Godefroid de Fontaines, *Quodl.* IX q.19, ed. J. Hoffmans, PhB 4 (1924): 271–75.
3. K. Tachau, *Vision and Certitude in the Age of Ockham* (Leiden, 1988).

| Ockham's Reply to the First Doubt

184. Ockham's reply is based on his distinction between intrinsically and extrinsically virtuous acts. Only acts of will are intrinsically virtuous, because only acts of will are necessarily voluntary, and therefore imputable—that is, we are praiseworthy or blameworthy only account of what we control (a.1 131–60). Extrinsically virtuous acts are acts that are called virtuous because they conform to intrinsically virtuous acts of will. Exercising at the fitness center is an example of an indifferent act that can be virtuous by extrinsic denomination. For example, if Patty exercises in order to maintain her health, her exercises are virtuous by extrinsic denomination. By contrast, her determination to retain her health, an act of will, is virtuous by intrinsic denomination. Replying to the first doubt in terms of this example, Ockham would say that Patty's exercises could be indifferent and virtuous in turn; if her goal changed, an extrinsically virtuous act could be rendered extrinsically vicious. Suppose that as she lifts weights she sees that people admire her beauty. Her exertions may, as a consequence, become an exercise in vanity rather than an exercise in maintaining good health. But Patty's intrinsically virtuous act cannot be rendered vicious, and the reverse is also true. Thus if Patty's aim really is good health, the mere awareness of admiration does not make her vain. Similarly, if her aim is vanity, that act of will cannot be rendered virtuous simply by her awareness that everyone should exercise for the sake of their health, something that virtually none of us can escape knowing. An act of vanity does not become a virtuous act just because we know the rules of practical wisdom. We must intend to follow those rules.

191. In setting out his own example, Ockham argues further that virtue and vice are incompatible—so that Patty cannot exercise both for the sake of vanity and for the sake of good health. Exercise is an exterior act, so it cannot be intrinsically good, but it can be good by extrinsic denomination. If that exercise has no purpose or no morally relevant purpose, it will be generically good. The reader will recall the account of generic goods presented in article 2 (212). Patty's exercise is generically good because it can be done for the right purpose in the right circumstances. It will be specifically good if what Ockham calls its partial objects and Scotus calls its circumstances are appropriate. Here Ockham is arguing that Patty's two forms of exercise are specifically distinct, because they can exist separately; they can come into and go out of existence at different times.

In considering Ockham's example, let us suppose that he has in mind the study of logic, the sort of intellectual activity that we can engage in voluntarily, just as we engage in exterior physical acts (OTh VI, 375). He posits two acts, both acts of will. The generically good act might be described as the resolve to study logic in morally indifferent circumstances—for example, a person might study logic for its own sake, because logic is interesting—at least if you are one of the world's great logicians. That first act is followed by a second act, which is morally good—the resolve to study logic because right reason dictates it—that is, because all people should learn to use their intellectual faculties properly. Ockham's first point is that the two are distinct acts; they can exist separately. His second point is that even though we know that right reason dictates the study of logic, if we study it only for fun, our study is not virtuous. To be virtuous, the study must be dictated by the desire to follow right reason.

210. Now Ockham considers Scotus's reply—namely, that it is the same act of exercise or of study, whether performed for a good purpose or not. This paragraph is very difficult to translate because of the term *'ratio,'* which could be rendered either as 'act of reason' or as 'description' (OPh I, 654). I have chosen the more conservative 'act of reason,' but what is meant is apprehension of the proposition 'study is good,' which dictates you should study—as opposed to 'study in accordance with right reason is good,' which dictates you should study in accordance with right reason. Ockham's point is that willing one is, or can be, *incompatible* with the other, because the second act would cease if study were not in accordance with right reason, and the first would not. His point is easier to illustrate with Patty's exercise. If she wills 'exercise contrary to right reason,' that is incompatible with 'exercise in conformity with right reason.' Even exercise with no morally relevant object—say, 'exercise to kill time'—will start and stop at different points from 'exercise in conformity with right reason.' So if Patty is exercising for the sake of good health, she will stop if the doctor tells her to, assuming she believes he provides reliable health advice. Even if she does not stop lifting weights, she will stop exercising for the sake of good health, since Patty cannot at the same time be obeying right reason and rejecting its dictates.

227. This reply duplicates the reply found at line 129, the first of two duplicate replies to Scotus. In reading this reply the reader needs to keep in mind that for Ockham 'natural' is the opposite of 'voluntary.' The contrast is between freely chosen and naturally dictated acts. As before, Ockham's point is that by themselves, neither acts of prudence nor the relations arising naturally from them can render other acts virtuous. But a new determination to obey right reason could account for a change from vice to virtue and from an indifferent act to a virtuous act.

233. In this reply, which duplicates the reply found at line 155, Ockham's point is that sins are acts that we are obligated not to perform, not something inhering or failing to inhere in the act. Rectitude is doing what is right according to the dictates of right reason and divine command. There is no rightness apart from right acts.

242. This is a response to Scotus's claim that rectitude is a relation. It is based on Scotus's own arguments against the concept of grace as something other than divine acceptance. In effect Ockham is arguing that since Scotus holds that merit is nothing other than the act of a free faculty, accepted by God and elicited as the grace inclines (*Ord.* I d.17 p.1 q.1–2 n.142–53, V: 207–12), he should also hold that moral virtue is nothing apart from an act elicited in accordance with right reason as commanded by God.

256. In this paragraph, Ockham is asking what entities are involved in sin. Again the aim is to deny rectitude independent ontological status and to affirm that everything involved is an absolute: the will, its acts, its future punishment, and God's precepts. Let us take the sin of failing to observe the Sabbath. If Maxine spends Sunday in the shopping mall, she commits a sin of omission; the deformity in the act is failure to worship on the Sabbath, as commanded in the Decalogue. A more difficult sin for Ockham to account for is the prohibition against false witness. Testifying that a neighbor beats his children is a sin of commission if the truth is that they beat him. But what is the deformity in the act? The answer depends on whether we believe that obedience to divine precept requires us to tell the truth. If, as the Decalogue suggests, the only thing we are required to do is avoid false witness, and the will is not obligated to perform the opposite act—that is, to communicate to the authorities what we know— then Ockham cannot provide an account of sin in terms of a deficit, the sort of account which would be preferable from a theological point of view. He is forced to conclude instead that a sin of commission is not the lack of anything, a difficulty that does not arise for Scotus, who can claim that it is a lack of rectitude (*Ord.* I d.17 p.1 q.1–2 n.62–68, V: 163–70; d.48 n.3–4, VI: 387–88; *Sent.* II d.40 n.3–4, XIII: 435).

I Sin

271. Scotus distinguishes a material and a formal element in his definition of sin, to will what is forbidden. What is material is the will, which acts; what is formal is the fact that its object is forbidden. The formal aspect of the definition signifies the lack of conformity with divine precept. Ockham rejects this account, focusing instead on the act and defining the act in terms that include its object. His criticism of specifying formal and material elements in the definition is based on the view that sins of commission unaccompanied by sins of omission, as well as sins of omission in the absence of sins of commission, are possible (OTh VIII, 437). In cases of commission, there is nothing the will was obligated to do and failed to do—for example, false witness involves no positive duty left undone, since the Decalogue does not require us to volunteer true testimony. There is no formal element in the sin, since nothing required is omitted. In the case of sins of omission, the material element is absent, since no sinful act is performed—by itself, shopping is not sinful; what is sinful is the absence of Sabbath observance. Where both commission and omission are involved, there is both a positive, the sinful act, and a negative, the lack of an obligatory act. For Scotus, all sins involve both a formal and a material element; for Ockham, though some sins involve both a positive and a negative element, there can also be sins in the absence of positive acts or in duties left undone.

287. Ockham concludes that Scotus is wrong to maintain that every sin includes two elements, one of which is a privation. As Wey indicates, there is a reading in this paragraph that is supported by only four manuscripts. Whether we accept this reading depends on how much weight is assigned to the Olmütz manuscript. Since the text preserved in this manuscript is the version of Ockham's lectures associated with Wodeham (OTh VII, *21–28), who was a close disciple, there is good reason to believe that the reading in that manuscript is authentic. It is reassuring that Wey was both correct and scrupulous, but neither adapting nor rejecting the reading would be of much philosophical significance in this case.

299. Ockham provides a very truncated version of his own account of sin as privation here, possibly because his own account seems to involve a relation. The conclusion here is simply that not every sin is privation. In his earlier commentary on the fourth book of Lombard's *Sentences,* there is a much fuller account. As here, the basic point is that a sin of commission is an act that someone is obligated by divine precept not to commit, and a sin of omission is the absence of an act that someone is obligated by divine precept to commit. One is positive, the other negative. But in addition, Ockham explains that there is a further element in both definitions—namely, the resulting punishment. So that whether or not they involve acts, it is on account of sins that we are destined for eternal punishment and deprived of beatific vision. Sin is a privation in that it deprives us of a future good (OTh VII, 223–25). There is no hint of this discussion in the brief note found in Ockham's *Quodlibets* (OTh IX, 261), so possibly Ockham dropped it, since it resembles a relational account of sin. Sin is an act, or the lack of an act, on account of which we are punished, something or nothing that is directly related to our future punishment. But this seems unlikely; Ockham's account of merit is parallel, and the relation is to future reward (OTh VII, 233). Moreover, Ockham has a perfectly adequate procedure for interpreting relations as connotative terms, which will allow him to avoid the problem. Sin is a connotative term (OTh VII, 225); the definition of a sin of commission signifies primarily the act itself, secondarily punishment, both absolute entities; sins of omission are neither relative nor absolute entities. Positing relations is unnecessary; the secondary significates connoted by 'sin' are all absolute entities—the person obligated by divine precept, the divine precept, and the future punishment (OTh IV, 622).

307. Headed "The Cause of Sin," this section deals with the problem of evil: If God is the immediate cause of everything, how can there be evil? A theologically acceptable solution of this problem must ascribe the evil to the creature rather than to God. Scotus's account is presented first. God is a concomitant cause of wickedness or sin, but the defect in the cause, which renders the effect wicked, is ascribed to the creature. Antecedently, God gives created wills the potential for rectitude, but because their wills are free, creatures may choose not to exercise that potential. Scotus's account avoids saying that God causes what is right, and the creature causes what is wrong about the act. Instead, he says that God causes rectitude antecedently, or rather God would cause rectitude, but because of a defect in the creature, that potential for rectitude is not realized, and wickedness is caused instead.

Implicit in this account is the distinction between the antecedent and the consequent will of God, which was to have a long history; Immanuel Kant, for example, still employs it in the eighteenth century, following Christian Wolff and A. G. Baumgarten.[4] Scotus presents it simply as a gloss on 1 Tim. 2:4, where

---

4. I. Kant, *Lectures on Philosophical Theology,* tr. A. Wood and G. Clark (Ithaca, N.Y., 1978), 106–7; *Gesammelte Schriften,* Akademie Ausgabe (Berlin, 1902–) XXVIII, 2, 2: 1068–69.

Paul says that God wills "that all men be saved": "The antecedent will, in which he wills that all be saved, is the will in which he wills those goods for people who can persevere to salvation, while the consequent will is the will in which he wills beatitude for someone on account of her merits."[5] Ockham rejects this distinction because it presumes Scotus's theory of instants of nature—a theory that allows the conceptual division of a single instant of time into more than one instant of nature, so that God can cause rectitude antecedently, but not consequently, in a logically (but not temporally) prior instant.

Ockham's solution is presented in his theology lectures on the fourth book of the *Sentences* commentary, where he takes care not to assert it, allowing that it may not be orthodox to assert that God causes wickedness. He distinguishes between causing wickedness and causing wickedness wickedly. Though God causes wickedness, he does not cause wickedness wickedly (OTh IV, 683–85). Instead he causes wickedness for a good end (OTh V, 353). Here Ockham appears less hesitant than in his theological lectures. God causes the deformity inasmuch as he causes the act. This appears unproblematic because the "deformity" has no independent ontological status. The only things caused would be the precepts and the people obligated by them (which, though connoted by the term 'sin,' are not themselves wicked), and in the case of sins of commission, the act itself. In the case of sins of omission, the word 'sin' has the same connotations but does not signify anything directly.

320. Regarding sins of commission, where an act is caused, God and the created will elicit the same act. So the question arises, How is it that the creature sins and God does not? Ockham's answer is that God is not obligated. Sin in the absence of a contrary obligation would be a contradiction in terms (OTh IV, 622; OTh VII, 198). The example Ockham considers in his theology lectures is a classic one, the biblical case in which the sons of Israel rob the Egyptians. Ockham considers that no sin is involved here (OTh IV, 685). God causes the appropriation of property just as much as the Israelis, but he cannot sin because he has no obligation not to take from the Egyptians. The Israelis also do not sin; indeed, strictly speaking they do not commit robbery. The definition of robbery is appropriating property contrary to divine or human precept (OTh V, 352; OTh VII, 198). But if God commands the sons of Israel to take the Egyptians' property, then there can be no binding contrary precept, and so no robbery.

---

5. Scotus, *Rep.* I d.46, XXII: 508.

Had the Israelis been guilty of sin, this would not imply that God, who must cooperate in order for the Israelis to act, causes a sinful act. God causes the act, but by itself the act is neither good nor bad. What makes it good or bad is whether or not it conforms to rules that obligate the person acting. Accordingly, though God causes the same act, only people cause an act that they are obligated by right reason and divine precept not to cause.

332. The issue here is how sin separates us from God, which in Scholastic theology becomes the question of whether acts of sin and acts of grace are formally incompatible—that is, whether it would be a contradiction in terms to sin and act meritoriously at the same time. This is a real issue, because Christians who love God regularly sin. It has to be dealt with by making distinctions. According to Bonaventure, the distinction is between deliberate mortal sins, undertaken with consent, which show contempt for divine precept, and venial sins, which do not.[6] For Scotus, the distinction is between virtually contradictory acts and acts formally contradictory to divine precept. Thus a sin resulting from weakness or ignorance may be only virtually, not formally, contradictory to love of God, provided it is not undertaken for the sake of dishonoring God. Ockham's account is similar; he points out that people cannot commit mortal sins without hating God. But before coming to his distinction, he explains how mortal sin turns us away from God. It is deliberate disobedience and necessarily implies failure to heed God's will, aversion from God.

On the issue of incompatibility, Ockham presents a more detailed account elsewhere (OTh VIII, 313–18), which distinguishes between complex and incomplex acts and assumes, as before, the identification of love of God with obedience to God (a.3 396). If we consider all the partial objects of acts of moral sin and meritorious acts, then there is formal incompatibility. If we instead consider only the incomplex object, there is none. Donald could love God and simultaneously be guilty of lust, but he could not love God above all and at the same time deliberately disobey the commandment to refrain from adultery. In the absence of a precept, Donald could even prefer his paramour to God without hating God; but once the precept is issued, he cannot. He cannot virtuously love God—that is, love God above all—and at the same time act contrary to God's will as reflected in the Decalogue.

344. One further distinction is required to deal with the issue of formal incompatibility: the distinction between actual and habitual grace. Another distinction required has already been

---

6. Bonaventure, *Sent.* II d.24 p.2 a.2 q.2 (Quaracchi, 1885), II: 581.

made implicitly—namely, the distinction between sins that have hatred of God as an object and those that do not, such as those whose object is inordinate love of creatures. Thus we get the following conclusions:

1. Actual sins involving deliberate disobedience to God are formally incompatible with acts of love of God (350).
2. Actual sins—even mortal sins—that do not have hatred of God as a partial object are not formally incompatible with love of God (355).
3. Actual sins contrary to divine precept are incompatible with love of God as result of the ordination of an extrinsic cause (357).
4. Infused habitual charity is formally compatible with actual sin, whether or not hatred of God is a partial object (370).
5. Infused habitual charity is incompatible with actual sin as the result of divine ordination (372).
6. Infused habitual charity is compatible with habitual sin (374).
7. Acquired habitual charity is formally compatible with actual sin, whether or not hatred of God is a partial object (385).
8. Acquired habitual charity and habitual sin are incompatible (393).

Most of these conclusions have been foreshadowed in article 3, in the section on the compatibility of the theological virtues with vice. But these conclusions deal with sin, not vice. The arguments are similar, and many of the same facts of experiences are adduced. In part this is because all vices are sins; Christians are punished for vices contrary to right reason. And, as we saw in the case of the despoiling of the Egyptians, if God commanded an act that would be a vice in the absence of such an extraordinary command, the prohibition would cease, the dictates of right reason would be altered, and there would be virtue, not vice.

353. What is interesting here is Ockham's emphasis on the statutory nature of divine precept—its potentially arbitrary nature. This differs from many Scholastics who emphasize the extent to which natural and divine law correspond. This characteristic of Ockham's views results from his interest in understanding the difference between what is absolutely possible and what has actually been ordained. What is important is Ockham's claim that God could have ordained a system in which acts that are correctly considered sinful in the established order of salvation would lead to beatific vision. Ockham's point is that nothing in the natural world dictates the order of salvation. Beatific vision and damnation do not depend on the intrinsic nature of things but solely on the will of God. Hence the rules of salvation are an external order not unlike the legal systems of human rulers, who regulate rewards and punishments by statute. But the reader should note, though Ockham does not point it out for us, that it is appropriate that the reward involved, enjoyment of God, should be a consequence of loving and obeying God rather than a consequence of obedience to an objectively defined, logically deducible code of ethics. This is a realm for love and generosity.

I Reply to the Second Doubt

401. Here Ockham argues that what Scotus calls the circumstances that render an act virtuous are all really partial secondary objects of a virtuous act. He claims that this is a necessary consequence of the fact that there are virtuous acts, since there are only intrinsically or extrinsically virtuous acts. But extrinsically virtuous acts are virtuous only by reference to intrinsically virtuous acts. Therefore there must be intrinsically virtuous acts. An intrinsically virtuous act is (1) an act directly within our control and (2) an act that could not be successively virtuous and vicious while remaining the same. But no act can meet these conditions unless it is an act of will and unless the purpose for which it is performed is built into its description or formula. Thus Ockham would argue that even the act of refraining from murder is not necessarily virtuous, since it is possible that God might command us to take a life; but the refusal to take a life is necessarily virtuous if it is performed for the sake of obedience to God. That is, this refusal is necessarily virtuous if it is elicited by a creature.

In this passage, as in the passage from article 1 (128) that it summarizes, a second qualification, "given the present divine ordination," poses a problem. For as Ockham has just finished arguing (a.4 357–58), divine commands are extrinsic to goodness. If an act is virtuous only given divine precept, it is not necessarily and intrinsically virtuous; whether it is virtuous is contingent on divine command. This is inconsistent with the position that Ockham has explicitly maintained from the outset—see, for example, article 1, conclusion 3—that there are intrinsically and necessarily virtuous acts; indeed, no act is virtuous except by reference to such an act. There are two ways in which this difficulty can be resolved. As I indicated in the commentary on article 1, Ockham assumes that there are many intrinsically and necessarily virtuous acts—most importantly, acts undertaken for the sake of obedience to God, such as being honest or refusing to take the life of another human being. But absolutely speaking, it is possible that God should have commanded that we misrepresent the facts or take a human life. In fact, the Bible appears to provide examples in which God has commanded such actions. So even if exercised for the sake of obedience to God, truthfulness itself is not necessarily virtuous. Only an act of obedience to God for the sake of love of God is necessarily virtuous. Following this line of reasoning, to resolve this difficulty is to suggest that Ockham is here allowing that perhaps not all fourth-degree virtuous acts are necessarily virtuous, but only one primary act: the act of willing obedience to God's will for the sake of love of God.

The other way to resolve this difficulty is to suggest that Ockham wants to go even further and to argue that even the act of obedience to God for the sake of love of God is not necessarily virtuous. He does claim once that it is logically possible that God should have commanded hatred of God. And given this command, it might appear possible that an act of love of God would not be virtuous, and an act of hatred of God would be virtuous. But this case is different from all the other extraordinary divine commands that are logically possible, since it would be impossible to fulfill the command. If in obedience to divine command, I hate God, then I am hating God because I love God, which is an impossible state of affairs. And similarly, if I disobey the command, I am loving God on account of hatred for God; to use the terminology that Ockham developed a few lines ago (344–99), the two acts are "formally incompatible." But Ockham's original qualification — "if elicited by a creature" — already covers this case. It is impossible that any creature should elicit such an act, since its description is a contradiction in terms. To paraphrase Ockham's most authoritative interpreter, Wodeham (OTh V, 353–54),[7] this is what Ockham should have said, whether he did so or not. Apparently at the time of his lectures on the *Sentences,* Ockham believed that creatures could obey such a command (OTh VII, 352). But since he withdrew this claim in his *Ordinatio* (OTh I, 503-6), where he is revising his discussion of the same material, and rejected it altogether in his *Quodlibets* (OTh IX, 256), the second solution to the difficulty is probably a misunderstanding of Ockham.

---

7. The attribution of these comments to Wodeham is likely but not certain. The comments come from the *Abbreviatio* of Ockham's theology lectures, which is attributed to Wodeham in the best surviving manuscripts of that work. The attribution to Wodeham is confirmed by the fact that Wodeham's quotations from Ockham are distinctive, and it is the same text found in the *Abbreviatio* (OTh VII, *21–28).

The first solution raises none of these difficulties, so it is a preferable interpretation of Ockham's contention that even the virtue of obedience to divine commands for the sake of God is contingent. More importantly, it leaves Ockham with what he says he proves in *De connexione virtutum* (OTh VIII, 415) and what he needs to maintain his position consistently, a necessarily virtuous act—obedience to God for the love of God. Provided that this act is defined in terms of its complex total object, which includes love of God as an end, it cannot be vicious. This is not to say that vicious love of God is not possible, since loving or obeying God for the sake of personal gain is vicious (OTh V, 354). But this act is specifically different from obeying God on account of love of God. Moreover, we do not get this result unless we posit that the purpose for which we elicit an act is part of its definition; it is a partial object, not an external circumstance. And that is the point that Ockham sets out to prove in this paragraph.

410. This paragraph proves that the necessary and sufficient causes of an intrinsically and necessarily virtuous act are God, the created will, its principal object, and its secondary object or objects. Note that as Ockham indicates later (618–19), an act's principal object is its purpose. Thus observing the Sabbath in obedience to divine precept is a necessarily virtuous act, which requires the created will as cause, God as a concurring cause, the commandment, and obedience to God as a purpose. Postulating these causes eliminates all the contingencies considered: we stipulate the causal activity of the created will, since otherwise it is logically possible that God could be acting alone; we stipulate that God is a concurring cause, since the act itself exists only contingently and would go out of existence if not maintained in existence by God; we stipulate the commandment, since it is logically possible that God should have commanded otherwise; and we stipulate the aim of obedience, since otherwise the act might be vicious.

| Right Reason

419. This is a proof that right reason is a necessary partial object of virtue, a conclusion that Ockham has already established (a.3 492–518) and will establish in much greater detail in his question *Whether the Will Acts Virtuously if the Intellect Errs about Its Object* (OTh VIII, 409–50). What is essential to virtue is not simply the apprehension of the rules of right reason, but our assent to their dictates. Ockham's example is dietary—temperance in eating. His argument for the necessity of right reason depends on a conclusion that he established early in his argument against Scotus's reply to the first doubt—namely, that the same act cannot be virtuous and vicious by turns. Suppose that Stephen sees pancakes with whipped cream on the menu at Perkins Family Restaurant and he refrains from ordering them. Stephen knows that whipped cream is not very good for him because his mother is constantly reminding him that fatty foods consumed in excess are bad for his health. But now suppose that Stephen exercises restraint in regard to whipped cream because he likes the taste of strawberries better, not because strawberries are better for his health than whipped cream. Ockham would hold that Stephen is not eating temperately, and moreover that if this counts as temperance, we would also have to agree that Stephen is eating temperately if he continues eating strawberries after he is told that they have been treated with a harmful preservative. But that would be absurd.

429. This objection notes that Ockham agrees with Scotus that prudence is a necessary partial cause of virtue and asks why Ockham insists that it also be considered a partial object. It looks as if there need be no real disagreement. Scotus even appears willing to reduce the relation of conformity, to which Ockham objects, to the necessary coexistence of the act of prudence (*Ord.* I d.17 p.1 q.1–2 n.94, V: 185).

435. Ockham offers three arguments for claiming that right reason must be considered an object. An argument not mentioned here is that right reason is no more essential to virtuous action than the purpose or even the time and place at which the act is performed, and no one would call the place at which an act is performed a cause of virtuous action (OTh VI, 389–90). A second argument is the one offered in the previous paragraph: What is necessary is assent to a dictate of right reason, not the intellect's mere apprehension of that dictate. The final argument is that if right reason were required only as a cause, then God could replace it, as was affirmed in the Condemnations of 1277. God could supply the place of right reason as a cause of apprehension, but God could not substitute for right reason as the object of a virtuous act of will.

It is interesting to note here Ockham's affirmation that God has ordained that we follow the dictates of right reason. God requires that we exercise prudence. Ockham evidently takes this for granted and mentions it only because it serves as a ground for rejecting the view that prudence is a only a cause, not necessarily *also* an object, of virtue.

443. Here Ockham affirms that right reason is an essentially ordered cause of virtue, and that what is essential is the will's assent to a dictate of right reason, not merely the apprehension of such a dictate. Stephen's decision to choose strawberries rather than whipped cream is not virtuous simply because he knows that it is the right decision; he must choose it for that reason, or for the sake of another worthy end. Note that if conformity to right reason is the purpose, we have moved beyond simple first-degree virtue. Ockham indicates that we have done so by using the phrase 'perfectly virtuous' at the beginning of the next paragraph (451). Conformity with right reason is sufficient for first-degree virtue; making right reason the purpose of action is third-degree virtue.

451. Ockham's use of the phrase 'perfectly virtuous' is a slip. As was indicated in the commentary on article 2 (179) and is stated explicitly elsewhere (634; a.3 312), the phrase 'perfectly virtuous' refers properly to fourth-degree or Christian virtue; what is wanted here is the phrase 'truly virtuous,' which describes the virtue possible for philosophers. In this paragraph, Ockham explains why right reason has to be the principal end of true virtue. In the terms of the example we have been using, Ockham would say that if Stephen eats strawberries because he enjoys the taste rather than because it is right to do so, then he would eat them even in the absence of the dictates of right reason. Stephen must choose strawberries because they are dictated by correct dietary precepts if his action is to be truly virtuous. If he wills strawberries for the sake of right reason, he is truly willing right reason. If the act of preferring strawberries and the act of willing conformity with the dictates of right reason are separate acts, then the connection between the two is accidental, and Stephen's preference for strawberries might persist in the absence of his willing conformity with right reason; he might even eat them if eating them were contrary to right reason (as might be the case if they were treated with preservatives). True virtue requires that we choose strawberries and the dictates of right reason in the same act. The case is similar to Christian charity, which requires us to love our neighbors for the sake of God and God for his own sake in the same act.

| End

471. Since Ockham has just established that true virtue requires that right reason be the purpose for which the act is performed, further discussion of the role of the ends of action in virtue would be superfluous. The quotation from Aristotle's *Posterior Analytics* was cited implicitly in the previous paragraph.

❚ Time and Place

476. Again Ockham uses the phrase "perfectly virtuous," when strictly speaking he should use the phrase 'truly virtuous.' Presumably, in this example Ockham intends to contrast marital coition, home in bed at night, with fornication before marriage in a public place. His aim is to show that time and place are essential to virtue.

482. Ockham proves his claim that time and place are essential by pointing out the absurdities that would follow if they were not. Even if the act performed were dictated by reason and performed on account of love of God, if it were not performed at the right time and place, it would be vicious. Suppose Allen waits calmly and patiently for a child to finish her homework, knowing that God and right reason counsel patience. His actions would be less commendable if he calmly and patiently waited for Matilda to set the curtains on fire.

491. This interesting objection suggests that although time and place must be part of the dictate that is the intellectual object, they need not be objects of the will. Ockham replies simply by asserting that the will must conform to the time and place dictated. If the will does not will conformity with right reason in every respect, its act is vicious or indifferent.

❚ A Second Look at Right Reason

509. Before answering the arguments advanced in support of the second doubt, Ockham returns to the question of whether right reason must be an object as well as a cause of virtue. An objector says that the reply that Ockham based on the claim that God could substitute for right reason as a cause, but not as an object, is invalid. For if you argue that right reason must be an object, then you could argue on similar grounds that the will must be an object. This is a *reductio* argument against Ockham. Although the term 'virtuous' connotes the will as well as right reason, we would not want to say that the will is an object of virtue. The objector claims that Ockham should reject the argument about right reason, since he could not accept it for the will.

521. Instead of defending his position by indicating in what sense right reason differs from will, Ockham offers what he calls a "better and stronger" argument. The stronger argument is that two absurdities follow if we do not posit right reason as the object of acts of virtue. The first is that no act is intrinsically virtuous, from which it would follow that no act is virtuous, as Ockham has shown earlier (a.1 99). The second is twofold: that a nonvirtuous act could be rendered virtuous by something merely natural, and that a nonmeritorious act could be rendered meritorious in the same way.

530. Ockham bases his proof of the first absurdity on the distinction between apprehension and assent, showing that we can will what a dictate of right reason stipulates without assenting to that dictate. In our earlier example, Stephen could eat strawberries while apprehending, but not assenting to, the dictate 'you should follow a healthy diet.' Suppose, for example, that he apprehends the proposition 'you should eat fruit as part of a low-fat diet,' but does not assent to it. He may even act as that precept would dictate while judging that eating a low-fat diet was unimportant, if he likes the taste of strawberries. Doing what he is told to do does not make his action virtuous unless he not only understands what has been said, but also agrees with the dictate. Unless he assents to right reason's dictate, Stephen's act of eating strawberries is not virtuous.

543. Not satisfied with this answer, Ockham's opponent replies that even if right reason is not the object of the act, since the act performed is what right reason would dictate, it is virtuous. And here Ockham might well have conceded that it is virtuous, provided Stephen's aim is good—say, he is trying to amuse people—but only in the first degree. Though the act conforms to the dictates of right reason, it is not chosen precisely because right reason dictates it. Here the opponent concedes Ockham's definition of what it means to conform to right reason—namely, to will what right reason dictates because it is a dictate of right reason (458–59). Forced to choose a different tack, the opponent then claims that there is aptitudinal if not actual conformity, and that suffices for virtue. In terms of our example, this is like saying that though Stephen is not actually virtuous, he acts as if he were virtuous, which is enough.

545. Cleverly, Ockham replies that if reason failed to dictate that we should choose right actions for the sake of right reason, it would be erring reason, not right reason. Stephen is wrong; he does not formulate a correct dictate. Interestingly, too, Ockham here affirms that there is no Christian virtue in the absence of willing conformity to right reason. So love of God is not enough for virtue in the absence of willing conformity to a dictate of prudence or right reason.

555. Ockham's opponent concedes that an act which did not have right reason as its object would be a dictate of erring reason, but claims that this would be a result of defective knowledge. Unstated is the assumption that this error is not culpable and the conclusion—namely, that there can be virtue even if a dictate of right reason is not chosen precisely because it is a dictate of right reason. Here Ockham denies that this would be a result of defective prudence; rather, it is the result of a defective will, since the right dictate could exist without an act of will conforming to it. In our example, Stephen can abstain from eating whipped cream while knowing that this is a dictate of right reason, which should be chosen for the sake of right reason, without willing conformity with the dictate.

563. Here Ockham is arguing against the view that virtue is constituted by the coexistence of prudence and an act dictated by prudence. He claims that this view has the consequence that no act is necessarily and intrinsically virtuous, and every act is contingently virtuous. His proof that all acts would be contingently virtuous depends on the possibility that the relevant prudent acts can come into and go out of existence. Suppose Stephen chooses strawberries rather than whipped cream. When he starts eating, his motive might simply be hunger for fresh fruit; subsequently, he might remember that fresh fruit is part of the healthy diet, which is dictated by prudence; and finally he might forget about dietary considerations, but continue to refuse whipped cream on the grounds that he is full. As the reader will remember, Ockham agrees that the same act of eating can go from being extrinsically indifferent to being extrinsically virtuous and back again (185–90). But he would argue that Stephen's three choices are different acts with different objects; the same internal act of will cannot be successively indifferent and virtuous.

576. Ockham introduces new terminology here, referring to a dictative act, the form of assent proper to practical reason. For Ockham, assent is produced by evidence; normally, it simply produces the judgment that a given proposition is true. In the realm of practical reason, it produces dictates like 'you should eat strawberries as part of a healthy diet.' In our example, particular directive knowledge might take the form of Stephen's apprehending that 'he should eat strawberries when they are ripe and plentiful' or that 'he should eat strawberries at the right time and place, for the love of God because they are dictated by right reason.' Ockham's point would be that only Stephen's decision to follow the last dictate is necessarily virtuous. Unless he is acting in conformity with the last dictate, his act could cease to be virtuous.

Ockham also introduces a new strategy in this paragraph, distinguishing between causing and conserving imperative acts. Typically this distinction is important in arguments that explore the limits of what is logically possible. Thus if Stephen's will originally dictates his eating in accordance with his prudential knowledge that we should eat fruit in season, and that corresponds to what right reason teaches when he starts eating, Ockham's opponent might claim that since Stephen's will is aptitudinally in conformity with right reason, he is acting virtuously. Ockham can then reply that God could preserve the imperative act unchanged, so that Stephen would keep eating until he had eaten ten gallons of strawberries. It would be the same dictative act, 'eat strawberries in season,' even though after he had eaten a quart of strawberries, right reason would dictate that Stephen should stop eating strawberries. But since there is nothing in the original imperative that refers to right reason, the act can be preserved for hours and days. At that point, however, no one would any longer be tempted to call his eating virtuous. Ockham's basic point in this discussion is that right reason itself has to be dictated if we want to be able to anticipate virtuous behavior reliably. He thinks that we can only get a transitory and accidental connection between prudence and virtue unless the will's purpose is to follow right reason.

584. The second absurdity that follows from the denial that right reason must be an object of virtue, according to Ockham, is that something merely natural could make nonvirtuous acts virtuous and nonmeritorious acts meritorious. To prove this Ockham returns to what he said about the consequences of positing that the simple coexistence of prudence is adequate for virtue. Ockham's example regards merit. Suppose Eva goes to church because it is a nice, warm place where she can escape from a Sunday thunderstorm, a sensible but hardly meritorious act. While at church she learns that God commands us to observe the Sabbath by attending church. Ockham thinks it obvious that her church-going is not thereby rendered meritorious.

Here Ockham is speaking of the present order of salvation, in which God ordains that we will be rewarded for following the dictates of right reason as well as divine commandments. Absolutely speaking, it is possible for acts not in our control to be meritorious. Specifically, Ockham points out that God could have decided to reward merely intellectual acts with beatific vision (149–54).

593. Having covered the case of transitions from indifference to virtue, Ockham now turns to transitions in which virtue is lost. Once again, if the imperative act does not include right reason as an object, then the act can be continued in the absence of prudence. Suppose Vea loves God and obeys right reason. Accordingly, she regularly contributes to charitable organizations. Then suppose that an illness renders Vea incapable of understanding what God and right reason require, but she continues to give money when asked. Her continued contributions are neither virtuous nor meritorious; her illness has altered the nature of her acts and made them morally meaningless. But if love of God and conformity to right reason are built into the imperative act that produces her charitable donations, then as long as she continues the same action, she is worthy and virtuous.

601. In his reply to the first argument for the second doubt, Ockham concedes that time, place, prudence, and purposes can be circumstances of an act. But this is true only for acts that are extrinsically and contingently virtuous. For intrinsically and necessarily virtuous acts, right reason must be an object. Extrinsically virtuous acts include acts of every faculty except the will. Even acts of will can be extrinsically virtuous if they are not in accordance with a dictate that fully specifies the time, place, and purpose of the act. As long as we are speaking of extrinsically virtuous acts, it is proper to speak of circumstances. But intrinsically virtuous acts, or acts virtuous by definition, must be in accordance with a dictate of right reason that specifies time, place, and purpose. Ockham is willing to concede that time and place are secondary objects, but he maintains that the purpose of an action is its principal object. Not 'strawberry eating' but 'conformity with right reason' is the principal object of 'strawberry eating for the sake of right reason.'

620. The second argument for the second doubt suggests that Ockham's claim that virtuous acts must be defined in terms of complex objects has an unacceptable consequence—namely, that the same act can simultaneously be an act of hatred and an act of love. Ockham accepts this consequence, as he has indicated a few lines above (469), using the example of hatred of sin. Here what prudence dictates is that 'we should hate false testimony, because it is contrary to right reason and divine command.' That same act can be described as rejection of sin, implementation of a dictate of right reason, and as loving God by doing his will. It can be both love and hate; love for God and hatred of sin. There is nothing inappropriate about acts with multiple descriptions, though some of these descriptions would reflect an impossible state of affairs if the object of the act were simple—that is, we cannot both hate and love God, both accept and reject sin, or both follow and depart from the dictates of right reason.

| Reply to the Third Doubt

624. Here Ockham replies explicitly to Scotus's claim that exterior acts may be intrinsically good, that they may have a goodness that does not pertain to interior acts. This reply is very brief, but in a sense the entire *De connexione virtutum* is a reply to this position.

The actual third doubt raises only two arguments for Scotus's position—arguments that were actually presented by the Scotist Walter Chatton (Adams 1980, 37). According to those arguments, exterior acts must have independent moral value (1) because we are more severely punished for exterior acts than for interior acts, and (2) because interior and exterior acts are separately prohibited. In the third book of his *Sentence* commentary, Ockham replies to the first objection by denying that God punishes exterior acts more severely and by pointing out that punishment here on earth serves chiefly to maintain public order. Though defamation is a graver sin than theft, since it does less damage to public order, defamation is less severely punished in practice (OTh VI, 376–78). An example shows the differences between how God regards sins and how they are regarded on earth. Suppose two local magnates—Henry and Roger—each commands a servant to assassinate someone. In a momentary fit of rage, Henry asks someone to rid him of a pest, but he soon repents of his sin and tries to countermand the order. Roger's hatred is more intense and more obdurate. But Henry's servant quickly executes the command before it can be rescinded, while Roger's servant fails to carry out the command at all. On earth Henry will be punished, and Roger will not; but God will punish Roger more severely.

An example of separate prohibitions against interior and exterior acts are the commandments against theft and against covetousness (Exod. 20:15.17). Here Ockham suggests that an act of covetousness that actually results in theft is likely to be more intense than the act that is not imperative. As he has pointed out in distinguishing between second- and fifth-degree virtues, there is a difference between conditional acts and formally imperative executive acts (a.2 151–80; a.3 167–81). Moreover, actually engaging in theft, enjoying its results, tends to strengthen the interior act (OTh VI, 375–76). Ockham's outstanding disciple and an important philosopher in his own right, Wodeham espoused views similar to Ockham's on this subject. More interested in the psychological questions involved here than Ockham, Wodeham presents more detailed replies to these arguments (Adams 1980, 15–17, 46–59).

Replies to the Fourth and Fifth Doubts

629. These two doubts challenge Ockham's account of the difference between virtue as he presents it and pagan virtue. Aristotle presents bravery, for example, as a virtue of the irrational soul, a virtue of feeling. As Christians, Ockham and Scotus deny such virtues—virtues pertain to things within our control; feelings are only minimally governable. But as Scotus points out, habits in the sensitive faculty produce acts that are like virtue, in that they are consonant with right reason. Ockham has to agree that habits of the sensitive soul can facilitate virtue or allow us to enjoy virtue. Ockham accounts for the resemblance by saying that acts produced by our sensitive faculty may be virtuous by extrinsic denomination—that is, they can be called virtuous, because they correspond to an intrinsically virtuous act of will. Scotus's distinction between material and formal virtue can also provide the basis for a reply. Habits in the sensitive soul can be materially but not formally virtuous—the acts can correspond, but not the imperative.

634. Here Ockham concedes that pagan virtue does not have love of God as its purpose. Aristotle did not suppose that God commands ethical behavior. Moreover, even if he had believed that God commanded ethical behavior, Aristotle would still not have agreed that our purpose in acts of honesty should be God's honor. But Aristotle was wrong, according to Ockham; his reasoning was inadequate, and consequently he was not capable of perfectly virtuous acts, which are necessarily virtuous (a.2 141). Ockham doubtless sees it as a strength of his position that on his account Christian and pagan virtues are specifically distinct. God is always the principal object of Christian virtue, while the pagan philosopher practices virtue for other reasons—abstinence, perhaps, in order to develop his proficiency in science. So it is altogether appropriate that Christian abstinence is a different virtue (OTh VII, 57).

Reply to the Sixth Doubt

654. This is a very technical discussion about what accounts for specific distinctions between habits. Ockham's problem is to explain why loving 'Socrates for the sake of God' and loving 'Plato for the sake of God' are not specifically distinct acts. His opponent wants to show that he is committed to that conclusion, since the two acts have different objects. Ockham rejects this conclusion: love of Plato and love of Socrates are not specifically distinct if they are both done for the sake of God. Since the principal object of the acts is the same (to show love of God), and since Plato and Socrates are not specifically distinct, nor are the acts of loving them formally incompatible, the habits produced by loving them are not distinct. By contrast, the habits produced by affirming that 'all triangles have three sides' and 'no triangles have three sides' would be formally incompatible.

I Reply to the Seventh Doubt

702. These final objections raise doubts about Ockham's account of temperance, and continence, perseverance, and courage. For Ockham, perseverance is not a virtue, but a degree of virtue; perseverance in virtue is the opposite of moral softness (a.3 98). The reader will recall the example of the poor, shivering religious, up before dawn saying matins. Ockham does not use the term 'perseverance' in his description of second- and fifth-degree virtues, but it would be appropriate there, where he is discussing the virtue that we ascribe to people willing to do more than human nature is normally capable of in order to preserve their virtue. 'Perseverance' may describe the quality of any virtue; by contrast, 'temperance' and 'continence' are terms we use for virtuous acts in regard to bodily appetites.

705. Note that here temperance and continence are not contrasted as virtues in regard to food and sexual pleasure, respectively. Rather, as was indicated in the commentary on article 3 (447–55), according to Ockham the degree of control in temperance is greater than in continence. In continence, the physical inclinations are too strong to allow the establishment of bodily habits that would permit the enjoyment of virtue. But the temperate are not necessarily more virtuous than the continent. They may simply have lesser temptations with which to deal. A person continent in the fifth degree would be more virtuous than someone temperate in the first degree.

Ockham's main reply to the seventh doubt is simply to list the conditions for each of the five degrees of virtue and to assert that temperance and continence may be found in any of them. In the remainder of his reply (716), he adds that temperance and continence need not be virtues. Thus if Henry refrains from alcoholic excesses simply in order to maintain his ability for witty repartee, his temperance will not be virtuous. Similarly, suppose that Stephen, despite experiencing an overwhelming temptation to eat whipped cream, refrains, and not even the thought of his teasing friends can persuade him to abandon his determination to follow the dictate of right reason 'do not eat empty calories.' We can suppose that his is second-degree continence.

I Reply to the Eighth Doubt

725. In his reply to the eighth doubt, Ockham clarifies his understanding of courage and distinguishes it from heroic virtue. Heroic degrees of any virtue are possible. 'Courage' is a term reserved only for case where people are willing to sustain injury at the hands of others—his examples are death, bodily harm, and imprisonment. But if, as a result of our own actions we sustain bodily harm, that is heroic if it is for a good end, but it is not courageous.

Ockham's opponent has suggested that courage and heroic virtue are not distinct, and that heroic virtue is only found among the courageous—a plausible enough claim. Ockham rejects this suggestion, however, treating the problem as just another case where one virtue may or may not be connected with another. He has established that third-, fourth-, and fifth-degree virtues will prompt us to perform acts of other virtues if they are challenged in a relevant respect (a.3 272–329). Ockham's example of heroism independent of courage is the Emperor Zaleuchos (actually a legendary ancient lawgiver), who put out his own eye in order to assure that the law would be enforced.[8] Here we have an example of heroic justice without courage, according to Ockham. A related example might be a case of heroic honesty without courage. If Louise is willing to sustain imprisonment rather than tell a lie, her commitment to truth-telling will produce courage. But if she decides that the only way to avoid perjury is to mutilate herself so that she will be hospitalized and not have to go to court, then her honesty is heroic, but her commitment to honesty will not prompt her to courage. Courage is not required because she does not have to undergo mistreatment by other people. For Ockham, courage is preeminently the virtue of the soldier and martyr, not the result of self-mutilation or policies of our own devising.

---

8. Valerius Max., *Factorum dictorumque memorabilium* 6.5 de justitia, no. 3 (London, 1823), 635; *Paulys Realencyclopädie der Classischen Altertumswissenschaft* (Stuttgart, 1960–78), s.v. Zaleuchos.

I Index of Medieval Authors

I Index of Modern Authors

❙ Index of Subjects

Rectitude *(continued)*
Reportatio, x, 3, 8
Right reason, 32, 41, 73, 81, 203;
apprehension or assent to its
dictates, 175, 271–73; aptitudinal conformity to, 175, 275; compatibility with vice, 105; and the
connection of the virtues, 226–
28; generalizing the commitment to, 208; and God, 157; God
supplying its causality, 173,
272, 274; God willing conformity
to it, 212, 272; as the object of
an act, 155; as an object, not a
circumstance, 143; as a partial
object of virtue, 167–69, 173,
272–78; relations of conformity
to it, 151; universal, 85, 215;
and vice, 223; and virtue's
definition, 121, 239; willing on
account of right reason, 169;
and worthiness, 224. *See also*
Prudence; Reason
Right reason's dictates: not always sacrificial, 225; the pursuit of goodness, 224; willing
what God wills, 213
Robbery, defined, 266

Sacraments: not instrumental
causes, 31
Saints, 27, 71, 83, 87; authority
of, 212; without opportunity
for political virtue, 99
Salvation: dependent on God's
will, 31, 268; and generosity,
269; independent of nature,
268; and the sacraments, 31;
without the form of grace, 23
Science: Aristotelian, 25–26, 29–
30; moral—*see* Moral science;
and observation, 26; real, 30;
and syllogistic reasoning, 26
Scripture, 27
Self-deception: and vice, 228
Sensitive appetite: attainment or
avoidance by, 129; capable of
impeding judgment, 133;
independent of judgment, 131,
246; necessarily and immediately following apprehension,
123, 129; not free, 133, 247

Sensitive habits: compatible with
vice, 121; inclining toward extrinsically virtuous acts, 179;
involuntary, 217; and moral
virtue, 219—acting as facilita-
tors, 280; not capable of completely impeding moral virtue,
237; not productive of virtue,
237–38
Sin: actual—formally compatible
with charity, 163, 165, 267; actual and habitual, 268; and
aversion from God, 163, 267;
causes of, 109, 125–27; of commission or omission, 161, 163,
263–66; of commission—acting
contrary to divine precept, 159;
a connotative term, 265; deliberate, 267; first sin, 248; God as a
concomitant cause of, 265–66;
habitual—not destroyed by
single acts of penance, 165;
ignorant—assumes universal
knowledge, 125–27; intellectual
sin, 248; malicious—assumes
particular knowledge, 125–27;
material and formal elements
of, 159–61, 263; and merit, 147;
mortal and venial (Bon.), 267;
mortal sin—good acts in the
state of, 234; as an offense
against God, 259; of omission—
not doing what divine precept
requires, 157; as privation, 161,
264; virtually and formally contrary to divine precept, 267; voluntary, 73; whether compatible
with love of God, 268. *See also*
Merit
Sin, defined: absence of an obligatory act of will, 260; acting contrary to obligation, 263; destiny
for eternal punishment, 265; a
lack of rectitude (Sco.), 147, 259
Skepticism, 25, 28
Socrates, 220
Softness, defined, 97
Species, 89; and acts and habits,
260; compatibility, 77; and psychology, 260; sensible and intelligible, 22, 260
Stoics, 43, 45, 47, 51